From Arrow to Atom Bomb

Other Books by Stanton A. Coblentz

PROSE

Marching Men
The Decline of Man
The Sunken World
After 12,000 Years
The Wonder Stick
Into Plutonian Depths
Villains and Vigilantes
The Answer of the Ages
When the Birds Fly South
The Literary Revolution
The Triumph of the Teapot Poet
An Editor Looks at Poetry
New Poetic Lamps and Old

POETRY

Time's Travelers
Garnered Sheaves
The Pageant of Man
Green Vistas
Songs by the Wayside
Winds of Chaos
Armageddon
The Lone Adventurer
Shadows on a Wall
The Enduring Flame
Songs of the Redwoods
The Mountain of the Sleeping Maiden
The Merry Hunt and Other Poems
Senator Goose and Other Rhymes
The Thinker and Other Poems

ANTHOLOGIES

Unseen Wings
The Music Makers
Modern American Lyrics
Modern British Lyrics

From Arrow to Atom Bomb

The Psychological History of War

by

STANTON A. COBLENTZ

NEW YORK: THE BEECHHURST PRESS

To Those Swordless Fighters
Who Have Waged
the Lone and Unceasing Battle
for Peace

"War is the enemy: but the first step
toward conquest of any enemy is to
understand him; to measure him not
on his weak side alone, but also in his
strength."

—G. G. Coulton,
Medieval Panorama

Acknowledgment

For invaluable advice and suggestions received in the course of the preparation of the manuscript, the author desires to acknowledge his indebtedness and express his thanks to Dr. James H. Breasted Jr., of the Los Angeles County Museum; Professor Thorkild Jacobsen, Dean of the Division of the Humanities of the University of Chicago; Professor A. L. Kroeber of the Department of Anthropology of Columbia University; and Professor John A. Wilson of the Oriental Institute of the University of Chicago.

Contents

V—THE BACKGROUND OF TODAY

VI—THE EPOCH OF THE WORLD WARS

APPENDIX

Introduction

Regarded from any point of view, we live in a warlike age—possibly the most warlike in all history. Yet almost all ages, as any observer will tell you, have been marked by strife and battle; the red records of raids and assaults, of sieges and massacres, of burning farmlands and shattered towns have checkered all the known centuries of man's experience on this planet. Indeed, the fact of conflict, whether by means of arrow, sword, gunpowder, or atomic bomb, has characterized civilized man almost as the zebra is characterized by its stripes or the stag by its antlers. This single phenomenon has built up and destroyed nations; has molded and obliterated cultures; has overrun industry, commerce, agriculture, learning, and art; has championed and toppled religions; has decimated whole generations and scattered whole peoples broadcast; has been the source of more human agony, bloodshed, and loss than all other forces combined; and at our own late day, by taking advantage of the scientific achievements of an uncontrolled civilization, presents our kind with the greatest menace that has confronted it since our ancestors came down from the trees.

All this, of course, is too commonplace to require emphasis. But what is not quite so commonplace, nor quite so easy to comprehend, is the fact that although war is unquestionably the master phenomenon of the ages and the overshadowing threat of our own time, men have never made much of an effort to understand its nature and to combat it in the light of understanding. There have, it is true, been histories of warlike means and methods; there have been studies of military strategy, discourses on the effects of particular battles and wars, inquiries into the economic and political causes and consequences of conflict, accounts without number of particular wars and particular generals, and occasional books, such as Bertrand Russell's *Why Men Fight*, which do attempt to strike down to the subsoil of root realities. But there has nowhere been a wide-reaching and organized effort, on the basis of all the armed conflicts man has ever fought, to analyze the motive-force behind conflict; there has nowhere been a clear recognition that the record of warfare is not primarily one of weapons or methods, but rather a chronicle of the human mind, its evolution and training, its passions and inhibitions, its discipline and submissiveness no less than its frenzies and desires. In other words, most surveys of warfare have concentrated on physical manifestations—which certainly have been blazingly apparent. But in order to know what war really is, and how and why it acts as it does, one must look beneath the physical mask to the psychological truth; one must analyze the conscious and subconscious impulses, the incentives and deterrents, the instilled habits of mind, the traditions, the mass motivations that underlie all mass combat.

It is this object that I am seeking to fulfill in the present book. I am not undertaking a new history of warfare; but I am endeavoring to follow the mind of man through the wars of the centuries, in the effort to discover how wars are caused and, accordingly, how they may be controlled. As no struggle, obviously, is an unrooted occurrence, but all must be nourished during periods of seeming peace, I am taking account of the intervals between conflicts no less than of the conflicts themselves. And as every organized encounter ever waged by men must bear upon the central theme, while our own gigantic upheavals represent the fruition of hundreds of combative generations, I am attempting to cover all the characteristic phases of the subject from the day of the first plundering nomad to that of supersonic missiles.

From this panorama, it is my hope, some conception of the hidden or inner nature of warfare will emerge, some realization of what it is that we must combat, and some recognition of whether we face a task that is hopeless or one that, with the admission of new light, offers some prospect of success despite the formidable obstacles.

Since the alternative to success is the annihilation of civilization or of man himself, who is there that would not look closely, to see if the picture does not offer some previously unnoticed clue to our salvation?

I

The Coming of the Warriors

Chapter 1

The Earliest Fighters

There is a popular belief as to the Old Stone Age. We picture its typical inhabitant as a club-wielding half-beast, who thinks nothing of dragging his wife by the hair or crushing the skull of an unruly offspring; we imagine that one of his chief delights is to indulge in warfare by means of stone axes, clubs, spears, and arrows, and that he is never happier than when invading a neighboring cavern and slaughtering its occupants.

The proponents of this picturesque old view, in order to be consistent, must hold with the philosopher Hobbes that the state of nature is a state of war. They must suppose that man is by instinct a fighting animal; and that his pugnacity necessarily breaks out in organized large-scale conflict. Correspondingly, they may—and usually do—take it for granted that man is driven to fight not only by biological but by economic compulsion; and that his fighting proceeds inevitably from a struggle for "the survival of the fittest."

If man is indeed a creature of this sort, he is an anomaly in the natural world. In nature there is conflict for living room, mates, and food; but except among the ants, there are no wars that even remotely resemble our own; the great majority of living creatures, from the bee and the beetle to the vulture in the sky and the lizard on the rock, are predominantly peaceful, and fight only for self-preservation, or (unconsciously) for racial preservation. One who has passed much time in nature will be impressed not by the combativeness of his surroundings but by their harmony; he will find that the sense of peace and joy is everywhere, and the evidences of strife and destructiveness only occasional; he will listen to the jays in their chattering troops, will see the deer bounding through the brush in their small bands, will watch the wild geese in their migratory flocks and will note the ants in their common task of moving some small crumb; and he will know that it is the rule and not the exception for the members of a species to live together compan-

13

ionably and even cooperatively. Can it be that man is different from most other things in nature? that he is driven to war upon his kind by a combativeness absent in his fellow mammals, and unknown even in birds, reptiles, and insects? Or is it that natural man, like other natural creatures, is not usually aggressive, at least in regard to the members of his own species? And is war then a by-product of civilization, or of the state of mind attendant upon civilization?

The answer to these questions is highly important, for just as the child is the index to the adult, so uncivilized man holds the clues to modern man. And this brings us back to our ancestor of the Old Stone Age and his supposed blood orgies. If he was really a gory monster, a fighter spurred on by some irresistible urge, he makes it a little hard to believe that war is an artificial and preventable phenomenon. And, correspondingly, if war occurred as if by instinct among his latter-day relatives, the so-called primitives of recent times, then the hope of checking combat in the modern world is slight if not non-existent.

By the nature of the case, not a great deal is known about our Paleolithic forebears. Yet we are not entirely without evidence. It is not even true that they did not leave a written record; the cave-dwellers of Europe have preserved a partial chronicle of their life and mind in the form of paintings. And, significantly, those paintings show us the aurochs, the horse, the wild boar, the reindeer, and other four-footed objects of the chase—which leaves no doubt as to the contemporary interest in animals and hunting. But where are the pictures of armed conflict? Nothing is truer of any martial people than that it delights in delineations of combat: the procession of warriors, the upraised spear, the cringing captive have been depicted in stelae and friezes, paintings and statuary by nation after nation. And the absence of such portrayals from the Paleolithic art must be taken as presumptive evidence of an unwarlike life.

All other indications point in the same direction. We have found no Paleolithic skulls or skeletons that seem to have been damaged by arrows or battle-axes; and we have discovered little if anything in the way of warlike weapons. Implements of wood, of course, would have disappeared ages ago; but stone weapons, which would presumably have been preferred for their greater power, would probably have been preserved. Yet with the doubtful and disputed exception of the so-called Solutrean blade, a laurel-leaf-shaped implement that could have been a spearhead used in warfare although some writers hold it to be similar to the flint hunting knife of the Eskimo, the men of the Old Stone Age have left no apparent relics of any warfare.

Important evidence on the same point is offered by surviving tribes in the Paleolithic stage, such as the Australian natives; their tools are of the same type as the flint relics of the Old Stone Age, are fashioned of the same substance, and apparently were made by the same methods. That they were intended for the same purposes —domestic and hunting uses—is a conclusion that follows irresistibly.

In the Neolithic or New Stone Age, and with the production of copper and bronze, we do find more warlike weapons. But this will be a subject for a later chapter. For the present we may note that all the evidence opposes the colorful view of Paleolithic man as a slinger of spears and a wielder of clubs in organized raids upon his fellow man. So far as we can gather from the signs, he felt no urge to fight anything except the cave-wolf and the cave-bear. If man is hurled against man by a natural pugnacity, he probably was completely unaware of the fact.

II

If the wide gaps in our knowledge leave these proofs a little less complete than we could wish, the evidence is powerfully bolstered by the customs of recent aborigines. Everything we have learned of these "children of nature" makes it reasonable to suppose that the Old Stone Age was actually a time of peace.

After one has perused a great number of works dealing with uncivilized man, one becomes aware of a peculiar fact. Other matters, from taboos and totemism to family relationships and magical ceremonies, are elaborated at great length; but there is comparatively little that has to do with warfare; the subject is hardly mentioned at all in the course of otherwise comprehensive volumes. Is this owing to a fault, an oversight, a blind spot among anthropologists? The evidence, it seems to me, warrants no such conclusion. Warfare is indeed discussed occasionally; but it is treated with relative infrequency for the reason that it occurs with relative infrequency. In fact, there are tribes among which war has never been known.

During the past several decades, investigators have compiled evidence tending to show that the earliest peoples, the "food-gatherers" as opposed to the "food-producers," upon the whole lead a warless life. And these "food-gatherers," being as near as we can get to man's original state, are of the greatest importance. Among far-scattered and unrelated tribes—the Negritos of the Congo, the Philippines, and New Guinea, the Bushmen of South Africa, the Veddahs of Ceylon, the Kubu of Sumatra, the Punan of Borneo, the Sakai of the Malay Peninsula, and many more—society has not advanced to the state of organized combat.[1] In other words, there is no civilization, and no civilized incentives to conflict—none of the new habits of thought and the spurs to bloodshed arising from possession, class distinction, and political leadership. This does not mean that there may not be occasional fights among individuals; but it does mean that there is no fighting which may by any extension of the term be classed as a military action.

Let us take a few examples. Here, to begin with, is what the great explorer Fridtjof Nansen says of the Greenland Eskimos:

Fighting and brutalities of that sort . . . are unknown among them, and murder is very rare. They hold it atrocious to kill a fellow creature; therefore war is in their eyes incomprehensible and repulsive, a thing for which their language has no word; and soldiers and officers brought up to the trade of killing they regard as mere butchers.[2]

Among the Yurok of California, in much the same way, "No distinction of principle existed in the native mind between murder and war."[3] Among the Papagos, it was held to be murder to kill an enemy warrior; the brave who had slain a man in battle had to face a severe ordeal of purification before being received back into the tribe.[4] And the aborigines of New Zealand and the Chatham Islands, the Moriori, apparently had a similar attitude; "in their relation to the Maori invaders," they "adhered to the strict pacifist principle of non-intervention and allowed themselves to be slaughtered without resistance like sheep."[5] Perhaps the Cook Islanders, of another part of Oceania, were not quite this docile, but it is significant that, "they say that their forefathers were a peaceable folk and knew not warfare till these Tongans came among them with their ironwood clubs and introduced real fighting." [6] The people of the Bowditch Islands were likewise peaceable, as were those of Funafiti in the Gilberts and those of Tikopia; and among the Andaman Islanders fighting did not break out except in the form of personal feuds. But these contests were evidently not very bloody. "No case of one Andamanese killing another has occurred of recent years. . . . It does not seem that there was ever such a thing as a stand-up fight between two partisans. The whole art of fighting was to come upon your enemy by surprise, kill one or two of them and then retreat." [7]

Something similar is to be seen in most conflicts of the so-called simpler peoples; violence and slaughter in the modern sense of the term were unknown. Take, for example, the Australian aborigines, a group that had not developed even to the level of pottery-making or agriculture. Some of their fights arose from ceremonies connected with the capture or marriage of women; but these could not have been very serious if, as has been reported, the wounds were sometimes sucked by the enemy when the fight was over. Again, as we shall see in the next chapter, the Australians indulged in a curious form of blood feud, in which occasionally a man did die. But their combats were far from indiscriminate massacre:

Most often the attackers, armed with spears and spear-throwers, boomerangs and shields, will march up to the enemies' camp, and the quarrel will be confined to a wordy warfare, lasting perhaps an hour or two, after which things quiet down. [8]

This testimony is confirmed by another authority:

There was hardly anything corresponding to a state of war, where armed adversaries went into battle intending to kill as many adversaries as possible; the judicial combats ended, as a rule, in reconciliation. . . . When one party got the worst of it, they retired from the field in a body; even in this case, however, the defeated tribe returned in the evening . . . it could not, therefore, have been more than a temporary state of hostilities, for the enemy had evidently left the scene. [9]

Consider, likewise, the *makarata* of the Murngin tribe of Australian Bushmen. This occurred after the injury or death of a clan member; the aggrieved group sent an invitation for the ceremony; the members of both clans arrived in war paint and singing war songs; they stood a little more than spear distance apart, with a safe wall of mangrove jungle behind them in case it became necessary to temper valor with discretion; then the challengers danced over to their adversaries, stopped, and retreated; after which the other side repeated the performance. Spear-throwing now began according to a prescribed routine: two men ran across the field, accompanied by two close relations who were also kinsmen of the other side, and whose object was to prevent the spears from being thrown too seriously. Every member of the offended clan hurled at least one spear, sometimes with the result that the enemy was chased into the forest; and meanwhile the old men of both sides warned the throwers to be careful. But in any case the hostilities apparently did not last long; they were ended when one group danced up to the other and one of the aggrieved party pierced the thigh of a foe with a spear—if the wound was not too slight, this usually sufficed for the demands of vengeance.[10]

Here we have, in a mild and ceremonial form, an upflaring of the blood feud, which we shall consider in the next chapter. We have also an example of the tendency, the worldwide and age-old tendency, to regard fighting as a form of game. But we find, in all the above, a motivation, an outlook strikingly unlike the modern.

It is much the same in other parts of the South Seas. We have the word of Bronislaw Malinowski that the wars of the western Pacific "were never very bloody and of long duration, and that they were in many ways fought in a competitive, sporting manner." [11] An observer of the Namau people of New Guinea tells us that, in the intercommunal contests, the adversaries would resort to frenzies of shouting, dancing, and gesticulating, but would avoid undue risk by a rule keeping them from coming to close quarters.[12] Similarly, according to another witness, the Papuans would make a tremendous commotion during one of their inter-village or inter-clan affrays, but would aim dangerous weapons at the legs instead of the chests of their foes.[13] And even when we glance at the more combative regions of the Pacific, we find the spirit of peace more pronounced than that of battle. The Maori, for example, were formerly renowned as fighters; but one wonders whether their pugnacity has not been overstressed:

It seems strange . . . that so warlike a branch of the race as the Maori should not have held the war-god in greater esteem. . . . But the fact that he holds, on the whole, an inferior position, would seem to indicate that the Polynesian race was not primarily a warlike race, though certainly capable of warlike genius when occasion arose. War was, as with the Scandinavians, a pleasure, a pastime, not a main object in life. Proverbs are the concentrated wisdom of a people, and there are many Maori proverbs against entering on war, many in praise of peace.[14]

It is in some respects the same with certain of the African natives, though these have acquired, not always unjustly, a name for combativeness. In Nigeria, as in parts of California, the killer had to pay for the luxury of killing; the damages were assessed by the elders of both warring tribes and of some neutral town, according to the value of the slain men; and the victors, consequently, paid the greatest indemnities.[15] Some suggestive further testimony is offered by an observer of the Bantu-speaking tribes:

I have been the eye-witness of a lot of native skirmishing in the bush and in the open, and it is certainly not the bloody affair that one has been led to anticipate. Very often the side that draws first blood is considered the victor and the other side retires. Lots of their shooting is mere noise and wild display. I have watched the fight on two successive days when guns banged on every hand, and men were shot at all around me, but the net result in casualties was nil.[16]

Similar observations have been made concerning the North American Indians, despite all their fighting reputation. For example, David Thompson, an early explorer of the West, tells of a war of the Cree and the Blackfoot against the Shoshones about the year 1725. Several days were passed in speech-making, feasting, and dancing; and a great display, including dancing and singing, was made when they encountered an enemy; but their shields were placed on the ground in a way to ward off all arrows; and after an affray participated in by eight hundred braves, not a scalp was taken.[17]

This is in accordance with the methods of certain California tribesmen, who went to war carrying headless arrows—which is about as if we moderns marched forth with blank cartridges. And we find much the same attitude of mind in the battles of the Maidu of California, during which the women and children would gather on the knolls out of arrow range to watch the fun, while the young men, advancing unarmed, would skillfully dodge volleys of darts. For hours each side in turn would expose itself to the enemy bowmen, until in the end an accident would happen and someone would be hit—after which all the stricken man's comrades would flee, triumphantly chased by the victors, who caught and beat the slow of foot. But evidently they did not beat them too severely, for everyone would return to the battlefield, the women would pass the food, and all would feast together, while the winners would pay the losers an indemnity for the wounded man.

Somewhat similar are the battles fought every five years in North Caledonia.[18] As when two baseball teams compete on a prearranged diamond, the villagers have a specified battlefield, at which they assemble after the heralds of both sides have made arrangements. Before fighting, the rivals meet in labor battalions to clear away the brush that has overgrown the field during the years since the last contest; then, lined up to face one another, they first engage in a wordy tiff; then stand by to watch while their chiefs display their prowess in single combat; and finally begin hurling spears and arrows and swinging clubs. When the first man dies, they call a halt for the day; but hostilities are continued next day, and until they have become too dangerous or tiresome; after which peace is formally made, both parties of warriors feast together, and each side recompenses the enemy with pigs or other commodities for the slain men.

Somewhat later we shall note further examples of war as an athletic contest. For the present, we may observe an additional motivation pointed out by a recent writer:

Man's balked wishes and denied ambition in time tie him into tight knots of frustration, crying for release. War is one such release. It allows desires disapproved within the group to find an approved outlet. The piping times of peace are often boresome except for the very fortunate. . . . By contrast, war is the most thrilling exercise in the world. The real struggle of fighting is more thrilling than the mock opposition of games; the real man-hunt is incomparably more stimulating than the slaughter of animals. War is the great trigger-release of pent-up emotions.[19]

One may question whether uncivilized man, with his less complicated existence and constant need of wresting a living from the fields or woods, is as likely as his civilized brother to be tied into "tight knots of frustration." Yet the elements of tension and frustration do at times enter in, as among some Plains tribes in which grief or disappointment would lead a man to seek death in war—in other words, a fairly elaborate and ceremonial form of suicide. Jealousy, balked rage, and outraged pride have occasionally produced the same results elsewhere; and such cases suggest the fact, of greater weight among civilized societies, that psychological tension may be like the steam pressing beneath a lid—it may explode into warfare. And this indicates the need of providing other forms of release, the psychological and "moral equivalent" of war.

In most of the cases mentioned above, we have an outlook far from the modern. Hence we may pause to ask just what forces have made uncivilized peoples relatively or entirely unwarlike.

III

Contrary to general belief, early man lives—at least, within the local or tribal unit—a thoroughly cooperative life. He is not an individual, in the sense of seeking his own good in conflict with his kinsmen; he is a cell in a larger organism. If he slays a beast in the woods, the flesh is not his alone, but belongs to the community; if he discovers a patch of rich fruit and berries, he does not wall it off, but all his fellows may partake. The typical state of mind of the non-possessing primitive is described by W. H. R. Rivers, who one day exchanged questions with four natives of Niue Island in Polynesia, and was asked what he would do with a sovereign if he earned one—would he share it with his parents, his brothers and sisters? When he replied that this would not be customary, they found his views so amusing that "it was long before they left off laughing. Their attitude toward my individualism was of exactly the same order as that which we adopt toward such a custom as the couvade, in which a man goes to bed when his wife has a child, and revealed the presence of a communistic sentiment of a deeply rooted kind." [20]

Primitive communism—which bears little resemblance to the doctrinaire and militant communism of a later day—appears to represent the original condition of the human family. It bespeaks a state of society in which the relationships of men were radically different than among us moderns; a state of society in which the predominant force was not man's separateness from man but his kinship to man. And that state of society, in which the pronouns *me*, *my*, and *mine* were scarcely accented at all, was not only based upon man's feeling of oneness with his fellow tribesmen, but tended to preserve that feeling, and to develop corresponding sentiments of kindness, generosity, and cooperation.

Where such sentiments are common, the idea of bloodshed or slaughter among the men of the community is not readily accepted. This must not be taken to mean that the untutored tribesmen are by nature more benevolent or altruistic than anyone else; it merely means that, by a species of extended egotism, they identify themselves with their kinsfolk and other members of the local group; they, literally, *are* their neighbors, and therefore hostilities among them are as unthinkable as between a man's arms and his legs. Manifestations of this belief are common, and usually have a strange look in civilized eyes. For example, among the Jibaro and Canelos Indians of South America, if a sick man has to diet, the other members of his family have to diet with him, it being supposed that the food they consume affects him just as would his own food. And when a man dies among the Jibaros, his brother falls heir to his wife—which continues, it is imagined, the relationship of the original husband. It is much the same with the *couvade*—that curious practice already mentioned, by which, in parts of South America and elsewhere, a father is confined when his son is born; this can be explained by the belief in a magical connection between father and child, whereby everything done by the one affects the other, and the former by staying in hiding will prevent invisible foes from finding the latter.

Even more notably, the sense of oneness between members of a community is shown by the blood feuds of innumerable uncivilized and half-civilized peoples: if a man has committed a crime and cannot be caught, his brother will be a satisfactory substitute, even though the latter had nothing to do with the offense. "An eye for an eye" is the principle—and whose eye is of small importance, so long as it is all in the family. The early settlers in America, in their conflicts with the Indians, had all too frequent opportunities to observe the workings of this principle: if John Jones had killed an Indian, Bill Smith might lose his scalp in retribution, even though Smith had not even known of the original crime. As a typical example, we are told that a Judge Dean of Ohio, who had been adopted by the Indians and made a chief, happened to be the most available paleface to pay a death debt, and "although innocent, was only saved from tomahawking by half a dozen squaws breaking into an Indian council." [21]

As this will demonstrate, the theory of the identity of the various members of the community does not always have beneficent results. Nevertheless, it is a welding and an annealing force, which on the whole tends to prevent conflict and to produce cooperation. It does not, indeed, necessarily create a feeling of oneness with the stranger, the man outside the tribe, who sometimes is regarded as synonymous with the enemy; but it does show man's native capacity, his native disposition to work amicably with his fellow man unless inhibited by his developed inclinations, his trained desires and beliefs.

Chapter 2

The Blood Avengers

For the sake of convenience, the conflicts of uncivilized peoples may be grouped in three categories:

(1) Blood feuds.

(2) Wars connected with religious belief or ceremony.

(3) Raids for the sake of booty, slaves, or human flesh.

These categories are not to be regarded as hard-and-fast and mutually exclusive. The fact is that they overlap frequently: a blood feud, for example, may involve religious and ceremonial elements; while these, in turn, may enter prominently into the raid for booty. But for our guidance along the way, these divisions may be useful.

There is, however, an important stimulus which is at times interlinked with all the other three. This is what, for want of a better phrase, may be termed the heroic ideal: the conception that glorifies fighting and skill and victory in fighting into something heroic, and sometimes illuminates even the goriest battle scenes with a cultivated glamour. The characteristic of the heroic ideal is that it exalts conflict for its own sake, makes of it an end as well as a means, and surrounds it with a vague immaterial entity variously known as *glory* and *honor*—a mist, a mirage that may appear more valuable in men's minds than life itself, and may rule their actions like a jealous god. From the most rudimentary levels to the most elaborate, the heroic ideal plays a part; we shall have occasion to note it from time to time no matter what kind of fighting we are observing.

Let us turn first, however, to that forefather of war, the blood feud.

In its simplest form, this is based upon elementary human emotion—the same that would move you or me were someone to deal us an unwarranted blow. What would our first unreasoning impulse be? Naturally, to strike back. And what would be the result of the return blow? Quite as naturally, to impel our adversary to hit again, particularly if he had been hurt in his body or his pride. If he saw that he needed assistance, he might call in some of his friends or relations; and you and I, in order to match the new force, might summon some of our own friends and relations. And when damage was done to our side, we would seek to retaliate with equal or greater damage, which our opponents would do their best to reciprocate. And thus a blood feud might be started, differing in no essential from those that have occurred among innumerable tribes throughout the world.

The blood feud, however, is not warfare, any more so than the sneak shootings of rivals by big-city gangsters. It is merely a form of revenge, which usually operates in the dark and may be carried on with ratlike slyness from generation to generation. Nevertheless, it can lead to war, and is in fact the nearest thing to war known among many peoples. But when it has become prominent among any tribe, it is usually complicated by psychological forces other than the stark desire for revenge. It generates a tradition; it is perpetuated by the power of training and the instilled belief that it is desirable for its own sake; and it is given strength by a systematically inculcated hatred.

Consider, for example, the situation among the Jibaro Indians of Ecuador, whom the anthropologist Rafael Karsten characterized as "no doubt at present . . . the most warlike of all Indian tribes of South America." When a Jibaro wishes revenge on an enemy from wrongs that he despairs of being able to redeem in person, he daily harangues his young sons, according to Karsten, in some such fashion as this:

"The *Shuāra* So-and-so killed my father, my grandfather, my brothers, when I was a child, carried off my mother, my sisters, and burnt our house. This blood guilt is not yet washed off. It is the duty of you, my sons, to avenge this crime and to kill the enemy or his sons, who are still threatening our family. If you do this, blessing and good luck will follow you in all your undertakings; you will have a long life, and be able to kill many other enemies. . . ."[1]

Hearing this chant in his ears from early childhood, the young Jibaro has the natural reaction: his mind is so filled with the thought of slaying the family enemies that it probably never occurs to him that any other course is possible. However, it may be doubted whether he has any single-minded thought of revenge. Note that the father appeals to the sons' desire to get on in the world; he promises them "blessing and good luck" if they reap a suitable crop of blood. And the young men may expect such "blessing and good luck" to accrue both from natural causes and from supernatural. The former will benefit them in the shape of the fame and honor that surrounds the successful warrior: the triumphant sniper of heads will shrivel and preserve his gruesome trophies, and in due course will enjoy a victory feast amid great ceremony and glory; also, he may open his way to a war chieftainship, since no one who has not killed an enemy can qualify for such an elevation. At the same time, he may appease the wandering soul of a murdered relation, which can enjoy no rest so long as the murderer is not brought to justice; and the severed head may prove to be a fetish of miraculous power to aid the growth of his crops, to bring him luck in the hunt, and to insure various other boons. If such religious and magical beliefs were not firmly planted in his mind, the Jibaro would have little incentive to carry on the feud.

This, however, does not tell the whole story. From his earliest days, the mind of the young Indian is conditioned to fighting; as a child, he may be taken to the battlefield by his father, so that he will become inured to blood-spilling; and as a child, he finds himself in a world of witchcraft, wherein malign enemies are always striking from ambush, with blows that can be redeemed only by means of life itself. As the Jibaros, in common with many savages, have no conception of natural death, and as the loss of life by accident or disease is always attributed to black magic, the question after every tragedy is not how it happened, but *who* made it happen. And when suspicion falls, a feud will follow. The belief in witchcraft, according to Karsten, is "nearly always the principal cause of the wars." But we moderns, whose own ancestors not many centuries ago were swept by a witch-hunting furor, should not have too great difficulty in understanding the urges of the simple forest-dweller, haunted by superstition and impassioned with the dread of natural phenomena that he cannot understand and has been taught to attribute to human malevolence.

One thing more should be noted before we turn from the Jibaros. These Indians clearly show how the blood feud, nursed by training and tradition and fanned by religion and superstition, may develop from private affrays into general conflict. For while many of the disputes are confined to families, others take the form of annihilating wars against whole tribes. The root character of the conflicts is shown by the fact that the attackers never move until they have consulted the spirits and found the verdict favorable; that they never, if they can help it, engage in direct fighting, but prefer the descent by night and the lance-stroke in the dark; and finally, that they never keep any enemy territory, which they suppose to be filled with supernatural terrors. We have here, in a word, nothing but large-scale blood feuds, in which the desire for revenge and the greed for glory are tempered by a formidable array of magical beliefs.

II

The blood feud, as most of us know, has been waged long and savagely among the Kentucky and Tennessee mountaineers; among the Scottish Highlanders; among the old Scandinavians, for whom it provided the chief theme of the sagas; among the Corsicans and Albanians, with the result that whole districts formerly faced depopulation; among the North American Indians, and even among the New England whites, who, in the days of the early settlers, followed native methods in their burning of towns, in their killing of women and children, and in the bounties they placed upon the heads and scalps of their enemies (those of small boys and girls being valued as highly as those of adults). Here we find that fear, the force of example, and the fury of revenge combine to submerge gentler and more humane emotions, no less surely than in the vengeance-fuming, superstition-ridden mind of the Jibaro.

But the blood feud among simpler peoples does not usually take on the same ferocious aspects as among peoples with a long training and precedent of harshness and cruelty. Spencer and Gillen,[2] for example, mention a feud in which a raiding party known as an *Atninga* was sent by some of the Arunta tribe of Australians against the Iliaura because of some deaths supposed to have been caused by the magic of the latter; the war party, however, held an amicable conference with two old men of the Iliaura, and decided to settle the grievance by killing three particular men whom the Iliaura did not like. This might seem a rather undesirable arrangement, especially from the point of view of the three victims; but the fact is that it not only halted the feud, but appeared a just and satisfactory settlement to the aggressors, who ended by decking themselves in war paint and holding a gay dance of victory about the slain bodies of two foes (the third having escaped).

The more typical blood feud is that which occurred among many of the North American Indians. Among the Plains tribes any brave who wished might enlist a party of followers and lead them off to deal vengeance to some neighboring people. But no matter how the raids were organized, the raiders came down "like the wolf on the fold"; the motive, unlike the wolf's, was always revenge rather than food; but the plan of attack was equally clandestine. However, after shearing off the scalps of one or two unwary enemies, the attackers would take care to leave a telltale mark, a sort of signature as the token of their triumph and a further means of infuriating the foe. The result, of course, was preordained. The relatives of the slain man, fired with the same vindictive fury as their adversaries, would brood over their wrongs and meditate vengeance; and some day—or, more probably, some night—the original attackers or their kindred would find themselves minus their scalps. And so the feud would go on and on, until whole families were destroyed or tribes decimated.

But again the greed for vengeance does not wholly explain the phenomenon. Again we may note the intrusion of the heroic ideal, with the glamour that it wreathes about bloodshed. Clark Wissler has well expressed the facts as to the Algonquins:

... the ideals of the tribe were such that the highest honors went to the man who was most daring and ruthless in such raids; the elders of the tribe continually exhorted the young men to be brave, aggressive and ruthless. These same elders often counselled peace, often met with representatives of their traditional enemies to talk peace, but at home preached the glories of the warpath. Obviously, under such conditions, all promises to cease raiding and killing were futile.[3]

As is shown by the braves who assembled their private followings to avenge injuries to their families or themselves, the blood feud is largely personal in nature, though it may lead to the most serious public complications. Its real character—and the way in which a tribal tradition and an artificially inflamed state of mind may produce destructive warfare—is demonstrated by the *kenaima* or *karaima* of certain South American peoples (particularly the Caribs). The *kenaima* is a blood avenger who is picked when other recourses seem unavailing; he is regarded as having supernatural powers, and is believed to become possessed by the destructive spirit or demon of retaliation. And he does act as if possessed by a demon. An outlaw from society, he is consecrated to the end of striking down his victim, and wanders through the woods as a creature apart, confined to a rigid diet, until under certain established conditions he slowly does his man to death. He then performs a prescribed ritual before being permitted to return to society.

As a *kenaima* may destroy not only the alleged murderer but all members of his family, the feud may not remain a personal one. Friends or relatives of the victims, enraged at the series of murders, may in turn commission a *kenaima* to take the blood of the original avenger—and thus may demonstrate once more the time-honored principle that hatred only breeds hatred, violence only breeds violence, and destruction only breeds destruction. If we are to take the word of A. Hyatt Verrill, "very often, before the feud . . . is over, entire tribes are decimated or wiped out." [4]

III

Observe that none of the above shows any economic motivation. The Plains Indian who takes his scalps in a sneak attack, the *kenaima* who skulks maniacally on the trail of a foe, the Australian who joyfully murders substitute victims after a conference with the foe, the Jibaro Indian who crouches in ambush to cull vengeance and heads, all have nothing whatever to gain in a worldly way (even though, as in the case of the Jibaro, they may expect magical benefits). The fact is that they may pay a heavy forfeit in a worldly way; they may give up the delights of this earth, they may fast, may turn themselves into outcasts, may subject themselves to rigid diets and disciplines and practice sexual abstinence for long periods in order to consummate the ends of vengeance. In the case of the Yurok of California—whose only conflicts were feuds to avenge grievances or imagined grievances—the burden of victory fell heavily upon the successful fighter; in fact, it fell upon him in exact proportion to the extent of his success. For, as we have also seen in the case of the Maidu of the same general region, he had to pay reparations to the loser for the damage he had caused. But despite the cost of winning a feud, feuds did occur, thus proving that the psychological impulses may be stronger than economic deterrents.

But among more warlike peoples, the economic penalties for feuds have been far greater. In South America, according to a statement of Thomas Whiffen (as quoted by Paul Radin), one result of the perpetual animosities between tribes "is that there are no recognized trade routes or trade centers nor are there any markets where the tribes of any language group may meet and exchange their wares. Even local markets are non-existent." [5]

While the statement just quoted may be somewhat exaggerated [proceeds Radin], still it holds to an amazing degree for most of the tribes of the Amazon basin and particularly for those of the northwest section. Such a situation taken together with the jungle and the climate is bound to react on the social organization. Not only is it almost impossible to develop large and cohesive social units under such conditions, but new tribes entering the area would be likely to have whatever integrated and unified social organization they may have brought with them greatly modified, if, in fact, they did not lose it entirely. [6]

Thus we see how the power of emotions and beliefs, acting through the cult of blood vengeance, may be a hindrance to progress not only economically but socially and politically.

It is much the same in North America, though there we do find a great exception in the Iroquois confederation, which was a peace league as between its own members, for whom it replaced the chaos of the blood feud with the stability of law. True, it was by no means unwarlike to outside tribes; but it showed that, among the members of the Five Nations (and eventually, Six Nations), the emotions that led to the blood feud could be curbed by the forces that demanded loyalty to the group. In the history of war-making —and the history of peace-making, and the history of the mind behind both peace-making and war-making—there is nothing more significant than this formation of a peace organization by five savage and fiercely independent warlike tribes. Hiawatha, the legendary figure whose preachments paved the way for the organization four or five centuries ago, must truly have been one of history's great men; the League that he established not only proved itself able to withstand the buffetings of time (at least, prior to the European's arrival), but showed that there is no psychological compulsion obliging hostile-seeming neighbors to indulge in feuds. The principle that the League could not make war without the consent of all its members; the principle that disputes among the members must be settled by arbitration—these indicated notable advances in human thought, and advances showing that the mind of man, when it fastens itself upon the ends of peace, can achieve those ends quite as definitely as it can reach the goals of vengeance and destruction when these are its objectives.

Chapter 3

Demons, Ghosts, and Gods

The black fury of the human vengeance-seeker is often less of a force in savage conflicts than the even blacker fury of unseen beings supposed to stride the winds, clouds, and waters.

The Jibaro Indian, who feels that the soul of a dead kinsman stands by approvingly while he shears off his neighbors' heads, has much company throughout the world; other lands also are commanded by ideas of demons and ghosts. Often, indeed, revenge plays no part at all; the warrior covets heads in much the way that the ivory-seeker covets ivory. And he goes out to get them in about the same spirit, by means of stealthy raids on unsuspecting victims, and at a minimum of risk to himself; frequently he picks women and children rather than able-bodied men, who might be so unobliging as to strike back. Strictly speaking, such head-hunting is like any other hunting, and is warfare only in the sense that the victims happen to be of the aggressor's own species. But the hatred and resentment it arouses can lead to the reprisals of actual warfare; and the murderous spirit that dominates it is not unfamiliar in actual warfare: for example, in the air raids and particularly the "sneak attacks" by which the more effective head-hunters of modern nations have swooped down upon helpless and unoffending communities.

But one should not picture the aboriginal head-hunter as necessarily a rogue of vile and ferocious aspect, or of a tigerish violence in most of his affairs. On the contrary, he has sometimes been described as gentle, gracious, and likable. Take, for example, the Dyaks of Borneo, some of the most renowned of all head-hunters. Alfred Russel Wallace has referred to them as "among the most pleasing of savages," and goes on to say that "They are good-natured, mild, and by no means bloodthirsty in the ordinary relations of life." And a later observer confirms this view:

It is difficult to understand how a people so docile and abounding in many characteristics so lovable still cling, thus tenaciously, to the ancient custom of headhunting. Crimes of violence, other than headhunting, are unknown among the Dyaks living in the jungles of Central Borneo.[1]

But though the author finds the custom "difficult to understand," he does throw a light upon it. He shows, for one thing, how intimately it is connected with ancient belief—with the idea of the head-hungry spirits of ancestors. Here is the Dyak point of view, as told by a native:

Always, always have our ancestors taken heads. The ghosts of our ancestors tell us to take heads. It is more important to satisfy the spirits of our dead ancestors who desire us to take heads than it is to please the government.[2]

Apparently we have here a revered old tradition, an embedded religious faith—as utterly beyond argument, and as irrational in its effects, as the pious view of the early Moslem that he must attain paradise by spilling infidel blood, or the devout conviction of Torquemada that he must redeem the heretic by turning him over to the "lay arm" to be burned to death.

Head-hunting among the Dyaks is described by William P. Krohn as "the cornerstone of their religious and spiritual life. In all great events, human heads are required." When a rajah dies, there must be a supply of heads so that he may be suitably accompanied to the Beyond; when an heir is born to a leading family, a head or two is necessary for a proper celebration. And in former times, when a young man wished to be married, he could not expect to be taken seriously unless he had captured at least one head. "In fact, he was not a man, but only a boy, and was not allowed to wear the habiliments of man's estate until he had secured a head in bloody conquest. . . . This terrible custom was the result of generation upon generation of teaching, tradition and practice." [3]

In other words, the disposition of the naturally mild Dyak had been perverted by old training and belief, in which religious conceptions were reinforced by elements of the heroic ideal, until even the women were on the side of murder. And thus, through no force in the world but that of the human mind, one of the most ferocious customs ever known became fastened upon an otherwise amiable people.

Among other tribes, it is believed necessary to hang a few heads from the posts of houses in order to insure the fertility of the fields.

And in the case of the Bagabo of Mindanao, the heroic ideal and the religious motive are closely intermingled. A man has the strongest inducement to commit at least two murders; this will give him social standing as well as spiritual protection; he will be entitled to display a chocolate-colored kerchief, and two great spirits will take him under their wing. For the merit of committing two further homicides, he may wear blood-red trousers; while if he can raise the score to six, he becomes an individual of prominence and can lead in war parties and assist at the annual ceremonies. However, it seems not to matter greatly which enemy head he snips off; a woman will do as well as a man; a sleeping foe will count for as much as one alert to strike back; and even his faithless wife and her lover may add to the points of the valorous brave.

Of course, all this is not precisely warfare. But it should not be impossible to see resemblances to the methods and mental processes of an age in which bomb-throwers are decorated for attacks in the dark against persons of all ages and both sexes.

II

The fear of and respect for the dead has had strange and various results among innumerable other peoples. The Ona of Tierra del Fuego and the Cape Horn Archipelago, for example, believe that their land has been apportioned for all time by a mythical ancestor; hence they never covet the territory of other tribes. And it is much the same with the Australian aborigines. But in other cases the desire to appease the dead might have pernicious results. Thus David Thompson, in his narrative of early America cited a few pages back, tells of a Nahathaway Indian who had died in a feud. The women of the tribe, zealous for the stricken one's welfare in the Hereafter, urged the survivors to "go to war and kill a Snake Indian," so that the slain Nahathaway "might have a slave to attend him in the other world. This would please him and make us friends when we met in the other world."

Often the stimulus comes from the medicine man; indeed, medicine men or *shamans*, along with all their associations of witchcraft and magic, are clearly behind many wars of uncivilized and half-civilized peoples. In some instances, as among the Jibaro Indians (already mentioned) and the Kenya tribes of Africa, the advice of the sorcerer is sought when the expedition is undertaken; in the case of the Salubba of southwestern Asia, the diviner stimulates himself with music "and works himself into an ecstasy, which helps him to hear the angel speak and hear the will of Allah." [4] But sometimes the power of the conjurer goes beyond mere advice-giving. In the northwest Amazons, he "has a considerable say in intertribal policy. War is never made without his advice, and in addition to his duties as tribal avenger and healer, he must warn the tribe of impending hostilities." [5]

It should be evident how a wily magician, working upon local fears and superstitions for the sake of his prestige, would be able to control and even cause wars.

But supernatural revelations are not usually confined to the official seers. Any man may have his own dreams and visions, which may offer guidance in war no less than in peace. Among the Maricopa Indians, every war party was led by a brave who had had the proper dreams; among the Crows, similarly, a chief had to have a vision of the impending battle before he could take command, and every raid was supposed to be preceded by a special revelation; among the Assiniboins, the leader had to stop four times on the way to the spot at which he had foreseen victory in the dream, and at the last spot he had to have another dream verifying the first.

Thus, beneath the suasion of the popular faith that dreams were inspired spirit-revelations, any fanatic might seize command; and, whipped into a frenzy by his self-induced hallucinations, he might inflame the superstitious tribesmen to savage and needless warfare.

Even apart from dreams and visions, religious ceremonials have done much to stimulate the martial spirit. War dances, war songs, and demonstrative war rituals are to be found among every combative people; the effect seems to be somewhat like that of religious revival meetings in producing a mass hypnosis, a mass hysteria. The war dances of the North American Indians are well known; the dances of the African natives, in which war drums boom and gaudily painted men cavort with enemy heads dangling from their mouths, have been reported by various writers. But few have given us more startling glimpses into the emotions behind these gory affairs than one finds in Thomas Whiffen's account of the Amazon. He tells of a dance, timed to the music of the drums, in which the men stir the great troughs of liquor with the forearms of their slain foes before drinking. He describes how they stagger back and forth to the intoxication of the dance; how their songs "become shrieks, maniacal, hellish"; how on one side one sees the dance of naked warriors, moving in perfect time with arms interlocked; while on the opposite side, dancing in the opposite direction, the paint-streaked and banded naked women wind about the sputtering fires to the light of torches and the music of flutes, pipes, and drums. And he testifies that even the white observer, despite all the accretions of civilization, cannot remain unmoved:

Forgotten cells in his brain react to the stimulus of the scene. He is no longer apart, alien in speech and feeling. He locks arms in the line of cannibals, sways in rhythm with them, stamps as solemnly, and sings the meaningless words as fervently as the best of them.[6]

If such effects are possible for a man reared with all the benefits of civilization, what of the simple uninhibited native? Beneath the delirium of the dance and the music and a contagious mass emotion, would he not be ready for any warlike extremes? Would he not, in fact, be converted from a self-operating individual into something more nearly like a cell in a great mechanism? And may not the emotions that moved the lone white observer, as he participated in the war dance of the Amazonian cannibals, be similar to the impulses evoked throughout the ages by military panoply and ceremonial—the impulses that produce a warlike mass distemper among people of normal simplicity and good will?

III

Behind the war dances, the war feasts, and the beating of war drums, we can see the leering crimson features of the war god —even though his actual form may not be that of a deity as we conceive the term, but rather of an avenging demon, or a blood-lusting ancestral soul. But the belief in some such divinity or divinities, in ghostly or fiendish or animal form, has haunted the background of much of the world's war-making.

Frequently the war god is a thing of horror, fitted to inspire courage in his followers and dread in the foe. Thus the war god Tairi of the early Hawaiians was a red-feathered, shark-toothed monster, whose grim image was accompanied into battle by his priest, amid frightful grimaces and yells that were accredited to the god. And thus, in the sanctuary of Montezuma in Mexico, there stood an enormous image of Huitzilopochtli. Clasped in the folds of a monstrous serpent, he held a bow in one hand and golden arrows in the other; his features were hideously distorted; he was adorned with a chain of alternate gold and silver hearts, which hung about his neck in mute testimony to the sacrifices he extorted from his followers; and on the altar before him three human hearts were smoking.

Such a guardian-power, if it did not inspire love, might at least have the suasion of the ogre in the fairy tale, which compels through terror that which it cannot obtain by good will.

As the very form of the Aztec war god suggests, we find in pre-Spanish Mexico an intimate relationship between warfare and one of the most pernicious of institutions, human sacrifice. The belief may be traced through a long ancestry, of which the Mexican extremes are no more than the ghastly culmination. The view that the god of fertility requires a human offering if the crops are to prosper; the view that the rain god demands victims if he is to open the floodgates of the skies; the view that the aging divine king must be rejuvenated by the blood of vigorous young followers; the view that the storm god or the river god or some other great malevolent power must be served, and that nothing pleases him so much as to feast on living men, women, and children; the view that ancestral souls must be attended in the Underworld or the Overworld by those who loved and followed them on earth—these are but a few among the notions that give rise to human sacrifice. But there can be no doubt that this institution and the beliefs behind it were intimately associated with warfare, and that wars have been waged for the sake of victims for the sacrificial knives; the case of the Aztecs is in itself proof of that fact.

The Spaniards under Cortes, in their battles with the natives, were repeatedly astonished by the enemy's efforts to capture them alive rather than slay them on the battlefield; this, indeed, was a leading source of native weakness, as it often enabled the invaders to escape when Montezuma's followers might have annihilated them. The Aztecs, it seems, were less aware that they were protecting their country in its dire need than that they were hunting for victims to offer up to their gods. The state of mind of the defenders is indicated by Prescott:

When Montezuma was asked, "Why he had suffered the republic of Tlascala to maintain her independence on his borders," he replied, "That she might furnish him with victims for his gods!"[7]

The priests, with an attitude as bloodthirsty as that of the heretic-hunters of contemporary Europe, acted as professional fanners of the flames:

As the supply began to fail, the priests, the Dominicans of the New World, bellowed aloud for more, and urged on their superstitious sovereign by the denunciations of celestial wrath. Like the militant Churchmen of Christendom in the Middle Ages, they mingled themselves in the ranks, and were conspicuous in the thickest of the fight by their hideous aspects and frantic gestures.[8]

We have, in a word, not warfare for economic or political ends; we have warfare for the sake of religion, or rather for the sake of certain fanatical religious beliefs.

The extent of the tribute exacted by those beliefs is indicated by the annual strife between the warriors of Mexico and those of Tlascala, which was prearranged for the sake of sacrificial victims. Once a year the two factions clashed "not with the intention of killing one another, but with the object of taking prisoners for sacrifice on the altars of their respective war-gods."[9] When one of the braves had been struck down, a tug-of-war occurred, in which his comrades struggled to pull him back to safety, while his opponents fought to drag him into captivity. If caught by the Aztecs, he was borne to their capital in a cage; after which he was tied to a slab, supplied with light weapons, and forced to fight for his freedom with a renowned warrior. His chances, however, were slight; he must rout six adversaries; otherwise, his heart would be torn out at the altar of the war god, Huitzilopochtli.

At this late date it may seem futile to ask the number of the victims. But the estimates, according to Prescott, vary between twenty and fifty thousand a year. And the extent of the practice is indicated by the fact that in a single building, in which the skulls of the slain were preserved, the comrades of Cortes, as Prescott tells us, "counted one hundred and thirty-six thousand."

And most of these victims were captives taken in war!

It may not be easy for us today to understand the outlook that caused men to make war and massacre thousands each year for the sake of the gods. But to the Aztec, the whole process doubtless seemed logical enough; in fact, at times it seemed logical even to the victims, some of whom, like the Christian martyrs before them, believed that they were embracing a glorious death and opening wide the highroads of heaven. Let us try to look at things through the eyes of the Indian. In his sight the gods were living beings, who required food and drink like other living beings, and might die unless properly nourished. And if they died, they could no longer bring fertility to the fields, nature would wither, and mankind starve. But what richer nourishment could the gods have than the source of all life: blood? What could fill them with greater satisfaction, more abounding energy? However, if a little blood was good, more was better, and still more was better yet. Therefore, let as many victims as possible be taken! Like a miser whose gold only whets the craving for gold, the gods but inflamed their taste for blood by lapping up blood. But their appetite could not be denied! What mattered then the disagreeable drawback of an occasional war? What mattered the lives of a few thousand victims annually when all life was at stake?

Once the premises had been accepted, the conclusion became logical. And the premises were accepted in the way of most articles of religious faith: unthinkingly. In that unscientific world of unknown and inexplicable phenomena, the basic assumption may have seemed reasonable, if not inescapable: rain from the gods, in return for the blood of human veins. And so the warriors fought for the rain god Tlaloc as well as for occasional choice victims for Tezcatlipoca the wind god and bevies of victims for the war god Huitzilopochtli. And yet they fought also for themselves; a little like the rabid Moslem or the battling Viking, they thought that death in combat would insure their rise to the abode of the gods, where they would enjoy the delights of paradise.

It is incontrovertible that, had the Aztecs had another set of beliefs regarding the gods, their social institutions would have been different; and their warfare might have been less perverted, or might not have occurred at all.

Chapter 4

Brigandage Exalted

When the Aztecs swooped down in quest of victims for their sacrificial altars, they were indulging in one of the most prominent types of warfare known to the centuries: the raid for booty. True, the usual object of the raid for booty has not been human flesh for the jaws of the bloodthirsty gods; yet occasionally the goal has been something even more repulsive—human flesh for the pots of the aggressors; and sometimes it has been human flesh in the form of slaves. That some of the most barbarous of early wars were actually slave-taking raids seems, in fact, beyond question.

Tales of blood-smeared looters, brandishing their dripping spears and swords and spreading ashes and devastation in their wake, come to us from across all the ages, and might almost seem to mark all man's history. Nevertheless, as we have seen, they do not mark all man's history; among the least civilized peoples, wars are not waged at all, or else are fought for ends unconnected with booty. When, therefore, does the ravager and plunderer arise? At what phase of man's existence do armed and organized robbers begin to prey upon peaceable communities?

It is evident that a people such as the Pygmies of the Congo, who had very little or nothing at all in the way of possessions, would not be a target for brigandage. Raids for booty, when something beside human captives or human flesh is sought, do not occur unless there is some booty to raid. A tribe must at least plant crops, or accumulate food, cattle, or other valuables before it offers an incentive to the raiders. And the rise of such possessions evokes an emotion unknown before: the emotion of greed, of acquisitiveness, which is not contemporaneous with mankind on this globe though largely coexistent with possessing mankind. And what was the origin of the raiders? It is impossible to believe that they pillaged because they could not have existed without pillaging; after all, man had supported himself on this planet for a long time by other means. But the growth of wealth did create a dangerous new psychological state.

It is easy to envision what happened. A tribe of nomads, in the course of their wanderings, chance to come to a rich valley, with villages more commodious than they have ever seen before, bright cloths and vases, and fat sheep and cattle browsing in the fields. In the mind of one of the savages a jealous thought arises: Why shouldn't he too enjoy ease and luxury? He communicates his idea to a comrade, who concurs: "Yes, why shouldn't we take what we want? Are we not stronger than the valley-dwellers?" . . . "Besides," the tribal wizard or medicine man might add, "our god Wuz, the thunder-thrower, commands it. He will protect his children." And so, after some exorcisms and other magical incitements, the plotters would wait for a very dark night, would steal down upon a village in the valley, slay the unsuspecting populace, and possess themselves of the village property, amid general rejoicings and ceremonies of thanksgiving to the god Wuz.

But this would be only the beginning. Finding it easier to support themselves by other people's industry than to forage in the woods, the tribesmen would make their raids regularly—one might almost say, professionally. They would honor the boldest and most successful raider; would establish a creed in which banditry, in the name of their chief god, was glorified as the most meritorious of callings; and would indoctrinate their sons in the ways of armed thievery. If necessary, they would even fight, since the victims might not always be as sheep awaiting the knife; and thus a martial code would develop among them, in which strength and skill at arms were exalted as the leading virtues; though if possible they would gain their ends by attacks in the night, without risk to their own skins. Moreover, the men of the tribe would find the new way of life a rousing and alluring one—much more interesting than preparing skins and grubbing for food; and so they would leave all the drudgery to the women, whom thenceforth they would disdain as beneath them, while they went forth on their gallant marauding.

This, of course, is only an imagined example; but all the evidence indicates that it conforms to the facts. A known case in point is that of the pueblo-builders of the southwestern United States.[1] These were peaceful corn-growing people, who had reached a higher level of culture than the wild tribes of the surrounding wilderness. The latter, not growing their own crops but learning by experience when the maize would ripen, would hurl themselves down to obtain it when it was least defended; their depredations differed from other armed robbery chiefly in their scale. Largely as a result of these ravages, the corn-growing district shrank to about the limits of the San Juan Valley, in which it was originally centered; and therein we see how a civilized area can be restricted, even shriveled, by freebooters from without. Yet though warfare may be inherent in the thefts, the original impulse is the brigand's desire for easy loot.

In many cases, to be sure, the raiders may be offshoots of the very civilization they plunder; they may have learned from experience the meaning of possession. But the pertinent fact is that the rise of ownership, whether in maize, cattle, fabrics, or metals, arouses a new set of desires and inflames a new psychological outlook in whole groups of men, who fall into a predatory way of life, develop the fighting creed and methods which that way of life demands, and exalt the arrow and the sword because these are the means of their livelihood.

II

If the fighting was merely incidental in the case of the southwestern raiders noted above, the same is true in many of the tribal wars; the one purpose is to obtain the enemy's property, and obtain it as cheaply and expeditiously as possible. In the Konde (Lake Nyasa region of East Africa), "When a chief wished to go to war he held secret council with his headmen and official advisers, the objective of the 'war' being to 'eat' the cattle of another chief." [2] Similarly, in the Kenya district of East Africa, the aim is plunder, without any superimposed glamour:

The various tribes of Kenya cannot be described as naturally warlike in disposition; there is no sort of feeling that war is honourable or desirable in itself, and when it occurred it was always for the purpose of obtaining some definite object, which was generally some form of plunder. A successful leader was respected and admired, but more because he had secured some material benefits than because of his valor or prowess. If possible, the same results would always have been obtained by craft or fraud, for preference. [3]

In such raids, the enemy would be in little personal danger unless he got in the way of the raiders or tried to defend his cattle; in other words, the fight was for cattle but not necessarily against men. And in this it shows resemblances to the horse-stealing raids of the Plains Indians, who would at times terrify and on occasion even scalp the owners of the horses, but whose real object was theft, and who were actually waging war only in the manner of a highwayman holding up a stagecoach.

But as a rule, in the case of the Indians and of most raiders for booty, the motive of robbery does not remain undiluted. Though man may readily descend to pillaging, he is so constituted that he demands some spirit-prop, some faith or belief to put a gloss over the ugly surface of banditry and elevate it into something dignified or noble. And so he fabricates the fiction known as honor or glory; he creates the heroic ideal, beneath whose magic he transforms the bare, raw face of thievery and brutality into something shining and resplendent. And having convinced himself that the wrongs he does are feats of gallantry, and having the example and approbation of the community to urge him on, the intrepid young warrior will not hesitate to gouge out the heart of an enemy whose one offense is to have some desirable property.

Both by the creed of valor and glory, and by the punishments and deterrents to those who fall short of the accepted standard, uncivilized man has elevated the plundering foray to the plane of a heroic exploit. Thus among the Crow Indians, according to Robert H. Lowie, "Social standing and citizenship . . . were dependent on military prowess; and that was the only road to distinction. . . . War was not the concern of a class nor even of the male sex, but of the whole population, from cradle to grave. Girls as well as boys derived their names from a famous man's exploit. Women danced wearing scalps, publicly exhibited the men's shields or weapons; and a woman's lamentations over a slain son was the most effective goad to a punitive expedition. There are memories of a woman who went to war; indeed, Muskrat, one of my women informants, claimed to have struck a coup and scalped a Piegan, thus earning songs of praise." [4]

Though two manifest stimuli were booty and revenge, "Lust for fame was axiomatically an end in all warfare." [5] And the artificial nature of this fame or glory is evident from the way in which it was defined. The rules were as definite as those of football or baseball. The touching of an enemy, whether he was wounded or whole and whether or not the stroke served any intrinsic purpose, was held to be a "coup"—something as meritorious in its way as a home run among modern diamond braves. The snatching of the adversary's bow or gun in hand-to-hand strife was deemed almost as great an honor—perhaps to be compared to a stolen home-base. And the theft of a horse from its picket in the hostile camp ranked third among the feats of renown; while to be the "pipe-owner," the planner of the raid, was to be worthy of celebrity in the fourth degree.

So deeply had the red-stained cult been instilled that temperate counsel had little chance to be heard. To quote from another authority:

The elders of the neighboring tribes talked peace and at times sincerely sought it, but the marauding traditions were so carefully fostered that raiding for blood, captives and plunder was on the level of second nature. The Indian who had not taken part in a raid was a curiosity. The honors and social esteem of the tribe went to him who had killed his man.[6]

"Why did the Crow fight?" asks Lowie. "Certainly not from an uncontrollable instinct of pugnacity. It was disgraceful to fall to fisticuffs within the tribe, and I have heard unfavorable comments on the brawls of white men." [7] Even the economic motive, as Lowie demonstrates, comes far from accounting for the facts:

The desire for horses was the most "economical" motive in Plains Indian warfare, yet a Crow rated higher for cutting loose one picketed horse than for lifting a dozen freely roaming about. And what was the use of horses after one got them? Gray-bull acquired 70 to 80 head, but a few fleet animals for the buffalo chase, several mounts, and a few pack-horses would have been more than ample for his needs. The Crow, unlike the Central Asiatic Turks, never dreamt of milking mares or eating horse flesh. A large herd had sheer ostentation value; the owner could offer twenty horses for a wife instead of five; and he could give frequent presents to his father's clansfolk if he liked to hear himself eulogized.[8]

The nature of the fighting is further evident from the fact that to deal the enemy even a glancing blow with the coup-stick was considered more meritorious than to kill him. And the established system of hero-recognition is also significant: a feather worn upright in the back of the hair denoted the first to strike, a feather with an upward slant pointing to the right designated the next in line, and so on. Men would try to save their lives when they could; and, indeed, constant prayers were heard among the Crows that the enemy might be killed easily and safely; but on the other hand, a competition not only with the foe but among the tribesmen was certain to develop. Just as a football star, a tightrope performer, or an actor may revel in his difficult work, but would drop it the moment the prospect of applause was withdrawn, so the Indian fighter might regard the raids with pride and delight, though he could see no reason to continue if the crowd did not stand by, ready to shout "Bravo!" But under the stimulus of admiration, even death might not seem too great a penalty.

Under the stimulus of admiration, even death may be painted in alluring hues. George Bird Grinnell has stated the case in regard to the Cheyennes:

Boys and youth were trained to feel that the most important thing in life was to be brave; that death was not a thing to be avoided; that, in fact, it was better for a man to be killed while in his full vigor than to wait until his prime was past, his prowess were failing, and he could no longer achieve those feats which to all seemed so desirable.[9]

But this does not tell the full story. When a youth grew to manhood, he would naturally wish to espouse a maiden of the tribe. But what sort of a reception could he expect unless he had proved his mettle on the warpath? What sort of reception could a modern young American man expect from the average American damsel if he was stigmatized by the community as a wartime slacker? Since the cold hand of social disapproval was upon him, the chill would communicate itself to whomever shared his fate—and the girl who overlooked this incubus would indeed be compellingly in love. So when the man sought to woo the maiden by wrapping his blanket about her, a stinging query as to the foes he had slain might end the courtship.

But the Plains Indians were not alone in using the mating desire as a goad along the warpath. Among the Salubba of southwestern Asia, a variation of the same method is employed:

Before the attack the tribal emblem Abu-d-Dhur is fastened to a camel which walks in the midst of the bravest youths on horseback. The warriors are accompanied by the prettiest women and girls of the camp, who, with their bosoms bared and hair loosened, keep shouting:

"He who runs away today shall never receive anything from us. . . ." In order to raise the courage and steadfastness of his warriors the chief orders the Afta, a fancy litter, to be placed on a she-camel and the handsomest of the girls to take her place on it.[10]

If a natural pugnacity led the men to battle, would there be any need to superimpose the stimulus of feminine beauty?

III

Among certain groups, we can observe the actual development of a raiding tradition.

Take the Abipones of the Chaco region of South America. These tribesmen are not believed ever to have included more than a thousand warriors, yet overran vast districts, stealing horses by the drove, and spreading bloodshed and destruction. Within five or six generations, an obscure, poverty-ridden agricultural tribe living in mat tents converted itself into a band of terrorists bringing reminders of the Mongol horsemen. And how was the transformation accomplished? Partly, of course, through the importation of the horse, but largely, also, through a change in the people's state of mind. First, by the hatred implanted by the white invaders, and the lust for revenge. And, secondly, by the development of a military tradition. Their chiefs apparently had no peacetime authority, but chieftainship became important in war, and was passed on from father to son—though not unless the son had shown himself brave and able. Secret societies admitted their members on the basis of valor; and a complicated ceremony, to test the man's hardihood and fortitude, was enacted whenever a candidate was raised to the honored rank of *hocheri*. And so the fighting spirit and fighting methods were engendered. To raid and deal terror appear to have been the chief objectives of the tribe; but the fury against the invader, even when aided by the vast maneuverability supplied by the horse, would not have sufficed without the military traditions which sent the men forth on the warpath with a fanatical frenzy.

Another tribe, the Mbaya-Kadiueo, went even further in their explosive development of militarism. We see here the actual birth of a military class, and the corresponding rise of slavery; the leaders seized from the Spaniards and Portuguese the idea that war could be waged most successfully if the soldiers existed as a caste apart, without the need to give time or energy to food production. But, obviously, food *did* have to be produced. Many warrior tribes have solved the problem, at least in part, by passing the heavy work over to the women, while the males pursued the manly ways of valor. The Mbaya-Kadiueo went a step further, by enslaving the Chané people, from whom they had drawn almost every notable previous development in their civilization; being thus freed by the labor of their vassals, they made their men an exclusive military class. Thus, as so often throughout history, we see how warfare leads to exploitation. And thus, even more importantly, we observe the contagion of an idea. The white invaders had a military class, who did not work the fields nor build the houses; therefore the Indians too would have an exclusive military class, though the cost was the enslavement of a friendly tribe. It is true, of course, that many other tribes had the example of the whites and did not follow it; but it was not always possible to follow it, at least without violation of ancient traditions; and, besides, ideas are like seeds, of which multitudes may take to the wind for every one that sprouts.

But to observe most vividly the deliberate production of a raiding mentality, we must turn to Africa. Among the Bantu tribe of Maputju, for example, if the warriors disobeyed their chief's command to return to the battle after a defeat, they might be humiliated by having to get down on their knees and fetch water like women; and, in addition, they might be obliged to put out a brush fire with their bare hands.[11] These incitements to a warlike state of mind, however, were mildness itself by comparison with the methods adopted by that notorious tribe of marauders, the Zulus.

At the close of the eighteenth century, the Zulus were a small, inconspicuous group. But they swiftly developed a terroristic power, which reached its apogee in 1824; under their war-chief Chaka and his successor Dingaan, they made themselves a scourge to the surrounding peoples, whom they either incorporated into their empire or annihilated (preserving only the young boys and girls). Their ostensible object, like that of the other African tribes, was cattle theft; cattle formed the basis of their society; and their wars were no more than organized cattle raids. But the significant thing is their manner of inciting the raiding psychology. Bloodshed was their goal and ideal; as among certain other militant peoples, a youth was not held to have reached manhood until he had taken human life. Since a slur against the young male's maturity and virility is the supreme insult, it would be a rare youth that would not try for his victim.

From early childhood, the Zulu had been drilled for army life. Every regiment had children in training; the military segregation of boys began at the age of seven. Yet even with all this preparation, the leaders did not trust to the fighting spirit to keep the recruit in line. Among various other inducements, not the least prominent was the force of terror; the evident aim was to make the dread of the commanders overmaster the dread of the enemy. Let the warrior not come back without his dagger, his *assegai*—not unless he wished to be killed. And let him not shirk his duty during the conflict! The chieftain Chaka, evidently realizing the importance of morale, ordained that cowards should not be allowed to live; and took the practical precaution of designating a few men as cowards after each engagement, whether or not anyone had flinched before the foe.

And as if this were not enough, the chieftain made no provision for return marches. The troops could move in one direction only! If they retreated—or if they were defeated—some hardened regiment would be ordered to kill them in a body.

It is therefore evident that Chaka was no believer in "nature" as a sufficient goad to the combative impulse. He had greater reliance, obviously, on the impulse of self-preservation, which made it more dangerous not to fight than to fight, and created cowards by playing upon men's fear of being designated cowards. His methods show that he found his followers malleable to the suasion of terror; and depended for his successes quite as much upon their docility beneath a ruthless command as upon their pugnacity in the face of the enemy.

It is possible, however, that given the military tradition and the military ideas which he had built up, Chaka could have erected a warlike machine even without Draconian measures such as the massacre of cowards and recalcitrants. And this brings us to an all-important point: that most men are no more able to escape from the atmosphere of opinion in which they are reared than they can leave the physical atmosphere that surrounds them; most men accept their beliefs ready-made no less unquestioningly than they do their tribal customs. If they are told from early childhood and never given reason to doubt that the ruler of the world is the demon Epi-wee-juk, who rides the back of the thunder clouds like a great black panther and spits down the rain from between his hissing jaws, in most cases they will never doubt the reality and the panther qualities of the demon Epi-wee-juk. If they are taught that the moon is a mother-goddess who requires monthly burnt offerings of grain or goats, or if they are incessantly warned that it is unholy to bathe in a certain stream at the time of the new moon, or that it is unpropitious to plant the crops when five long-tailed birds are seen coming from the south, or that the death of a man with red sores on his skin or red patches on his cheeks proves that a witch has committed murder and must be hunted and slain—if men are sufficiently indoctrinated with such ideas, and indoctrinated sufficiently early, they will accept them implicitly, and make them the launching platforms for their deeds. This is easily demonstrable, for unsophisticated men throughout the world have acted upon precisely this type of belief. Furthermore, if the inculcated faith or tradition proclaims that a sword is worth a thousand plowshares, that a man whose hands are not crimsoned with enemy blood is no man at all, and that no self-respecting woman would defile herself with the embrace of such a sub-male, then the atmosphere of opinion would give the youth no choice except to be a warrior or an outlaw. Here we have an artificially developed creed serving as the support and background of military institutions, which would collapse with the collapse of the creed.

Actually, there is no extreme of conduct which men will not espouse as natural and reasonable, if only they move in a dense enough atmosphere of belief. The institutions of cannibalism, of head-hunting, of human sacrifice, of the *suttee* or widow-burning, of slave-trading and slave-hunting, of witch-hunting such as agitated civilized Europe and America, and of the Inquisitorial torture-chamber and stake, are but a few from among the catalogue of horrors that men will approve and perpetuate if the atmosphere of belief be sufficiently thick. So why should warfare be an exception to the rule? If men will chase ghosts and witches and redden altars with human blood beneath the persuasion of their beliefs, will they not wage war for the same reason? And just as the belief may be the sole incentive to the shocking social conduct of certain uncivilized peoples, so it may be the exclusive cause of their wars.

Though we also are powerfully ruled by opinion, we seldom

realize the extent of this force in simpler societies; we seldom understand how often it is the guiding power of their life. Clark Wissler has expressed the facts as to the American Indian:

White people living with the American natives are repeatedly astonished at their extreme sensitiveness to disapproval and ridicule. In fact, the whole control of the local group in aboriginal days seemed to have been exercised by admonition and mild ridicule instead of by force and punishment.[12]

And Bronislaw Malinowski, in a revealing monograph,[13] has shown how native society among the Melanesians is governed by the power of prestige and opinion; how men, who might otherwise shirk their obligations, are held back by what they would lose in the regard of the community; how the disapproval of the majority may be a sufficient deterrent or punishment for crime; how the rules owe their power not only to material self-interest but to ambition and vanity; and how a damper on extreme action is the fear of suicide, which may occur if a man or woman has some sin or outburst of passion to expiate, or has been unjustly injured and wishes to protest or reveal an intolerable situation. The objectives, of course, vary widely, but the incentives that bow the natives to communal opinion and even drive them to the extreme of suicide are of the same breed and nature as those that goad men on to warfare. In all cases alike, the actions are subject to the atmosphere of belief and the psychological currents set up within that atmosphere. And thus, despite all the surface differences, the situation is exactly the same when a girl in the Trobriand Islands jumps from a palm-tree so as to redeem herself in her people's eyes from the insult inflicted by her suitor, and when a Plains Indian or a Zulu takes to the warpath in order that the tribesfolk may not despise him as a coward and a half-man.

Chapter 5

Kings, Human Victims, and
Gold-Seekers

We have seen that, judging from all the available evidence, Paleolithic man led an unwarlike existence. As already suggested, it is the almost universal opinion of Paleolithic archeologists that, with the possible exception of the enigmatic Solutrean laurel leaf, the Old Stone Age of western Europe contains no artifact which can be interpreted as a specialized man-killing weapon. Correspondingly, we have observed that recent makers of stone implements either have no group fighting at all, or else have nothing more warlike than occasional relatively unsanguinary feuds. But we have also noticed that, as agriculture replaces food-gathering and the network of customs and beliefs grows more complex, merciless conflicts do break out, sometimes rooted in religious and ceremonial ideas, but frequently revolving about the greed for possessions and usually bolstered by artificially nourished concepts of honor, glory, and the heroic ideal.

When we turn back to the Old Stone Age and trace the ancestry of war, we find indications of the same line of development as among the latter-day aborigines: first, a pristine era without organized fighters, and then the gradual or sudden appearance of attacking bands. This does not mean that random affrays or personal feuds may not have occurred, or that there was necessarily a "Golden Age of Peace" such as the ancient Greek poets and certain moderns have loved to describe. But it does mean that there was a period without organized strife—without military methods, training, or tradition. The statement of V. Gordon Childe regarding the early dwellers in the Danube Valley might apply to many peoples at the dawn of civilization:

The earliest Danubians seem to have been peaceful folk; weapons of war as against hunters' tools are absent from their graves.[1]

51

But how did the change to warfare occur? The answer should be found in our previous observations. We saw that, while the blood avengers and the religious zealots might stain themselves with gore, it is the lure of possessions that leads most quickly to organized large-scale conflict. Just as the Zulus would not have banded together for their cattle raids and imposed their ferocious military discipline had there been no cattle to steal, so the first significant warriors of the white race would not have swung their swords had they seen no prospect of loot. All the evidence suggests that civilization had attained a considerable development, various arts and crafts had sprung up, and a settled, comparatively comfortable mode of life had been evolved before the plunderers were induced to strike.

Apparently the earliest civilizations of the Mediterranean, by originating the idea of luxury and wealth, implanted the craving for luxury and wealth in the minds of the barbarians swarming at their verge. Thus the generalization which Childe makes as to Mesopotamia may be extended to other lands: "The growth of militarism might be justified first by the necessity of defending the wealth of Babylonia against plundering raids of barbarians from the desert and the mountain." [2] It has also been suggested that the shortsighted business zeal of the contemporary industrialists contributed to the war-making. We have reason to believe that the traders of the civilized world, four thousand years ago, provided the wild tribes of the north with their best bronze weapons—thereby falling into the folly that later peoples have repeated again and again to their deadly cost. "Commercial greed would seem, even at this early date," writes F. G. Scott Elliot, "to have been unaffected by any, even the most obvious forebodings." [3] Enlarging on this interpretation, Childe explains that, "at least in Denmark and southern England, the costly bronze armament merely consolidated the authority of the ruling groups as did the knight's armor in the Middle Ages. . . . But the petty chieftains were now equipped with weapons not only to enforce obedience on their followers but also to lead them to conquer the new lands that their still neolithic rural economy demanded—even to plunder the rich civilization that had unwittingly armed them." [4]

It is not quite clear how the Neolithic rural economy demanded the plundering of "the rich civilization that had unwittingly armed them"; in any case, one finds it hard to believe that the wanderers of the northern woods and marshes, had they been denied the boon of bronze, could not have continued to exist quite as before, doubtless as backward and as contented as ever. But granted their new super-weapons (which must have seemed as revolutionary as does the atom bomb today), and granted also the jealousy and greed evoked by the sight of ease and comfort—and what could we expect? Inevitably, the raiding psychology. And so the makers of the bronze weapons were felled by their own customers, or their customers' sons.

Centuries later, after the invention of iron tools, the same stupidity was repeated; again the tribesmen of the north, drawn by the lust of possessions, swept down upon the civilized cities; and swinging the swords furnished by the forges of those very cities, dealt irreparable blows in Greece, Crete, and elsewhere. The case, however, may have been complicated, as some writers have insisted, by the rise of offshoots from the civilized communities, who developed a military state of mind and a greed for easy gain, and turned back to pillage and destroy their own defenseless parents.

All the above suggests that war may have been, as H. J. Massingham contends, "the purely artificial product of a civilization gone rotten." [5] This conclusion is reinforced by the fact that agriculture and the attendant civilized developments may exist and have existed without a descent into warfare. ". . . in Africa none of the first agricultural migrations were warlike. It was these peoples who caught the first brunt of African warfare, for the obvious reason that they were settled in mine-bearing (viz., wealth-producing) regions, which aroused the covetousness of the predatory warrior, who followed some restless and scheming princeling belonging to the very family and community he first quitted and then attacked, he or his descendants." [6]

Behind these "scheming princelings"—whether they were degenerate offspring of civilization, or outsiders indoctrinated with the creed of the destroyer—two sets of intimately related beliefs are to be seen. The first is concerned with kingship and leadership in general. And the second is connected with a peculiar, developed set of acquisitive ideas, involving not only the accumulation of inanimate property and gold, but the capture of human victims for sacrifice or slavery.

II

Among many uncivilized tribes, well-defined leadership is unknown. Sometimes, as with certain South American Indians and various tribes in Liberia, Madagascar, New Zealand, and elsewhere, the medicine man has considerable power, and may even be one with the chief; now and then, as with the tribes of northwestern America, it is the rich man that has most influence, though there are, strictly speaking, no chiefs; frequently, as with the Plains Indians and the Jibaros of Ecuador, the chief functions in war only. But history provides notable examples of war-chiefs who have been able to maintain their authority after the hostilities were over; and the case of the Mbaya-Kadiueo Indians, mentioned in the last chapter, shows how it is possible for war-chiefs and their followers deliberately to elevate themselves as a warrior caste, taking advantage of a warlike atmosphere to force economic and political domination upon a captive people. Here we find, in the war-bred state of mind, not only a situation that leads to violence among ruling groups, but one that produces the ruling groups themselves. For the psychological attitudes that make men try to impose their will in warfare are the attitudes that make them try to impose their will in peace as well.

Nevertheless, there is a more important relationship between war and leadership than in the direct transformation of war-made leaders into peacetime autocrats. For chieftains were probably not in most cases originally associated with ideas of war; the evidence indicates, rather, that they were involved with ideas of magic when not concerned with the simple need for administration—and that their warlike connections developed later. The fact that some savage kings are killed when they show signs of physical impairment, or even when in the prime of life, indicates the belief that they are filled with a magical essence which must pass on undiminished to a successor. And in many regions the idea of kingship is intermingled with that of nature and of divinity; the king is identified with a natural force, such as the sun or a river, upon which the people depend for life; and accordingly he is worshipped as if he is that natural force. "I am Cyrus, King of the universe," the celebrated Persian conqueror proclaimed.[7] . . . "I have made the heavens and the earth," is the boast which a scribe of the twentieth Egyptian dynasty accredits to a dead king. "I have ordered the mountains and formed all that is thereon. I am he who made the water, creating the inundation. . . . I make the hours and create the days; I send the festival of the New Year and form the river." [8]

We may be inclined to smile, not too indulgently, at this "I am God" attitude. But we should remember that the people of the ancient world had not our facilities for judging the scientific evidence. What awe, what reverence, what dread must have attached to the person of him who, in popular belief, could throw up the mountains and create the river! How men must have bowed in terror and adoration before the being upon whom, in their own unquestioning view, their very lives depended! Surely, the object of all this fear and veneration would really have been superhuman if he had not himself been impressed—yes, if he had not been converted to the idea that he was of a superior substance, which entitled him to command and trample upon mere commoners! From this state of mind there arises the absolute monarch, the despot. And from the absolute monarch there springs the ruthless warleader. The process may be long, involving many generations, as in Egypt; but once you have a leader who is held to be the source of all power and the distributor of all rights, you have a man who will drive his people forth for the sake of his own aggrandizement, glory, or authority. And usually the road will lead through exploitation and slavery to war.

By way of a beginning, when vast irrigation works are built as in Egypt or Mesopotamia or vast monuments are constructed, what more simple than for the divine sovereign to command the labor of his people? Being divine, has he not the right to command it? Has he not likewise the right to requisition part of the produce of their fields as his own just share? And later, when he has waxed fat and desires to exploit some other country, what more natural than that he should assert his godhood in order to arm the youth of the land? And what more natural than that the people should bow and yield to the great life-giver, the source of all bounties and punishments, dreading to disobey even if the thought of rebellion ever entered their superstitious minds? With the reverence for their divine leader on the one hand, and the lure of honor and booty on the other, the stage was all set for the fury of pillaging armies.

All this would not have been possible, however, without what W. J. Perry terms an "education in violence"—which was accomplished not only through the example of the ruthlessness of leaders, but through the growth of various ideas, mostly connected with acquisition. And the earliest of these, as we have seen, have to do with the seizure not of inanimate property but of human victims.

Though head-hunting today survives at most in a few remote jungles, the principle behind it has been almost universal among peoples at the dawn of civilization. In order to provide nourishment for the crops, or to launch a war canoe or open a canoe house under proper auspices, or to appease the wind god or the rain demon or the souls of ancestors, one must either secure a few heads of neighbors or enemies, or else capture the neighbors or enemies whole and offer them on the altar of the gods. As a substitute, however, if the neighbors and enemies are uncooperative and keep at a safe distance, one may cut down a few of one's kinsfolk, or even one's own sons and daughters. We have seen the extremes of human sacrifice among the Aztecs, and the close connection of this institution with warfare; but the Aztecs, as already noted, merely carried a world-wide custom to its logical if hideous climax.

Among scores of peoples—the Druids of Britain, the Arabs, the Phoenicians, the Greeks, the Romans, the Incas, the Mayas, the Fijians, and innumerable other groups—a cult of human sacrifice has existed. Frequently, as with the Aztecs or the Norsemen in their offerings to Odin, it was the prisoner of war who was sacrificed. But the victim was not always the warrior; the Skidi Pawnees, for example, would capture an enemy maiden, treat her with especial consideration, then one night would suddenly seize her, string her up between two poles, and shoot her through the heart. Even more striking, however, was the case of the Khonds of India, who, before the British in the last century put a halt to the practice, had a well-developed cult of human sacrifice, raising prisoners to be immolated somewhat as we raise cattle for the slaughterhouse. While the connection with the god of fertility is here usually more evident than a relationship with the local Mars, in Jeypore it was "the blood-red god of battle Manecksoroo" who had to be placated. "Thus on the eve of battle, or when a new fort, or even an important village is to be built, or when danger of any kind is to be averted, this sanguinary being must be propitiated with human blood." [9]

When we have a mind so dominated by false ideas, and so immured against normal sympathies that it will seek the bloody death of fellow beings for magical ends, we have a mind that will not rebel at the brutalities of warfare, and may even embrace such brutalities eagerly for the sake of those same magical ends or other ends equally desired. Thus we return to the conclusion that an "education in violence" is necessary to reconcile men to human sacrifice, and that the same force leads them toward war. And this it does in two ways: by a hardening of the spiritual fiber, which makes war and its atrocities appear tolerable; and by a demand for victims, who can be supplied (with greatest satisfaction to the local population) from foreign sources.

One may note the convergence of several lines of belief. The sacrifice of the divine king, which may prove inconvenient or may encounter objections from the king himself, can be avoided by the immolation of substitutes, who may be offered in ever-increasing numbers, and may be obtained most painlessly from other peoples. At the same time, companies of retainers for dead lords may be found from the same source, which likewise may be tapped for human offerings to place under the doorposts of houses, or to seal up in gates or bridges, or to throw into wells or bury in the fields as a guaranty of good crops or as safeguards against storm demons and disaster. Thus warlike raids may arise for the sake of human victims. And when in time the idea dawns that the captives may be more useful as living servants than as dead offerings, human sacrifice gives birth to slavery, itself a fruitful source of war; there seems to be reason to accept the view, expressed by Edward Westermarck and others, that slavery originated in war and conquest. Even though not all the earliest slave raids may have stemmed from human sacrifice, note how the vicious circle continues: slavery having sprung from warfare, wars will spring from slavery, or rather for the sake of taking slaves or in the rebellions of slaves or armed precautions against such rebellions. And so man's education in violence will continue.

One thing to mark in all this is the genuineness of the original belief, however mistaken. The Phoenician mother who saw her first-born devoured by Baal doubtless surrendered him with torment in her heart even if with tight-drawn lips and stoical eyes; she felt that her actions were right, and for the general good; her spirit was not unlike that of many a mother throughout the ages when her son girded on a sword or shouldered a musket and went forth at the command of his god, the State. And similarly when Abraham in the Old Testament was willing to sacrifice his first-

born to Jehovah. Beneath the very barbarism of the act there may
be something heroic—the sacrifice must be made, therefore let it be
made with inflexible will. Even when the current mores demand
self-immolation—as many a Hindu woman proved when she con-
signed herself to the flames of the *suttee*, or as Spartan boys showed
when in their city's declining period they let themselves be
flogged to death in hysterical orgies—the victim who has been sufficiently drilled in the current creed will not ordinarily hold back.
It is all a question of what tuition the mind has received. If it has
been taught the ways of human sacrifice, slavery, or warfare, it
will accept human sacrifice, slavery, or warfare as natural and right.
And that is why innumerable victims have bled on the altars of
innumerable peoples; and that also is why the kings of early times,
having won popular recognition of their divine status and enlisted
the gods on the side of their depredations, have been able to break
through the normal peaceable inclinations of their subjects and to
found military aristocracies whose exploits during forty centuries,
according to one annalist, make up "the greater part of what usually passes for history." [10]

III

The accumulation of human booty, though it may have pointed
the way to the accumulation of booty in cattle and inanimate property and even to the conquest of territory, does not represent the
acquisitiveness that has been most prominent throughout the ages,
or most conspicuously connected with warfare.

Ordinarily, acquisitive impulses and activities have centered
about one word: gold. And this, when one comes to think of it, is
a strange thing. For gold is something that cannot be eaten. It is
something that cannot be made into a cloak against the cold; it has
no power to fertilize the fields, nor any medicinal qualities; it is
too soft to be of use in axes, hammers, or plowshares, and too
scarce to be of much utility in the walls of buildings; in most practical ways, it is inferior to iron and copper, and even to flint; and
consequently it is considered worthless as any pebble by savages
not indoctrinated in civilized ways. And yet this metal, intrinsically
almost valueless, has played a dominant part in human affairs; has
been a goal and an allurement throughout the centuries; has incited
explorations and migrations; has caused thrones to topple and em-

pires to crack; has built up great areas, and devastated areas, and been a major historical stimulus to the disputes of individuals and the wars of nations. Surely the reason, since it cannot be found in external nature, must be in the mind exclusively, and in the beliefs and desires distilled by the mind. Therefore, if we would understand the background of the gold-engendered wars, we must understand the background of man's reverence for gold.

We may notice, to begin with, that although other media of exchange (such as strings of shells) have been devised by certain peoples, acquisitiveness has nowhere evolved to its full rapacity where gold has not been at the basis of trade. Among the Incas, in whose communistic state both gold and silver occurred in fabulous-seeming quantities, the precious metals were prized only because they "could readily be made into beautiful objects fit for the use and adornment of the rulers of the land, but not at all fit to be used as a symbol of value." [11] And much the same is true of the Mayas, who would make bells and other artistic articles of gold, which was no more an incentive to avarice or to warfare than are marble and onyx among us. What, therefore, was there in men's minds to produce the sharp difference between the Incas and Mayas and scores of other peoples?

Perhaps the entire reason will never be known. But G. Eliot Smith, in his *Human History,* provides an answer—and one that is plausible not only because of the specific facts adduced, but because it is consistent with what we know of the mental reactions of early man. In ancient times, according to this analysis, the Red Sea cowrie shells, whose shape was suggestive of life-giving properties, were highly valued as charms; they were deposited by the myriads in the old Egyptian graves, and were used by the living as amulets on necklaces and girdles. After a time, however, people at a distance from the sea had difficulty in securing the shells, and contrived imitations of clay, which by degrees gave place to more attractive imitations made from the yellow metal which they found in the desert. Accordingly, gold itself came to be prized; the magical qualities originally attributed to the cowrie shells were ascribed to the gold as well—even when its shape was not that of the cowrie. Thus, unintentionally, the early believers in magic enthroned the yellow metal.

To sustain this conclusion, the author offers many bits of independent evidence. Take, for example, the case of India. In the ancient *Satapatha-Brahmana,* according to Professor Smith, gold is "said to be immortal, born of fire, the rejuvenator of mankind, conferring long life and many offspring upon its possessors. . . . Gold was endowed by the sun with its beautiful color and luster, and shone with the brilliancy of the Sun-God. Hence it was regarded as a source of life, as well as of light and fire." [12]

Not only in India, but in Mesopotamia, China, and Egypt, gold was esteemed as the charmed life-giver. In the latter country, it was valued as one of those substances that could prolong the existence of a dead king and turn him into a divine being—a view which not only gave it the enchantment of Aladdin's lamp but prompted rulers to send out expeditions to obtain this supernatural prescription for immortality. It was inevitable that it should also prompt them to any fighting that might be incidental to their quest.

The process, to be sure, was a slow one. But from the mind-made magical qualities of gold, other mind-made qualities took birth, so that a small quantity of the metal came to be treasured as the equivalent of days of work, of a plot of land, of a yoke of oxen, of a house or a boat or of sorely needed food. Thus commerce and magic began to mingle, and the artificial value given to gold found expression in ancient Sumer in a gold currency. Not that there was any natural relationship between the dense, glittering metal and the objects it would purchase, the services it would command, and the sacrifices it would entail; it was merely that the mind of man provided the link, and conferred prestige and piled power upon him who could dig or buy, extort or steal enough of the favored substance. With such an incentive, the path was paved for small-scale and large-scale quarreling over gold.

Thus we see how the artificially inflamed beliefs and desires behind one metal have given a fiery prod to the acquisitive impulse, and have been responsible for wave after wave of warfare. It is known, of course, how large a part the lust of gold has had in stimulating bloodthirsty raids among scores of peoples: how it encouraged the Vikings to their looting expeditions, how it spurred the Assyrians, the early Greeks, the Romans to pillaging affrays, sometimes organized on a vast scale; how it made possible the mercenary armies of Greece and Carthage, and of medieval and modern times; and how—most important of all—it nourished a spirit of callousness and of violence that tended toward war's indefinite propagation, somewhat as a fire will tend to indefinite burning, so long as fuel remains.

But we shall return to all this in later chapters. For the present, let us note one important further bit of evidence, in regard to the barbarian hordes that were the bane of civilized communities in ancient and medieval times, and that were responsible for some of history's most devastating wars. In the migrations of these plundering multitudes, historians of the economic school have been wont to see nothing more than a search for food. Modern research, however, has shown that the Huns, Turks, Mongols, and other nomadic warriors sought something more alluring and glittering than bread:

They are not seeking food, but someone whom they may dominate. They have moved from gold-field to gold-field, imposing themselves as rulers on the peaceful sedentary agriculturists. . . . To say that Asia has been devoid of adequate pasturage is absurd; for as Douglas Carruthers has shown in his work on *Unknown Mongolia*, there are thousands of square miles of fertile pasturage in Dzungaria that never have been tenanted by nomads or irrigators. The reason for the absence of the irrigators lies in the fact that, with one exception, none of the rivers contains gold. . . .[18]

Here, as in so many historic cases, the idea behind gold is the idea behind migration, invasion, and warfare. And it is not economic or biological necessity that dominates; it is a psychological persuasion. It is a thought, a desire, which, founded upon a magical belief, has been converted into a devouring passion, and thunders across cities and civilizations with the blindness of an avalanche.

II

Sword-Wielders of the
Ancient World

Chapter 6

The Land of the Pharaohs

Whether or not certain moderns are correct in regarding Egypt as the mother of civilization, one of the first and greatest of recorded civilizations did arise in the valley of the Nile. And because we here see men emerging from the prehistoric dimness into the light of an advanced society, we have one of the best opportunities for observing the reactions of a new civilization to the problems of peace and war.

All the indications are that the Egyptian in the beginning knew little and cared little about warfare. But there are some scattered evidences of early fighting, as in the "Narmer palette," which dates back to the first dynasty, and shows a king putting his enemies to flight and gathering the booty. In the Middle Kingdom and the Old, according to James Henry Breasted, "warfare was little more than a series of loosely organized predatory expeditions, the records of which clearly display the still unwarlike character of the Egyptian." [1] An inscription of Ameni, a general under Sesostris I (twelfth dynasty, Middle Kingdom) mentions an army of only four hundred men, whose purpose, however, may have been gold-seeking and not fighting; in any case, these appear to have pushed on almost unresisted. Subsequently, indeed, the numbers were greater, but could not have been great; Breasted estimates that "it is not probable that any Pharaoh ever invaded Asia with more than twenty-five or thirty thousand men, while less than twenty thousand is probably nearer the usual figure." [2]

In other words, the whole active army of ancient Egypt was roughly equivalent to one modern army division! Even allowing for the fact that the population of ancient Egypt was much less than that of many modern nations, and that the difficulties of transportation and supply sharply limited any expeditionary force, we certainly do not see militarization on anything like the modern scale.

And what were the objects of the Egyptian wars? Some of the

earliest arose over property rights and the avarice excited by possession or hoped-for possession. Specifically, some of the first mines gave birth to some of the first conflicts; as long ago as 3300 B.C., according to A. Moret and G. Davy, "The Egyptians had to defend their mines against the Asiatics and advance the domain of their arms. So from economic greed was born military conquest. The oldest known military autocracy seized the mineral regions of Sinai, which it needed, and 5,300 years ago began the long career of aggressions and of so-called economic wars which are the counterpart of civilization." [3]

In view of the observations of other commentators, the date 3300 B.C. may seem a little early; but this does not affect the central point. In any case, despite such affrays as those mentioned above, the average early Egyptian probably saw and certainly heard less of warfare than does the average citizen of Basle or Stockholm today. As we may divine from Breasted's references to "loosely organized predatory expeditions," the wars for the most part were little more than raids for booty, such as we have observed among various half-civilized peoples. Breasted tells us, for example, that the Syrian campaign of Sesostris III, which brought great glory to the Egyptian name, was "no more than a plundering expedition . . . far from achieving the conquest of the country." [4] The place of booty in the early Egyptian battles is shown by the fact that, once the enemy had been driven from the field, the victorious force did not as a rule conduct a long pursuit; often it forgot all else in its eagerness to pluck the spoils abandoned by the fugitives, and to strip the bodies of the slain. The usual spirit of the Egyptians was exactly like that of their foes the Hittites when, in the Battle of Kadesh, Rameses II was enticed into a trap and faced annihilation; it was his immense good fortune that the great mass of Hittite charioteers, just when they might have crushed the Egyptians, were drawn to the loot lying scattered about the field, and, abandoning their chariots in a covetous rabble, forgot all about the possible defeat of the foe amid their pillaging.

Even apart from such orgies of snatch-what-you-can, the common soldier could expect a reward if his side prevailed. While he had to surrender all that he collected to the general hoard, he would not be forgotten in the final distribution: the Pharaoh, after reserving a portion for the temples of the gods and keeping another part for his royal purposes, would remember each member of the army, with due regard to rank and services: one might be given a male or female slave, another a sword or spear or a necklace or bracelet taken from the vanquished, and still another might be honored with a measure of gold, "the gold of bravery." Thus, down to the most miserable retainer, all who had participated in the campaign might regard themselves as shareholders, who could expect their cut of the dividends.

War, in a word, was a sort of business speculation, seasoned no doubt with incidental spice of travel and adventure. And the business was not made unattractive by so grave a risk as has accompanied later conflicts; casualties in these early wars were comparatively few; the shields were shrewdly made to diminish the peril of mortal injury; and while we do know of one battle of the eleventh dynasty in which nearly sixty men seem to have been killed, we have little evidence in early Egypt that war on the whole was a reeking, gory affray in which a merit was made of blood-letting for its own sake.

II

Time, however, was to make a conquering empire out of Egypt. As far back as the Middle Kingdom, we can see the rise of a military class—connected, as so often throughout history, with the institution of royalty, and built upon the desire of kings to keep themselves in power. Though they were professional soldiers— among the earliest which history records—they seem to have had many of the qualities of a police force; their exact numbers are unknown; but they were garrisoned in companies of one hundred in the palace and the various royal strongholds throughout the land, and thus gave the impression of having been intended quite as much to guard against domestic insurrection as against a foreign menace.

But whatever its size and functions, this force was small in scale and influence compared with the armies of later days. Egypt did not receive an "education in violence" until the coming of the Hyksos or "Shepherd Kings," who invaded the country and ruled for several centuries, before being expelled by the seventeenth and eighteenth dynasties (roughly, about thirty-five hundred years ago). In its resistance to the intruder and its development of an organization suitable to eject him, and under the spur of his example and beneath the glow and éclat of a great national triumph and liberation, the once-unwarlike nation became militarized. And this is true even though, according to Manetho, the original conquest had been accomplished "without a battle." Not only the physical fact but the psychological impact of war made itself felt for centuries; men's minds had been trained to tolerate and to accept war; and the twin magnets of gain and glory, as in so many later conflicts, were the lodestones that drew the masses. A strong, well-organized army had been developed as the fruit of the campaigns of many years; Ahmose I had served both as general and king; and the example of fighting—particularly since it was attended by the promise of victory—had provoked the spirit of fighting. Breasted has ably described the militarism which had overtaken the Egyptian of the time of Ahmose I in spite of his "usually unwarlike character":

The long war with the Hyksos had now educated him as a soldier, the large army of Ahmose had spent years in Asia and had been for a long or shorter period among the rich cities of Syria. Having thoroughly learned war and having perceived the enormous wealth to be gained by it in Asia, the whole land was roused and stirred with a lust of conquest, which was not quenched for several centuries. The wealth, the rewards and the promotion open to the professional soldier were a constant incentive to a military career, and the middle classes, otherwise so unwarlike, now entered the ranks with ardour.[5]

But though a warlike strain had developed in the people, the outlook of the leader could in itself bridge the gulf between war and peace. This fact is remarkably illustrated by two successive sovereigns. The first was Queen Hatshepsut, an outstanding ruler of close to thirty-five hundred years ago. A great-granddaughter of Ahmose I, she did not share her ancestor's imperialistic leanings, but tried her best to develop the country in ways of peace. And during her twenty-two years of power, the land did remain at peace. Following the death of her half-brother and husband Thutmose II, she had become the principal wife of the youthful Thutmose III, with whom she differed widely in policy, since he —along with the priests of Amon and many of the court officials, who apparently hoped to profit from the spoils—favored campaigns of aggression as strongly as the Queen supported peace. And immediately after her death Thutmose III—who was to become known as the "Egyptian Napoleon"—launched his wars in Palestine and

Syria while doing his best to destroy the monuments and obliterate the name of Hatshepsut.

III

As the country became more militarized, two characteristics of all combatant nations gradually developed. The first was the rise of a definite military class; the second was systematic training of the body and mind for the purposes of battle. It is hard to say if the recruitment of the army was ever on a voluntary basis, but in any case the terms of service were such as to make self-interest rather than the fighting spirit the guiding force. To the poor peasant, a virtual serf compelled to till his land and pasture his cattle under backbreaking conditions for a meager subsistence, the prospect of holding some land of his own must have been well-nigh irresistible—and this prospect was held out to him if he joined the army, along with exemption from taxation and immunity from forced labor during his term of service. But even if a man were not one of the oppressed rabble, even if he were one of the fortunates who had independent means, the lands given him as the reward for his services would add to his estates and augment his income.

Nevertheless, despite all the lures to the self-seeking, and despite the rise of a military autocracy which even the Pharaohs and the great lords could not scorn, the essentially unwarlike mood of the Egyptian remained evident—remained evident in the fact that the army had largely to be recruited outside native ranks. Comparatively early in Egyptian history we find the rise of that peculiar, that hybrid, that paradoxical species of soldier, the mercenary. Surely, if man warred because of some inescapable prompting, some biological urge, no foreign adventurers need ever have been paid to fight other men's battles! But already in ancient Egypt, as in many and many a later land, we find the people hiring their fighters instead of fighting themselves—a little as when a man, having a distaste for the drudgery of digging a ditch or rearing an embankment, engages laborers to do the job for him at a stated price. And so we see the Beduins of the desert, the Negroes of Nubia,.and even ex-enemies and prisoners of war entering the bodyguards of the kings and nobles.

The native element, in fact, constantly declined after the first great surge of conquest. In the day of Rameses II (thirteenth century B.C.), there was a whole division of five thousand men that included not one native Egyptian; and by the time of Rameses III the greater part of the infantry was formed of mercenaries originating in Asia Minor, Phoenicia, Libya, and elsewhere. Mercenaries, coerced prisoners, and slaves, however, were merged, so that at our distance in time it is hard to distinguish among them; and this was especially true in the fleet, at least half of whose crewmen were Libyan captives—captives who bore on their skins for life the scars of the branding-iron to discourage desertion.

Again, we find evidence of anything but a love of fighting in the revival by Rameses of a system a little like the conscription of modern nations. Whereas the peasants were still ready to exchange their peonage for the relative advantages of the army, the privileged classes had come to disdain the military profession, and, in fact, were wont to mock and gibe at the soldier—scarred and beaten and worn to a shred, "like a bird that trembles" if he reaches the enemy, and "like a piece of old worm-eaten wood if he returns to Egypt." But let the lovers of ease and luxury complain as they would; the overseers of the Pharaohs nevertheless made their way through the land, on a great man-hunt for the young and able-bodied, who displayed much less of a spirit of fight than of flight.

IV

Even when military service was not exacted by the scourge and the bastinado, there was often a potent compulsion. Only a few men of the privileged classes, upon whom military service fell as a hereditary obligation, were summoned during peacetime; but let the war drums sound, and all must join the marching ranks (unless, like the modern man of draft age, they could find some legitimate ground of exemption). If a father was too old to serve, his son must replace him; and if he had no available son, some other relation must bear the burden. But what if he held back without excuse? The king or the lord of the manor, from whom he had a tax-free parcel of about eight acres of land, would seize his property—and he and his family would be plunged into poverty.

For those dedicated to a military career—specifically, the children of such commoners as wished their sons to enjoy the army's advantages—a long and systematic training was provided. Like other warring peoples, the Egyptians did not rely too much upon schoolmistress nature; they felt it best to train both the muscles and the minds of the young. There were special schools in which youths were drilled in the most lordly of warlike professions, that of the charioteer; and there were barracks where the rank and file were trained in the use of the lance and shield, the mace, the bow, and the battle-axe, and were prepared by marching, running, jumping, and other exercises. We can still see, in the tomb paintings, representations of the recruits engaged in energetic wrestling contests, tackling and challenging and throwing one another with every evidence of athletic prowess. Also, we can see portrayals of the war dance by which they whipped up their spirits for the battle; we can observe them leaping in the air, in a fashion reminding us of the red Indians; brandishing a bow in one hand and a quiver of arrows in the other; and prancing and pirouetting vehemently.

Here is evidence that the Egyptian, even as the modern who takes an intoxicant to keep up his nerve, felt the need of some sort of battle stimulant. It is a well-known psychological fact that any mass emotional movement—from the hysteria of a revival meeting to the sadism of a lynching mob, the frenzy of a flagellant procession and the self-inflamed furor of a fighting host—produces a mania in which the individual becomes inundated and virtually absorbed by the multitude, so that their reactions become his reactions and he is driven to extremes of which individually he would be incapable. One may question whether a reasoned knowledge of this truth has existed among the many peoples that have resorted to war dances and kindred war-provoking ceremonies; but, certainly, the intuitive knowledge has been present; and, certainly, they have acted as if they realized that mass psychology would effect what individual psychology could not accomplish. And so we find the Egyptians, though far from the most warlike of peoples, joining the great historic stream by provoking a group hypnosis, and drowning the will and desires of the individual amid the emotions of the crowd.

Other common methods, likewise, were followed. Though we find no more boastfulness and vainglory than in other lands, these elements were by no means neglected. Some of the Pharaohs were wont to shout their victories to the skies, doubtless only with the thought of enhancing their own renown, but with the incidental effect of adding glamour and seductiveness to warfare. Take, for example, the case of Rameses II, after the Battle of Kadesh, in which, as we have seen, he was almost destroyed by his own bad leadership, and undoubtedly would have been destroyed had the enemy soldiers not been more avid of booty than of victory.[6] Forgetting all about the negligence that had led him into a potentially fatal trap, and disregarding the loss of nearly a whole army division, the failure to attain his main objective, and the undermining of his country's influence, he honored himself with a triumph, while making an offering of captives to the gods, and took pride in adorning the temples of Luxor, Thebes, and Karnak with reliefs depicting the glories of his feat. To add to the effect, the scribe Pentaur copied out an ode which the monarch duly published on temple walls throughout the kingdom. After telling how "the vile king of the Hittites" mustered "warriors that were as the sands of the sea" and overthrew part of Pharaoh's army but dared not attack Pharaoh himself, the poet tells of Rameses' single-handed exploit:

Then arose Pharaoh, in strength like unto his divine father Mentu, and took weapons in his hand, and put on his armor, like unto Baal.

And he took his horses, called "The Victory of Thebes," which were from the royal stable of Miamun.

And Pharaoh smote the horses, and they charged into the center of the host of the Hittites, and there was none with the King.

And the King looked, and lo! the enemy surrounded him, two thousand and five hundred of their best warriors, three men in each chariot; and they came behind the King and upon each side of him.[7]

Here was a predicament to daunt even a Horatius. But was Rameses daunted? The poet goes on to recite how the Pharaoh, having prayed to "Father Amon" to make him "like unto Mentu, the God of Battles," showed himself versed in heroic traditions:

My left hand shook the spear, and my right hand held the sword, even as Baal, before them that saw me.

And I charged into the midst of them, two thousand and five hundred chariots with horses, and the hoofs of my horses trampled upon them.

None raised his hand against me, for their hearts failed them, and with fear were their limbs loosened, and the spear and the dart they dared not wield against me.

And I cast them down into the water, as falls the crocodile from the bank, so fell they. Yea, one by one they fell upon their faces, and at my pleasure I smote them.

I smote them. There was none to escape me.[8]

A most human monarch, assuredly, was Rameses, and one who saw no merit in understatement. And if he was only doing as thousands have done before him and since, was he to object if he incidentally aroused a sense of the glory of battle in the minds of generations of hero-worshippers?

One must not imagine, however, that Rameses II, any more than the other warring Pharaohs, was exclusively warlike in his aims. He appears to have known the value of peace, whose importance is recognized in a treaty drafted in 1272 B.C. by his representatives and those of Hattusilis, the Hittite king. After some preliminary pomposities about the "valiant this" and "valiant that," both monarchs agreed to renounce conquest against the other, and accepted a defensive arrangement whereby each would aid against the enemies of his allies. A thousand gods and goddesses of the Hittites, and a thousand of the Egyptians, were called upon in solemn witness to the pact; a curse was pronounced upon any violator, and a blessing invoked upon all that honored the treaty. And the treaty *was* honored, whether because of dread of the curse or owing to more practical considerations, but possibly in the main because Rameses and his advisers recognized the virtues of peace. And through the remaining forty-six years of his reign and into that of his son Mernepthah, the agreement was kept, though it meant the surrender of Egyptian ambitions in Asia.

Before the time of Rameses, one of the most remarkable characters in ancient history had been responsible for a brief flaring of the spirit of peace. Amenhotep IV or Akhnaton, a Pharaoh who had fallen heir to the military glories of the conqueror Thutmose III, was as unmilitary an individual as ever occupied a seat of power. His absorption in the ways of religion and peace brings inevitable reminders of the Hebrew prophets of later centuries; he appeared to care little that his unmartial activities would cost the Egyptian Empire in Syria and Palestine. Though execrated by subsequent generations of his own people, he stands forth in world history as one of the first great foci of revolt against the ways of the sword. His failure to propagate his ideas or achieve his main objectives implies not so much any personal shortcoming as an inadequacy in the times; the soil had not been sown psychologically for his great innovations—all the less so since the wars of Thutmose, featured by seventeen campaigns in Syria and lesser expeditions into Libya and Ethiopia, had occurred not many generations before and had drilled the people in military ways of thinking. Under such circumstances, he was bound to fail; he had trampled roughshod not only upon the religious creeds but upon the warlike traditions of a people—and traditional ideas are too powerful to be uprooted merely by a blast of royal authority.

Even so, he did not fail completely. While he was a unique and a solitary figure, and perhaps something of a fanatic in the singleness of his convictions, he goes far beyond his predecessor Queen Hatshepsut in showing that the turbulent world of more than thirty-three centuries ago did produce thinkers to whom the gains and glories of the warpath were less than the ideals and the devotions of peace.

Chapter 7

From Tiglath Pileser to Hannibal

Second only to Egypt among the great empires of the early ancient world, we think of Babylonia. But though her wars were many, it is not chiefly her warfare that impresses us; we recall her commerce, her agriculture, her star-gazing, her art of brick-making, her palaces, her monuments, her scribes, and her clay books.

The indications are that her first wars were in the nature of raids for booty, sprung of the greed of barbarians or semi-barbarians for the wealth of settled communities; such raids occurred frequently in the course of early Mesopotamian history. Yet well over four thousand years ago, we can observe a different type of warfare in the conflicts of the small Sumerian city-states. One of the earliest known warlike records was left in the famous "Stele of the Vultures," which reports the victory of Lagash over Umma: we note the strutting and vainglory of the victors, and read a symbolism whereby the vanquished are represented as held in a net like caught birds by the god of Lagash.

It was in about the twenty-third century B.C. that one Lugal-zaggisi conquered much of Babylonia, and showed the conqueror's typical frame of mind by inscriptions acclaiming himself as having been given "dominion of the country" by the great god Enlil. Despite such divine favoritism, he was defeated and captured by another warring king, Sargon of Agade, who was known as lord not only of Babylonia but of Spurpurla, Kish, and Uruk, and who even during his lifetime wore a nimbus of heroic legends—though, even so, he appears to have ended his life ingloriously beneath the sword-thrusts of his own troops.

Warlike rulers and peaceful rulers followed: Naram-Sin, his conquering grandson, who called himself "king of the four quarters of the earth"; and Gudea, who has left mostly inscriptions dealing with the construction of temples and palaces, and so suggests that, even if peace was by no means universal in the early

Oriental world, there were long periods and wide areas that never heard the tramp of war-bound troops.

Out of the little that we know of early Babylonian warfare, a few facts emerge in clear relief. And not the least prominent of these is the religious nature of the wars, their invariable association with the gods and the will of the gods. We see this when Eanna-tum, the priest-ruler of Lagash, appeals for help to the god Nin-girsu, who appears to him in a dream and promises victory over his enemies; we observe it in the booty which various monarchs devote to the gods; we witness it in the oaths uttered by the war-ring factions. "I have sworn the oath," says Eannatum, "and the men of Umma have sworn the oath to Eannatum, in the name of Enlil, the king of heaven and earth. . . . If at any time they shall deviate from this agreement, may the great net of Enlil, in whose name they have sworn the oath, overwhelm them." [1]

As the above suggests, the Babylonians seem to have been desirous of establishing a rude justice or at least a rude principle of conduct by means of their wars. A further indication of this fact is the celebrated code of law promulgated by Hammurabi after the series of struggles whereby he united the country. But, at the same time, violence appears to have been sanctioned in the name of the gods, under whose devices the kings might blaze forth as con-querors and unifiers of the country. The relationship of religion and national unity has been summarized by a present-day authority:

The fact that the Mesopotamian universe was conceived of as a state—that the gods who owned and ruled the various city-states were bound together in a higher unity, the assembly of the gods, which possessed executive organs for exerting outward pressure as well as for enforcing law and order internally—had far-reaching consequences for Mesopotamian history. . . . It vastly strengthened tendencies toward political unification of the country by sanction-ing even the most violent means used toward that end. For any conqueror, if he was successful, was recognized as the agent of Enlil.[2]

Thus early in human history do we find God walking with the strongest battalions.

Yet the gods simultaneously served a pacifistic purpose; the kings, as their representatives, might officiate in the quarrels of the city-states. Since the word of the mediator was the word of heaven, would it not be difficult to ignore it? And so possible warfare was averted, as when Utu-Hegal of Uruk settled a boundary difference between Lagash and Ur. And a rudimentary foundation for international law was established.

II

When we turn to Babylon's great sister empire Assyria, we find a state largely specialized on a military basis. While opinions have differed widely and this nation has not been without her modern apologists, the burden of evidence seems to support the view that she was largely a predatory community, whose basic industry was robbery. In her we can see the systematic development of the raid for booty, which had been the occupation of kings in Egypt and elsewhere but had nowhere else reached such a flaming apogee. Many of the Assyrian monarchs appear to have made it their regular business to go forth with their iron-encased spearmen, their cavalry, and their two-wheeled chariots, for no reason other than to pillage the farms and towns of their neighbors, and to carry away booty and captives. And in the minds of the Assyrians, as in those of all plundering peoples, a blood-letting fury seems to have been aroused. Across the dimness of more than three millennia, we can read this attitude of mind amid the boastfulness of an inscription by Tiglath Pileser I (twelfth century B.C):

The bodies of their warriors like the storm-god I hurled to earth, their blood in the ravines and on the heights of the mountains I made to flow down. Their heads I cut off, by the side of their cities like grain heaps I piled up. Their spoil, their property, their possessions, to an unnumbered quantity I brought out.[3]

The emphasis here is not only on cruelty but on loot; and the loot of the provinces was the preoccupation of the Assyrian before the conflict and after, when the governor made sure that the conquered kings brought in their assigned yearly tribute and that the toiling masses paid their heavy taxes. Not only from the point of view of the sovereign, but from that of the common soldier, the wars promised rich returns in spoils. After each battle—and sometimes after some leading men of the defeated army or city had been impaled or flayed alive as a warning to the recalcitrant—the rank and file would bring in the heads of the slain, throw them upon the general pile, mention their name and company to the scribes, and leave with the assurance of a reward proportionate to the slaughter they had committed. Thanks to this system, the wounded and the defenseless had small hope of being spared. As for the ruler himself —his reward, as befitted his imperial dignity, was the lion's share of everything; with the cold-blooded calculation of a mortgage-holding banker, he made sure that he would not be cheated.

The records tell us how the royal scribes, like the king's watchdogs, surrounded the loot. Their wary eyes apparently lost track of little; prisoners and inanimate articles alike were listed; everything worth the trouble of transportation was added to the inventory and carted off to Nineveh. The property of the vanquished king led the way, his jewelry and his household utensils of gold, silver, copper, and brass gleaming in the vanguard; while his wives and daughters, his slaves and servants, chariots and horses, rich cloths and ornate furnishings were included in the triumphal procession. The very images and wealth of his gods were snatched from their temples; the poor suffered along with the rich, and were either sold as slaves, or borne off with their families to till the soil of a foreign land. As for the enemy troops—the most likely-looking were drafted into the Assyrian army to fill the war-made gaps.

In the profaning of the temples and robbery of the alien gods, the Assyrians were guided by something more than bare-faced greed (though this was rarely absent). Somewhat as when a modern army feels it necessary to keep its own flag waving while that of the enemy lies low in the dust, the Assyrians held it essential to humble the foreign gods as a matter of prestige, of psychological effect; if they proved their own deities superior and better able to protect their votaries, they would go far to check the foe's will to resist and crush the enemy morale. (Incidentally, the same desire to crush the enemy morale may in part be behind the inscriptions that recount, in terrifying detail, the atrocities committed by the victorious forces of Ashur.)

For the Assyrians themselves, the gods were at home on the battlefield; the religious element in their conflicts was ever-visible, particularly in regard to their chief divinity, Ashur. And though this may seem strange when we remember the frightfulness of the Assyrian wars, it is actually no more paradoxical than the zeal with which men in many ages have associated the tragedies of battle and the sanctities of theology. "We must at least credit the Assyrian with honesty," writes Olmstead, "when he carried on war in the name of Ashur, for to him the whole progress of Assyrian expansion was the triumph of the deified fatherland. To the extent that all states must acknowledge Ashur chief and father of the gods, the Assyrians were perfectly prepared to act the armed missionary. . . . Once Ashur was accepted as the chief god and taxes were regularly paid, the conquered or deported were reckoned good Assyrian citizens." [4]

All this will indicate that Assyria spared no effort to cultivate the psychology of war. Her entire administrative system was based upon a single conception, one common enough among the nations of the world, yet never developed to a more logical extent: the view that thievery in the name of one's country is commendable, and killing under proper auspices worthy of reward. And thievery and killing were not only legitimate but desirable according to the Assyrian code. The soldier who set out for the battlefield was hardened to a toleration of slaughter by thought of the respect paid to the slayer; his sensibilities to human suffering were blunted by sight of the tortures inflicted upon prisoners as a sort of terror measure; his greed was aroused by anticipation of booty, and a spirit of rivalry was awakened in him by competition in the seizure of spoil and the taking of heads. Both the sanctity of religion and the authority of the State were on the side of the war god. It was Ashur himself that commanded the conflict; it was Ashur that rode forth amid the shrieking and frenzy of the battlefield; it was Ashur that ordered the victory and directed the punishment of those sacrilegious enough to oppose him. How, then, presume to believe the strife not a glorious thing? Did not the living representative of Ashur, the sovereign himself, proclaim that it was glorious? And was the sovereign also not a god? Assuredly, here was no matter for common men to question—theirs but to heed the mandate of the deities, and with pious humility, to march forth and take their share of plunder and of heads.

III

The Assyrians and Babylonians were not the only ancient people who went out to kill and be killed in the name of the gods. The religious motive was prominent also among the Hebrews, a small people who otherwise would be of little importance in the history of war.

The Jews did not merely fight battles for their religion; they also on occasion refused to fight: Yahweh was for them not only the god of the dripping sword but the god of peace, in whose name the lion would lie down with the lamb. And here is something noteworthy in the highest degree. From the point of view of a practical-minded contemporary, it might have seemed the apex of folly, it might have seemed criminal of the prophet Isaiah to paralyze the military activities of King Hezekiah by his anti-militaristic declamations, crying out in the name of his god with such effect that no preparations were made against the advance of the Assyrian Sennacherib, the breaches in the walls of Jerusalem were not repaired, and steps were not taken to protect the city's water supply. Yet here (if we except the preachments of Akhnaton) was something new in history. Here was the spirit of peace pleading against the will to fight. Here was the religion and the philosophy of the peace-maker triumphing over the combative impulse—and it is immaterial whether or not the triumph was for the people's immediate practical advantage; its significance is in the proof it brings us that man's thoughts and emotions may be as powerful to preserve peace as to provoke war.

Even though the outcry of the prophets could not prevent the onrush of the invaders, they could counteract much of the destruction. It was owing to the prophets, and the spiritual counsel they offered, that the blast hurled at Jerusalem by Nebuchadnezzar did not doom the kingdom of Judah to the obliteration that descended on her sister realm of Israel. The return from Babylon in 535 B.C., fifty-three years after the transportation, has been recognized as a triumph of the human spirit, its courage and its faith, over seemingly insuperable obstacles. And that triumph was made possible by the very forces that had stayed the hand of the war-maker.

The effect of religion is once more to be seen in the tenacity—one might almost say, the fanaticism—with which the Jews subsequently clung to their beliefs, though the cost was often death, as when the Syrian Antiochus dispatched an army under Appolonius to stamp out the worship of Yahweh, and massacred men without mercy, and enslaved women and children. Or take, again, the attitude of those large bodies of Jews who refused to fight the Syrians on the Sabbath, and were mowed down without resistance sooner than violate their principles. One may regard their position as incredibly quixotic, foolhardy to the last degree—and perhaps it was so considered by the Maccabees, who decided to fight whenever attacked. But consider what was implied by the refusal to ignore the taboo against Sabbath fighting. Every natural impulse, every demand of self-interest and self-preservation, was on the side of resistance; even the most unpugnacious of men, in a similar situation, would ordinarily have struck back; even animals so uncombative as deer and rabbits would have fought for their lives if likewise driven to the wall. But not the Jews. Rather than desecrate the Sabbath, they let themselves be slain. In other words, an idea and the emotions connected with it—the idea and emotions of the Sabbath, and of the great god Yahweh who commanded the Sabbath—were stronger than the self-protective drive. And though the fruits of non-belligerence were death, non-belligerence *was* achieved, and achieved as the product of no forces but those within the minds of men. Here, surely, is proof that just as man can be trained to fight, so he can be trained to resist fighting, and to resist it even to the death.

There is something peculiar and a little ironic in the fact that the Hebrews were the first to teach us this truth. For, like most other peoples of the early Near East, they had been warring for centuries: fighting the Canaanites when they entered Palestine, fighting the Philistines, fighting in guerilla and plundering bands of doughty raiders (as among the tribe of Benjamin), fighting in civil wars as in the conflict between David and Saul, fighting in the gory border struggles of the twin kingdoms of Israel and Judah, and fighting in the early days with a heroic life a little like that of the Greeks, and with a class of professional soldiers, the *Gibborim*, to which men aspired to belong, and whose one vocation was battle. That a strong, war-resisting force should arise among such a people —a people which, on a small scale, had shown most of the features of the great combative empires—is surely evidence that the seeds of peace do lie unobserved even in the heart of supposedly warlike peoples, and that the very will and strength that swings the sword may also, if the mind be suitably trained, be used to oppose the sword-swinging.

IV

More famous in the history of warfare was a great African offshoot of an Oriental stem: Carthage, the daughter of Phoenicia.

The first and most obvious fact about her citizens is that they were commercial-minded but rarely war-minded, and for the most part did not do their own fighting. In Egypt, as we have seen, it became customary for the Pharaohs to enlist foreigners in their ranks; in Carthage, this practice was carried even further. Alien tribesmen by the corps—Gallic footmen, Balacrean slingers, Numidian cavalry, and others—were assembled under their own chiefs; they were obtained *en masse* by negotiation and sale from their own countries, while the Carthaginian citizens ordinarily served but in small numbers in special divisions (compulsion being exerted only in times of public peril). At a period when the army had an estimated strength of seventy thousand, the native troops were confined to one thousand in the cavalry (a source of honor, which only the rich could afford), in addition to fifteen hundred in the superbly outfitted "Sacred Band." But what does this reliance upon mercenaries mean? That the average Carthaginian had as much liking for soldiering as the average American has, let us say, for garbage collecting; he did not deny this to be a necessary occupation; but so long as he could pay others to do the work for him, why soil his own hands? We have here something pretty close to the absence of a fighting psychology.

And what of the mercenaries that filled the Carthaginian army? Are we to assume that they, unlike their masters, were moved by the imperious urge to fight? They had proved a source of lucre to their own government, which had hired them out by the drove in exchange for the bounty of the Punic coffers; and they were spurred toward the battlefield not only by the exhortations of their leaders but by the lust of gain. Their loyalty was that of a dog to its latest bone—let a larger bone loom in sight, and they would snap at it instead. And so today they might battle for the Carthaginians; and tomorrow, if offered a better fee, they might shoot down the Carthaginians. Under such circumstances, it is hard to disentangle the fighting spirit from the spirit of profiteering. And it is as pointless to say that the mercenaries fought out of a natural desire as that a butcher or a tanner, who dresses meat or leather because he knows no other trade, performs his tasks through an inborn compulsion.

One thing we can be certain of: had there been no mercenaries, the Carthaginian wars as we know them could not have occurred.

And when warfare depends upon bought services, it has sunk to a purely artificial state.

But what of the character who has shed the most renown upon the arms of Carthage? Is Hannibal not proof of a combative spirit? Here we have a special case, and one that shows clearly how a war-like attitude of mind can be developed. Hannibal was one of a family of soldiers; his father Hamilcar Barca was an outstanding general; his three brothers and his brother-in-law Hasdrubal all followed the career of arms. At the age of nine he was taken by his father to Spain; and it is not hard to understand the effect upon the mind of the impressionable boy if (as has often been claimed) his parent bade him swear eternal hatred of Rome. For nine years, removed from feminine influences, he was drilled in the craft of arms, with all the encouragements of special tuition from the commander-in-chief. For nine years he endured the privations and vicissitudes of the campaigns; and though he returned to Carthage after his father had drowned during a battle, he subsequently served three years in Spain under Hasdrubal. If we have not here a training consummately suited to funnel a man's thoughts into channels of war-making, such a training has never been vouchsafed any human being.

All of which may prompt one to ask: is there any reason to suppose that, with an equal education and encouragement as an engineer, an architect, or a statesman, a man of Hannibal's gifts and energies might not equally well have become an engineer, an architect, or a statesman, and perhaps a leader in his field? But his mental conditioning was all in the direction of warfare, and so he became a warrior.

This is particularly significant because in his day the dominant force in warfare was the individual. Although the so-called Elders' War Council of one hundred and four members was supposed to direct all phases of military operations, one cannot observe that in practice they exercised much control over Hannibal; while the great bands of mercenaries, who as a rule would fight so long as they were paid and saw no higher bidder on the horizon, would readily follow wherever he directed—all the more so as he kept them well oiled with donations from the public purse and from his own bountiful fortune. Thus, in a definite sense—even though he took advantage of the political mood and undercurrents of the day—it was the will, the desires, the outlook of one man that decided the issue of war or peace.

Let us take a single example. The Second Punic War, one of the most deadly conflicts of ancient times, had its roots in previous strife and antagonisms and in Rome's high-handed attitude; but it began specifically over the question of Saguntum, a city in eastern Spain. Though there was some question as to their legal rights under a treaty, the Romans had warned that an attack upon this stronghold would mean war. Nevertheless Hannibal—some time after being invested with the supreme command—laid siege to this crucial point, and captured it in an engagement lasting eight months. Rome thereupon called for the surrender of Hannibal and his chief officers; and this demand being refused, war was declared.

There is reason to believe that, on Hannibal's part, all this represented what we of today would call a "calculated risk"—reason to think that he desired to reconquer all Spain, especially since he had early declared this to be his ambition. And this was but the first step in the epoch-making project that would bring his armies thundering down upon the plains of Italy. Though there was a strong peace party in Carthage, and one that would have brought powerful pressure to bear against any obvious plunge into war, Hannibal was not slow to find the means—means that remind one of later leaders in not more worthy causes. He claimed that the people of Saguntum were attacking some subjects of Carthage, the Torboletes; and it is not hard to read a desire to goad the Romans into war in the rudeness with which he brushed their envoys aside. Even so, many months passed before Rome decided to knock the chip off the Carthaginian shoulder.

Though other forces might have conjoined to produce a Second Punic War even had Hannibal never lived, it is evident that war in the form it took and at the time it broke out and under the particular circumstances we know, occurred mainly because of the anti-Roman sentiment fuming in the mind of one man or of one small circle of men. And that sentiment existed because of his training, his long-inculcated hatred of Rome, his equally long-inculcated love of his fatherland, his education in warfare, and his acceptance of a set of values that made all other goals subordinate to those of the fighting arm.

Chapter 8

The Heroic Age in Persia and India

Far to the east of Carthage, in the empire of the Medes and Persians, the footmen swung their battle-axes and swords and the mounted warriors deployed. In Persia, as in Assyria, we find something close to a military specialization; even though we need not believe the fabulous stories of million-men armies, we do know that immense hosts accompanied the march of the Great King, as the Persian ruler was called. And we do know, also, that the training of the Persian youth was all in the direction of fighting—that is to say, the training of the Persian proper. Throughout the empire there were millions of non-Persians, peasants and herdsmen and traders, who entered the military life only when thrown into it. And the failure of the native military manpower is indicated by the large number of mercenaries employed by the later Persian monarchs.

At the age of five, the training of the Persian lad began. Removed from the women and the taint of their possibly anti-militaristic sentiments, he was forced through a rigorous course of instruction. He rose before dawn, and competed with the other boys in running and stone-slinging, bow-shooting and javelin-throwing; at seven he was taught to ride; and when, soon afterward, he began to hunt, he had to master such dangerous arts as that of throwing the spear and discharging arrows at full gallop. Later, he was inured to various hardships; he had to make long marches, bear extremes of heat and cold, cross rivers without wetting his weapons, go for as much as two days with but one meal, and occasionally support himself from the wild nuts and berries of the land. And all the while he had to harden and strengthen himself by frequent athletic contests. By the time he was fifteen, he was held to have reached manhood, and was enlisted in the army; and for the next thirty-five years he was liable to service. But his education had been strangely lopsided; he had not been taught to read, and his mind had been trained toward nothing but warlike ends.

Under such circumstances, it was to be expected that he would make a good soldier—how could it be otherwise, when his entire life-energies were directed toward this one end? Since the feats, exercises, and competitions of a warrior's life had been his sole occupation from his fifth birthday, would he not indeed have been an exceptional individual if he had supposed for one moment that those feats, exercises, and competitions were not of supreme importance? It is the way of most human beings to bow to the practices of the day, as if their mere prevalence makes them right; and this is particularly true of the very young, who have no outside point of reference, and must accept what they see because it is all that they know. And so the Persian training, even if it did not expressly instill the idea that fighting was the supreme virtue, must have instilled that idea by implication, since fighting was the one value it emphasized. Thus, by the time the boy had grown to manhood, he would be a convinced lifetime warrior.

Nothing more than this is necessary to explain the Persian's performance as a soldier. And since a large part of the adult male population was incorporated in the service, one can believe that the training was designed to produce the very effect it did produce.

Even so, one must not assume that the Persian always fought willingly. The penalties for rebellion were ferocious—a sure sign that rebellion was greatly feared, if not continually threatened. The leader of an insurrection and his chief followers were killed, usually by the cruel method of crucifixion; while minor punishments were applied by means of the searing hot iron, or by wholesale deportation of the rebels. But even the unrevolting masses, if we are to believe Herodotus, sometimes were in need of unusual stimuli. The Greek historian tells how the hordes of Xerxes, as they forced their way toward the pass where Leonidas awaited them, were flogged and driven continually forward by the whips of their captains . . . until many fell into the sea and drowned, and many were trampled to death beneath the feet of their comrades.

A further question as to Persian fighting inclinations is provided by the use that the Great King made of Greek mercenaries. At various times he had alliances with Sparta, Athens, and Thebes; Greeks, attracted by the lure of gold, commanded the Persian armies and fleets; and the rank and file of the standing army took on a strong Greek admixture, bringing us again face to face with the old truth that a nation whose own subjects desire to fight need not enlist foreigners.

A fact to note about the Persian wars is that, like many of the early Eastern conflicts, they were often motivated by one man. And they were so motivated because absolute authority, according to the principles of the age, was permitted to inhere in one man: the Persian monarch was treated like a god, who perched at an unreachable distance above his people, lived for the most part alone, ate alone, and rarely showed himself in public. To enter his throne-room uninvited, although innocently, was to suffer death; to seat one's self upon his throne, even by accident, was to incur the same penalty. Strange stories are told of the whims of the Great King: for example, how one ruler, capriciously and as an exhibition of archery, shot down an unoffending youth and how the lad's father, doubtless fearing for his own head, congratulated the marksman on his skill. Even if this tale is a fable, it nevertheless does indicate the power possessed by the Persian sovereign.

So far as we are able to make out in view of the incompleteness of the records, it was the personal motive that underlay the aggressions of Cyrus, one of the great conquerors of ancient times, who with startling suddenness vanquished the Lydians, the Medes, and the Babylonians and established perhaps the vastest empire the world had yet seen. Like many empires, it apparently was founded on little but the ambitions and the thrust for power of a single autocratic commander; there was no economic or political need for the consolidation of the various kingdoms, and the gains to humanity were mostly in reverse. The comment of one historian is pertinent:

The fall of Lydia was a tragedy for civilization, and the obscuration of Ionian culture by the semi-barbarian customs and laws of Persia a lamentable thing. Here, as often since in the history of European peoples, beauty had gone down before might, with promises of future greatness left sadly unfulfilled.[1]

The same writer's remarks on Cyrus' conquering urge are likewise suggestive:

He was, however, like other conquerors who have not known where to rest from conquest and carry on construction and consolidation; or like many masters in vast commercial or industrial forms of modern business, who know not how to cease combining, uniting, consolidating until the concern is too great for any mind to control successfully.[2]

Conquest, in other words, becomes an obsession, a passion, which, like strong drink, drives a man in disregard of reason. But it does something more: also, like strong drink, it establishes a habit, a precedent, and so leads to further conquest or attempted conquest: after Cyrus a whole line of military despots, waging warfare for personal motives, attempted to spread their power by means of the flaming sword. And not the least notable among these was Cambyses, the son of Cyrus and the conqueror of Egypt.

How such a leader might provoke conflict, simply because he desired it, was shown before the Egyptian campaign. As the heir of a great conqueror, doubtless he desired some conquering of his own; and he had not far to look for ways and means. A little as when Helen of Troy provoked the Trojan War, a girl named Nitesis was the immediate occasion of the Egyptian conflict—not that she was stolen, but that she was demanded by Cambyses of the Egyptian monarch as a secondary wife. Or, rather, what he demanded was a daughter of the Egyptian sovereign, and what he got was Nitesis, who, as he was informed by no one but the young lady herself, was not actually the king's daughter at all, although represented as such. At this late date, there is no way of being sure whether Cambyses had intended war from the first; or whether, in his anger at discovering the deception, he had subsequently resolved to make this the excuse for war. In any case, the substitution of one damsel for another is surely small logical reason for the invasion and subjugation of a great empire; the alleged justification is so disproportionate to the effects that the cause must be regarded as psychological rather than logical. In the mind of an inordinately egotistical monarch, for whom a blow to his pride was the supreme outrage, this cause *could* have seemed sufficient; and even if it did not appear sufficient, it might have struck him as an adequate face-saving excuse. However this may be, this was the pretext for the invasion of Egypt, as a result of which many thousands perished and a great country was placed under a foreign yoke. And the pretext, one must remember, was no more than the fruit of the desire of one man, to whom autocratic power had been entrusted.

II

Once more we may turn eastward, this time to India. Here we find something of a paradox among the nations—a paradox because on the one hand early India was a convert to that same heroic ideal, that same cult of blood-letting which has stained the annals of many lands; while on the other hand she developed a creed of harmlessness, of non-injury, of peacefulness unique in the ancient world.

If you consult that great Hindu epic, the *Mahabharata*, you will find an almost continuous record of warfare. You will see the hero Arjuna entering the lists, somewhat like a medieval knight at a tourney, and dazzling by an exhibition of swordplay. You will witness the battles of the kings Drona and Drupada, in which the former redeems an insult by wresting away half the kingdom of the latter, who in turn swears vengeance. You will be present at a competition, wherein Drupada's daughter the Princess Draupadi offers her hand to the most expert warrior; and you will be entertained by a great battle, lasting eighteen days, wherein all the notable Indian princes take part, and in which Drupada and Drona and countless others meet death.

The resemblances to the *Iliad*—at least in theme—are here far from inconspicuous. We have the same society dominated by the war-making aristocrat; the same artificial set of values, which hold the things of the sword to be the things of consequence; the same strutting and vainglory and knightly exhibitionism; the same personal rivalries and the same contentions for individual ends; the same evident purposelessness of slaughter, and the exaltation of that slaughter as a grand achievement. The Heroic Age of India was, indeed, very similar to that of Greece, from the time when, four thousand years ago, men first marched forth in compact masses, to the accompaniment of war horses and chariots, to the sound of drums, and to the flashing of banners. All the familiar technique for arousing a warlike state of mind was present: the acclaim of the warrior and the resultant emulation of the warrior, the martial competition and rivalry, the channeling of the ambitions of youth toward the battlefield, the goad of pride and the corresponding goad of the fear of disapprobation, the appeal for feminine favor no less than for masculine applause.

And yet, in spite of all, we do notice certain points of distinc-

tion in India. There the heroic ideal, as never in Greece, was fortified by the doctrine of a future paradise of warriors, in which the
god Indra played a part corresponding to that of Odin in the
Norse Valhalla. But when such naïve and beatific conceptions
did not suffice to instill a fighting spirit, the Hindu had recourse to
a more elaborate philosophy, and tried to justify the slayer on the
ground that it was really impossible to slay. This is apparent from
the words of the god Krishna in the *Bhagavad-Gita*:

> Eternal, then, is that by which
> 　　Creation's web was spun;
> Destruction of eternal life
> 　　Is possible to none.

> These bodies pass; but he within,
> 　　With life immortal dight,
> Is neither limited nor lost:
> 　　Therefore, brave hero, fight!

> If the red slayer thinks he slays,
> 　　The slain think he is slain,
> They err: the slayer vainly kills;
> 　　The victim dies in vain.[3]

The argument proceeds that, since man does not actually die but
"Endues himself with fresh attire," pity for any life is misplaced.
And this doctrine, so contrary to the tenor of much Indian thought,
so hostile to Buddhist and Jainist precepts of non-injury, so heedless of the claims of the transmigrationists that each incarnation has
a purpose, is bolstered by pleas of a more common type:

> Besides, to tremble at the view
> 　　Of duty is not right,
> Since warriors have no duty more
> 　　Ennobling than fair fight,

> Which freely offers open gates,
> 　　O prince, to heaven's bliss;
> And happy warriors run with joy
> 　　To meet a fight like this.

> With shrinking of this righteous fight
> 　　Your infamies begin:
> Your virtue and your name are lost,
> 　　And you are sunk in sin.

All living things will gossip of
Your everlasting shame;
And to a man once honored, death
Is less than evil fame.[4]

And so, as in every land dominated by the heroic ideal, the man who conscientiously objects to taking life is scourged by the cry, "Dishonor!" And the pusillanimous throng echo that charge in the name of courage, "Dishonor! Dishonor!" And the gore-stained fighters point contemptuous fingers, the women mutter in scorn and derision, and even the children echo that taunt, "Dishonor! Dishonor!" And the objector, if he be not braver than a hundred knights, will finally yield, and take the coward's path of valor; for not many men in any land or age can be found with the hardihood to withstand that gibe, "Dishonor! Dishonor!"

Yet warfare in early India, for all its ferocity, was not quite so ferocious as elsewhere. Even in the early days, when the most definite religious and military rules regulated the warrior clan, the farmer and his crops were held inviolate, the trees were not cut down, nor the land ravaged by fire. And at an early time, the idea of non-killing and non-injury arose. "Long before Buddhism, it was one of the five preliminary conditions necessary for the attainment of a higher degree of spiritual life." [5] The laws of war, according to Apastamba, a teacher of the fifth century B.C., forbade the slaughter of fugitives, of those who had laid down their arms, and of those who with flying hair or clasped hands begged for mercy. And another teacher, Baudhayana, counseled the warrior not to fight persons who were fear-stricken, intoxicated, or out of their minds, nor women, infants, old men, and persons who had lost their armor.

We have here, manifestly, a set of regulations making for decency and fair play. But they are, quite as manifestly, regulations which take for granted the existence of a merciful element in man, and assume that he is not so pugnacious by nature that he need forget humanity. Where we have definite rules, as here, we have something immensely significant: we have warfare treated not as a spontaneous outcropping of nature, but as something subject to human control. Man, in other words, is regarded as the superior of war, and capable of governing it; and war, as among many early peoples, has something of the character of a game, bound by set principles and specifications, and having little in common with the remorseless struggle for the "survival of the fittest" which we moderns sometimes identify with all war.

A further artificiality introduced by the Hindus—and a highly instructive one—was in the establishment of a single caste, the Kshatriyas, on whose shoulders rested the entire privilege and burden of war-making. The members of this group were set apart, in the days of the epics, to fight and die upon the battlefield; their entire education was directed toward martial ends, and archery, combats with clubs, and the use of the shield and the sword were a part of their expected training. As members of the retinue of petty rulers and princes, they had no work in life except to give battle; and lest their periods of unemployment be too frequent, the leader not involved in war on his own account might dispatch his followers to assist some far-off sovereign to whom he was indebted. "Thus," says one writer, "soldiers came even from the East, West and South to take part in the Kuru-Pandava war, simply because their king thought it his duty to join one party or the other, it being customary for the parties to send requests for help to all kings likely to render aid." [6]

In later times, it is true, boundaries were broken down and men of all castes joined the warring ranks. But the original delimitation of fighting on a caste basis shows how largely war-making was a matter of man-made rule and rote; the combative impulse, if it were an inherent part of man, could not by any possibility be confined to one caste. The nature of a Kshatriya has been well described:

Who ever pretends to be a true Kshatriya ought to know that he can only be a soldier, and nothing else, and that his one object in life is to make war. . . . The true Kshatriya when engaged in fighting an enemy should give up all desire to live. Far be it from him to think of retreating or taking to flight! On the contrary, let him advance bravely, resolved to conquer or to die! The happiest death for a Kshatriya, the one he should wish for most, is to die sword in hand, fighting. It procures for him the inestimable happiness of being admitted to Swarga [the Paradise of Indra]. Boundless ambition is the highest virtue a Kshatriya can possess. However vast his possessions may be already, he should never say that he has enough. All his thoughts should extend to enlarging and extending his territories and to making war on neighboring princes with a view to appropriating their possessions by main force.[7]

It was of the essence of caste that a man born a Kshatriya had to remain a Kshatriya; he was, as it were, conscripted into the army at birth; if he had any weak inclinations toward peace, it was well for him to hide them. More than that, in the traditions surrounding his class, the sanctity that accompanied the fighting arm, and the injunction that he must fight in order to justify his existence, he would find excuse for any wantonness of aggression. His attitude toward molesting unoffending neighbors would be exactly that of another caste in regard to the profession of brigandage:

The caste of *Kullars,* or robbers, who exercise their calling as an hereditary right, is found only in the Marava country, which borders on the coast, or fishing, districts. The rulers of the country are of the same caste. They regard a robber's occupation as discreditable neither to themselves nor to their fellow castemen, for the simple reason that they consider robbery a duty and a right sanctioned by descent. . . . This caste is looked upon in the district of Madura, where it is widely distributed, as one of the most distinguished among the Sudras.[8]

What essential difference, one wonders, was there between the warrior caste and the robber caste? Behind them both one can see the same type of forces—the same artificial sort of regulations, the same traditions, the same state of mind. To say that a Kshatriya is a fighter by nature is like saying that a Kullar is a robber by nature— each is made what he is by the network of customs and beliefs that envelop him. Through a similar training and tradition, it would be possible to develop a caste dedicated to kidnapping, arson, poisoning, or any other end however preposterous.

III

With the birth of Buddhism, we can notice a change in the outlook toward war and peace. In Brahmanism the doctrine of non-killing was held to apply to the ascetic and the simple peaceful citizen but not to the warrior, for whom killing was an appropriate part of his trade; the aim of Buddhism, on the other hand, was "as much at reclaiming the warrior from his war-making as the outcast from his bestial superstition." [9] In Buddhism war "is everywhere implicitly, and in many passages, explicitly, condemned." [10] The activities of the soldier, along with those of the hunter and the slave-holder, were not considered legitimate means to a livelihood.

For war-making and the consummation of spiritual freedom or liberation are regarded as irreconcilable. The Buddhist attitude in regard to the *Arahant*, or enlightened soul, has been significantly expressed:

I should say that the four qualities which seem to stand out most prominently seem to be peace, freedom, joy and insight. The first of these is the most commonly and the most specifically emphasized. Nirvana in this life means primarily the attainment of the great peace. It means deliverance from the fear of death and every other fear, a large equanimity, a carelessness of all happenings, an inner calm, often compared with the stillness of the sea. Peace is closely connected with spiritual freedom; in a sense it comes from it.[11]

To such a philosophy, warfare would be abhorrent; warfare would stand as an impassable road-block in the way of all worthy attainment. One could not be a sincere and consistent Buddhist and at the same time be a soldier.

But how much in actual practice did Buddhism accomplish in the way of peace? There seems ample evidence behind the view of William Loftus Hare that, "we are probably warranted in saying that Buddhism went far toward forming the non-combatant temperament which is so often exemplified by Oriental nations, such as the Indians, Chinese, Siamese, and Burmese peoples." And though Buddhism was eventually to vanish from its native India, we know that it did notable service there in checking the war god. It is said to have stayed the warring hand of King Kanishka, who (though the dates are somewhat uncertain) appears to have lived in the second century of the Christian era. But whatever the facts about Kanishka, there is no question whatever in regard to Asoka, one of the most remarkable monarchs who ever lived, and one who has shown how easily an idea in the mind of man may bridge the gulf between war and peace.

Asoka was born at about the beginning of the third century B.C. He was the heir to a military tradition, and a military empire; his grandfather Chandragupta, a man of "blood and iron," had conquered the Indian provinces of Alexander the Great after fighting his way from poverty to the throne. And Asoka, as the result of the strong rule of his forebear, was firmly established on his royal seat. His dominions, which included all of India from the thirteenth latitude to the Himalayas along with Kashmir, Sind, Baluchistan, and Afghanistan as far as the Hindu Kush mountains, might have appeared large enough to satisfy any prince; yet in the ninth year after his coronation Asoka launched an aggressive war against the kingdom of Kalinga, a strip of territory stretching along the Bay of Bengal. Considered sheerly from the military point of view, the campaign was quite successful. True, there was a large amount of suffering and bloodshed, one hundred thousand persons were estimated to have been slain, several times that number were killed by the incidental famine and pestilence, and a hundred and fifty thousand were borne off into captivity—but what would all that have meant to the usual blood-and-thunder conqueror, especially as the cost was paid by helpless foreigners?

Asoka, however, was not of the common conquering clay. At about the time of his occupation of Kalinga, he became a convert to Buddhism; and in accordance with the precepts of that religion he expressed his "remorse, profound sorrow, and regret." The sight of all the misery he had caused, the knowledge that he alone was responsible, had affected him to the depths; he resolved never again to inflict such agony upon his fellow creatures; and four years after the conquest he could state that "the loss of even the hundredth or the thousandth part of the persons who were then slain, carried away captive or done to death in Kalinga would now be a matter of deep regret to his Majesty." [12]

He not only proclaimed these principles; he adhered to them. Never again, in a reign of thirty-five or forty years, did he set out on the warpath; he went so far as to become a Buddhist monk, even while wielding the scepter; he followed the Buddhist principles of respect for all life, including that of animals, and not only abolished the royal hunt but prohibited the slaughter of all the thousands of creatures previously slain for the royal kitchens, and made laws forbidding the killing of many specified kinds of animals in any circumstances. In all this there is more than a surface significance, for the psychology of non-violence to animals is one with the psychology of non-violence to human beings. He who remorselessly sheds blood of any kind, even the blood of rabbits, will be less disinclined to shed human blood; the warlike races of history have usually been hunting races, the warlike leaders have frequently enjoyed the hunt; and where there is great regard for the lives and suffering of animals, inevitably there is a regard for the lives and sufferings of human beings. For the quality of mercy not only is "not strained"; it is indivisible; it is not of the nature of the merciful mind to be considerate toward one class of creatures, and bloodthirsty toward others. And thus Asoka's humane attitude toward the birds and beasts was but a reflection of his humane attitude toward his own race; and thus, conversely, a cruel and savage state of mind toward our furred and feathered kindred is apt to be paralleled by a cruel and savage state of mind toward our kindred on two legs.

It is noteworthy that, as Vincent A. Smith tells us, "In early life Asoka is believed to have been a Brahmanical Hindu, specially devoted to Siva, a god who delights in bloody sacrifices, and he had consequently no scruple about the shedding of blood." [13] His early training in the worship of such a divinity, along with the fighting tradition that had descended in his family from his steel-fisted grandfather, would explain Asoka's bloody incursion into Kalinga. But since many another young king, beneath the goad of a similar schooling, has made equally bloody assaults and has expressed neither compunction nor remorse, there must have been some special determining factor in Asoka's case, other than a superior sensitiveness. And that special determining factor could only have been the Buddhist creed, the Buddhist philosophy of harmlessness and peace. This it was—this invisible element operating silently in the mind—that checked a career of conquest which might have been one of the goriest in ancient times. This it was that saved an unknown number of lands from being overrun, an unknown multitude of people from privation and death, an unknown extent of territory from ravage and devastation. And this it was that transformed Asoka's place in history: instead of a lifelong destroyer, famed and terrible and execrated in many lands and centuries, he became the supporter of art and architecture and religion and peace, of whom it has been said that if a man's glory can be measured by the number of persons who revere his memory and speak his name with honor, he is more famous than Charlemagne or Caesar.

Chapter 9

Greece: Plunder and Glory

Time and legend and romance, which lend a glamour to far-off objects and events and wreathe a halo even about the grim brow of horror and massacre, have made it hard for us to look upon the wars and warriors of ancient Greece except through a magnifying rose-mist. Lulled by the superb rhythms of the *Iliad*, we see Achilles and Agamemnon and Hector as the actors in a majestic pageant quite divorced from the realities of everyday; we find it difficult to distinguish gore from glory, or to throw off the age-old traditions that give these deeds and characters a heroic place. And similarly with the other episodes and features of Greek warfare: the Spartan system, which may loom out of the fog as a model of ruggedness and simplicity; the wars with Persia, and particularly the episode at Thermopylae, in which we see the bravery of the stalwart band under Leonidas, and forget the treachery responsible for their desperate plight; the struggles of the city-states, wherein the gross hues of passion and corruption are hardly visible at our great distance; and the campaigns of the Macedonian Alexander, so remote and so enveloped in an aura of song and story that we do not see them to have been on the moral plane of Hitler's invasion of Poland or of Tojo's thrust into the Philippines.

It was the fortune of the Greeks that, ever since the time of Homer, they were gifted with poets and story-tellers able to give a romantic glitter to their past. And thus coarse reality was hidden by agreeable fiction, or by half-fiction more alluring than any sheer invention; and ideas of valor and glory were allowed to color the grimy substance of fact. No equivalent literary skill had been able to illuminate the bloodshed of such a warrior chief as Ashur-nasir-apal, the Assyrian who did himself no credit with posterity by reciting how he cut off noses, ears, and fingers, put out eyes, and reared a pyramid of heads; or of the Persian Artaxerxes III, the destroyer of Sidon, beneath whose cruel command forty thousand persons are said to have perished in the flames. Yet if these bloody

conquerors had been emblazoned in the ringing measures of a
Homer, they would have stood out for the future as no less worthy
or memorable than Ajax or Odysseus; and their deeds might have
seemed of a noble fortitude. Thus a tradition of heroism would
have formed itself about their names; the dread actualities would
have been overlooked or forgotten; the image of them in the minds
of men would have borne little more relation to their true selves
than a butterfly bears to the wriggling larva; they would have
been extolled for the qualities they never represented, and their
warring careers would have been cited for the approbation and
the emulation of youth. And all the while a martial tradition would
have been strengthened and expanded, the idea of the sanctity of
battle would have grown, and, beneath the stimulus of the magnificent fabrications, new generations would have girded on arms.

This is what might have happened, but did not precisely happen,
in Assyria and Persia. But this is exactly what did occur in Greece.
It may not be that the heroes of Greek lore were altogether of the
stamp of Ashur-nasir-apal or Artaxerxes; their operations, in any
case, were on a smaller scale; but in all alike we see the glorification
of butchery—the idea that bloodshed for its own sake may be
meritorious. And this idea, decked in the stage settings of literature,
was softened for the Greeks, and disguised, and passed on to succeeding centuries, and made a vehicle for the perpetuation of the
fighting spirit.

Let us glance at the *Iliad*. It is fairly well established that this
epic was written long after the events it records, and therefore
probably does not faithfully reproduce the standards and ideas of
the Trojan period, although it does inevitably, even if unconsciously, make report on the era in which it was composed. And
what does it tell us of that era? That it was, to begin with, an
epoch of vainglorious ideas, in which warriors could compete for
possession of a corpse somewhat in the spirit of Plains Indians
engaged in bloody rivalry for scalps, or of Malay head-hunters
contesting for heads. And it was an epoch in which the flaunting
of victory was quite as important as the victory itself; this is
graphically evident when Achilles drags the body of Hector after
his chariot wheels, the fair hair flying in the dust.

At the same time, the *Iliad* tells us of a day of remorseless
slaughter. Scarcely anywhere does the soft, tender voice of pity
come to us amid the sonorous harmonies of the master poem; it

was deemed glorious not only to be strong and brave, but to be hard and cruel. And so we find a callous denial of pleas for mercy, as when Tros, the son of Alastor, comes begging on his knees for his life to the gallant Achilles, but is none the less slain.

Accompanying the slaughter, there is an unashamed greed of plunder:

All round the second city two armies of warriors were stationed,
Shining in arms. Two also the plans that found favor among them:
Either to pillage the two or divide between the two parties
All of the substance the lovely city was holding within it.[1]

There is a fierce emotion of pride, apparent not only in the famous sulk of Achilles, but in many a boastful passage such as

"Seest thou not what a hero I am. How comely and mighty?
  Goodly is also my sire, and the mother that bore me—a goddess!"

There is a savage lust for revenge:

"Nay, even so ye shall die by an evil fate, until all ye
  Pay for Patroclus' death, for the slaughter of heroes Achaean."

There is an evident reveling in the death-stroke and its gruesome accompaniments:

                    . . . he slashed him over the liver;
Out through the gash it slipped forth, and the dark blood out of it
  jetted,
Filling his bosom with gore.

And, a few lines further on:

        Then smiting his neck with his broadsword
Far off swept Achilles the helmet and head, and the marrow
Out from the vertebrae gushed.

And, continuing in the third line following:

Him he smote with his lance in his breast; in his lung was the
  weapon
Fixed, and he fell from his car. His squire he smote with his keen
  spear
Square in the back . . .

These are not pleasant lines, but there are many such in the *Iliad*. And such passages are significant, since they suggest in grisly detail what the Greeks supposed the heroic life to have been like (even to the dealing of valorous blows in the back). To Homer, and doubtless to a majority of the Greeks, the author of this carnage was "Goodliest far of Achaeans," "Godlike Achilles," "Achilles, the glorious hero." And perhaps he was literally godlike, since the Greek gods—as we read in the *Iliad*—came down to fight in the wars of men. But in any case, even if he never had a physical prototype, he did represent the early Greek ideal. And that ideal was one of a militant ruthlessness, physical strength and intrepidity, dauntlessness in slaughter, and supreme carelessness of human suffering. To the unimpassioned modern gaze, his salient qualities appear to be a stout arm and a stony heart. How, then, does he come to be exalted as a people's hero? But just how, one may ask, have our own Babe Ruths and Joe Louises awakened veneration? Consider the enticement that would attach to one of these if, after several centuries, he were to be made the hero of a surpassingly well-told epic. Or, to be more exact, consider the situation if a highwayman or a gangster—a Jesse James, a Murieta, or a Capone —were to be exalted in a great romance long after the victims of his brutalities had ceased to breathe. His deeds might somehow seem haloed and enchanted; and youth, overlooking the bloody realities, might pay reverence and wish to follow in the champion's footsteps.

It would not be correct to say that Homer and the other Greek poets and story-tellers created their country's fighting tradition. What they did was to take a pre-existing tradition, reinforce it, glorify it, enhance and perpetuate it, and thus hand down in exaggerated form the creed of fighting and the point of view that makes for fighting. And when they did not actually wreathe a golden mantle about war's crimson-soaked butcher-block, they tended to make the truth acceptable or to obscure it altogether beneath a mist of phrases: "noble," "great-hearted," "illustrious," "valiant," "divine."

II

At the dawn of Greek history, we see all the three main types of conflict already noted among uncivilized peoples. The blood feud, which often underlies war, arose at an early date from the desire of clansmen to avenge the death of fellow clansmen; and this incentive to indefinite combat was encouraged by the religious belief that the shade of the slain man hovered near, avid for retribution. But even more conspicuous was the raid for booty; this, in a land where the dweller beyond the next hill might be considered a foreigner, developed according to the good old principle that thievery from other tribes was not dishonorable. Brigandage in its various forms flourished, unrestrained by the organized power of the State, although checked to some extent by the authority of religion and the fear of punishment by the gods. The comment of J. B. Bury is revealing:

Piracy was a common trade. . . . So many practiced this means of livelihood that it bore no reproach; and when seamen landed on a strange strand, the natural question to ask them was, "Outlanders, whence come ye? are ye robbers that rove the seas? [2]

The attitude of mind appears to have been a little like that of the Hindus toward the robber caste mentioned in the last chapter. Since banditry was so common, and conflicted with no law, it had a recognized status; it was an acknowledged form of business, doubtless unfortunate for the customers; but in a world where every man, or at least every clan, was supposed to be self-protected, what happened between the corsair and his clientele was no third party's affair.

From small-scale marauders a gradual process of growth would develop the large organized raiding parties. And when the latter were met by correspondingly large defensive groups or conflicted with other bands of their type, the raids would give place to actual warfare. Thus the way was open for strife of the sort that we observe in Homeric times—strife in which lawless gangs roam the country, looking for adventure and loot; strife stimulated and bolstered by the heroic ideal, the tradition of bloodshed and glory; strife in which the armed aristocrats, the freebooting knights and pirates, dominate society and tend to check the advancement of the more civilized communities. The rapacity of the raider, when we find it in the ascendant as during the Heroic Age in Greece, tends to check the urge to development in peaceful regions; more than cities such as Troy and Knossos were obliterated by the armed bands that destroyed these centers. The will to reconstruct them was paralyzed; the people were like dwellers on a volcano's rim who, having seen their houses swallowed by the seething lava, have not the heart to build again near the danger-spot. And thus, as so often in history, war-making has given birth to a dark age.

For a long while—in fact, until treaties to the contrary arose—it remained the right of the Greek city to send out expeditions to seize the property and even the inhabitants of neighboring towns. And no Greek city, if it had the power and felt that reprisals were justified or righteous claims had not been heeded, would hesitate to hurl an attack. Nevertheless, warfare was not altogether a lawless thing. Though there was no written restraint, there was the potent regulator of custom, of tradition, of religious belief; well-established rules of war, supposed to be under the supervision of the gods, tempered the harshness of conflict.

Thus the heralds, made inviolable by the caduceus or "wand of Mercury," had the sole power to declare war, and had the right to enter the hostile lines without molestation, and likewise to shed a mantle of protection over any envoys or peace-makers dispatched to the enemy camp. After a battle, it was the prerogative of the defeated—unless they were a sacrilegious army—to ask an armistice to permit them to bury their dead; and this demand had to be granted. If the vanquished threw themselves down before the victors as suppliants, ordinarily their lives were spared in accordance with the rules of war; though if they resisted in their strongholds, and could be subdued only after the hardships of a siege, the men were massacred, and the women and children enslaved. When booty was taken—which appears to have been frequently—a definite tradition as to the division was observed, and a tithe was put aside for the gods.

The place of the gods, furthermore, is evident in the provision that temples, unless used for military purposes, were to be inviolable sanctuaries. The gods, once more, play their part in a law protecting travelers to pan-Hellenic festivals, even in districts infested by battling armies. And during the entire month of the festival of the Carnea, which was held at about the end of our August in honor of Apollo, the Peloponnesians would never launch a campaign; nor would they set out against any city between the time of the announcement of the festival and its celebration. In these ways and many others—and notably through the eventual negotiation of treaties of peace, which might run for as long as thirty, fifty, or a hundred years—the Greeks by degrees tempered the severity of warfare. Yet perhaps not even their acute minds recognized how they were showing war to be a circumscribed, artificial thing, capable of being checked or directed by the will and intelligence of man and by his moods, emotions, and traditions.

In line with the peace treaties were the attempts at arbitration, in which an outside city or sometimes the priests of Delhi were asked to settle a dispute. When treaties of peace were made in the late fifth century B.C. between the Athenians and their enemies, it was usual to include stipulations providing for arbitration in case of disagreement. Thus Athens and Megara, when engaged in a controversy over Salamis, threw the decision into the lap of Sparta; the Argives and the Lacedaemonians, by a treaty made in 418, agreed to permit all their difficulties to be settled by a third power; and other agreements of the same nature show the desire for peace —which, unfortunately, did not always blossom into accomplishment, since there was no way of enforcing the decisions and a loser in an argument would not always abide by the decree of the judges.

But though the end result may have been failure, at least one good had been accomplished. The Greeks had shown, as Rameses II and the Hittites had shown many centuries before, that there are other means of negotiation than the bloody blade; and that the spirit of peace, in the face of immense obstacles, may be able to place orderly process above the forces of storm and fire.

III

During the earliest centuries of recorded Greek history, various rich and powerful men known as "tyrants" seized control of many cities, largely by means of the heavy armed infantry or *hoplites*. Ambition for renown and greed for power appear to have been foremost among the motives of these usurpers, although the name did not originally bear the stigma we now attach to it and some of the tyrants were actually beneficent. But the interesting fact, from the point of view of war-making, is that the armed forces of the tyrants—in so far as they were not composed of friends, personal followers, and hangers-on—were mainly made up of mercenary soldiers. Thus, as far back as the seventh century B.C., we find men needing other battle incentives than patriotism or glory, religion or revenge; we find that, as among the Carthaginians and other peoples, they fought because paid to fight.

The new order represented by the tyrants, though it took wide root, was resisted by that city whose name, perhaps more than any other in the ancient world, conjures up the thought of military specialization. Sparta, as everyone knows, was a community organized on a military basis; it was a community that has been described as little more than a camp devoted to the production of the best soldiers and the best soldiers' wives. All ordinary interests were subordinated to the one great interest of fighting; all desires except the desire for the battlefield were frowned upon by custom and discouraged by the law. The breeding of muscular limbs and the development of a warlike state of mind were the two great aims of the Spartan system; the art and culture that glorified Athens were not for the Spartan youth, and even in the time of Plato the typical citizen had not learned to read. For thirteen years, beginning at the age of seven, he passed his days in a sort of military academy, and at twenty he entered the army; but even then, though allowed to marry, he was compelled to live among other men in the barracks. He had no private life; his every action, almost his every thought, was under constant supervision. He was not permitted to engage in trade, and was discouraged from every sort of civil work; all necessary labor was performed for him by the Helots; while his own training was psychological as well as physical, and he was drilled in a sort of camouflage calculated to conceal the miseries and terrors of war and to exaggerate its glory and glamour.

The stoicism of the Spartan is proverbial—it was not in his code to admit that sorrow was sorrowful, that misfortune was unfortunate, or that life was preferable to death. Thus in the year 371, when the news was brought of the grievous defeat by the Thebans at the battle of Leuctra, the men's choir was not stopped nor the games ended, and the women were warned to make no lamentations; while on the following day, according to the contemporary writer Xenophon, the families of the slain walked about in public with smiling faces, and those whose sons and fathers had survived went abroad "in gloom and shame."

Such a suppression and subversion of natural emotions is possible only as the fruit of a long and unnatural course of training. The individual Spartan was caught in a net out of which he was powerless to struggle. Since early childhood, he had known no education other than the education for battle; he had heard no commendation other than the commendation of warlike feats; he had been chided

if he seemed less skillful than his fellows in the martial games, and
had been taught that no crime was more monstrous than to shirk
one's duty in conflict. And even if he was one of those rare few
—how rare throughout the ages!—who oppose their own reason to
the force of tradition and accepted belief, what chance would he
have to make his individuality felt? If he dared to protest in words,
he would be condemned as a coward or traitor; and if he showed
less vim or determination than his brothers during the campaigns,
he would walk as with a brand of shame, an outcast among his own
kin. There would be none to break bread with him, none to engage
him in wrestling contests; his place at the dance would be the low-
est, his place at public meetings would be surrendered even to
those beneath him in years; he would have to behave humbly if
he wished to ward off showers of blows, and would suffer the contempt even of the women and boys. Certainly, a sword-stroke
would be a light penalty by comparison.

From all this, one might not suspect that the ordinary Spartan
felt any irrepressible eagerness for the military career. And the
Spartans themselves, by their own regulations, have provided a
flash of insight into their state of mind—a flash which, like the
inadvertent revealing word or gesture of an individual, is all the
more illuminating for having been unconscious. Let a man have
three sons to give to the State, and he could not be mobilized into
the army! Let him have four sons, and he had no further obligations at all to discharge toward the State! But just what did this
mean? Obviously, both provisions were intended as rewards. And
if they were intended as rewards, what is the inescapable conclusion? That honorable release from military service was held to
be a pearl of great price. That the citizen, fighting because the
social order compelled him to rather than because he desired to,
was eager for any acceptable way out. And since the privilege of
not fighting was put second only to the privilege of avoiding all
obligations to the State, we have here a strong implication that the
fighting mood of the individual was more a matter of social convention and compulsion than of native inclination.

This becomes the more understandable when we realize that
there was an economic basis for the Spartan regime. The community was essentially parasitic; it was founded upon slave labor.
Beneath the edifice of the State, the Helots seethed and brooded
in ever-threatened revolt; the military organization may originally

have been deemed necessary because of the mumblings of the subject class against their numerically inferior masters; and it continued to be held necessary not only against foreign foes but to keep the local underlings in subjugation. The precarious state of affairs is indicated by the existence of a secret service in which most of the eighteen-to-twenty-year-olds were enlisted, and whose members skulked on the roads, legally privileged to kill any suspicious-seeming Helots. Nevertheless, it was not dread of the slaves that was primarily preached to the Spartan youth; it was the glory of military attainment, the splendor of heroism against an outside adversary. Hence one wonders if any effective organization against the slaves could have been maintained had the Spartans not been educated in ideals that had little to do with the slaves.

Beyond this, we must remember that the position of the Helots was not exclusively economic. Ironically, they gave aid to the instrument of their own oppression; like almost everything else in Sparta, they served a military purpose. For, just as the knight of a later day had his squire, so the Spartan (though unmounted) had his Helots, his invaluable wartime helpers and retainers; and these were so numerous that, on the battlefield of Plataea, each Spartan is said to have been followed by seven servants.

The Helots, in short, were not only useful workers but invaluable adjuncts to the military or heroic mechanism. It would be strange indeed if the average Spartan, who had been taught to despise economic goods and reduce his material wants to a minimum, should have looked at slaves through the eyes of a modern industrialist rather than of a warrior pricked on by a fighting creed.

Chapter 10

Greece: Pericles, Cleon, and Alexander

Sparta, of course, was an exceptional phenomenon not only in Greece but in world history. In order to get a better rounded picture of Hellenic warfare, we must turn to her great rival, Athens.

In Athens, though the youths of the upper class trained for the army during their nineteenth and twentieth years, service was not compulsory before the fourth century. But in Athens also we notice a military spirit, much less pronounced and exclusive than in Sparta, yet growing with the rise of Athenian imperialism. We can trace a variety of motives behind the wars, even the religious impulse, as in the so-called Sacred War of 448 B.C., in which the Spartans rescued the shrine of Delphi from the Phocians and returned it to the Delphians, after which the Athenians under Pericles retrieved it from the Delphians and restored it to the Phocians. Motives of political ambition and inter-city rivalry may here have played their part; and such impulses, along with local pride and jealousy, the lure of foreign riches and the fear of foreign encroachment, were notorious in other wars of Athens and her sister states.

We find what we today should call a "preventive war" being urged on Sparta against Athens when, according to Thucydides, a Corinthian speaker declares that "they were born neither to have peace themselves nor to allow peace to other men," and proceeds to dogmatize that "peace is best secured by those who use their strength justly." [1] Yet this counsel was the forerunner of anything but peace.

Interfused with such practical considerations, we find the almost invariable idea by which men strive to assuage the grimness of slaughter and numb the agony of loss. The idea of glory and honor is one without which few fighting communities have been able to maintain their morale. And this idea is artfully woven into the celebrated Funeral Oration of Pericles. Speaking of the dead, the great leader declares (as reported by Thucydides):

For even where life's previous record showed faults and failures it is just to weigh the last brave hour of devotion against them all. There they wiped out evil with good and did the city more service than they did her harm in private life. There no hearts grew faint because they loved riches more than honor; none shirked the issue in the poor man's dream of wealth. All these they put aside to strike a blow for the city. Counting the quest to avenge her honour as the most glorious of all ventures . . . they chose rather to suffer the uttermost than to die by weakness. So their memory has escaped the reproaches of men's lips . . . and in a moment of time, at the climax of their lives, were rapt away from a world filled, for their dying eyes, not with terror but with glory.[2]

A similar exaltation of death in battle occurs in another passage:

For the whole earth is the sepulchre of famous men; and their story is not graven only on stone above their native earth, but lives on far away, without visible symbol, woven into the stuff of other men's lives. For you now it remains to rival what they have done.

Therefore I do not mourn with the parents of the dead who are here with us. I will rather comfort them. For they know that they have been born into a world of manifold chances and that he is to be accounted happy to whom the best lot falls—the best sorrow, such as yours today, or the best death, such as fell to those, for whom life and happiness were cut to the self-same measure.[3]

Not all the orators of the ages have had the eloquence of Pericles; not all have had the persuasiveness with which he haloes the skull-bones of dread reality in an aura of rainbowed words. But he has set a pattern not overlooked by military speakers in later days. By his appeal to the emotions, his bid to personal pride and the pride of country and the spirit of emulation, he has not only saved the warlike mood from shipwreck on the rock of gory fact, he has given it new impulse, power, and direction, and has inspired his hearers toward fresh memorable accomplishment. The magic, the magnetism, the almost hypnotic suasion of language, when pouring from the tongue of a master, can hardly be overrated as the provoker of warlike far more than of peaceful attitudes of mind.

Wherever we turn, we can see the same emphasis on glory as in the speech of Pericles: for example, an inscribed stone for the

Athenians who fell before the walls of Potidaea commemorates those who "giving their lives in barter for glory ennobled their country." It was worship of glory that was manifested when, after a victory, the winning side would boastfully erect a "trophy"—a post fitted with a crossbar, and hung with pieces of captured enemy equipment. It was the same worship of glory that, if Thucydides has spoken truly, made the errant leader Alcibiades boast of a plan to conquer Sicily, Carthage, the Peloponnesus, and Italy and rule the entire Greek world. But it is not glory that we see when we turn our eyes to the facts of Grecian war. It is of anything but glory that we read in most of the pages of Thucydides. Even leaving out of account the major catastrophes of the Peloponnesian War, such as the plague at Athens and the Syracusan disaster, the words of this acute reporter do not make pleasant reading—least of all, in his delineation of the state of mind of the war-makers and war-provokers. The confusion in the wits of men, the way in which the combatants reverse their normal judgments and look at things upside down, is described in a memorable passage:

When troubles had once begun in the cities, those who followed carried the revolutionary spirit further and further, and determined to outdo the report of all who had preceded them by the ingenuity of their enterprises and the atrocity of their revenges. The meaning of words had no longer the same relation to things, but was changed by them as they thought proper. Reckless daring was held to be loyal courage; prudent delay was the excuse of a coward; moderation was the defense of unmanly weakness; to know everything was to do nothing. Frantic energy was the true quality of a man. A conspirator who wanted to be safe was a recreant in disguise. The lover of violence was always trusted, and his opponent suspected. He who plotted from the first to have nothing to do with plots was a breaker-up of parties and a poltroon who was afraid of the enemy. In a word, he who could outstrip another in a bad action was applauded.[4]

The chronicler proceeds to tell how "Revenge was dearer than self-preservation," how agreements were binding only so long as the power to break them did not exist, how men took greater pleasure in perfidy than "in an open act of revenge," and how the cause of all this moral anarchy was "the love of power, originating in avarice and ambition, and the party-spirit which is engendered by them when men are fairly embarked in a contest. . . . When men are retaliating upon others, they are reckless of the future, and do not hesitate to annul those common laws of humanity to which every individual trusts for his own hope of deliverance should he ever be overtaken by calamity."

Had Thucydides used the terminology of today, he might have said that the people were suffering from a war-bred psychosis, a sort of group monomania in which the emotions took command of the rational faculties. And he might have added that avarice and ambition, which he identifies as the twin roots of the trouble, were themselves imbedded in the standards and ideas of the day—standards that elevated wealth and political position above morality and justice as ends to be applauded and devoutly sought.

In a further passage, the historian reveals the hardening of the fiber of the Athenians beneath the thrust of power. He shows how, having erected an empire, they subjected themselves to the sophistries of what we would call "political realism," and submerged normal humanity beneath the passion of command. The State of Mytilene had revolted and been subdued; the entire male population had been condemned to death; and Cleon, the successor of Pericles, opposed a proposal to rescind the decree. Thucydides credits him with these words:

I still maintain that you should abide by your former decision, and not be misled either by pity, or by the charm of words, or by a too forgiving temper. . . . Forgiveness is naturally shown to those who, being reconciled, will continue friends, and not to those who will always remain what they were, and will abate nothing of their enmity. In one word, if you do as I say, you will do what is just to the Mytileneans, and also what is expedient for yourselves. . . . If, right or wrong, you are resolved to rule, then rightly or wrongly they must be chastised for your good. Otherwise you must give up your empire, and, when virtue is no longer dangerous, you may be as virtuous as you please.

In several ways, this is extraordinarily interesting. First, it will be noted, Cleon speaks of forgiveness for the sake of expediency; a little later, he links justice to expediency, or rather implies that what is expedient for the Athenians will be just to the Mytileneans; and only a sentence or two further on, dropping all pretense of considering justice at all, he declares that, "Rightly or wrongly, they must be chastised for your good," and adds a gibe as to the permissibility of virtue when it is no longer dangerous. In part, of

course, Cleon was but the child of his age; in a period in which it
was not unprecedented to massacre an entire male population, any
leader could have represented such a procedure as for the good of
his people; the ferocious precedent of much ancient warfare, in
which genocide was not infrequent, was as much responsible for
his words as any personal brutality.

Yet the phrase, "Rightly or wrongly, they must be chastised
for your good," has gone ringing down the ages. "Rightly or
wrongly, they must be chastised!" cried the Romans above the
ruins of many a sacked and burning town. "Rightly or wrongly!"
exclaimed the fighting hosts of the Middle Ages, the Italians under
Cesare Borgia, the armies of Peter, Charles V, Louis XIV, Frederick, Napoleon, and many another leader. "Rightly or wrongly!"
has gone dinning into our ears from the imperialists and aggressors
of our own day, the disciples of expediency who have been responsible for the greater part of the world's suffering, and who
within our own time have perpetrated outrages far vaster in scale
and even more cold-blooded than the massacre favored by Cleon.

II

It is instructive to observe the background of the most famous
and momentous of all the conflicts of the Hellenic city-states. Like
most armed clashes, the Peloponnesian War has its roots deep in
the less stormy period that preceded; we can clearly trace the line
of descent in the attitudes of mind created by the Persian wars.
Those struggles, it will be recalled, had united the Greeks in the
short-lived Hellenic League; and following the defeat of Xerxes
the fear of a new invasion gave birth in the year 477 to the Delian
League, an anti-Persian alliance of the free communities of Ionia
and the Aegean. Athens, whose power in this League was as overmastering as that of Prussia was to be in the German Empire of
twenty-three centuries later, guaranteed the independence of each
member state, and seems at first to have respected her agreement.
But in time the League foundered upon the rock of Periclean
imperialism.

Here we can see the operation of a number of diverse forces
within the minds of the Athenian ruling group. There was the
desire to be strong and secure, and consequently the huge expenditures for preparedness, including new fortifications and enormous

defensive walls; there was the desire for commercial supremacy, and the jealousy of and rankling rivalry with Sparta; and there were the social measures of Pericles, which, whether introduced for political motives or as genuine humanitarian reforms, compelled a deep drain upon the treasury by doling out State funds to an estimated third or more of the Athenian citizenry. Because of his immense expenditures, Pericles needed an income; and since there was still no direct tax on Athenian citizens, he must look elsewhere for his revenues. But where could he look? Where but to the allies of the Delian League? In 454 Pericles found a pretext for transferring the League's treasury from Delos to Athens; and thenceforth virtually all the tribute flowed into Athenian coffers. It is obvious that this was not calculated to make friends among the League members, all the less so as Athens denied them the right of secession. And it is not surprising that revolts occurred, the most notable being that of Samos, which was crushed in 439 after the defenders had been starved into submission; various penalties were then inflicted, including the leveling of the city walls, exile of the rulers, seizure of the fleet, and imposition of a large indemnity.

In all this we can see the nurturing of an antagonism that was to lead toward general war; Sparta, Corinth, and the other states could hardly have looked except with apprehension on the high-handed methods of the Athenian imperialists. It is, in fact, the view of Thucydides that the basic cause of the war was the fear which the rise of Athens had incited in the Lacedaemonians. And fear was accompanied, as almost always, by envy and suspicion, and gave birth to counter-strokes: counter-strokes that did not confine themselves to military preparations, but included intrigue, the fanning of disaffection, and the fending for advantages in the supposedly inevitable struggle at a time when peaceful negotiations might still conceivably have been effective.

We see this when a dispute flares up between Corinth and her colony Corcyra. Both send envoys to Athens; Corcyra pleads for assistance, which Corinth—backed by the powerful Peloponnesian League—naturally opposes. Obviously, if Athens would avoid war, she must shun the Corcyrean alliance, which is directly calculated to bring on a clash with the Peloponnesus. On the other hand, if war is to come anyhow, the alliance offers evident advantages. It is the defeatist attitude—the attitude automatically debarring a peaceful arrangement—which comes to the foreground, as we can see in this appeal (reported by Thucydides):

The Lacedaemonians, fearing the growth of your empire, are eager to take up arms, and the Corinthians, who are your enemies, are all-powerful with them. They begin with us, but they will go on to you, that we may not stand united against them in the bond of a common enmity. And it is our business to strike first, and to forestall their designs instead of waiting to counteract them.

Again, the idea of "preventive war"!

The Corcyreans further argued that the Athenians would have the use of their fleet if they sided with them; otherwise, they might have to oppose the Corcyrean fleet along with the Corinthian. Thus a shrewd appeal to self-interest supplemented the plea of war's inevitability. And these arguments prevailed; instead of leaving an avenue for settlement open, Athens accepted an alliance with Corcyra and sent ten warships to that city, though she agreed to fight only in the event of an attack or threatened attack.

The result was that she fought almost immediately, intervening in a naval battle between Corcyra and Corinth. And the breach with Corinth made it necessary for Athens to be watchful of her interests elsewhere: for example, in the city of Potidaea, an offshoot of Corinth but a tributary of Athens. Asked to abandon a system whereby they received annual magistrates from Corinth, the Potidaeans proved refractory; and this, along with a revolt of the Macedonian king Perdiccas (who opposed Athens because she had favored his brothers instead of him), precipitated a battle over Potidaea, in which the Athenians routed the Corinthian general Aristeus. By this time the Corinthians had been goaded sufficiently to do some goading of their own; they appealed to the Spartans to declare war on Athens, using the argument, already quoted, that the Athenians "were born neither to have peace themselves nor to allow peace to other men."

Events were moving on such a swift emotional tide that war had become almost if not quite unavoidable. Pericles, striking with an economic weapon, now crushed the Spartan ally Megara, which had aided the Corinthians at the Battle of Sybota; by cutting off her trade with the Athenian Empire he dealt her a blow such as might fall, let us say, on modern England if all her foreign commerce were suddenly forbidden. Athens was thereupon accused of breaking the Thirty Years' Truce; but in a debate at Sparta, King Archidamus urged postponement of action until his side made sure that it had money enough for the needs of war. However, he was overruled by the majority, which voted that the question at issue was whether Athens had been in the wrong—and this question, of course, they decided in the affirmative.

But it is significant of the times that, before war could be declared, the approval of the Delphic oracle had to be gained. Even in this sternest of stern business, in which pride and passion and fear and jealousy and economics were strangely blended, men could not act without regard for the old superstitious and religious beliefs. It is worthy of note, incidentally, that those same religious ideas made themselves felt later in the war, when the situation of the Athenian expedition to Sicily had begun to appear desperate. Demosthenes, one of the generals, had urged that the invaders sail away; but another general, Nicias, had opposed the move. Finally, following the arrival of fresh enemy reinforcements, Nicias consented to the withdrawal; the preparations were all made . . . when to everyone's consternation the moon was eclipsed. Surely, a warning from the gods! Thucydides tells of the sequel:

The mass of the army was greatly moved and called upon the generals to remain. Nicias himself, who was too much under the influence of divination and such-like, refused even to discuss the question of their removal until they had remained thrice nine days, as the soothsayers prescribed. This was the reason why the departure of the Athenians was finally delayed.

This also was the reason why the Athenians never were able to get away; and why the expedition ended in catastrophe. "Fleet and army perished from the face of the earth," Thucydides reports; "nothing was saved, and of the many who went forth few returned home." One cannot help wondering as to the results if the Athenians had had modern astronomical knowledge.

III

During the following century, a meaningful though not entirely new idea began to spread throughout Greece. This was the idea of Panhellenism. Beneath the stress of the Persian wars, as we have noted, the Greek states had joined hands in a momentary unity;

but during the period of disorganization that succeeded the Peloponnesian War, dreamers began to think more seriously than ever before of a possible Panhellenic world, in which all Greeks would be united. Perhaps most prominent of these nationalists was Isocrates, an Athenian who urged war upon Persia in the interest of Greek unification (though not with the idea of establishing a Greek empire, which he specifically opposed). Isocrates was not to live to see his idea fulfilled; and it is notable that when, in the year 355, his scheme for a common Greek attack upon Persia seemed no longer in the dream stage, he was eloquent in raising his voice for peace. Nevertheless, his views are worth a passing glance: that the Athenians were the teachers of mankind; that to be a Greek was to be heir to a superior intelligence; and that a common citizenship for all Greeks was desirable. Isocrates here displays several qualities not absent in later history: a belief in the superiority of his own people; a desire for unification in one great peaceful (at least, internally peaceful) nation; and an idea that the olive branch can be won with the sword. And his views were to be, to a great extent, behind the career of a more celebrated figure, Alexander of Macedon, who may not himself have had any strong Panhellenic convictions yet acted consciously or unconsciously as the apostle of Panhellenism.

Alexander owes an enormous debt to another remarkable character, his father Philip. And Philip in turn appears to have been influenced by the ideas of Isocrates. Whether from personal inclination, or in recognition of the emotions that Isocrates had been arousing for decades, he not only established a Hellenic union in the League of Corinth (which he dominated), but moved to wage the Persian war that Isocrates had long urged. But the war had hardly begun when Philip was assassinated. And the twenty-year-old Alexander took over more than a crown and an army; he inherited the Panhellenic ideas which Isocrates had been broadcasting.

It would be interesting to know what that stanch anti-imperialist would have thought of the use to which Alexander put his beliefs. Certainly, nothing could have been further from his mind than wide-flung conquering expeditions. But perhaps his short historical perspectives did not show him that the idea of fighting is like the evil brood of Pandora's box, which, once released, may be beyond our power to recapture or control.

No man was ever more deliberately trained than Alexander to be a war-chief. The resemblances to the early Hannibal are in some respects marked: like Hannibal, he was the son of an outstanding general; like Hannibal, he was taught by his father in the actual field (he led the cavalry at Chaeronae beneath Philip's very gaze). But unlike Hannibal, he was educated to be a king as well as an army leader; unlike Hannibal, he came into contact for several years with one of the supreme philosophic minds of ancient times —and it is reasonable to suppose that any ideas of Panhellenism which he had may be largely traced to his great teacher, Aristotle.

Few characters in world history have been the target of greater controversy than Alexander. He has been something more than a man; he has been a divine hero, a legend; he has been worshipped not for what he was but for what men have imagined him to be. In the concept of the youthful conqueror, who lifted a blazing sword and in a few short years went crashing across the unknown East, there is something to appeal to the romanticizing mind; and consequently the reality has often been obscured amid an aura of glamour and glory, and it is still a little difficult to look at the actual man.

A number of facts, however, may be noted. And first let us glance at his methods, particularly in conquered territories. His treatment of the city of Thebes was notorious; all authorities agree that it was unjustified by the circumstances, even though it has many parallels in ancient warfare: he had the city leveled to the ground, sparing only one or two buildings; he ordered the men to be butchered, and the women and children to be sold into slavery. He is said to have regretted this savagery, and afterward to have gone out of his way to treat Thebans kindly; yet he dealt the same bloodshed and devastation later upon the cities of Tyre and Gaza, both of which he took after long sieges. Yet toward some other cities he was considerate, even indulgent; at Jerusalem, according to Josephus, he was met by a band of citizens headed by the High Priest; and appeased by a prophecy of Daniel, in which he saw himself as the warrior who would subdue the Persian king, he not only spared the city but exempted it from every seventh year's taxation. It may be that this story is not literally true; but certainly it accords with Alexander's character as we see it in other episodes.

In all those incidents we behold him as headstrong, self-worshipping, egomaniacal—as, indeed, few could help being if reared with no thought in mind but to rule and be obeyed. We note a youth steeped in the heroic ideal, taking pride in his alleged descent from Achilles and Hercules, and wishing to prove himself a worthy descendant of those legendary great; we observe one who is not only proud but vain, and whose likeness—clean-shaven, to preserve his boyish beauty—is handed down upon countless sculptures and paintings and on the faces of coins. We see a man who, inflated with the pomp of empire, insists on wearing the tiara and robes of Persian royalty; we view the poets and historians he takes with him on his expeditions in order to press-agent his mighty deeds; we hear his demand that his subjects, on approaching him, throw themselves to the ground in the Oriental fashion; we watch his self-veneration giving place to self-deification, until, as if with an actual belief in his own godhood, he orders the Greek states to grant him divine honors.

Various stories, with a rather bitter ring, tell of the violence and impetuosity of this man-god: how, during a drunken bout, he ran a spear through Cleitus, his boon companion, who had once saved his life; how he hanged Aristotle's nephew, Callisthenes, who refused to prostrate himself before the ruler; how he executed Philotas, the son of one of his best generals, on the flimsiest of evidence of treason, and then had the unoffending father, Parmenio, also slain before he could learn of his son's fate. Such deeds, and others even more frightful, have been common in the lives of Oriental despots, of whom Alexander in effect was one; and these are mentioned here not so that we may revel in ancient gore and gossip, but because they show the purely personal and capricious nature of Alexander's rule, and lead toward the conclusion that the wars he waged and the empire he established were likewise personal and capricious in their nature.

A combination of more or less unrelated forces made Alexander and Alexander's empire what they were. On the physical side, we see the army that Philip had bequeathed to him, the conquests that Philip had made, and the well-nigh irresistible phalanx that Philip had developed. But even more important were the beliefs and attitudes of mind to which Alexander had fallen heir: his training by Philip and Aristotle, the Panhellenic views of the day, the idea of Greek racial and intellectual superiority, the millennium-old tradition of aggressive warfare and the long antagonism against

Persia, the heroic ideal with all its trappings of a distinguished
ancestry and deeds of glory and bluster.

We might, however, have had all these without having Alexander or Alexander's conquests. One thing more was necessary:
a man of the peculiar mental stamp of the Macedonian leader, a
man of great self-will and tremendous daring, a man of a rose-
clouded romanticism and a wildly adventurous spirit, a man who
was young and fiercely energetic, all-powerful and all-convinced
of the ascendant star of his destiny.

Consider the situation at the time when Alexander embarked on
his major adventure. What reason was there, on the face of things,
why an army from Madeconia or Greece should have set off across
the thousands of miles of Persian valley and plateau, across the
mountains of Turkestan and Afghanistan, through the Khyber Pass
into India, down the Indus for hundreds of miles to its mouth, and
back along the desert to the Persian Gulf, enduring inconceivable
miseries, founding cities, fighting battles, subjugating previously
unheard-of peoples in the course of a six-year expedition? What
reason was there on the face of things? None at all!

Alexander himself, unless endowed with supernatural powers of
prophecy, could originally have had no idea where he was going;
in that day of scanty geographical knowledge, he penetrated a
world virtually as unknown as Columbus explored on his first
westward voyage. And the impulse behind him may have been not
wholly unlike that of Columbus; if he was seduced by no thought
of a quick western route to the East, he was allured by the kindred
idea of reaching the end of the earth. It is noteworthy that, like
Columbus, he faced grumblings and threatened mutiny from his
followers; in the end, only their revolt prevented him from continuing on his way across India—a fact which in itself indicates
the aimless, adventurous nature of his undertaking. For if he had
had his way, where would he have gone? No one knows. Perhaps
across to the valley of the Ganges, perhaps on into present-day
Burma, Assam, China, or Indo-China. And for what purpose? To
continue a wild and glorious adventure, in which he might finally
have become entangled beyond possibility of escape. Surely, we
have not here a man moved by any compulsions except those of
his own nature.

But, for several reasons, it was possible for him to follow the
bidding of his own nature: because of the traditions of leadership,

which made it the practice for one man to give orders, and for all others to obey; because of the growth, throughout the centuries, of military institutions and ideas, so that attacks upon outlying countries were neither unusual nor disapproved; and because men consequently were inured to fighting, and would take up the sword either as wage-seeking mercenaries, or as adventurers looking for honor and booty.

That Alexander hoped to dominate a great empire appears evident; yet this was merely a phase of his self-glorification. His defenders have argued that he consciously sought to spread Pan-hellenism; but in view of the homage that he paid to himself, the indications are that his chief thought was to spread Pan-Alexander-ism. Certainly, a man with a clear project for consolidating cultural gains would have done more than to wander hither and thither, brandishing a lance; and would have striven to found his empire on some more solid rock than personal glory. One is obliged to agree with the summary of a recent commentator:

Though his views developed greatly during the years he spent in Asia, we have only hints from which to guess what was in his mind, and the only progress that we can clearly trace is one toward the aggrandizement of his own personal power and prestige.[5]

Though he probably could no more have foreseen the effects of his actions than he could have traced the course of the Indus before setting foot in India, Alexander did leave a tremendous heritage to the future: not only in the diffusion of Hellenic culture, but in the propagation of ideas that had a profound bearing on war and peace. And these ideas were of two types, and, paradoxically, worked in opposite directions. In the first place, though his empire fell to pieces immediately after his death, he showed that it was possible to unite many lands beneath a single banner. His was not, indeed, the first great empire the world had known; but it remained for him to suggest the possibility of peace through unity, and so to give the peace-loving world an ideal to work for (an ideal partially fulfilled in the *Pax Romana* of several centuries later). However, while he thus unconsciously provided a new hope for peace, he supplied (likewise unconsciously) a new spur to the war-makers.

Throughout the centuries, the story of his exploits has lent impetus to that very heroic ideal of which he was himself a victim.

During his lifetime, as we have seen, he was deified—an honor calculated to impress the unanalytical and the superstitious, and even to create a basis of unity, a sort of banner beneath which the Greeks and Orientals could combine. During his lifetime, Callisthenes circulated stories of the divine qualities of this "son of Zeus"—stories which apparently the "son of Zeus" never troubled to deny. And though for a while after his death the pendulum swung to the opposite extreme and he was pictured as little more than a drunken bandit, the Alexander of fact gradually became lost in the god-Alexander of romance, which shone as the model for all later conquerors and would-be conquerors. From Pompey and Caesar through the Crusader captains to Alexander's nearest modern kinsman, Napoleon, that romantic and magnified vision of the Macedonian adventurer has never left the world's consciousness, a goad and a justification to war-makers and above all to egomaniacal aggressors . . . a lingering illusion that puts golden spangles across the black face of battle.

Even today, the name of Alexander retains its magic; even today, we are apt to accept the legend rather than look at the man. Most of us make our acquaintance with Alexander through elementary textbooks that give no more than flying glimpses at a few peaks and headlands, among which the Macedonian leader only too often seems a dominating figure, the essence of all that is bright and glorious, a paladin, a superhuman figure. We do not visualize the battered and burning cities, the bleeding stumps of men, the wailing women and children dragged forth into slavery; we do not see the treacheries, the violent rages, the murders, the pomp and bluster, the inordinate ambitions, the mad and aimless wanderings. In our juvenile enthusiasm, we feel that here is someone to emulate. And millions throughout the centuries have had just this romantic and puerile idea of Alexander; millions have been drawn toward warlike adventures, on what they took to be the model of their divinity. How much this has bequeathed to the ages, in the way of terror and bloodshed, will never be known; but there is reason to hold that the brilliant myths surrounding Alexander, even more than Alexander's actual deeds, have been among the factors forming and perpetuating the war-making mood of twenty-three centuries.

Chapter 11

Rome: Discipline and Profiteering

History sifts with a strange unpredictable hand, but rarely has she chosen with more seeming caprice than when she picked a small hill-city by the Tiber to be the head of one of the world's greatest empires.

Not more than twenty-five centuries ago, Rome was a little peasant community, occupying no more than four hundred square miles, and with a population estimated not to have exceeded 150,000. Yet this minute state, whose farms and homes together covered less territory than many modern metropolitan areas and whose people are outnumbered in scores of second-rate modern cities, came within a few centuries to extend its dominions over seas and mountains, to govern immense sections of three continents, and to reach for a time from the Irish Sea to the Persian Gulf. How did this miracle happen? This is a question that historians for thousands of years have asked, but on one fact all are agreed: the wide extension of Roman sovereignty would not have been possible without the Roman fighting arm. It was the Roman sword that was the physical instrument of the whole remarkable expansion. And therefore it is necessary to ask just what sort of a sword this was.

In early Rome we find a rigid, rigorous regime, with little resemblance to the corrupt and luxury-ridden system of later days. There appears to have been no lavishness, little art, little literature, little learning; the individual was reared on a stern, practical creed, of which the chief tenets were piety, dignity, simplicity, and subordination: subordination to the gods, to the family, and to the State. And in a sense these three forms of subordination were one. Awe and reverence for the gods was easily translated into awe and reverence for the priest-father, the head of the family; and this in turn could be converted quite naturally into awe and reverence for the State, obedience to the State, patriotic respect for the State, and the bearing of arms at the State's command. In the family there was in effect both a religious and a political control, which resembled the command of a military dictator: the *paterfamilias* not only officiated at religious rites but was an absolute monarch within his small domains, an autocrat with the power of life or death. When he spoke, his children obeyed, though they might be men of consular rank and high civic attainments; when he decreed punishment, punishment was inflicted; and cases have been recorded in which a father, officiating as a one-man court of no appeal, ordained the death of his own offspring. Thus, in one well-known instance, the senator Fulvius, a contemporary of Caesar, decreed his son's execution for participation in the conspiracy of Catiline. And it was not until the time of Constantine that a father was prohibited from exposing an unwanted child to the elements.

Under such a paternalistic system, the fine, delicate buds of individuality would have little chance of flowering. Not only the lawbreaker but the breaker of tradition would be discouraged; he who rebelled against the State or the family could in most cases do so only to his cost. Here in early Rome, as so often throughout history, we see a demonstration of the fact, which has been generally overlooked, but which glares at one across the ages like a snow-patch on a mountainside: that much of man's fighting is based not upon his pugnacity but upon his docility, that he is led forth to slay and be slain because of his submissiveness rather than because of any bellicose quality, that it is this submissiveness which permits him to be regimented and trained. What do we observe in Rome? From earliest childhood, the systematic development of obedience. The small boy, from the time he is old enough to notice anything at all, witnesses how his father gives orders to his brothers and sisters, even though these be full-grown; or how his grandfather commands his father, uncles, aunts, and cousins, along with all the slaves and retainers of the house. And since he is early taught that he must obey, since he is drilled in the idea that the gods demand obedience to their representative, the family head, and that it is sacrilegious to put one's own desires first, he never thinks of obedience as anything except his plain duty.

Shaped by such home training, the ordinary youth is ready-made for the army. He has learned respect for authority, he has learned discipline; he knows what it is to be in step with other men, and recognizes the dire fruits of disobedience. And so, when he takes his place in the camp, he is in a not unfamiliar atmosphere;

his home too has been a camp of a sort. And if we remember that he has been taught love of country just as he has been indoctrinated in love of family, and has been led to value physical courage as one of the primary virtues and a prized proof of manhood, we will understand that he has the full psychological equipment of a warrior.

Here, undoubtedly, we have one explanation of the early successes of the Roman arms—one reason why a single community, out of all the Italian communities, prospered and spread militarily, and reached out and subdued its neighbors. But other reasons also become evident when we look at the early Roman army.

II

As in most warring countries, the growing boy was trained physically as well as mentally. He was systematically drilled in handling weapons; he was given continuous practice in marching, running, jumping, swimming, the carrying of heavy weights, and the wielding of the sword and javelin. And thus his body was hardened to bear the trials of the campaign at the same time as his mind was conditioned for warfare and his desires were stimulated toward the practical application of the knowledge he had acquired.

Between the ages of seventeen and forty-five, the Roman was subject to serve; after that, if he desired and was still fit, he might take up his post with a corps of the older men until he had reached sixty. Every citizen was obliged to serve for at least ten seasons; and every citizen's service was regarded as a privilege rather than a duty. To be declared unworthy to serve was to be punished grievously; it was to be disgraced, and to be debarred from all public employment. For the honorable citizen, every path to political advancement had a military approach; one must, literally, be a soldier before one could be a statesman or a politician. But even the honorable citizen required some qualification other than willingness or ability; he had to be a man of property, and had to bring his own equipment to the field. By the days of the early Republic, the infantry was divided into five classes, according to the possessions of its members; these varied from the contingents or "centuries" composed of men equipped with shields, spears, helmets, and cuirasses, down to companies that fought only with slings and stones. Beneath the latter were the supernumeraries and labor battalions; above them all were the *equites* or cavalry, whose members had the means to provide themselves with horses and full armor.

A man's position in the army, being thus determined by his wealth, was in a sense the measure of his social rank. And, conversely, the citizen with the most property to defend was the one given the most important defensive place.

Nevertheless, the lawmakers did not rely wholly upon the obvious incentives, such as the soldier's patriotism and his desire to protect his own land or annex or plunder the land of his neighbor. Nothing is more evident than that, when a man obeys a compulsion of his own being, he requires neither rewards to lure him forth nor punishments to keep him from going astray: he who really loves, will act through love; he who of his own impulse defends the right, needs no spearpoint to prod him on. Then why should a soldier require a spur to make him do the proper thing, a jab to save him from doing the wrong? The Romans were not the first, nor have they been the last fighting people to feel that they must help nature along; to recognize that in war, as in most other affairs, man is moved by the hope of reward and the fear of punishment. And so they were at pains to fan the fighting spirit by an elaborate series of rewards and punishments.

It was a Roman maxim that a soldier should fear his commander more than the enemy. And in accordance with this principle, the punishments might be severe to the point of savagery. The trooper, as he trudged on his way, knew that the general, one mile beyond the city limits, had the same power as the *paterfamilias*: the power of life or death over every man beneath him. True, he might call a council of war before deciding in important affairs; but humble Gaius or Marcus, who tramped with his heavy pack amid the dust of the infantry, could hardly expect such a formality. There were many offenses for which, according to the law of the Twelve Tables (449 B.C.), he might be scourged to death (or beheaded, if he were an officer): for fighting in battle without keeping his proper order, for leaving his post or otherwise failing in duty, for throwing away his weapons or mutinying, or for going over to the enemy (which a soldier was held to have done if he strayed beyond trumpet call). For lesser infractions, he might be beaten with the centurion's rod; he might be sold into slavery (the occasional penalty for desertion); or he might be subject to the cruel punishment of the *fustuarium*, a sort of running of the gauntlet, in which his comrades stoned or beat him—and fortunate was he who died during the ordeal, since nobody, not even the members of his own family, would dare to succor him if he survived.

But the military lawgivers were not satisfied to strike at individual offenders. In some cases, they prescribed the punishment of decimation: every tenth man in a legion would have to die beneath the stones or scourges of his fellows; while the survivors might not be allowed to camp with the other contingents, and might receive barley instead of wheat as their mainstay.

It is said that the commanders did not often have to invoke such punishments. One can easily believe this; but the fact that the punishments had been authorized, an ever-threatened terror and a constant "heavy, heavy hangs over your head," is in itself eloquent.

III

The dread of punishment was tempered, however, by the hope of reward. And the simplest reward was in the nature of the soldier's regular wage, though this was not paid in the earliest times (the mildest punishment, correspondingly, was in the withholding of the wage). Special recognition came in various ways: in decorations such as the *hasta pura*, a headless lance that betokened some outstanding deed; *phalerae*, or medallions that adorned the hero's breast; arm-bands or collars; and crowns such as the *corona muralis*, reserved for the first man to scale the ramparts of a beleaguered town; and the *corona aurea* for distinguished courage in other ways. Even the general might be tempted by the prospect of decorations; he might wear a wreath of grass, the *corona obsidionalis*, in recognition for his relief of a besieged camp or fort; and he was entitled to display a laurel leaf at his triumph, to hold a scepter, wear a purple and gold-embroidered tunic, and ride in a chariot escorted by red-robed *lictors*. Incidentally, the triumph itself, with its display of the spoils, the sacrificial animals, the hostages and the chained captives, was the commander's supreme reward, no less than a spur to the spirit of his followers and of the populace in general.

But these were only a few of the artificial enticements. There were other lures, such as promotion, additional pay, exemption from taxation, pensions, and shortening of the term of service. And just as whole bodies might be punished by having to eat barley instead of wheat or by the dreadful penalty of decimation, so entire contingents might be rewarded. And as all distinctions were conferred in public, and were accompanied with great ceremony and honor, they were made to appear especially glamorous.

In some cases, the chief inducement was the persuasiveness of a commander—his kindling of the pride or awakening of the shame of the troops, his playing upon those emotional strings by which even strong men are moved. An example, if we are to accept the word of the *Commentaries,* occurred during Caesar's campaign in Gaul against the German leader Ariovistus. Many of the Roman soldiers, raw and inexperienced, had been intimidated by the fantastic reports of German prowess; and Caesar, faced with mutiny, called a council of war. After setting out the general situation, he stated that if the other legions held back, he would go forth alone against the Germans with his favorite Tenth. However, he professed not to believe that the others were afraid to go; after all, their ancestors under Marius had routed those same Germans— were they, he implied, less worthy than their fathers of the name of men? Against such a challenge to their manhood, the troops could not hold out—sooner than appear as unworthy as their refusal would have implied, they swore that they would follow Caesar to the world's end.

Such persuasiveness did not, of course, always suffice. Nor were all the official gifts, badges, ceremonies, and insignia likely to have been bait enough to the thousands of legionaries. Beyond all these, there were hopes of unofficial returns in the shape of booty. As the power of the Roman arms gradually spread, and as the city by the Tiber was moved partly against her own will to gather an empire about her, the fascination of foreign riches took powerful hold upon the Latin mind. By the second century B.C., we can observe the process well advanced. Ferrero, in a succinct passage, has summarized the situation:

In the looting of cities in Greece and Asia, and the devastation of the countryside in the Po Valley and Spain, generals learnt a new indulgence toward themselves and their men. Sometimes the legionary traded with the native on his own account; during the Macedonian War there were several instances of soldiers who acted as usurers. Many a poor peasant returned home from the wars with a small fortune to his credit; and if a campaign promised to be lucrative, volunteers would flock in from all parts of Italy. And where the private soldier drew profit the State drew far more. With tribute and plunder the finances were set in order, debts were paid, and money lavished on all manner of improvements.[1]

In Spain the magnetism of booty was so powerful that the wars became a sort of gold rush; the legionaries and their commanders alike joined in the scramble; all sorts of traders, battening on the plunder, accompanied the troops; and even the privates at times became so affluent that they had slaves to do their work and carry them around in litters. It is not hard to see why these military gold-diggers rushed away in their thousands to the provinces; the idea of loot, of easy riches, was in the air, exercising a sort of fascination, producing a sort of hysteria, like that of the California gold fields in 1849. We need only remember the streams of captured wealth which for many years had come flowing in from conquered lands, and which after 167 B.C. were so enormous that the Roman citizen no longer had to pay property taxes. Parasitism has its allurements, and its advantages—for the parasites. And the Roman adventurers, even at the possible cost of some inconvenient incidental fighting, were not unwilling to drain the sweet sap of foreign treasure.

Nevertheless, not every self-enriching citizen had to submit to the uncertainties and hardships of traveling abroad. Many stayed comfortably at home, and grew fat on war profiteering, selling goods to the army at whatever the market would bear. It is hardly to be supposed that such men, who shared all the advantages and none of the perils of victory, were soft-minded believers in peace.

One should note, incidentally, that Rome at this period would sometimes fight without annexing territory. Despite the great wealth which she gained in plunder and tribute, she was not greedy for land; after defeating Antiochus, she divided the conquered territory between Pergamus and Rhodes; and, subsequently, she overcame the Galatians, but left them in possession of their country. Evidently the idea of fighting for empire takes hold but slowly.

Quite as notable as the desires and incentives of the war-makers during all this period was the state of mind induced in the civilian population by the series of victories, and particularly by the Second Punic War. Toynbee, in a pertinent passage, has drawn attention to this. After quoting from Polybius, who describes the materialism and the surrender to sense and passion that marked the younger generations of Romans, he goes on to comment:

This was the moral pass to which the Roman governing class had been brought by the overwhelming victory which had descended upon the Republic after years of agony in which she had been tottering on the verge of an abyss. The first reaction of a generation which had lived through this bewildering experience was a blind presumption that a victor's irresistible material power was the key to a solution of all human problems, and that the only conceivable end of Man was an unbridled enjoyment of the grossest pleasures which this power could place within his grasp. The victors did not realize that this very state of mind bore witness to the moral defeat which a militarily vanquished Hannibal had succeeded in inflicting upon them.[2]

It is an incidental irony that the victories which had plunged the upper classes into orgies of material indulgence had been the ruination of the lower classes, and notably of the peasants, large numbers of whom lost their lands to aristocrats and the newly rich . . . with the result that we can see the deep-rooted beginnings of that decay of Italian agriculture which some authorities hold to be among the leading causes of Rome's eventual downfall. But of all this most contemporaries appear to have been oblivious, while they proceeded blithely about their enjoyments, their profiteering, and their plundering, filled with what Toynbee aptly calls "the intoxication of victory."

Chapter 12

Rome: The Paths of Empire

As the Roman Empire expanded, the looting of conquered territory and the exactions from the provinces became more systematized, more businesslike. Polybius tells us that, after a city had been taken, half the army would disperse to pillage, while the other half kept the ranks to protect the plunderers.[1] This meant that robbery was no longer disorganized, as among uncivilized raiders, but had advanced to the point of planning and order; impulse had largely given way to design.

Further testimony as to the place of organized plunder is found in the words of one of the more humane and civilized of the Romans. The following is from Cicero's speech *pro lege Mantilia*:

. . . the whole system of credit and finance which is carried on here at Rome, is inextricably bound up with the revenues of the Asiatic provinces. If these revenues are destroyed, our whole system will come down with a crash. See that you do not hesitate for a moment to prosecute with all your energies a war by which the glory of the Roman name, the safety of our allies, our most valuable revenues, and the fortunes of innumerable citizens, will be effectually preserved.[2]

The case of Julius Caesar is conspicuous in this respect, yet was by no means exceptional in type. Here was a man who, unlike other great captains such as Alexander, Hannibal, and Napoleon, did not embark upon his conquering career until middle life; here was a man who, apparently, would not have been a military leader at all if he had seen equal prospects of promotion in other directions. Even if he was born in the year 100 B.C. (and not in 102, as has sometimes been asserted), he was almost forty when, as *praetor*, he was assigned command of the province of Further Spain; and it would be naïve to suppose that when he subjugated the refractory tribes and at the same time collected loot enough to discharge his huge private debts, he was thinking exclusively of his patriotic duties. While he was adding to his military prestige in Gaul, he may have believed that the quelling of the tribes would make for the greater safety and prosperity of Rome; but if there was any impelling necessity why he should have passed years in warfare beyond the Alps, going so far as to bridge the Rhine and cross the English Channel, one can find it in nothing but the tradition and precedent of aggression that prevailed in his day, and in the urges of his own ambitious nature.

The latter element, indeed, is indicated by several diverse facts: the agreement that he reached with the other two members of the First Triumvirate, providing that he should govern a province and command an army; the law which he forced through the Senate, giving him "extraordinary command" in Cisalpine and later in Transalpine Gaul; his own subsequent career, in which he moved through civil war to the status of an uncrowned king; and the writing of the *Commentaries*, in which he took care that full credit should be given him for his military exploits.

II

Apart from the desire for tribute, loot, and land, one of the causes of Roman warfare was the need and greed for slaves; we find expeditions that were in effect nothing but great slave raids. Consider, for example, the case of Marcus Popilius Laenas, who was consul in 173 B.C. In his official role, he took it upon himself to start hostilities against a friendly tribe in Liguria; at the cost of three thousand Roman lives, he captured ten thousand prisoners to be sold into slavery, and went so far as to defy the order of the Senate to free the captives; after which, not content with the profits he had taken and the misery he had caused, he repeated the aggression in a more limited way, as if deliberately trying to show how war may be caused by the cupidity of a single powerful individual.

After the day of Laenas, one source of Roman warfare continued to be the need for slaves which the ancient social order implied, as well as the abnormal demand for slaves which the peculiar institutions of Rome produced. Though slave-taking may have been only a subsidiary motive, it was an important one: slaves were taken in huge numbers, even the relatively mild Caesar having sold as many as sixty-three thousand on one occasion in Gaul; and captives were not only disposed of for profit, but were taken to

Rome or the provinces for use in the fields, the mines, and the home, or to be trained in special gladiatorial schools before amusing the populace by the blood-spilling of the arena.

Here, if ever, we see how one artificial institution leans upon and supports another: the gladiatorial contest a stimulus to the slave trade, and through the slave trade an incentive to warfare; while warfare is itself the spiritual father of the spectacles of the arena, which in turn beget a state of mind favorable to further warfare, an insensitiveness to carnage and cruelty, and a consequent callousness to the brutalities of battle. Yet all this does not even take account of the warfare arising directly from the revolts of the gladiators, as in the case of Spartacus, who for a while roamed the Italian countryside with an army of forty thousand men.

In not a few other instances, we find the wars of the later Republic precipitated by the will, the desires, or the obstinacy of individuals. For example, in the year 171, when the Third Macedonian War was being waged against King Perseus, one of the consuls became jealous of the military command exercised by his fellow office-holder; and without authorization from the Senate or a sufficiency of supplies, he attempted to beat his rival to the battlefield—with the result that he came into conflict with the Illyrians, whose territory he was attempting illegally to cross, and so involved Rome in the Third Illyrian War.

A more flagrant example, and one with greater historical repercussions, is that of the Third Punic War. The propaganda of Cato the Censor—"*Carthago delenda est!*" ("Carthage must be destroyed!")—has often been reported; he is said to have closed every speech with this inflammatory phrase. At this late date, of course, we cannot say just how far this warmongering went toward producing the dire sequel; but it could hardly have served otherwise than to stir up anti-Carthaginian sentiment, even if it did not initially represent a large segment of popular opinion. Certainly, the subsequent actions of the leaders indicate that they had Cato's views in mind. Carthage, which had been religiously respecting her treaty with Rome, had been a prey to the depredations of King Masinissa of Numidia; but whenever she appealed to Rome, Rome decided in favor of the despoiler. At last Carthage, goaded to the breaking point, struck back at the Numidian, and was crushingly defeated—after which Rome, taking advantage of a fifty-two-year-old treaty, declared war on Carthage. She then induced seven Punic cities to join her, and even persuaded the Carthaginians to lay down their arms—after which, by one of history's supreme treacheries, she announced that Carthage was to be destroyed, took the city by storm, and sold into slavery all of the inhabitants whom she had not massacred.

There can be no doubt that the Roman action was uncalled for and indefensible on any basis of justice or reason. Carthage was not a menace to Rome; her recent activities had not been hostile; she even proved docile to the extent of yielding up her arms. Yet the memory remained of a century-long commercial and military antagonism, the dread and horror inspired by Hannibal, and the sting of the humiliating defeats he had inflicted on the Roman arms; while the reiterated demand of the aged Cato, "Carthage must be destroyed! Carthage must be destroyed!" helped to keep alive the old hatred and the terror of Carthage's eventual resurrection.

III

It would not be too much to assert that, in addition to the other causes, there was an "ideological" motive behind the empire-making wars. Ever since the time of Alexander, as we have seen, men had held the hope of peace beneath the unity of one mighty world-control. Not only from Alexander, however, but from the Oriental monarchies which in a measure he imitated, observers took the idea of a universal government—the rule of one beneficent universal king. The unity of mankind had been proclaimed in the third century b.c. by Eratosthenes of Alexandria, who thought that men should be divided not into Greeks and barbarians but into good and bad; and this philosophy had been furthered by that of the Stoics, who saw an intelligent unity beneath the universe and consequently believed in the oneness of man as well as of nature. It is known that the Stoic philosophy was widely accepted among the educated classes at Rome; and this philosophy not unnaturally colored their political conceptions. One commentator has thus summarized the matter:

The thought on which the best of the Romans fed was a thought of the World-State, the universal law of nature, the brotherhood and the equality of man; and thought of this nature inevitably penetrated and determined the general conception which they entertained of their empire.[3]

It is obvious that thought of "the brotherhood and the equality of man" was far from the minds of most of the Roman empire-makers; nevertheless, this idea undoubtedly rendered many of the ruling class more tolerant than they would otherwise have been of the imperialistic expansion. And this was subsequently a factor behind the maintenance of the *Pax Romana*.

IV

Not all the Roman conflicts, of course, were external; during the last century of the Republic, the civil wars were notorious. Some of these disturbances, like the attack of the Cretan mercenaries that cost the life of Gaius Gracchus and several thousand of his followers, originated in the struggle for an economic "Fair Deal" and the passions aroused by that struggle. But most of the civil wars represented no more than the clash of ambitions, the greed for possessions, and the scramble for power by political rivals. What they demonstrate most clearly is that the old Roman traditions of patriotism had broken down, that the fighters had thought neither of their country nor of the gods, that they were the spawn of a seething, aggressive society, in which the only laws were shove-and-thrust and snatch-and-grab. In the eyes of the common soldiers, the greater cause—the good of the people or of the nation —did not matter at all; these men were mostly adventurers who, somewhat like the *condottieri* of medieval Italy, were loyal to a particular leader rather than to the country (all the more so when, as in the case of Caesar's followers, they were provided with free land or other gratuities proceeding from the spoils of the conquered). None the less, their loyalty to their leaders appears sometimes to have been of a flexible nature, as may be judged from the fact that Caesar, after his defeat of Pompey at Pharsalus, enlisted about half of the twenty-four thousand prisoners in his own army.

It is hard for us today to note much moral difference between contenders such as Caesar and Pompey: each was determined to get his own way by any available methods; and Caesar's celebrated crossing of the Rubicon, in defiance of the Republic, is but indicative of the spirit in which self-seeking men in all ages have put themselves and their ambitions above the world. We can agree with a modern observation that "The civil war between Caesar and Pompey was at first little more than a continuation of the gang warfare with which Clodius and Milo had distracted Rome for so long." [4] The sword, according to this analysis, was but a weapon of last resort, drawn after the commoner devices—such as intrigue, vituperation, and rioting—had been exhausted.

And why was the sword drawn even as a last resort? Because there was a fighting tradition in Rome; because warfare, for centuries, had been the means for the settlement of disputes and the satisfaction of desires; because the leaders had themselves been trained in combat, and because there was available a great mass of adventurous, greedy, and foot-loose men, who had been physically drilled and psychologically molded to fighting methods, and whose only ideals were those of the battlefield.

V

As all the foregoing will have suggested, the Roman army had been constantly declining during the last centuries of the Republic. From a non-professional corps of property-holding citizens, drilled in their duty to home and country and holding it a privilege to defend their land, they had become a medley of armed adventurers, for whom war was a trade. This change, which had been evident from the time of Marius, grew increasingly conspicuous; and the essence of it was a shift in the focus of attention from the nation to the military leader, and from warfare as an avocation to warfare as a gainful vocation.

Under Augustus a standing army was maintained along the frontiers of the far-flung provinces; yet the legions, charged with the vital task of maintaining the *Pax Romana*, numbered no more than twenty-five at the time of the death of Augustus, as against about sixty at the close of the civil wars. Despite the reduced number of the legions, however, great inducements were held out to the recruit, who usually came from some Romanized part of the West. The valuable privilege of Roman citizenship was granted him when he took the oath of allegiance to the emperor; he received the considerable pay of 225 denarii a year, in addition to occasional gifts from the emperor; and he had the chance of honors and promotion while in the service, and the prospect of land or a donation of money when he left the ranks. In the auxiliaries, though the pay was much less, there was the same attempt to make war attractive for reasons outside of itself; these troops, who came from the less Romanized regions, were promised Roman citizenship upon their discharge after twenty-five years of service.

But regardless of the sweet bait that was offered, demands for higher pay and complaints as to the over-long period of service were common in the reign of Tiberius; and for a while the Emperor silenced the grumblings by reducing the ordinary service to sixteen years. From this time on, increasing signs of disintegration were evident; the army became less and less representative of the Latins, and more and more composed of barbarians. And this was not only because the barbarians found it desirable to serve; it was because the people of Italy found it desirable not to serve. As time went on, the army became to a large extent hereditary; the legionaries, settled for life in the same provinces, would marry women from their adopted districts and bring up their sons to follow in their footsteps, so making army life almost a matter of caste. Thus a youth might be reared for the army in much the way that some moderns are raised to be clothiers, shoe manufacturers, or plumbing contractors, not because they have any particular taste for the business but because their fathers had followed this line. And thus, again, as so often, the more docile and malleable of men would take up the sword; the more pugnacious, the more individualistic would obey their own will.

Meanwhile, in various ways, the armed forces had got out of hand. The Praetorian Guard, originally the emperor's bodyguard, had become the maker and unmaker of emperors; using strong-arm methods, they had turned toward politics and plunder, and had become a sinister political force. Knowing the ways of modern racketeers, one need not be surprised that they descended to the point of auctioning off the emperorship; yet one does notice with a shock how, having set their playthings up in power, they would swing the assassin's blade to knock them down again, sometimes after a few weeks or months. The confusion was made all the more confusing by the fact that large sections of the army, in various parts of the empire, would back their own contenders for the purple, as when Posthumus in the year 260 was declared Emperor by his troops in Gaul, and being too powerful to be deposed by Rome, ruled in effect as an independent sovereign until his death eight years later. Even leaving out of account such a usurper, and similar claimants throughout the provinces, historians list twenty "barrack-room emperors" who reigned between 235 and 285, when to be an emperor was apparently more hazardous than to fight wild beasts.

Meanwhile, as the value and warlike spirit of the army diminished, the artificial inducements to fighting were increased. Even in the day of Domitian (late first century), the pay of the infantry had been so raised that the ordinary soldier is said to have received four gold pieces a month (far from an inconsiderable sum, considering the contemporary purchasing power of gold); while the centurions and mounted men were granted still more. Even so, the rank and file would not perform the old-time duties; the onerous drills and maneuvers of former days were dropped; and the men mutinied at the idea of making themselves useful, like their predecessors, in building public works and roads.

But even with their higher pay and less burdensome existence, the legionaries did not always find army life attractive. We read of occasional desertions, as when a private named Maternus, in the year 185, not only fled his post of duty, but gathered a band of brigands about him, and set slaves and prisoners free, inviting them to join him in plundering Spain and Gaul. Under Septimius Severus, at the end of the second century, discipline was so relaxed that soldiers, bespangled with gold rings, might lounge about the barracks in the company of their wives—in return for which they received more pay than ever, and expected gifts at every time of public crisis or celebration.

This degeneration, in which the army served the convenience and desires of its members rather than the good of the State, was not helped by certain arbitrary regulations, such as the decree passed by Gallienus in the middle of the third century, excluding Roman senators from the army, and eventually the senatorial and other classes in the provinces. Thus the army life, from having been the proudest right of the well-to-do Roman citizen, in the course of time became forbidden by law to the well-to-do Roman. Rarely has history witnessed a more complete reversal in the war-making state of mind. The change would not be so significant if it had been forced upon an unwilling aristocracy and bourgeoisie; but the fact is that it accorded with the mood of the times. Military service, far from being a prerequisite to public repute and political office as in the time of Caesar, came eventually to be regarded as disgraceful—a judgment confirmed not only by the inclinations of the people but by the dogmas of the Church. Whenever possible, the Italian populace avoided service; cases of self-mutilation were not unknown; and the difficulties of recruiting an army became so great that any barbarians, even those who had fought against the empire not long before, were admitted by commanders desperate to build up their forces—admitted at first into the auxiliaries, but later into the legions themselves. Such soldiers had no loyalty to Rome; like the havoc-wreaking hordes of the civil wars, they paid allegiance to their leaders and not to the State; their chief incentives were pay and loot; and they would turn the sword against the empire as readily as they would defend it.

By the middle of the fourth century, the barbarization of the army had gone so far that the words "soldier" and "barbarian" had become synonymous. The army of Julian, who was declared Caesar in 354, was composed of Germans who attacked with wild bellowings in "boar's head" formation, and lifted their general on their shields barbarian-fashion; while even the Emperor dressed in the skins of wild beasts.

When we turn ahead to the beginning of the fifth century, we find the degeneration verging toward a collapse. Compulsory service had become the rule: that is to say, the owners of the great estates had to supply the army with manpower in proportion to the size of their holdings. So urgent was the demand that even the Emperor's estates were not excluded; however, the senators, according to an enactment of the year 397, escaped by a provision permitting a money payment in place of each recruit. But despite the strong arm of compulsion, putting a man into the service was not the equivalent of keeping him there. Like criminals, or like cattle on a ranch, the men were branded upon enlistment; but no deterrent could prevent them from escaping in large numbers. The frequency of desertion may be judged from the fact that Emperor Honorius, in a sixteen-year period, found it necessary to issue nine decrees on deserters and their concealment. But despite severe penalties, his edicts evidently had not the desired results; several decades later, in the year 440, Theodosius and Valentinian III felt obliged to impose the death penalty for the crime of harboring deserters.

As far back as the end of the preceding century, the guards along the frontier castles and forts, the *burgarii*—who were bound

to their positions, a little like serfs tied to the ancestral soil—had
been gradually disappearing. And this, among other things, seems
to have been behind the extraordinary appeal of Honorius and
Theodosius in the year 409. Sweeping away the millennium-old
tradition that excluded slaves from the army—a tradition broken
only in the case of the dire emergency created by Hannibal many
centuries before—these emperors offered a bounty and freedom to
slaves who took up arms. When one remembers the contempt with
which slaves were held in the ancient world; when one recalls that
freemen were in the habit of looking down upon them as pariahs,
as untouchables, or as beasts of burden; and when one takes account
also of the fear of the slaves, the dread that they would become too
powerful and turn upon their masters, one must recognize the enactment of 409 as nothing short of a measure of desperation.

Like most measures of desperation, it did not achieve the hoped-
for effect. The empire by this time was beyond saving; and it was
beyond saving not because the barbarians were strong but because
the defenders were weak—actually, the invaders were not relatively
numerous, nor were they at all united, nor did they follow a plan
of attack that the legions of a few centuries before would have
found it hard to combat. But the spirit of the empire was that of a
jaded, worn-out man. Why did the citizens not fight? Because they
had not the will to fight; because they had come to loathe the
pursuit of arms; because they had ceased to be vitally interested
in the empire. And so, in the empire's last centuries, we see a
frantic effort to generate a combative will and outlook; we see a
despairing recourse to the services of barbarians and even of
slaves; we see the whip and the branding-iron employed, along
with the most savage threats—even the threat of burning the recalcitrants alive. But all to no avail. Forced military labor is like all
other forms of forced labor; if a strong enough opposition exists in
the minds of the coerced, the results will not be proportionate to
the effort expended. And the road will end in failure. Rome, during the last centuries of the Western empire, was morally and
psychologically and in other ways the antithesis of Rome during
her youth; there was a numbness in her spirit, as contrasted with
the vigorous if often ruthless spirit of earlier years. And this numbness expressed itself in a paralysis of the army, a defensive breakdown that actually reflected a breakdown in those intangibles of
thought and mood that are at the roots of a nation's robustness or
decay.

III

From Horse Raider to Gunpowder

Chapter 13

The Barbarians and the Dark Ages

In the barbarian swarms that swept down in successive streams upon the settled civilizations from the hills, plains, and forests of Europe and Asia, we can observe one of the outstanding phenomena of ancient and medieval history. Looking back with the simplifying tendency of the remote beholder, we are apt to regard these movements in the main as warlike invasions, whereas actually the greater number of them were more nearly in the nature of migrations, wherein whole communities transported themselves along with their women and children, their goods and flocks.

The truth is that a false idea regarding the barbarian invaders has long been current; we have overemphasized their martial inclinations, and magnified mere migrants into destroying fiends. There were indeed some who, like Attila, were blood-spilling terrors; there were pirates and pillagers like the Vandals and the Vikings; but there were others who made war on no one and sought to maintain peace by law rather than by force. Actually, the motives of the barbarian tribes were as many as the tribes themselves; some came as land-hungry settlers, some as looters, some as random nomads, some as armed adventurers, or bands of mercenary soldiers seeking hire, some came to help the Romans and some to oppose them, some arrived as fighters trained in an aggressive tradition and resolved to put their swords to use.

The motives behind the warfare of these barbarians were in general the same as among the uncivilized fighters we have already observed. We find them given to the blood feud, to conflicts for religious and ceremonial ends, and, most of all, to the raid for booty; and we note among many of them a well-developed tradition of valor and glory. This was particularly true, to cite a celebrated example, among the Vikings, who earned a well-deserved reputation as plunderers and killers—looters of towns and castles, and destroyers of churches, monasteries, and nunneries, against which they seemed to have almost a religious hatred.

Viewed externally, the Vikings were in a class with any cut-throat gang that cries to the unoffending stranger in pulp-story style, "Your money or your life!" Yet from their own point of view, they often had the hero's motivation. And their activities, which to the outside gaze looked like brigandage seasoned with murder, might seem to them gallant and glorious, and worthy of a golden reward here and still more splendid returns hereafter. While they were fighting, those divine maidens the Valkyries might be riding unseen through the air, commissioned by the god Odin to pick the bravest of the brave; and those slain in combat might be expected to be lifted to Valhalla, where they would pass their time in carousing and fighting, in drinking mead that flowed inexhaustibly from the udders of the goat Heidbrun and the stag Eikthyrmir, and in feasting on the flesh of the ever-renewed boar. When death was so clearly a doorway to perpetual bliss, surely none but the fool would refuse to be brave!

Incidentally, if the blood of one's enemies was spilled and no little avoidable destruction and suffering was caused, what did that really matter? After all, foreigners were not as one's own kin; indeed, they were hardly human at all; they counted scarcely more than did the beasts of the fields.

In accordance with such beliefs, it would not be wrong to make sacrifices to the gods—sacrifices not only of hawks, dogs, horses, and oxen but of prisoners taken in battle. And as a supreme act of devotion, one might dedicate to the gods the entire enemy army, along with all its possessions—which is to say that, in the name of religion and righteousness, one might destroy all the enemy and all their belongings in a wholesale and indiscriminate sacrifice.

It may be questioned whether such a holocaust would ever have been tolerated except for the low value that the Norse placed upon life. Like many warring peoples, they had been trained to a contempt of death; time and again this fact is brought out in their literature: in *The Poetic Edda* and the subsequent prose sagas based on the old lays. To quote one example: in *The Saga of Ragnar Lodbruk*, one Eric "fought most bravely, caring not whether he could get away or not. At the last he was overpowered by numbers and captured. Eyestein bade him cease fighting and he offered him peace, 'and in addition,' said he, 'I will marry my daughter to thee.' Then Eric spoke a stave:

> " 'Eyestein has slain my brother; I will
> Neither peace therefor nor a maiden buy;
> My mother will weep not; last of my men,
> Upon these spear-points let me die.' " [1]

And so "he gave up his life most valiantly."

A similar case occurs in another saga, when the hero Hogni is captured by King Atli, and expresses indifference to the prospect of death. His attitude is contrasted with that of the swineherd Hjalli, whom one of the King's councilors proposes to execute in Hogni's place. The poor thrall, not being inspired with any romantic notions of the virtue of feeling cold steel through his entrails, runs about in a panic, screaming his protest; and thereupon Hogni, in true heroic fashion, asks that the swineherd be spared for his hog-keeping; he himself would rather die than hear the other's screams. "Hogni," in the words of a modern commentator, "scorns Hjalli, not so much for his fear of death, as for his attachment to a worthless life. It would be difficult to find another episode in literature which so forcefully expresses the proud superiority of a warlike aristocracy, not only toward the class of thralls, but also toward life as a whole." [2]

The same contempt of life and of death finds expression in many a bloody scene in the sagas—scenes reminiscent of the gorier parts of the *Iliad*. One sees the arrows and the spears flying, the "axes blood-reddened and shields cloven and byrnies slit," the "shattered shields and riven skulls and many a man fallen to death." And one knows that such details are reported in the people's heroic literature because they are reveled in, sought, or admired in actual life.

In many places the sagas are naïvely, disarmingly frank as to the heroes' methods and motives; there is an unconscious revelation in the simple naturalness, the casualness with which they tell of crime and terror. Take this, from *The Saga of Ragnar Lodbruk*:

And when they were thus evenly matched, the men of the castle were slain, though some of them escaped by flight, and the end of it was that they slew every mother's son that was in the burg and took away all the treasure, and they burnt the castle before they departed.[3]

Or observe the following, from the same saga:

Now it came to pass one day that Ivar spoke with his brothers, and asked them how long they thought to continue sitting at home instead of gaining glory for themselves. . . . "It is my wish," said Ivar, "that we ask to have a ship and men, well ordered, and after that I desire that we earn wealth and fame for ourselves." [4]

And how was the wealth and fame to be earned? By taking other men's property. But, obviously, robbery was not the only object. After they had gained much treasure, "Ivar said that they wished that they would betake themselves where there was a mighty force to be met, and thus make trial of their hardihood." And hearing of a stronghold named Whitby, which was also a temple and was so redoubtable that all who had tried to take it had been destroyed, he decided "to try by venture which might be the more potent, their valor or the idolatry of the folk of that country."

Again we have the idea of warfare as a game—a deadly, desperate game no doubt, and one in which religious beliefs and emotions might be interjected, but nevertheless just as much a trial of skill and superiority as any game of tennis, football, or chess.

II

An even grimmer raiding tradition—and one still more devastating in its total effects—is to be observed among the tribesmen who emerged in several terrifying waves from the great tableland of central Asia. They are known to history by a number of names—the Hiung-nu, the Huns, the Avars, the Turks, the Mongols, etc.—and they poured like an affliction of nature across many centuries and lands. But basically they were all similar: they were nomads who moved from place to place with their families and herds; their life was a pastoral, a hunting, and a fighting one; they had no learning, no arts, and no crafts except of the most rudimentary; and such skills as they possessed were mostly in riding their wild mounts across the steppes and deserts, and in aiming their arrows against man or beast as they wheeled on horseback. When they rushed down upon settled communities, or when their skirmishing swarms whirled against the relatively static armies of the older type, they were apt to prove irresistible; their cruelty was a byword; and from the day when Attila was known as "the scourge of God" to the time when Tamerlane piled his pyramids of skulls, the number of farms and towns which they burned and of innocent lives which they snuffed out defies the power of the annalist to compute.

The question naturally arises whether these warriors, who were terrible and bloodthirsty even beyond most fighters in a terrible and bloodthirsty age, were of a racial stock that made them especially callous and cruel. But it is doubtful if any ethnologist would answer in the affirmative. Not race but training and manner of life provides the solution; any other group of men, reared under the same circumstances, might have reacted as did the Mongols. From his earliest days, the young nomad had faced a rigorous existence; a tent had been his home, the back of a horse his school; as far back as he could remember, he had been taught to shoot in order to kill, at first slaying mice and small birds with minute bows, and later hunting hares and foxes; he had witnessed the slaughter of sheep and of horses for food, and perhaps as soon as he could wield a full-sized bow, he had set off after human quarries. Here, surely, was no life to develop sensitiveness or tenderness!

There is no question but that cruelty or tolerance of cruelty in one direction makes the path easier to cruelty or tolerance of cruelty in other directions. And from the complaisant taking of animal life, not only the lives of beasts slain in the hunt but of the very creatures with which one has lived, the road is not long to the complaisant taking of human life as well. The Huns and other nomads, we may conclude, were scourges and terrors because everything in their life had taught them to be scourges and terrors.

This is not to say that their motives were entirely simple and unmixed; a number of unrelated forces were behind their warfare. In the case of the Seljuk Turks, we find the fanaticism of men newly converted to Islam, and eager to win credit in heaven by liquidating the unbeliever. In the case of most of the raiders and invaders we see a greed for wealth and booty, such as induced the Huns to serve as mercenaries in the Roman army under latter-day leaders such as Stilicho and Aetius. And in the case of the followers of Genghis Khan, we observe the pressure of a powerful military organization, and a spirit of conquest embodied in the principle that peace must never be made until the enemy was on his knees. Each soldier was subjected by his particular commander to an iron discipline; instant execution was the universal punishment for any offense or fancied offense. If, for example, two or three men out of a division of ten horsemen were seen to turn and flee on the day of battle, the other seven or eight would be tried and put to death; while the same punishment awaited the first to fly when no general retreat was ordered, the last to plunge into the attack when a general assault was made, and any of those so inept as to be unable to rescue captured comrades.

Beyond this, we have records of how the commanders deliberately stirred the fighting mood of their troops. There is extant a report of an address of Attila to his followers before the Battle of Chalons—an address in which he cunningly plays upon the emotions of these raw barbarians. He refers to the "sweetness" of revenge; he gives expression to his savagery when he speaks of cutting the sinews and tearing away the bones of the fallen foe; he counsels the wounded to seek the death of at least one enemy, and those who are unhurt to "revel in slaughter"; he works upon the men's fatalism by assuring them that those doomed to die would perish in any case in the midst of "slothful peace"; and he further exploits the same fatalism to suggest that fate, which had permitted the Huns to stamp their heels in conquest over so many lands, is surely preparing for them the "delights" of this battle too.

And thus one of the most remorseless fighters of ancient times strives to bolster the fighting spirit.

III

By contrast, let us turn back to various Teutonic tribes. Tacitus, in his *Germania,* has described many of these in revealing detail, with considerable attention to their warfare; he shows that, though there were tribal differences, these peoples were on the whole devoted to the heroic ideal, and were stimulated in their conflicts not only by the hope of booty but by the cult of glory and honor. The youth's first public distinction was to be equipped with shield and spear in the presence of a tribal assembly; thenceforth he belonged no longer to the household but to the State. And being ready for manhood and battle, he had to heed certain established rules. To abandon his shield was to be disgraced; and to be disgraced was to be debarred from the religious rites and the tribal council, and, in many cases, to end his miseries with a noose.

Nor was the loss of one's shield the only sure way to dishonor. "When the battlefield is reached," writes Tacitus, "it is a reproach for a chief to be surpassed in prowess; a reproach for his retinue not to equal the prowess of its chief: but to have left the field and survived one's chief, this means lifelong infamy and shame: to protect and defend him, to devote one's own feats to his glorification, this is the gist of their allegiance: the chief fights for victory, but the retainers for their chief." [5]

Public reprobation, however, was not the only punishment for those who failed at fighting; the tribal assembly might decree capital punishment. "Traitors and deserters are hung from trees; cowards and poor fighters and notorious evil-livers are plunged in the mud of marshes with a hurdle on their heads." But while strong deterrents to unheroic conduct were found in the savage laws and traditions, there were also positive inducements to bravery:

The strongest incentive to courage lies in this, that neither chance nor casual grouping makes the squadron nor the wedge, but family and kinship: close at hand, too, are the dearest, whence is heard the wailing voice of the woman and the child's cry: here are the witnesses who are in each man's eyes the most precious; here the praise he covets most: they take their wounds to mother and wife, who do not shrink from counting the hurts and demanding a sight of them: they minister to the combatants food and exhortation.

Tradition relates that some lost or losing battles have been restored by the women, by the incessance of their prayers and by the baring of their breasts. . . .

Brave fighters though these Germans apparently were, they could be daunted by a sign or an omen. Like many peoples, they consulted the flight and cries of birds; while a particularly esteemed method was to judge from the neighing and snorting of certain white horses, which they regarded as the confidants of the gods. Or else they would contrive to capture a member of the enemy tribe, and engage him in single combat with one of their own champions; the issue of the duel, they thought, would test the outcome of the prospective battle.

But not all the German tribes, according to Tacitus, were warlike. Take, for example, the Chatti, who "prefer to protect their vast domain by justice alone":

They are neither grasping nor lawless; in peaceful seclusion they provoke no wars and despatch no raiders on marauding forays; the special proof of their sterling worth is, indeed, just this, that they do not depend for their superior position upon injustice; yet they are ready with arms, and, if circumstances should require, with armies, men and horses in abundance; so, even though they keep the peace, their reputation does not suffer.

Even less warlike, in some ways, were the Suiones, who lived in present-day Sweden. Though they did possess men, weapons, and fleets, they permitted "no general carrying of arms," but locked up their fighting implements "in charge of a warder, and that warder a slave." "The ocean," explains Tacitus, "forbids sudden inroads from enemies; and, besides, bands of armed men, with nothing to do, easily become riotous: it is not to the king's interest to put a noble or a freeman or even a freedman in charge of the arms."

Evidently these northern barbarians recognized a fact too frequently overlooked: that it is dangerous to give men arms and nothing to fill their time; that wars, among other causes, may arise from sheer boredom and the urge to activity of unemployed warriors.

IV

Among the various barbarian groups, few have played a more conspicuous part in history than the Franks. Here, as in the case of the Huns and the Vikings, we encounter marauders, but marauders with some principles and methods of their own. A memorable picture of them is provided by their enemy, the Byzantine Emperor Leo VI ("Leo the Wise"):

The Franks and Lombards are bold and daring to excess . . . they regard the smallest movement to the rear as a disgrace, and they will fight whenever you offer them battle. When their knights are hard put to it in a cavalry fight, they will turn their horses loose, dismount, and stand back to back against very superior numbers rather than flee.[6]

But their valor was not without its limitations:

Perhaps the best tactics of all are to protract the campaign, and lead them into hills and desolate tracts, for they take no care about their commissariat, and when their stores run low their vigor melts away. They are impatient of hunger and thirst, and after a few days of privation desert their standards and steal away home as best they can.[7]

Among the Franks we observe an attempt, conscious or unconscious, to reconcile two irreconcilables: personal freedom and military service; the individual did not become, as in more mechanized armies, merely a spoke or a cog in a gigantic fighting engine; each man retained some personal rights, and his leaders had poor control of his actions. But the system had disadvantages, one of which was in the provisioning; every soldier was tempted, even obliged to turn looter. For his superiors neglected to provide him with certain details, including pay and food. And the result was that he foraged for his own provisions, which he would exact from an unfriendly country or a friendly. Even so, his ravagings did not always keep pace with his hunger; after stripping the territory bare, he sometimes literally had to strip himself bare; one army in Lombardy had to sell their weapons and their very clothes for bread. And other armies, again and again, simply faded out of existence, since the men preferred desertion to privation.

But let the king or the duke assert his authority, and mutiny, according to Gregory of Tours, would lift its head. More than that, let the men see a prospect of booty, and they might force their captains into battle, whether the latter desired it or not. A case in point occurred in 555, when the Saxons offered to make peace with Chlothar I and the latter wished to accept the favorable proposals. Not so the army, however! Honeyed promises of loot had been made them, and they felt certain of winning the battle and filling their pockets. Hence they forced their king to dismiss the Saxon envoys and take up arms—with the result that they were thoroughly beaten.

Fifty-seven years later, the opposite form of insubordination occurred when the troops of Theuderich II refused to advance at his command, slew his chief minister in the royal tent, and compelled their sovereign to make peace. And why should they not have compelled him? The wars of the Merovingian kings were mostly waged over matters of personal ambition, rivalry, and greed —matters having no relationship whatever to the needs or desires of the subjects. Their regimes were shot through with conspiracy and corruption, according to a system whereby "benefices" were conferred on favored subjects, who were expected to render reciprocal benefits; the rank and file had to give services and be taxed, but nothing to their advantage was done in turn, nothing was paid out in the public interest, and indeed, as has been remarked, "the very notion of public interest disappeared." [8] The word "docility" seems to be well applied to the run-of-the-mill Frankish soldier:

... so worthless were the Meringovs, and so futile their pretexts for war with each other, that one can only wonder at the docility of the subjects who let themselves be butchered in such a cause.[9]

The private citizen, obliged to give himself for useless wars under the system of *heerban* or compulsory military service, might lose his freedom in more senses than one. He might prefer serfdom to soldiering; he might voluntarily relinquish his civil liberties to one of the great landed proprietors, whose soil he would till sooner than bear the lance and shield of the king. Not only singly but in groups, men would surrender themselves; there is recorded, for example, the case of a band of fourteen who early in the ninth century (after Merovingian times, but still under Frankish rule) forfeited their lands to the abbey of St. Germain at Nauphelette and gave themselves up as serfs, professing to be no longer able to fulfill the king's military demands. Thus the process of feudalization was accelerated by an anti-militaristic sentiment.

V

The most celebrated of the Franks, of course, was Charlemagne. He was much more than an ordinary leader; he was a great conqueror and empire-builder, though one whose dominions, like those of Alexander, did not long survive his death. A vivid picture of him is provided by a monk of Saint Gaul, who wrote a life of Charlemagne at the end of the ninth century, and claimed that he reported what had been told to him as a child by Adalbart, one of Charlemagne's followers:

Then could be seen the iron Charles, helmeted with an iron helmet, his hands clad in iron gauntlets, his iron breast and broad shoulders protected with an iron breast-plate; an iron spear was raised on high in his left hand; his right always rested on his unconquered iron falchion. The thighs, which with most men are uncovered, that they may the more easily ride on horseback, were in his case clad with plates of iron. . . . His shield was all of iron: his charger was iron-colored and iron-hearted. All who went before him, all who marched by his side, all who followed him and the whole equipment of the army imitated him as closely as possible. The fields and open places were filled with iron; the rays of the sun were thrown back by the gleam of iron. "Oh the iron! Woe for the iron!" was the confused cry that rose from the citizens. The strong walls shook at the sight of the iron; the resolution of young and old fell before the iron.[10]

Conceivably this has been a little colored by time and distance. But in any case this does indicate the effect that Charlemagne had upon his contemporaries or near-contemporaries—the psychological impact, the awe and fear and the sense of helplessness produced by the thought of the iron figure bristling at the head of an iron army.

In the campaigns of Charlemagne we can see not only political but religious motives. His fervor for the cause of Christendom, apparently, was second only to his zeal for extending his sovereignty; wherever he lifted his sword, he founded monasteries; and wherever he held control he placed allegiance to the Church side by side with loyalty to the State. We can observe this in his eagerness to baptize subjugated Saxons (the baptism being compulsory); some time between 775 and 790, he promulgated a law prescribing the death penalty not only for those who proved unfaithful to his royal self, but for those who refused to be baptized. Some time later (after he had been coronated Emperor by Pope Leo in the year 800), he showed a predilection for loyalty oaths by requiring every male subject above the age of twelve to swear allegiance once more, vowing devotion to the sovereign and fidelity to the State. And by way of further evidence of his ecclesiastical leanings, he decreed the death penalty for acts of burglary committed in a church, and imposed heavy fines for participation in pagan feasts, for pagan vows made at springs or groves, and for neglecting to bring a child to baptism before its first birthday.

In all this he was, obviously, a true son of the Middle Ages. And in him we can see clearly accented the medieval tendency to swing the sword for the "holy" purpose of extending and perpetuating the sway of Christendom.

Despite his religious principles and a reputation for mildness as compared with other autocrats of the day, Charlemagne could upon occasion show a ferocity worthy of a Genghis Khan. One well-known instance has been recorded in which, angered at a revolt, he caused forty-five hundred Saxon prisoners to be beheaded—a deed which, though latter-day apologists have attempted to explain it away, cannot possibly be explained except by the ancient doctrine so dear to the hearts of conquerors, that the end justifies the means. One cannot help wondering if, in this episode, the ruthless creed induced by war-making did not take precedence over the King's vaunted Christianity.

But regardless of any incidental little blots, Charlemagne has lived as something more than a historical figure; he has survived as a legend. Like Alexander before him, and like King Solomon and a few other romantic personages, he has shone for the future not only through his actual deeds, but through the glorious feats woven for him by the spinners of tales and the singers of songs. In the chants of the minstrels, and most prominently in the *Song of Roland*, he and his comrades Olivier and Archbishop Turpin stand forth as men of matchless bravery, boundless mutual devotion, and unswerving religious faith—incomparable paladins, who fight indeed a losing battle against the infidel, but fight it with such wonderful verve and spirit as to triumph even in death. Here, in the glorified creation of the myth-makers—a creation which the uncritical audience of a credulous age would not question too closely—we find once more a manifestation of the heroic ideal, an incitement to the military mood and the military ambition, no less than a stimulus to that religious bias which, after several centuries, was to bear a tragic bloom in the Crusades.

Chapter 14

Feudal China and Japan

It may be significant that two of the earliest known civilizations were two of the most unwarlike. We have already glanced at Egypt, but the case of China is not less instructive. Although recent events may have seemed to fly in the face of the traditions of millennia, throughout the greater part of China's history the man of peace has on the whole been much more esteemed than the war-captain. In few other countries if any has so sharp a line been drawn between soldier and civilian, and in particular between soldier and scholar. War has in the main been held to be the occupation of the rude illiterate; the statesman and the ruler have sought to lead through other means. And in this discountenancing of the warrior and elevation of the learned man we have a major explanation of the relative peacefulness of the Chinese throughout many centuries.

It would not be correct to say, however, that China has been wholly peaceful. Long before our own turbulent era, she has had numerous wars; and some of these are known to have occurred as far back as the feudal period—which was not contemporaneous with feudalism in Europe, but closed about a thousand years before the latter began.

The warfare of that remote epoch, centuries before the birth of Christ, appears not to have been extremely bitter or remorseless; it had, in fact, striking resemblances to our own medieval warfare in its more chivalric phases. Fighting was treated frankly as a game, in which courtesy was as important as courage, and magnanimity more conspicuous than ruthlessness. Surpassing even the American Indian who risks his life in a foolhardy attempt to take the enemy's gun or the Philippine native who slays in order to wear red trousers, the Chinese have not only fought by rule but have restrained their fighting by rule, and have shown the enemy a consideration bearing no evident relationship to economic or biological ends.

In feudal days, the urbanity for which the Chinese are noted was not confined to the tea-room or the domestic shrine; politeness was also considered essential on the battlefield—politeness not only to one's comrades in arms, but to the enemy. This might serve a practical purpose, since a contingent in danger of capture might be allowed to escape if one of its members paid a proper debt of homage to the foe. But on the other hand, the noble warrior would make gifts to the enemy regardless of such a mundane consideration as his own safety, as in the tale of the archer of Ch'u, who having shot an arrow at a stag and killed it, ordered it to be presented to his enemy Chin on the ground that it was not the hunting season—as a result of which Chin, not to be outdone, halted the attack and graciously complimented his adversary.

Like the Indians of northwestern America, who gained prestige by their prodigality in disposing of wealth at a *potlatch*, the feudal Chinese earned glory by their freehandedness. They would exchange gifts of arms as they would exchange food and drink; and honor came to them from their generosity even more than from their military skill. This generosity extended even to the treatment of the foe. "When victory has proved the righteousness of the cause, a noble warrior cannot make up his mind to slay more than three men. Again, when he lets his arrows fly, he shoots with his eyes shut: they will hit the enemy if fate wills." [1]

We have here a marked contrast with the spirit of the *Iliad*, in which the swords literally swung in all directions and there was no limit on the bag of men. And the same contrast pervades the entire code, which, unlike that of the remorseless Achilles, makes a virtue of mercy. The whole battle appears to be a matter of point-scoring; and points can be gained by treating the enemy gently quite as much as by dealing him hammer-strokes. Correspondingly, it is necessary to prevent one's antagonists from scoring points. "To run the risk of being the laughing-stock of an enemy who will cry your name aloud, or even to be haughtily spared by him—these are the worst misfortunes that can happen. To avoid them calls for as much cunning as bravery." [2]

The battle is not even waged against the enemy exclusively; one also tries to surpass the members of the home team. "Much more than a clash of arms, it is a duel of moral values. One tries to qualify oneself by disqualifying others, not only the enemy but also, and in equal measure, those of one's own side. The battle is the great moment in which each warrior proves his nobility." [3]

One way of showing nobility is to follow the rules even at the risk of one's neck. There was, for example, the case of two war chariots which were approaching one another; one party had just discharged a volley of arrows, and was about to make a second attack. But the other side, dismayed at such unfair tactics, cried out that it was now his turn; whereupon the men in the first chariot drew back their arrows and offered themselves as targets.

A similar case was that of Duke Siang of Song, who, waiting for a pitched battle while the enemy was crossing a river, was urged to strike without delay, for his forces were few, and those of the enemy were many. The Duke, however, was unwilling to take any such advantage; he proclaimed that no worthy leader would profit from his enemy's misfortune, or fight before their ranks were formed. And so he proved himself a worthy leader— and having waited until his foes were drawn up in battle array, was defeated and wounded.

So mild were these feudal conflicts that the honor of a chief was enhanced less by his victories than by his moderation. And from this it follows that "Gentlemen prefer half victories, or tempered defeats." [4] The vanquished foe was not humiliated beyond appeal; he might plead with his conqueror for mercy, and if he were sufficiently humble and contrite his words would not fall on deaf ears; the penalty exacted of him would be relatively slight, and he would be restored to his former place in life.

It is true that the victor took the spoils of battle along with the glory of moderation. Yet he could claim little for himself in a practical way; he had to distribute the trophies among his retainers; and the division of the booty was decided by a tournament in which the rivalries were as heated as in the war with the enemy. However, the growth of his prestige, and in particular the honor of having proved himself to be merciful, was sufficient compensation for the captain.

Not until the feudal period ended did this "playboy" form of war give place to more savage conflict. Then powerful leaders, uniting innumerable petty states beneath the thrust of ambition and ideas of political expansion, created a unity that brought with it warfare on a larger scale, and submerged the old ideal of heroic and comparatively bloodless fighting. Yet the influence of the earlier principles did continue, despite subsequent wars of politics and intrigue, revolutions, conquests and attempted conquests, and struggles with the northern barbarians. And China, whose feudal age was so much less gory than that of most countries, was to continue until the dawn of our own times to be one of the most peaceful of nations.

Even before the feudal era had ended—in the year 545 B.C.—a notable attempt at war-prevention was made. The would-be pacifier was Hsiang, a minister of the state of Sung; being impressed with the folly even of the relatively unsanguinary conflicts of his day, he sought international agreement to outlaw war. Conferring with the delegates of several neighboring states, he pointed out the wastefulness of strife, and maintained that they must stamp it out, even though many believed this impossible. The representatives of Chin and Ch'u, along with those of Ch'i and Ch'in and nine other states, all accepted the proposal, after the more reluctant had been reminded that refusal would arouse discontent among their people. The agreement—one of the earliest known international covenants—was discussed for two months, and finally was signed by fourteen states. Unfortunately, however, it was not unlike certain subsequent international arrangements in giving undue privileges to the great states; and though it was renewed five years later, it soon broke down. Still, it did not fail altogether; even after twenty-five centuries, it stands forth as a proof of the will to peace in ancient China.

II

In the far more warlike empire of Japan, the fighting resembled that of feudal China, to the extent that utilitarian motives were subordinate to artificial standards of heroism.

Among many military peoples, honor has been paid to the sword; but it is questionable if such honor ever went further than in feudal Japan, where the respect given to the weapon of death is indicative of the creed of the times. The sword was held to be a proof of nobility; the gods themselves were represented as wearing two-edged weapons. The very sword-makers—who occupied as much as sixty days in finishing a blade—were held in high esteem, and sometimes rose to great honors. And the swords themselves, treated with an almost religious veneration, were inscribed with telltale mottos, such as "There's naught 'twixt heaven and

earth that man need fear, who carries at his belt a single blade";
and, "One's fate is in the hands of Heaven, but a skillful fighter
does not meet with death"; and, again, "In the last days, one's
sword becomes the wealth of one's posterity." [5]

Not only was honor paid to the sword; a minute etiquette arose
in connection with it. Let a man so much as clash the sheath of
his sword against that of a neighbor, and the second man's blade
might hew him down. Let him place his sword on the floor and
kick the guard toward another man, and a duel to the death was
likely to result. More than that, the conflict might not end with
the death of one of the participants. For a code of blood-venge-
ance prevailed among the Japanese, as among many peoples. If
a man was slain, his wife would not forget the injury; in the spirit
of a Jibaro Indian tutoring his offspring to avenge their murdered
kin, the woman would drill her sons in the need for retribution.
And in this she found approval in the sentiment of the times; the
blood feud was a recognized institution, unhampered by law. It
was, furthermore, an institution calculated to deal the hardest blow
at the most painful moment. "Many a bride," writes William Elliot
Griffis, "found herself a widow on the wedding-night. Many a
child became an orphan in the hour of her father's acme of
honor." [6]

As the slain man would in most cases have brothers, sons, or
other male relatives who felt in honor bound to strike back at the
slayer, the vendetta would continue along the same cruel vicious
circle as in many lands.

The spirit of the blood feud was accentuated by and in turn
accentuated the general fighting mood of the day. Even in early
times, the Japanese had a military organization; by the close of the
seventh century A.D., the army included from one third to one
quarter of all able-bodied males, and later the proportion was increased until all except weaklings were enlisted. It was at about
the middle of the tenth century that the distinctive military caste,
the *samurai*, arose; this caste, owing its origin largely to political
machinations, formed a sort of knighthood dedicated to the profession of arms and destined to be outstanding in Japanese warfare for nine hundred years.

To understand the *samurai*, one must understand something of
the conditions attending their origin. It was a rift in the civil
mechanism that gave them birth; the usurpations of two influential

families, the Taira and the Minamoto, established them as distinct and powerful elements of the community. The civil officers, who were in the control of the emperor, had gradually yielded to indolence and luxury, had ceased to take the warpath themselves, and had allowed the war department to become indolent and disorganized; so that, while the generals at Kioto were losing their ability to enforce their orders, the peasants were becoming soldiers. It had been the practice to bring commoners to court as attendants; and these, instilled with the court spirit, which was the spirit of glory and power and of ruthless striving for rank and position, would return to their homes, surround themselves with armed followers, and convert themselves into military despots in miniature. Like the mercenaries of Western lands, they would rove through the country in bristling gangs, ready to serve any war-lord for pay, and bringing a trail of brawling, terrorism, and chaos.

These professional fighters were of course a temptation to the *shogun* or general who despaired of recruiting an army by the older methods; and it therefore came about that his troops were gathered from the professionals, and began to follow the leader somewhat as the medieval European retainer followed his lord, owing allegiance not to the people or nation but only to their own immediate commander. The civil authorities, helpless to fight on their own behalf, put the power of crushing revolts into the hands of the professional followers of the Taira and Minamoto; and consequently, by the twelfth century, all military authority had been lost to the court. A strange gulf now separated state and army; unrecognized by the crown, which issued unavailing edicts to check the military classes, the fighting clans conquered a large part of the island; after which they rewarded the soldiers by means of grants of land, thereby initiating feudalism, establishing the principle of the rule of the few by means of the sword, and transferring the loyalty of the warrior from the Mikado to the soldier chieftain.

And thus arose the *samurai*, the representatives of as positive a military aristocracy as the world has ever known.

As a caste apart, the *samurai* had no profession but that of arms. Their code forbade them to sully their hands by any trade or business unconnected with war-making; they were relieved from the need of menial work by the income of rice which they received from the government; and outside of idling and amusing themselves, their only duties in times of peace were to keep watch at the houses or castles of their lords, to appear as members of the noble retinue, and to display themselves at prescribed times in their ceremonial splendor. Obviously, men so limited in their normal occupations would either sink into dissipation or find some active vent for their energies—and what active vent was possible except in the warlike spheres for which alone they were trained, and which alone they considered legitimate? Hence the standards that forbade them to work encouraged them to fight.

This is not to imply that they were given to remorseless fighting, with no object other than to slay. Perhaps to a lesser extent than the feudal Chinese, but certainly to a marked degree, they treated their combats as games played according to rules. When two armies met in the field, they did not hurl themselves upon one another with annihilating fury; rather, like two rival athletic teams, they waited until the proper formalities had been observed and due challenge and counter-challenge had been offered. A single champion of each side would step forth, and loudly proclaim his virtues and the virtues of his ancestral line, while pouring scorn upon the boasts of his opponent; and after the interchange of compliments had reached a peak, the two men would meet in mortal combat. The performance would then be repeated with variations by the other warriors, each of whom would wage a wordy duel before clashing with the sword: so that the entire battle would represent nothing more than a series of individual contests, fought first with the tongue, and then with hard steel. Furthermore, it would be a series of contests conducted according to strict principles of honor: fair play would be considered above military advantage, and the warrior embroiled with the foe would not be assisted by his comrades, however desperate his plight—to confront one fighter with two adversaries would be a breach of the *samurai's* code.

It is hardly necessary to point out that combats staged under the goad of biological or economic compulsion could know no such rules or restrictions. Two wolves do not hesitate to attack one lamb; two hungry men in pursuit of a deer do not pause to consider that the animal is unfairly harried; two armies at life-or-death straits have no thought of the boasts or glory of individual champions. Nothing could be clearer than that the real basis of Japanese warfare was not any external pressure but the urgency of ideas—the force of tradition and of inherited precept, the establishment of standards of honor, and men's desire to be adjudged worthy in the light of those standards.

Chapter 15

Byzantines, Saracens, and Crusaders

Few things in all history are much stranger or more tantalizing than the attitudes of mind that different peoples bring to their war-making: the fact that standards abhorred by one group are religiously embraced by another, and that one country's list of "Principles to Be Avoided" is another land's "Code of Military Commandments."

In the last chapter, for example, we saw how warfare in feudal China and Japan was dominated by an artificial creed, a system of rules that sometimes put chivalry ahead of survival. But if we turn west from Japan and China to the Byzantine Empire, we find an artificiality of an opposite type, though equally far from the thrust-and-grab of a fighter whose only desire is to fight. Whereas the Chinese and Japanese were like wrestlers or boxers who competed in a ring according to established regulations, the Byzantines were more like contestants who would trip up their opponents on the way to the ring, so as to avoid the need of ever meeting them face to face. They were more interested in defending themselves than in striking aggressively; but if necessary, they would fight; and when they did so, few holds were barred.

This does not mean that the Byzantine brought no enthusiasm to his fighting. He held himself to be a bulwark of Christendom, its savior against the assaults of Saracen and barbarian; but, on the other hand, his creed held little trace of the heroic; he did not disdain ignoble means, and if he could settle an issue without bloodshed he saw no reason for the crimson wastage of battle, which he regarded as better fitted for raw, rude savages than for civilized men. There were, of course, some exceptions in practice; in an empire covering vast stretches of territory and enduring for centuries, there were bound to be exceptions. But the dominant point of view is indicated by the *Tactica* of the Emperor Leo, which unashamedly advocate certain methods that have not, unfortunately, been confined to any one era. Those of us who look back to a certain December day in 1941, and recall how Japan attacked Pearl Harbor at the very moment when a delegate at Washington was presumably negotiating for peace, will wonder if Tojo's strategists had not taken the Byzantine Emperor's advice to heart: that when you are intending to break off negotiations with an enemy, you should beguile him with gentle words on the day before the last, and then, when he has been soothed with the assurance of peace, you should launch a sudden assault.

Leo, moreover, was not ashamed to win by bribery; to fight with coins rather than swords. And he had no compunction about waging what we have come to call a "war of nerves": to plant rumors that some prominent man in the enemy country is secretly befriending your side, and to lend color to the reports by exempting his lands from plundering; or to spread suspicion within the enemy camp by means of forged treasonable letters which come into the commander's hands and make him distrust his captains. The use of envoys who were really spies was another device not unknown to Leo; and propaganda to encourage his own troops— fictions regarding crushing victories on remote fronts—was employed without any burdensome technical regard for veracity.

In all fairness, however, it should be added that there were limits to the sheer expediency of Leo's methods. He did believe in respecting truces and treaties, in keeping ambassadors inviolate, in prohibiting the massacre of civilians and the maltreatment of women, and in seeing that a courageous enemy was not struck down with oppressive terms. To this extent, if to this extent only, warfare with Leo was a game with rules that were meant to be followed. But his pronouncements regarding ruses and stratagems give the impression that he treated war as an unscrupulous diplomat would treat politics; it was a form of fending for advantage, in which the principal weapon was a sly and remorseless intelligence. And just as a clever foreign minister might manipulate his nation into a favorable position, so a wily war-leader might prevail by his machinations even more than by military might.

We have here, in a word, a conception of war as sheerly cerebral and man-made as any aberrations of the heroic ideal, even though its objectives are coldly practical rather than perfervidly gallant and grand.

The man-made quality of Byzantine fighting was equally evident in the empire's final centuries, when foreign mercenaries largely replaced the small free landholders and possessors of military grants who had made up much of the older armies. Franks and Lombards, Russians, Patzinaks, and Turks began to be hired to do the nation's fighting; and, as always when men wage war for money, fighting was to a great extent subordinated to plundering, and victory was on occasion by-passed for the sake of gain. As evidence of the spirit that animated the Byzantine mercenaries, two examples will suffice: the first occurred in 1079, when, in the course of an engagement, the Patzinaks began to plunder their leader's camp instead of giving him the aid for which they were hired. And the second took place during the crisis of 1204, when the Franks were breaking into Constantinople, and when the mercenaries, instead of plunging forward to the defense of the city, struck for higher pay and refused to fight.

II

Many of the Byzantine operations were conducted against the Saracens, in whom we can see the upsurge of a different spirit, originally as unbridled and passionate as the East Romans were calculating and down-to-earth. Now and then throughout the centuries some national or religious group has been inspired with a vehement conviction of the righteousness of its own views; a burning persuasion of the necessity of conveying those views forcibly to others; and a fanatical willingness to throw their lives away in the service of this militant conversion. When this belief is accompanied, as in the case of the Moslems, by an instilled fatalism; and when the thought of death is honeyed, as in their case, by the anticipation of a paradise of never-ending sensual delight, we have the stage ready-made for fighters who are apt to prove as well-nigh irresistible as human fighters can be. And when the faith has spread to a vast host, and we have the emotional contagion of a common movement in a common cause and the frenzy and hysteria of a general hatred of the unbeliever, we have the possibility of just such conquests as were made by the Moslems, who in a few years tore through the old Sassanian kingdom of Persia, wrested Syria, Egypt, and other parts of Africa from the East Roman Empire, and eventually spread their dominions from India on the east to Spain on the west.

It has been said that the early standard-bearers of Islam went into battle with the actual desire to die. At this remote date, it may be a little difficult to confirm this statement, which is of a sort that would not be easy to prove even in regard to contemporary warriors. Nevertheless, the fact is that the Moslem zealots fought as if they did want to die; like some of the modern Japanese with their "suicide attacks," or like the North Koreans or Chinese Communists recklessly hurling themselves into the jaws of United Nations mortar fire, they appeared to show an utter indifference to death. This indifference may, as suggested above, have been due in part to the passion, the near-dementia that sometimes sweeps masses of men, and the tremendous éclat of mass action; but it also evidently stemmed from the conviction that all had been written in the book of fate, that each man would die at his appointed hour no matter how he behaved, and that therefore one had nothing to fear in being fearless. On the reverse side, this fatalism made it difficult if not impossible for the Moslems to rally after being defeated; since their repulses had been preordained, what use to fight against them, or seek to regain lost territory?

Like their enemies the Crusaders, whom we are about to consider, the Saracen fighters were swayed not only by religious motives, but by the inducements of this world. On the surface, the religious element is the more prominent, since it was in religion that the Moslem conquests were avowedly founded—a religion that marched with the sword in one hand, and the Koran in the other. From the time of the Prophet, religion, politics, and war were intimately intermingled; a theocracy, established at Medina, spread its moral force throughout the vast conquered domains. And within those domains, loyalty to the State implied loyalty to the religion, and loyalty to the religion involved loyalty to the State and willingness to fight for it; insurrections, revolutions, and dynastic changes all had their roots in theological belief.

Hopelessly divided before the time of Mohammed, the prey to internecine quarrels and blood feuds, the Arabs had been inured to small-scale fighting, which they were able to extend to a larger arena and give a unifying purpose beneath the prod of Islam. And like most fighters for religion, they were not marked by restraint in their treatment of those who chanced to disagree with them. While the early Mohammedans were more tolerant than their successors and less avid to obtain conversions and scrupulously offered the alternatives, "Koran, Tribute, or Sword," the Prophet himself had caused the cold-blooded massacre of hundreds of Jews of the tribe of Koreitza and the sale of their women and children into slavery in exchange for horses and harness—their crime having been to prefer their own beliefs to those of the founder of Islam. But not until the time of Haroun-al-Raschid did the fanatical mistreatment of the Christians begin. And meanwhile the Moslems indulged, on pious pretexts, in civil strife with their coreligionists, as in the case of the sect of Khawarij, which benignly spared Jews and Christians while slaying fellow Mussulmans—men, women, and children—who did not accept the Khawarij symbol. No matter if the slain were brave and loyal men who could be ill spared from the defense of the frontiers—after all, did the killers not have the example of the Prophet, who had answered his opponents with the effective argument of the sword? When the head of their faith, Allah's right-hand man, had been a warrior and a slayer, should his followers not also be warriors and slayers? Did the Koran, in fact, not embody the theory that the Prophet might at certain stages resort to fluent bloodshed?

However, bloodshed was not in itself a sufficient object. Though the sword had been proclaimed to be the key to heaven and hell, it seems that for the Prophet's own men it was principally the key of heaven, since the angels fought on their side, while the wicked Iblis and the evil jinns befriended the foe. But the angels of the faithful, strange to say, appear not to have been over-angelic. They were of the plundering variety; they did not object to sacking and looting. Mohammed himself had set the standard: after his conquest of some unoffending Jews, the Keibar, he not only spilled copious blood, but enriched himself with the sheep and camels of the victims, their oil, grains, and honey, along with all the rest of their valuables. But this example, apparently, did not suffice; wishing to see order in robbery as in other things, the Prophet had codified the law of pillage: of all that was captured, he proclaimed, "verily one fifth is for Allah and the Prophet, and for the orphan and the poor and the wayfarer." And the remainder was divided among the soldiers. And so, added to the rewards of Paradise, there was the hope of enrichment in this life if the warrior's survival was written in the book of fate.

The fact that a man takes tribute does not, of course, infallibly prove that his first object is tribute. But if I see an intruder forcing his way into a neighbor's house, and coming out with heaps of jewelry and silverware, I may not be illogical in assuming that he has other incentives than a pious reverence and worship of the Most High. And the Mohammedans, likewise, may be judged not only by what they said but by what they took.

It is evident, of course, that their plundering did not arise from one vast aggressive master-plan, conceived in advance and astutely followed to the end. The facts indicate, rather, that like a house-breaker lured from room to room of a mansion and from theft to ever-greater theft, they extended their pilfering beneath the spur of success; and going from depredation to depredation, magnified their raids in ways they themselves had originally little foreseen. But in all this they appear to have been of much the same breed and species as other marauders, for whom a robbery accomplished is often but the stimulus to new and more lucrative robberies.

Consider some of the specific facts: how, for example, having crossed the Oxus River during the reign of the Caliph Walid I, the Moslems taxed the subjugated people two million pieces of gold—plunder that Walid could not well disdain, since this was the main support for his vast military equipment. Or take the booty in rich lands obtained after the Battle of the River of Blood in the year 633, when, according to reports whose round numbers perhaps need not be taken literally, seventy thousand Persians were slain in order to give the followers of the Prophet access to the rich river valleys of the East. Or, again, witness the loot seized by the Moslem warriors and the permission granted them after the victory over the East Romans at Wacusa to take all the spoils in captive women that they wished—a deliberate catering to the passions of the men, just as the flaunting of inanimate booty was a deliberate catering to their greed. Or, once more, observe the terms offered to captured cities, such as, for example, Damascus, which avoided the extreme penalty by capitulating without a last-ditch struggle: the Moslems were to receive the entire imperial domain, all the possessions of citizens who had escaped during the siege, half of all the other real property, gold and silver both public and private, and, in addition, an annual tribute.

Finally, if all this does not seem sufficient, glance at the business-like laws of plunder enacted by the Caliph Umar. This ruler, after his rise to power in 636, systematized the taking of booty by or-ganizing a *diwan*, a sort of Department of the Treasury; he established rules for the assignment of spoils to the various qualified classes according to rank, down to ordinary women (each of whom received the tenth of a man's share); and did not even exclude the slaves from the profit-taking.

Thus, by making war profitable to every subject, he gave every subject an incentive to warfare. And thus, perhaps even more than through religious fanaticism, he preserved and extended the fighting spirit. It is not too much to say that the strife which he encouraged was brigandage exalted to a national scale—brigandage conducted as a sort of corporate enterprise, in which everyone down to the humble slave was a shareholder.

In view of the utilitarian elements in this warfare, it is not surprising that Islam did not continue to rely wholly upon the swords of the faithful, who at first had flocked as zealous volunteers to serve Allah and his prophet and win themselves a place among the *houris* of Paradise. As befitted a system infected with mercenary aims, the military regime became a prey to that affliction of many lands, the vice of mercenary soldiers. Like many another monarch, the caliph employed great numbers of guards, who shielded his royal person, and formed the core of his army when he moved against a foreign enemy. These men were not fanatics blazing with religious enthusiasm, they were hirelings looking for pay. And while at first they were Arabs, soon the natives were supplanted by foreigners; the Abbasid caliphs, who brought the Islamic power to its peak, engaged Persians, Sudanese blacks, and Turks. The latter—dangerous to their employers, as mercenaries are always likely to be—ended by mastering their masters, and enthroning their own rulers much as the Praetorian Guard in Rome named and seated emperors. Thus they became a political force of the first magnitude. And they stand forth strangely, a sort of silent contradiction, a refutation of the military spirit, which could send the armies of Islam flaming across three continents and yet could not provide reliable guards for the leader of the faith.

III

At first glance, one is impressed by the similarity between the Saracens and their famed adversaries, the Crusaders. While the latter were mainly the aggressors, the Moslems too, as we have seen, had waged religious wars; the Moslems too had sowed death

and devastation for the sake of God and God's earthly representative. The names which they invoked may have been different
of sound, and the express motives unlike; but in essence there had
been a curious resemblance, for when men are swept by the great
flame of fanaticism, the details on which they set their minds represent mere changeable symbols, while the fundamental thing is
the sizzling, tempestuous passion that sears away all obstacles in
order to consummate its end.

Yet where could one find a sharper contrast than in the origins
of the two religions? While one sprang into being full-blown with
a doctrine of fire and sword, the other took its birth in the preachments of the soft-spoken Jesus, the apostle of "peace on earth and
good will to men." Christianity in its early days had been a pacifistic faith; nothing had been further from its original spirit than
the idea of forcing its way with the burning torch and the cold-
bladed steel. But as this sect of a persecuted few spread out and
became a world religion, it absorbed the ideas current in the world,
and became a prey to the passions smoldering in the world; and
gradually it let down its bars to permit defensive warfare, and even
offensive warfare against the heathen. By the time of the Crusades,
one can see little surviving trace of the benign original idea of
"turning the other cheek."

It has been pointed out that the sources of the Crusades lie deep
in medieval history: in the practice of making pilgrimages to the
Holy Land, which dated back to the fourth century, and had on
one occasion (in 1065) involved as many as eleven thousand persons in a single episode; and likewise in the fact that great warlike movements foreshadowing the Crusades had already occurred.
"The wars in Castile against the Moors (1072–99), the Norman
conquest of Apulia and Sicily (1016–90), the Norman conquests of
England (1066), were veritable crusades, and involved upon a
smaller scale most of the motives which afterwards actuated the
Crusades proper upon a grand scale. By example and contagion of
influence these three events powerfully stimulated the warlike
spirit and economic appetite of the western nations."[1]

There is no doubt that the Church, by deliberate propaganda,
fanned the idea of the Crusades. The most obvious example is of
course the celebrated speech of Pope Urban II at Clermont in
1095, which cleverly played upon the emotions of the people in
order to arouse a warlike excitement, and so was the spark that

ignited the fuse of the First Crusade. While Urban's precise words have not survived, the accounts of four hearers as well as some less direct reports give us a fair idea of the contents. His method was one not neglected by subsequent rabble-rousers: he declaimed on the atrocities committed by the Turks, and the agonies endured by the Christians beneath heathen hands. And while he seems to have strummed every string of fanaticism, he did not forget a quota of inducements to the worldly minded; the prospect of plenary indulgences was held out to the sinful, and the hope of enrichment from the adventure of war was implied if not expressly stated.

Other propaganda in an incessant stream was poured out both before and during the Crusades, some of it in the form of papal bulls and diplomatic reports, some in the shape of prose narratives and religious poetry, some apparently in the nature of deliberate fictions, of a kind with which the world has since become sadly familiar. But how was the illiterate believer to check the authenticity of a letter such as that of the Patriarch Simeon to Urban II and the Western rulers, in which he described how the Holy Sepulcher had been profaned and outrages perpetrated against pilgrims? With the ordinary human tendency to accept hearsay as truth, the everyday listener would not be overcritical; his indignation would rise at the supposed offenses, all the faster since it would be shared by the neighbor who bore him the report, and by the neighbors to whom he in turn transmitted it. And he might whip himself into a fighting mood, and end by becoming no less eager to plunge a sword through a Turkish breast than some twentieth-century enthusiasts have been to rebut communism with atom bombs.

There has been much discussion as to the motives behind the Crusades; but one point of general agreement is that the objectives were far from unmixed. While the earlier commentators were inclined to ascribe the movement principally to a flare of religious fanaticism, later critics have been prone to emphasize economic aims, and even to explain the Crusades "primarily as a colonizing movement." [2]

There seems reason to regard the colonizing explanation a little cautiously, as representing the modern tendency to overemphasize the economic interpretation of history. Yet undeniably the colonizing inclination did play a part. Dana Carlton Munro offers us, for example, such a revealing statement as, "Bohemond, son of Robert of Guiscord, had failed to secure his father's principality in Southern Italy, and used the crusade to obtain a new dominion for himself." And, again, "Count Raymond of Toulouse, in spite of his great possessions, is said to have taken an oath before his departure that he would never return. . . . From the very beginning, his great desire was to secure a new principality, and to the end of his life he worked steadily to accomplish this object." And, once more, "Baldwin and Tancred, as soon as they reached Cilicia, endeavored to make conquests for their own profit. When the former was offered an opportunity of ruling in Edessa, he promptly abandoned all further participation in the expedition against Jerusalem." And, finally, "The leaders showed such an evident desire to neglect the conquest of Jerusalem, in order to obtain possessions in the more wealthy Syria, that the common people rebelled and forced the nobles to continue the march." [3]

All this indicates that the economic motive—or, rather, the motive of greed—was dominant among certain Crusaders, but it does not necessarily follow that it was dominant in the movement as a whole.

Various other economic aims, however, are also evident—and were invoked with a designing foresight. If, for example, a man were in debt and elected to bear the Crusading Cross, he might enlist in the service of God at the price of a legalized fraud upon his creditors; he could not be sued for the money he owed, nor obliged to pay interest upon it. At the same time, his religious zeal received the prop of exemption from taxation; and he was placed under the protecting arm of the Church, so that he could not be brought to court except for crime or suits related to land—which might make it cheaper for him to join the Crusade than to meet his civil responsibilities. Furthermore, if he happened to be a man of rank and had committed some dastardly crime, he might avoid the usual penalty by the penance of a number of years under the Cross. And if he were a monk he might escape from his cell, if he were a priest he might forsake his parish, if he were a serf he might desert his land, and even if he were a condemned criminal he might leave his dungeon in a manner impossible without some divine pretext. Hence, when one takes account of the motives of excitement and adventure, not to mention the gifts of arms, horses, and equipment often bestowed on departing enthusiasts by devout kindred, and the commercial incentives opened to the fleets of cities such as Genoa, Venice, and Pisa, one must acknowledge that the Crusaders had just a few inducements that were not precisely religious.

One should also note that the Church, in stimulating the Crusades, had seeming motives apart from sheer piety: the desire to be rid of brawling ruffians and adventurers, and to siphon off domestic dissension by stirring up trouble abroad. And possibly—though here we are judging on *ex post facto* grounds, and must remember that it is not always possible to decide motives from results—some of the Church leaders were not immune to the thought of ecclesiastical enrichment, since the departure of so many peasants and landowners depressed land prices enormously, and the Church was able to buy vast estates literally for a song.

And yet, even considering all the admixture of motives, one may reasonably put the religious incentive first. It is not difficult to accept the view that, "He errs who thinks to find the source and power of the First Crusade elsewhere than in the flaming zeal of feudal Christianity. . . . Overmastering and unifying all was the passion to wrest the sepulchre of Christ from paynim defilement, and thus win salvation for the Crusader. Greed went with the host, but did not inspire the enterprise." [4]

One cannot understand the Crusades without a glimpse into the mind of the average plodding contemporary. He was in most cases a countryman, brought up in an ignorance that has few parallels in the West today. He could not read, he could not write his own name; he did not know that such a thing as science existed, he had never heard of philosophy; he knew no more of the world than the few miles he had traveled on his own feet, supplemented by reports—many of them fictitious and fabulous—from the lips of travelers almost as ignorant as himself. He had been wont to look for guidance, in all things of the mind and spirit, to the one great authority of the age, the Church, which throughout his life he had been taught to fear and reverence, and probably no more thought of questioning than he thought of doubting the rising of the next day's sun. And so when the parish priest told him of the sacrileges against the Holy Sepulcher committed by the heathen Saracens, and preached that it was his duty to rescue this sacred relic and that God would bless him and forgive his sins if he did so, awe and fear and superstition would join with a pious zeal and the long-instilled traditions of Christendom to bid him follow the example of the many. That his cause was righteous, and that righteousness bade him to join the Crusades, were ideas that he would accept with the simplicity of a child taking spoon-fed opinions from its mother's hand.

Only on such grounds can we explain the unprepared mad mass movements characteristic of the Crusades. The crowds that followed such rabble-leaders as Peter the Hermit and Walter the Penniless, and that for the most part were slaughtered by the Hungarians or Turks when they did not perish of hardship or disease, seem to have been victimized by a group hysteria and to have flung themselves against the barriers of the East somewhat as lemmings in their senseless multitudes are said to crowd one another into the sea. Certainly, the most elementary foresight, the most rudimentary precaution would have forbidden them to move in their encumbering hosts, often with throngs of women and children, toward a Holy Land that was more of a fable to them than a reality, a Jerusalem that they were wont to seek in every town and castle by the way. The almost incredible extent of their fanaticism, or rather of their crazed delusion, is shown by a fantastic minor episode, the Children's Crusade, in which the unfortunate boys and girls expected to see the walls of Jerusalem crumble before them and the infidel surrender without even a sword-thrust. Greater folly than this, surely, has never been perpetrated in the name of faith; and though this is an extreme example, it goes only a little beyond the absurdities of the grown Crusaders in demonstrating that it was indeed faith, blind and unreasoning, which induced many of the warriors of the Cross to take up arms on their long, chimerical expeditions.

Not only a misguided faith, but pillage and persecution marched with the Crusaders—pillage that arose partly from need, and partly from greed and brigandage; and persecution that was directed with a murderous zest against the Jews, and can be traced in part to the bigoted views and the passions of the times, and in part to a commercial jealousy. Massacre, however, was aimed also against the inhabitants of captured cities, and particularly of Jerusalem in 1098, when multitudes of Saracens were beheaded, shot with arrows, forced to jump from towers, burned or tortured, until piles of heads, hands, and feet were to be seen in the city's open places. A stark commentary on the motives of the triumphant Crusaders is provided by Raymond of Agiles, a clerk in the Provençal army under that renowned leader of the First Crusade, Raymond of Toulouse:

In the temple and porch of Solomon one rode in blood up to the knees and even to the horses' bridles by the just and marvellous judgment of God. . . . When the city was taken it was worth the long while labor to witness the devotion of the pilgrims to the sepulchre of the Lord, how they clapped their hands, exulted, and sang a new song unto the Lord.[5]

But despite the fury and ferocity manifested in the taking of Jerusalem, cooperation between the Christians and Moslems is often as evident as antagonism. We observe them living on neighborly terms, in frequent communication; sometimes we even catch them in the act of expressing admiration for the other side; we find the Franks calling in Mohammedan physicians, who were far superior to their own; we see an interchange of children as hostages, with a resulting closer understanding; we behold Saladin, during an armistice, arranging with Richard I for the continuation of contracts and commercial relations; and we discover that many a war between the rivals is waged in words alone. All this, it is true, occurs only after the Saracens and Crusaders have had an opportunity to observe one another and to cast off some prejudices. But in all these cases, clearly, the pugnacious impulses of both sides are submerged in a spirit of ordinary, peaceable humanity.

Even in the battles of the sword, the Crusaders and Saracens were not always ranged against one another. From time to time the Christians solicited the aid of the Mussulmans in their quarrels with other Christians or even with the Moslems; in 1108, for example, Joselin of Courtenay was assisted by the Arabs in his contest with Tancred; and Frederick Barbarossa, when preparing to set forth on his Crusade, secured an alliance with the Sultan of Iconium. The Christians, returning the favor, occasionally supported a Saracen ruler against some other Saracen; while, as a parallel to the partnership of Frederick and the Sultan of Iconium, we may note the association of the Greek emperor with Saladin.

All of which will suggest not only that political motives sometimes predominated over religious, but that cooperation between the two great adversaries, the Easterner and the Westerner, the infidel and the unbeliever, the follower of the Prophet and the follower of Christ, was by no means so difficult as the vehemence and pious ardor of some of the earlier conflicts might have indicated.

It is paradoxical that, while the Crusader and Moslem often worked hand in hand, the disputes among the Christians themselves sometimes blazed more vehemently than their quarrels with the Mohammedan enemy. Thus in the thirteenth century the rivalry between the cities of Venice and Pisa on the one hand and Genoa on the other, became so acute as virtually to kill the Crusading movement and insure the loss of the Holy Land. By capturing Constantinople early in the century (a city which had been the possession of the Greek Christians, and not of the Saracens), Venice had been able to establish a monopoly over the trade of the Aegean and Black seas; and the result had been further to inflame the antagonism between her and Genoa. Eventually the stored-up hatred, jealousy, and bitter commercial rivalry found vent in actual war at St. Jean d'Acre in 1255, when the military order of the Knights Templars sided with Venice and the Knights of the Hospital took up arms for Genoa; in the end, the entire Genoese fleet was sunk, and twenty thousand men are said to have been slain. And thus a vast movement, begun more than a century and a half before as an international religious enterprise, degenerated beneath the economic and political hostility of two petty maritime states; the desire for political and commercial advantage took precedence over the unifying impulse of religion; and fury and plunder supplanted the thought of the Holy Sepulcher.

All these changes, obviously, reflect the changing state of mind of the times; yet from the beginning, apparently, the seaboard cities of Italy had been more concerned with the spices and rugs of the Orient than with pious relics. But not until the time of the Fourth Crusade were they able to make their desires predominate, to put the acquisitive ideal unashamedly ahead of the religious, and to dissolve the Crusades amid the squeeze-thrust-and-crush of the mania for empire and trade.

Chapter 16

Feudalism, Chivalry,
and The Hundred Years' War

In our twentieth-century world, wherein we have recognized the principle of using not only the moral but the physical force of the United Nations to check aggression, we have swung the dial of peace-making almost a hundred and eighty degrees from its position in the Middle Ages. For whereas now we have acknowledged that wars are not limited or local affairs and that the united force of all peace-loving nations should be used to combat them, in medieval times the majority of affrays were minor or neighborhood concerns, in which the man across the river or over the hill might be one's enemy. There were exceptions, of course, such as the Crusading movements and the invasion of England by the forces of William the Conqueror; but, generally speaking, the state of the country was a little as that of the region above New York City might be if we had a Count of Yonkers who was at war with the Duke of New Rochelle, and incidentally ravaged the neutral territory and terrified the people of Bronxville and Mt. Vernon; while the principalities of Scarsdale and White Plains might at their discretion join one side or the other, and both factions were in constant danger from robber barons who made hit-and-run attacks from their castles along the Hudson, or their strongholds deep in the woody fastnesses above the Bronx River.

Such a condition would be one of almost unimaginable chaos; yet such a condition would approximate only in part the anarchy of the Middle Ages. It is not absolutely true, as we shall see, that no law except that of might was recognized. But feudal obligations as a rule were respected only when they could be enforced; vassals would turn against their lords, lords against their sovereigns, sons against their fathers, and younger brothers against older whenever opportunity appeared to offer—there was no code, no creed of loyalty, no persuasion of religion that deterred, and he who was not led toward warfare by greed for plunder was stimulated by a long training in arms, and by the current sentiment in favor of the fighting profession as the most fitting for the young man of rank.

One must concede, of course, that at our distance we may tend to lose our sense of proportion, and may see the outbreaks of war somewhat as an aviator may notice the highly colored points in a landscape while neglecting the much wider areas of commonplace gray. Nevertheless, the entire European continent was much in the condition of a city which lacks a police department, and which is constantly the theater for the battles of organized pillagers and rival gangs. It was, furthermore, like a city filled with old animosities as well as with riches beckoning to the strong and bold; there was a continual temptation to man's baser and more greedy incitements, and small matters involving the claim to a trout stream, or a boundary, or a patch of brush or timber, or other ill-defined but valued "rights"—matters which today would be settled in court, if not amicably out of court—would cause swords to rattle in their scabbards and armed men to clatter forth in bloody duels.

In all this we can trace the deeply entrenched habits of a people bred for centuries in militarism—bred in the idea of defending themselves without recourse to any outer power for physical or moral support. We can observe, besides, a people trained to an extreme isolationism, of which the castles with their thick walls and narrow slitted windows are only the outer symbols—a people so divided among innumerable petty rulers, and so inured to a narrow self-reliance that they distrust all strangers and even all neighbors.

And yet, with it all, the chaos was not complete; there were rules governing even the private wars. A man could not assault an enemy without giving a week's notice; "sneak attacks," in other words, were prohibited. And if a vassal took up arms against his suzerain, no nobles outside his own family circle were permitted to assist him; while a respite of forty days was provided before a belligerent could strike the relations of his foe; and during this time, the relatives had the right to protect themselves by proclaiming their neutrality. But even among relatives, priests as well as women and minors were immune from attack; while all were safeguarded during the period of a truce, and violators were severely punished.

Thus, to a large extent, the private wars were treated as games

played according to rule rather than as wholly undisciplined outbursts of violence.

Even so, they were bitter and bloody affairs; and the opinion
of humanity, even in those unenlightened days, does not seem to
have altogether favored them. The Church, for one thing, made
powerful efforts to suppress them. Seeking to protect the poor—
the heaviest sufferers in the incessant raids—the French bishops
proclaimed the Peace of God, and bade serf and noble alike to
take an oath to refrain from further war-making. Unfortunately,
the bishops, not unlike some later enthusiasts, seem to have over-
estimated the power of the sworn word; some of the barons would
not pledge themselves, and others would not keep their pledge;
and despite some slight gains to the priestly and noncombatant
elements, the bloody brawls and raids continued. And so the
Church had to modify its requirements. Apparently its principle
now was that one killing is not so bad as two; contenting itself
with the traditional "half a loaf," it sought to limit warfare to
certain days in the year. One is curiously reminded of the game
laws of a later day; the season for human slaughter was from
Monday morning to Wednesday evening of each week; but to
kill outside of the prescribed time, or during certain saintly feast-
days or religious holidays, was to subject one's self to severe punishment, which might vary from the forfeiture of one's property
to the loss of a hand.

But if these regulations did accomplish something, there was
much that remained undone. Consequently, the Church was led
to establish "sanctuaries"—holy places where bloodshed was forbidden. He who gained one of these refuges would be protected
by the clergy from the sword of the foe—a safeguard which, while
only partial, saved many a wretch from a bloody death.

Yet the fact remains that, while the Church gained some scattered successes, its campaign against private warfare was on the
whole ineffective. And it may be that the anti-militarists of the
time, sighing at their continual failure, were resigned to believing private warfare inevitable. "It is the nature of man to fight,"
we may suppose some of these disappointed idealists to have
remarked. "It is his nature to attack the village or castle of his
neighbor. It is the son's nature to war with his father for his inheritance, and the younger brother's nature to battle with his
elder brother, and the baron's nature to launch his troops against

any fellow baron who arouses his jealousy or greed. These things are lamentable, but are not to be avoided; they always have been, and always will be so long as the world endures."

In the later Middle Ages, the private wars gradually gave place to larger-scale conflicts, in which the clashes of ruling houses and commercial rivalries played a part; mercenary soldiers became common, and professional armies were established. But at the risk of some slight chronological inconsistency, we shall leave this subject until a little later, and turn now to the institution most prominently associated with feudal warfare, an institution glorified in thousands of poems and romances of the Middle Ages.

II

Chivalry represents a flowering of the heroic ideal, akin to that which we have seen in early Greece and India, China and Japan. The resemblances to feudal Japan, with its *samurai*, are especially marked; like the latter, the knights of medieval Europe were the scions of a military aristocracy, and had no profession but fighting; like the latter, they were largely influenced in their conduct by their cult of honor and devotion. And just as the civilization of Japan was shaped and colored by the *samurai* and their code of loyalty, combat, and suicide, so the life of Europe was given its peculiar complexion by the knights and their traditions of chivalry.

To state this is to repeat a commonplace; few would deny that the culture of medieval and even of modern Europe would have shown a vastly different face had the knights never tilted and the idea of chivalry never been born. However far the men may ordinarily have descended from their ideal; however they may have masked the rending blade behind the colored screen of gallantry; however great the admixture of religious intolerance and the smudge of worldly motives in the minds of the noble adventurers, the fact remains that the heroic standards were ever-present, frequently triumphing over practical considerations, and at all times exercising an influence. It may not be that any flesh-and-blood Don Quixote ever charged an actual windmill; yet ten thousand, a hundred thousand Don Quixotes assuredly girded themselves to charge windmills of the imagination—and not because they were dull-witted or blind, but because this peculiar form of attack was approved by the ideas of the age.

One must not imagine, however, that the knight was so chivalrous and romantic a figure as legend and fable would make him.
Often he was a mere bully and a brigand; the earlier knights, in
particular, had many scoundrelly characteristics; they killed unarmed men without compunction; they burned nuns in their con-
vents, and carried off women like pirates; and their virtuous
attributes are largely the contributions of the hero-worshippers.
These earlier knights were, in a word, merely a military class run
wild; and, like most military tyrants, they seized whatever they
would for the all-sufficient reason that they could.

Nevertheless, the knight did develop from a freebooter to a warrior with a certain ideal of honor. And this growth can be traced
to his own egotistic qualities, as well as to the evolution of the
ideas with which he surrounded himself:

When a knight was also a feudal lord and had associates of all
ranks under his command, he had to protect and defend them,
under penalty of being abandoned by them and scorned by his
peers as a coward. This duty was a point of honor. In time this
point of honor grew by reason of their great boastfulness, which
the heroes of the old chansons exhibited in rodomontades, and in
bold and rash undertakings. Any wrong done to a protege was an
outrage to the protector. When a knight made himself the champion of all the feeble, he gave the most striking proof that he
feared no rival, because he was under the necessity of fighting at
any moment against all comers. Magnanimity might thus arise
from the intoxication of pride, and from the exuberance of
strength and individuality.[1]

One might be inclined to cite the Crusades themselves as evidences of the practical effects of chivalry, were it not, as we have
seen, that the source of those fantastic expeditions was largely
religious when it was not merely predatory. Yet the heroic ideal
did play its part in inducing the knights to set forth on Crusading
adventures whose inherent absurdity was in many cases equaled
only by the high faith of the participants. This becomes especially
plain when we turn to the late Middle Ages, which were confronted with problems far more pressing than the recovery of a
mere sacred emblem from the infidel, yet allowed the imperative
needs of the moment to be obscured by the vagaries of tradition.
In the year 1400, when common prudence might have envisaged
the necessity of repulsing the Turks, who had just taken Adrian-

ople, the efforts of the West were not focused upon the Balkans, but the Turkish question was viewed as subordinate to the ancestral idea of the Crusades:

The conquest of Jerusalem could not but present itself to the mind as a work of piety and of heroism—that is to say, of chivalry. In the councils of Eastern politics the heroic ideal preponderated more than in ordinary politics, and this it is which explains the very meager success of the war against the Turks.[2]

But it is when we turn to lesser undertakings, uncomplicated by a religious emotion, that we can watch the pursuit of mirages most plainly, and see the warriors of the windmill squadron tilting most vigorously at clouds and shadows. Take, for example, that renowned and glamorous figure the knight-errant, that singular being who rode in full armor across a peaceful countryside, attended by a faithful squire, and in constant quest of adventure, which he might attempt to coax forth by jousting with some passing knight, or by posting himself at some bridge or crossroads and permitting no knight to go by without a passage at arms. One can well believe that he constituted a public nuisance, if not a public menace. Yet generally speaking (though anger might spur him to kill), the contests that he waged were not dangerous. And often there arose situations such as Cervantes has so pointedly satirized. One of the knights would proclaim, for example, that his lady love was the most beautiful on earth; and the other, even if he had never seen the charmer in question, would instantly deny the allegation, asserting that his own love was fairer by far. There being only one way to settle so delicate a matter, the two knights would fly to arms; and he whose thrust was the quickest, whose lance was the stoutest or whose horse was the strongest would demonstrate the superior comeliness of his lady.

In the songs and stories of chivalry, we can see countless examples of an unwarlike warfare, with none of the remorselessness of the typical "no-holds-barred" fight to the death. For example, in that heroic old Spanish poem *The Cid*, the protagonist on one occasion defeated the haughty Count Raymond Berenger of Barcelona, by whom he had been attacked; and having routed the enemy and captured his famous sword Colada, what should he do out of courtesy but ask the fallen foe to feast with him? The latter, however, did not share in his courtliness, but went on a hunger strike, which he ended when it became too burdensome; after which the Cid made friends with him, gave him his freedom, and parted with him on cordial terms.

Though this is admittedly no more than popular romance, not even romance would be accepted unless it reflected the standards and ideals of the people (think how we would laugh at the story of a bombardier who, having done his best to lay waste a city, is shot down by his intended victims, and then set at liberty and politely invited to a banquet!). But not only in individual contests celebrated by the poets and tellers of tales; in historical records of engagements involving large numbers of men, we can observe actions that our world would regard as equally quixotic, equally irrational.

Take, for example, the account that we find in Froissart of the war of the Black Prince to restore Don Pedro of Castile to the throne. Here, as in many medieval conflicts, we see a leader marching his men to a foreign land for no reason that economic demands or the needs of politics or common sense can explain—for no reason but the topsy-turvy chivalry of bringing back to power a deposed monarch (and, incidentally, a tyrant of whom his people were well rid). Likewise, chivalry at its typical best (or worst) is to be seen in one of the episodes of the war, when Don Pedro's brother is a target of the British attack. Finding that he may be able to trap the Black Prince in a mountain pass and starve him into a ruinous retreat, he scorns to take advantage of such an unheroic short-cut to victory. With something of the attitude of the feudal Chinese captain who disdains to attack an unprepared enemy, the Spanish commander expresses a desire to match his strength with the foe on equal terms—as a result of which a pointless and unnecessary battle is fought.

Nor is this an isolated instance. A similar case is that of Don Henri de Trastamera, who, before the Battle of Najera, was so desirous of competing on an equal basis with the enemy that he voluntarily surrendered a position of strategic advantage, and so lost the battle. And almost equally untouched by any "tooth-and-fang" law of survival were those Knights of the Star who, according to Froissart, had bound themselves by oath never to fly more than a specified distance from the battlefield—as a consequence of which ninety of them perished. Not less egregious, again, was the conduct of that king of England who, it is said, made a rule forbidding knights in armor to retreat, and then himself by mistake passed the night-quarters of his troops and found himself in a dangerous dilemma. "Courage before discretion!" seems to have been his motto; sooner than violate the principles of valor he himself had laid down, he did not retreat; he imperiled the army by ordering the vanguard to advance to meet him.

Another rule that met with frequent favor was the one prohibiting ruses and ambushes: the Irish of the age of chivalry, for example, ordinarily disdained surprises or stratagems, and sometimes gave notice of an intention to attack, and even reached an agreement with the enemy as to the time and place of battle. And from the Continent many similar cases have been reported: for example, in the siege of the castle of Cormicy by the English knights in 1360, the assailants mined the stronghold but first warned the inmates to come out if they valued their lives; and the French, doing as bidden, surrendered with thanks to their considerate rivals.

In all these instances we are face to face once more with the old familiar tendency to regard a battle not as an inexorable duel but as a form of game.

Even more characteristic was the case of that twelfth-century emperor, Frederick Barbarossa. One of the most striking of medieval figures, this red-bearded war-leader was a man of grandiose ideas, who regarded himself as a successor of the Caesars and Charlemagne, who thought he could revive the Roman Empire, and who looked upon his dominions (as he himself announced to the Pope) as a gift from none other than God. And the actions of this "perfect knight," as he has been termed, seem to testify to the sincerity of his belief in the God-theory. Instead of staying at home and administering the affairs of his country as rulers in a less visionary age would have thought natural, he wasted his treasure and the blood of his men in a succession of Italian invasions that absorbed his energies for thirty years and could not by any conceivable means benefit his people; and finally, indulging in the luxury of a Crusade in old age, drowned while crossing a stream in far-off Cilicia. The striking fact about Frederick is not that, in pursuit of the heroic ideal, he was drawn by vainglorious or quixotic dreams into chimerical adventures; the striking fact is that he did so with the tactic consent and even the approval of his people, who not only did not cry out in protest, but clasped him to their hearts in admiration. In other words, he embodies the views of his age. And he shows how little that age was concerned with the sheerly practical, the economic or the nationalistic aims that we should value today.

III

All this, however, represents but one side of the picture. It represents chivalry at its most gallant if sometimes its most fatuous extreme; it does not unbare the evils festering at the roots of the system. Even if occasional knights would sacrifice themselves before a will-o'-the-wisp, the heroic ideal in the Middle Ages showed the tendencies it has exhibited in most lands and eras: it provided a hothouse for the forced cultivation of ideas of combat and love of combat, and so bred incessant strife and bloodshed. It exalted fighting for the sake of fighting; it flaunted the allurement of glory; it taught the young to emulate the warrior, and set no standard above that of the successful lance-wielder. And the natural result was that the lance-wielders became many and powerful, and could not be repressed for centuries. Long after the call that brought them into being had ceased, the knights-errant continued their depredations; the knighthood and nobility, bristling and arrogant and at incessant war among themselves, swept down across the countryside from their unconquerable castles, trampled the land with their armored horses, and put impassable hurdles in the way of a unified government, political stability, and peace.

The artificial nature of the cult honored by these adventurers is manifest in the exaggerated respect paid to the sword. As the prime implement of combat, this weapon was prized much as among the *samurai* of Japan. The author of the following may be suspected of a romantic exaggeration, but the heroic literature of the Middle Ages will bear out his thesis:

. . . the weapon *par excellence* is the sword. Barons often love their swords perhaps more than they love their wives. They treat them almost as if they are persons. They try to keep them through their entire lives. According to the epics, the hero Roland likes to talk to his sword "Durendal," and Ogier to his "Brans." Conon swears one of his fiercest oaths, "By my good sword *Hautemise*," and Aimery has named his sword "Joyeuse," after the great blade of Charlemagne.

There are many fashions in swords. You can always revive a

flagging conversation by asking whether your companion likes a tapering blade or one of uniform thickness and weight.[3]

One will remember the sword Excalibur in the *Idylls of the King*:

> "Thou therefore take my brand Excalibur,
> Which was my pride: for thou rememberest how
> In those old days, one summer noon, an arm
> Rose up from out the bosom of the lake,
> Clothed in white samite, mystic, wonderful,
> Holding the sword—and how I row'd across
> And took it, and have worn it, like a king . . ." [4]

This, of course, is the interpretation of a modern poet; but it is an interpretation consistent with the medieval spirit, in which the fighting blade was not only treasured, but even at times treated as a thing of mystical and almost religious significance.

A not less telling example is to be found in the *Song of Roland*, which speaks of "the good sword Joyeuse" and "the honor and the virtue" wherefrom it had received its name, and goes on to exalt it as a perpetual warlike symbol:

And ever shall it remain in the minds of the Frenchmen, for it is therefrom that they have their battle-cry Montjoie, and it is the reason why no foe can stand against them.[5]

All this accords with the whole system of chivalry. The kernel of that system is to be seen in deliberately instilled ideas and emotions connected with the sword; in the growth of the future cavalier in an atmosphere ringing with the songs and romances of combat and the unstinted praises of knighthood; and correspondingly in tournaments wherein the warriors might court popularity and put their prowess to the test. As if aiming to develop a warlike state of mind, noble fathers would send their sons at the age of about seven to the castles of barons and dukes, where, free from the softening influence of their mothers, they would grow familiar with weapons, would be trained in mock combats and in the chase, would listen to incessant chatter of martial feats, would assist their masters in defending their castles and preparing assaults, and would be taught to place supreme faith in the knightly ideal. And as if this were not enough, the youth would be given a sort of laboratory course in actual warfare; he would attend mimic battles that were at once training schools and gala affairs, and that, a bit like the "Big Game" of college football teams, were regarded as sporting events and were attended by enthusiastic crowds, including all the nobility of the countryside.

Some of these mimic battles, in a manner reminiscent of the Roman arena, were deliberately arranged, and were waged by men who entered in cold blood without any grievance or fancied grievance and butchered competitors who similarly had no grievance or fancied grievance. This refers, of course, to the tournaments—not the more or less orderly spectacles of the fourteenth or fifteenth centuries, but their predecessors of three or four hundred years before. Just as, in the Coliseum of Rome, pseudo-wars were fought with some of the deadly consequences of actual wars, so on the fields of Germany and France armored hosts would clash with sanguinary results; knights on horseback, beneath the goad of the crowd's admiration and applause, would drive at one another in duels fatal to them and their chargers alike. Sometimes entire small armies would hurl themselves at one another; at one tournament at Lagny-sur-Marne, more than three thousand knights battled with murderous zest in the vineyards and ditches and among the thick forests of vine-stocks. And so late as 1240, a contest near Cologne is reported to have cost more than sixty lives.

Despite the prohibitions of popes, bishops, and kings, the bloody displays persisted: the spectators enjoyed the recreation; the competitors were egged on somewhat as our Joe Louises and Joe Di-Maggios have been egged on by the grandstand in more recent forms of sport; and the merchants and common folk—a culminating reason—favored the exhibitions because they were good for business.

But beyond providing a spectacle and amusement, the tournament seems to have been consciously regarded as a training school for the warrior's mind and body. "A knight cannot shine in war if he has not prepared for it in tournaments. He must have seen his own blood flow, have had his teeth crackle under the blows of his adversary, have been dashed to the earth with such force as to feel the weight of his foe, and disarmed twenty times; he must twenty times have retrieved his failures, more set than ever upon the combat. Then will he be able to confront actual war with the hope of being victorious." [6]

However, as we have seen, the line of demarcation between the tournament and "actual war" was sometimes a little difficult to determine. And whether or not the contest was relatively restrained, one result was certain: through the rivalries and the spirit of emulation which it aroused, it would lead toward even deadlier armed actions.

IV

But while chivalry is conspicuous for nothing if not for the militarism which it encouraged, it also had results of an opposite nature. Paradoxically, it has been credited with pacifistic tendencies! By regulating war as a game played according to rule, it made possible the cessation or the avoidance of war by rule; and by instilling a degree of consideration for the enemy, it opened a path over which the disputants might draw together and settle their difficulties in amicable council. And thus it prepared the soil for internationalism.

As one writer points out, "The law of nations originated in antiquity and canon law, but it was chivalry which caused it to flower."[7] For, side by side with warlike desires, there flourished a knightly aspiration for peace. This we can see in certain of the chivalric orders, such as that which Philip de Mézières planned for the sake of world harmony; and we can read a similar longing in the expectation that Charles VI of France and Richard of England would be able to meet, and, on chivalric principles, arrange for peace after a personal consultation.

But the share which the ideas of chivalry have had in the development of a law of nations is not limited to these dreams. The notion of a law of nations itself was preceded and led up to by the ideal of a beautiful life of honour and of loyalty. In the fourteenth century we find the formulation of principles of international law blending with the casuistical and often puerile regulations of passages of arms and combats in the lists. [8]

The growth of an international system was favored by the fact that the knights of all lands could look upon one another with a fraternal spirit. They were all, as it were, acknowledged members of the same exalted order; they were like brothers of one caste; they could meet, confer, and fight on a basis of equality. Between a knight of England and a *chevalier* of France, and between either of these and a Spanish *caballero*, there was far more in common than between any of the three and a peasant born and reared within a stone's throw of one of the group. Consequently, there was a tendency for the three not only to challenge and charge one another but to link hands.

The corresponding effects in encouraging and widening class distinctions, and hanging fresh burdens about the necks of men already tottering beneath oppression, are a little aside from the theme of this discussion, except in so far as such discrimination sharpened the tensions and deepened the cleavages that led toward peasants' revolts and social revolutions. But when, in addition to such evils, one considers the role that chivalry has played in encouraging wars of religion, in scattering persecution and suppressing freedom of thought, one must conclude that it was at best a rather mixed blessing.

At the same time, one has to acknowledge that the vices resulting from it as well as the virtues it propagated were inherent in its very fabric. When it provided a bond between remote countries, the reason is to be found in its spirit of tolerance within class limits, no less than in the international nature of the dominant religion. And when it magnified the gulf between the noble and the common man, the explanation lies in its spirit of intolerance outside of class limits. At its best as at its worst, it is characteristic of the heroic ideal as we find it in many lands: ruled by a sort of adolescent egotism, a childish love of praise and an evaluation of that praise above solid realities, it was necessarily exclusive and narrow in its loyalties even while extravagant in its courting of applause. Although nominally and sometimes not insincerely devoted to the service of the Christian Deity, it actually owed allegiance to the twin gods Honor and Glory, the lodestars of the immature mind throughout all time. And these almighty beings displayed their usual sublime fickleness, and allowed their altars to be defiled by giddy ceremonials and crimson sacrifices.

Little of the chivalric idea remains today. One can see not even its ghost in those recent conflicts in which dive-bombers have screeched down upon streams of terrorized defenseless refugees, or in which hostile craft have machine-gunned shipwrecked sailors, or in which the residential hearts of belligerent and even non-belligerent cities have been blown down upon crushed and bleeding men, women, and children. Perhaps just a touch of the spirit of chivalry, as it existed even in its most vainglorious era, would have served to offset to some extent the horrors of our time, and brought at least a suggestion of relief from our own grievous burden of war.

V

Even before chivalry as an idea was dead, we find foreshadowings of a new state of mind, and one characteristic of the late eighteenth, nineteenth, and twentieth centuries. Throughout the Middle Ages, the world was without any conception of nationalism in the modern sense of the term; men paid allegiance to feudal lord, king, city-state, pope, or caliph, or were linked together in such wide and amorphous organizations as the Byzantine Empire and the Holy Roman Empire. But the thought of country, of patriotism, which has subsequently played so large a part in warmaking, was still in the stage of things-to-be. We do indeed find hints, gleams, suggestions of a dawning new outlook, as among the cities of northern Italy, which in the twelfth century displayed a fine local spirit in successfully opposing the invasions of Frederick Barbarossa. But we have to move forward as far as the Hundred Years' War (1338–1452), before we can observe a marked widespread change, and find something like a sense of national existence and a desire for national predominance.

Though a number of nations were to be involved in this late-medieval version of a world war, the struggle was basically due to the efforts of the English to control much of the territory now belonging to continental France, and the corresponding desire of the French to drive the English out. This, however, is to express the matter much too simply: a great variety of forces were at work, including the ambitions of the English King Edward III, who laid claim to the French crown; the rivalries of French and English sailors and fishermen, involving brawls in which numbers of men were killed, and which at times flared almost to the proportions of blood feuds; the intrigues of the French with the Scots in the conflicts of the latter with the English; personal exacerbations, as when Edward provided a haven for Robert of Artois, the mortal enemy of the French King Philip; and economic excitations, as in the case of Philip's levies upon the wine-trade of English-held Aquitaine, and Edward's prohibition of the export of wool to Flanders, whose economy was largely built upon this product.

We can here see the creation step by step of antagonisms, psychological excitations, involving both the rulers and the people, until each side was ready to fly at the other's throat. The irony of the matter is that both sovereigns, when the war opened, expected it to be a short-term affair; Edward, in fact, when he formed the series of alliances that would give him the strength to attack France, arranged to obtain the services of the allies for a few months only, and apparently foresaw triumph in the fourteenth-century version of a *blitzkrieg*. Little could Edward, or Philip, or any of their lieutenants, imagine that the struggle would drag wearily on, through bloodshed and devastation, when they and their sons and even the sons of their sons were no more! It is not too much to suppose that if the two kings had been keener realists and wiser prophets; if Edward had not been lured forth by the will-o'-the-wisp of a quick victory; if the two sovereigns and their subjects had visualized the trials and the miseries that lay ahead, some way would have been found in the high councils of the states to bring the dispute to an end.

It was chiefly during the latter decades of the struggle that the rising new sentiment of nationalism made itself felt. Whatever national feeling had previously existed had been directed in the main toward the person of a ruler rather than toward a specific country. Hence the significance of the turning tide. One recent writer has ably summarized the case:

The English in their endeavor to conquer France were . . . struggling against a current of increasing strength, the French sentiment of national separateness and unity. Neither the French nor the English, probably, were aware of the growth, perhaps not of the existence of this force, but it was nevertheless a potent one. There are many evidences of it. One is the successful defection of England's French allies. . . . These French adherents of the English king ultimately left him, drawn away by the attraction of their own nationality. . . . If the steps by which these defections took place should be traced it will be seen that in each case an assertion of nationalism was the fundamental cause.[9]

While the new force of nationalism was lifting its unrecognized head, the old element of chivalry was on the retreat. Though there were some exceptions, one can notice little trace of chivalry in most of the campaigns of this war, in which countrysides were burned and ravaged, crops uprooted, fruit trees cut down, villages and towns put to the torch, citizens imprisoned and held for ransom, guards strangled, women violated, helpless captives stabbed, and populations decimated to such an extent that Toulouse lost half its inhabitants, Rouen was reduced (according to a census still surviving) from 14,992 in the thirteenth century to 5,976 in the fifteenth, while after the sack of once-populous Limoges a mere five persons were left alive among the ruins. Such melancholy statistics but prove once more, as the records of other great wars have proved, that after a conflict is under way there is no checking the unleashed passions of men, the growing ferocity of leaders beneath prods and reverses, the rapacity of uninhibited attacking rabbles, and that mob psychology which, once aroused, is a fierce and ravening thing, and rarely halts at anything short of impassable physical barriers.

Nevertheless it should be noted that, long before the Hundred Years' War was over, the struggle appeared to be dying of inanition. During the final twenty years, the rulers and the people of England were no longer fired with the warlike spirit of Edward III and his followers; they were more interested in trade than in battle, and were moved by the current revival of learning and by intellectual objections to the conflict. The war continued more of its own momentum than because anyone wanted it to go on; but it continued rather sporadically, until, after two last bloody affrays at Castillon and Bordeaux, the English troops were withdrawn. Nothing more clearly shows that no one wanted any further fighting than the fact that there was no treaty or agreement, either written or unwritten, but that the war none the less ended.

The Hundred Years' War is notable, among other things, for one incident without a parallel in all the world's recorded conflicts. It is now more than five centuries since Joan of Arc, like some strange comet from another universe, flamed across the horizons of the French and English. Surely, never has there been a more perfect illustration of how the mind may influence war-making. That a woman should have elevated herself to become a leader of warriors is in itself extraordinary; but that she should have done so for motives of selfless devotion, and in response to a series of visions, is very much more remarkable. The question whether the visions were real, needless to say, is merely academic; the important fact, proved beyond doubt by Joan's conduct and her heroic defense of herself at the Rouen trial, is that she devoutly believed them to be real, was fervently sure that a mission had been entrusted to her by Saint Michael, Saint Catherine, and Saint Margaret. Here was the proverbial faith that moves mountains!

What Joan did was indeed equivalent to the moving of mountains—a truth which the English realized after she had captured a number of their strongholds and forced the abandonment of the seven months' siege of Orléans. She represented the welding of two powerful psychological forces: the religious and the patriotic—a firm belief in saints and miracles and a divinely given mission; and a strong persuasion, apparently engendered by the stories she had heard since early childhood, of the necessity of driving the English invader from her fair land of France. Nothing could have been further from the normal woman's impulse, nothing basically more unreasonable than to ride forth mail-clad at the head of the French troops. But forces stronger than reason moved in her—forces that could not, however, have prevailed in an age which did not share some measure of her religious faith; the resource that won her triumphs was the confidence and enthusiasm she inspired in her followers. Her strength was of the spirit only, her great weapon her moral courage; and these, as long as the recorded word endures, will keep her name alive; these will preserve the memory of one who, heedless of the restraints of position and sex, fought because a spur within her consciousness bade her fight, and won because she had the power to communicate something of the ardor of her own dreams.

Chapter 17

The Dawn of Modern Times

During the late Middle Ages, one of the most common types of warfare had little in common with that of lance-wielding knights and castled barons. This was the warfare conducted by mercenaries, who leaped back into a prominence they had not known since the days of ancient Greece and Carthage. Perhaps nothing could be further from the professed ideals of chivalry than to offer one's sword for hire, regardless of right or wrong, honor or love or glory. It is therefore not least among the paradoxes in the checkered history of war that the mercenary system returned to full bloom at a date when men still professed a belief, even if a waning belief, in the chivalric ideal.

It was at the time of the Hundred Years' War that the mercenary system became deeply entrenched. In many of the engagements, troops representing England, France, Spain, and Portugal were hired in much the way that bricklayers or plumbers might be engaged in house-building projects. These warriors, who called themselves "Free Companies," were often organized in the manner of contemporary guilds of masons, leather-workers, or goldsmiths, and elected officers like any of these guilds. War to them, obviously, was not a consecration but a trade (though one at which they strove to excel for no one's advantage but their own). They ravaged, they burned, they slew, they levied tribute, they stole women and children, and terrorized and mastered whole wide districts. The popular attitude toward them, as well as their own nature and the nature of their impositions, is indicated in a passage from Froissart, who tells us how certain captains received 250,000 francs as the price of quitting the country, which, says the writer, "would gladly have seen them depart, for the inhabitants could neither till the earth nor carry on trade for fear of these pillagers, unless they had entered into composition with them according to their wealth and rank; and these compositions amounted in a year to as much as was now demanded for the evacuation of the forts." [1]

Whether or not the "Free Companies" as a whole were more villainous than the rank and file of mercenaries, all these soldiers of fortune manifested the same general tendencies. And any ruler who hired any of them was likely to be a discontented employer. Machiavelli, who had occasion to observe these hirelings at first hand, has portrayed them with a realistic pen:

The mercenary and auxiliary are unprofitable and dangerous, and that prince who founds the duration of his government upon his mercenary forces shall never be firm or secure; for they are divided, ambitious, undisciplined, unfaithful, insolent to their friends, abject to their enemies, without fear of God or faith in men . . . in time of peace they divorce you, in time of war they desert you, and the reason is because it is not love or any principle of honor that keeps them in the field; it is only their pay, and that is not a consideration strong enough to prevail with them to die for you; whilst you have no service to employ them in, they are excellent soldiers; but tell them of an engagement, and they will either disband before or run away in the battle.[2]

Since the first object of the mercenaries was gain, their payment was, as Machiavelli implies, the test by which their actions were gauged. When wages ceased, discipline ceased; or else they sought compensation by ravaging the countryside, and thus were as ruinous as an invading army. But even when they received regular pay, they would expect extra dividends from the spoils of battle, and particularly from the ransom of prisoners; hence their very existence provided a warlike stimulus, and their incorporation in the army encouraged raids for booty. Often they chose to plunder a wealthy region rather than engage in unremunerative combat; and sometimes they became so unruly that their leaders had little or no control over them. Worse still was that occasionally they would turn upon their employers, and establish themselves as military dictators. The story is told—evidently with conscious exaggeration, but in a way to indicate the reputation of these paid fighters—that the inhabitants of a particular town were uncertain how to reward a mercenary chieftain who had defended them. Finally, wishing to take no chances, they decided that safety lay in first making away with him, and then venerating him as a saint.

The situation in Italy was especially interesting. At about the beginning of the fourteenth century, bands of mercenaries known as *condottieri* became established—bands which represented a sort

of big business, since they were under the command of a leader
who organized them and hired them out at his discretion. Being
willing to serve any master, they were the vehicles of the machinations of ambitious princes; they served democracies and autocracies with equal readiness. Venice, for example, employed them for
purposes of conquest; the Florentines likewise made use of them,
under the command of foreign generals; and Venice and Florence
and all their fellow states alike tasted the advantages of the system,
which involved not only the possibility of a thrust in the back
from the less scrupulous *condottieri*, but the certainty that even
the more scrupulous would enlist with the ex-enemy if this seemed
profitable when the engagement was over—thus making it dangerous for a ruler to discharge his hirelings, lest he meet them again at
the point of a spear.

But not all the failings of the *condottieri* were of a moral nature.
It was urged against them that they were not even effective fighting instruments; they were woefully inefficient in killing. They
would not spill blood when they could help it; they would make
prisoners of each other without striking a blow. Like members of
a modern labor union refusing to work overtime, they would attack
no fortifications at night; or if inside the fortifications, they would
not risk themselves by sallying out. In order to avoid hardship and
discomfort, they would not make winter campaigns; and in order
to allow room for their horses to maneuver, they would fight only
in certain favorable areas unencumbered by steep slopes, narrow
defiles, or boggy plains. The object of their fighting—like that of
chess players maneuvering pawns across a board—was to drive the
enemy into a position where he could not manipulate with ease.
Accordingly, battles came to be merely competitions for the favored situation, and there were few if any direct clashes; the side
which was outflanked would admit itself beaten, and felt it no
disgrace to surrender; and there are records of engagements which
lasted for so long as half a day without the loss of a man on either
side.

And so once more we see the spectacle of war not as a remorseless
duel, but as a game. The *condottieri*, we must remember, had little
incentive to kill one another. They were not fighting in hot blood,
beneath the spur of personal hatred, love of glory, infuriating propaganda, or national, racial, or religious prejudice. They had no
cause at stake, since they and their foes were battling for the same

ends; they might even have a friendly fellow feeling toward the
enemy, for possibly in the last campaign they had fought side by
side with their present rivals, and in the next campaign they might
nudge them again in comradely understanding. Besides, why
slaughter your adversaries when they were worth more alive? Each
prisoner might bring a ransom, in addition to having to forfeit his
horse and valuable armor; or he might be induced to enlist under
the standard of the victors, and so the battle might benefit one side
without damaging the other.

Still another reason for the indecisive battles was that the *condottieri* did not desire peace. If they slew all their enemies, the war
might end; and sooner than precipitate such a calamity, they would
engage indefinitely in their inconclusive skirmishes, so "making
work" and preserving their source of income.

One thing is particularly evident about the *condottieri* and other
medieval hired soldiers, as about the mercenaries of all time; their
existence implies not the presence but the absence of a fighting
spirit. They prove the absence of such a spirit not only in themselves, but in the public that would sooner entrust its fate to these
bought defenders than go forth themselves with the sword or pike.
If war-making had not been unpopular with the rank and file in the
late Middle Ages, the rank and file would have filled the columns
of the war-makers; but since militarism was unpopular, the mercenaries were employed as artificial means of counterbalancing
the naturally pacifistic tendencies of the people.

The attitude of the Italian populace—a matter of common historical record—has been aptly summarized:

Although the Italians could fight as well as anybody else when
their back was to the wall, they were not war-minded. In spite
of the chronic strife they believed with Leonardo that war is a
bestial insanity—*pazzia bestialissima*—and feared and distrusted soldiers on principle. One of the most engaging and impressive figures
of the Italian Renaissance art is the *Pax* in Lorenzetti's fresco of the
Buon Governo in the Palazza Pubblico of Siena; it was painted to
celebrate one of the rare moments "When the city, thanks to her
state of peace, enjoyed greatness and happiness and a bountiful
measure of good luck." [3]

It is true that most of the struggles in which the mercenary system originated—struggles such as those of the Guelfs and Ghibe-
lines, and of the various tyrants of the Italian city-states—did not

represent principles or purposes that would evoke great popular enthusiasm. But even when the cause of a beloved homeland was at stake, the people were quite willing to leave the fighting to mercenaries. The case comes to mind of Florence, whose hirelings on one occasion had not overcome a small, badly equipped Pisan army in four years of warfare. Yet when practical-minded Machiavelli suggested an armed force recruited from among the citizens, he was turned back with laughter. Should peace-loving and respectable citizens leave their trades and crafts, their arts, their professions, and their homes to wield arms which other men could be paid to handle for them?

II

A specialized fighting class of a different nature was developed among the Turks—an infantry force by which they made the beginnings of a standing army. Like the Romans and Spartans before them and like the Zulus of a later day, the Turks realized that the most docile and efficient fighters are those early trained in the cult of war. Accordingly, it was their custom to levy upon Christian village communities a tribute of boys from seven to ten years of age; these, chosen at the discretion of the sultan's emissaries, were to be exempted from the dread conscription only if their parents had embraced the faith of Islam. One of the objects of the system, in fact, was to extend Mohammedanism, for the fate of the captives was far from enviable. They were all reared in barracks; were subjected to a remorseless discipline; were educated in warfare and in the Moslem religion; and were trained to believe that their sole objects in existence were to give battle and spread the creed of the Prophet. All their early years were consecrated to these ends: he who faltered or disobeyed was condemned to be strangled; he who was tractable and quick to learn might expect to be rewarded. After ten years of apprenticeship, the youths were drafted into the corps of Janissaries; then, wedded to their swords, they were held to strict celibacy, while before them a bright prospect was perpetually flashed—the prospect of promotion out of the corps, of admission into the freedom and license of a native Turk, and even of elevation into the highest offices of the Ottoman state.

The effects of the system were curious. That it achieved its object will be apparent from the fact that the Janissaries won a dreaded name and gained some of the sultan's most decisive victories. But that it achieved more than its object is likewise evident. In the first place, the Janissaries, though Christian by birth, were so thoroughly tutored in a militant religious psychology that they are said to have surpassed the native Turks in their fanatical zeal to serve. And, in the second place, they created a soldier caste instilled with a combative spirit that tended toward the indefinite perpetuation of combat. They had been trained to fight and conquer; they knew no way of life except fighting and conquering; and like well-educated professionals in any line, they wished to preserve their vocation. Hence they were an inflammatory force, a spur to aggression, a deterrent to the ways of peaceful sultans, whom they had come to view with contempt.

It is not surprising that, like the Praetorian Guard in ancient Rome, the Janissaries became a sinister political force, masters of the State and threats to its stability. But it is significant that when in time they were permitted a wider, more normal range of activities—when they were allowed to marry and engage in trade—the war-making fervor deteriorated. Surely, this in itself indicates how their peculiar earlier training and indoctrination, the channeling of their minds in a single direction, had forced them toward the one available outlet.

At about the middle of the sixteenth century, under Suleiman I, the Janissaries numbered about twelve thousand. Not exactly a vast force, when one considers the standing armies of later days! Yet it was then unique; for with the exception of the comparatively small contingents in France and Spain, the only standing armies were comprised of the few hundred men in the bodyguards of kings.

England in the fourteenth century had had a revealing experience. In the hope of satisfying his dream of military glory and achieving the conquest of France, Edward III had raised professional armies; and, as a result, the spirit of professionalism had persisted of its own natural impetus. The soldiers, upon being discharged by the English monarch, sought service elsewhere; and those that could not find employment formed a disgruntled class of adventurers, anxious to occupy themselves on any pretext at the only trade they knew. It was this class that, augmented by foreign troops, composed the armies that devastated England during the following century in the futile conflicts of ruling houses, the Wars of the Roses. Those unhappy struggles, which smoldered for thirty years, were characterized by a curiously cold-blooded attitude bred of professionalism. The soldiers, as befits men whose vocation is bloodshed, went about the business of warfare as coolly and systematically as a merchant might go about the business of selling linen or lemons; wholesale executions were ordered, not in the heat and frenzy of conflict, but with planned and reasoned intent; and the troopers, obedient to the orders of their sovereign, would habitually strike down the nobles and let the common folk escape. Yet this clemency toward the poor people is to be explained by the fact that nothing could be gained by slaying an artisan or tradesman; whereas the lords were not only legitimate enemies, but had houses and estates that might be despoiled.

So once again we find a repetition of the old, old story: the bearer of the firebrand and sword is not the everyday citizen, but a man whose arm has been trained and whose mind has been drilled to the craft of havoc and killing, and who consequently views the rape of the countryside and the massacre of its inhabitants with the shoulder-shrugging nonchalance of the slaughterhouse worker paid to take the lives of sheep and cows.

Not less illuminating was the experience of France, when in the fifteenth century Charles VII made the innovation of creating a standing army, which he paid in times of peace to be ready in time of war. The feudal lords, to be sure, had had similar forces on a smaller scale; but the action of Charles signifies the first establishment in western Europe of a national standing army. The fighting quality of these regulars far surpassed that of the lawless bands of mercenaries whom Charles dismissed—and this, of course, was only to be expected, in accordance with the experience of the ages that men who have no business in life but fighting, men whose minds and bodies are trained for battle and who need look to no other source of support, make the most capable and efficient soldiers.

An incisive commentary regarding the army of Charles is to be found in a recent history of modern militarism:

. . . the situation was most difficult in France, at the end of the Hundred Years' War, after a century of strife between France and England, when the former was left with a multitude of warriors who did not remember peace and often had no homes to which they might return. The only way to overawe such hosts and persuade them to disarm and disperse seemed to be that suggested to Charles VII by a rich merchant, Jacques Coeur: to select a small, picked minority to chase away the rest, after they had been paid off with the money Coeur provided. Thus the nucleus of the first real standing army was formed.

The first standing army was thus, paradoxically, the outcome of the idea that armies should not be permanent. It arose as an institution to liquidate bothersome military groups seeking to perpetuate their existence by marauding.[4]

This seems to have been but one of many historical instances in which the remedy has proved worse than the disease. For the standing army, having come into existence, tended to fasten itself upon the community with the bloodsucking qualities of the leech; it was self-perpetuating, since its existence in one land created an excuse, a desire or an apparent need for its existence in neighboring countries. At the same time, it provided a means of livelihood and a place of esteem and honor for indigent noblemen, who, as we shall have occasion to note again, began to look upon it as their own property by a sort of vested right, and thereby propagated and enlarged not only armies but the wars without which armies cannot fulfill their purpose in being.

III

It is not only the men of the sword that have played a part in the history of war. Now and then a worker with the pen or quill has had a deeper, more enduring influence than the head of conquering hosts—an influence sometimes for good, but occasionally the reverse. One such writer, and one never absent from the world's consciousness since his death in 1527, is Niccolò Machiavelli. In his celebrated treatise *The Prince*, he laid down the laws of leadership as he saw them; he codified, in a sense, the principles and methods of the unscrupulous rulers that machinated in the Italy of his day, and gave something of the sanctity of authority to a ruthlessly cold-blooded and calculating expediency. Many men before Machiavelli had no doubt thought in the same terms as he; many, certainly, had acted according to the rules he laid down; but it remained for him to avow openly the desirability of methods that previously had been followed covertly and shamefacedly. To those who have closely observed Machiavelli's world, no less than the world of four centuries later, there will be nothing startling in his ideas: for example, that a prince should play the hypocrite with shrewd design; that he should break his promises whenever this suits his purposes; that it may be better for him to seem than to be merciful, courageous, and religious; that he should mouth the principles of justice and humanity while actually being as harsh as self-interest appears to demand. Nor is there anything novel in the famed Florentine's views as to the relationship of rulers and war:

A prince, then, is to have no other design, nor thought nor study but war and the arts and disciplines of it; for, indeed, that is the only profession worthy of a prince, and it is of so much importance that it not only preserves those who were born princes in their patrimonies, but advances men of private condition to that honorable degree.

Ambitious and unprincipled men for two thousand years and more have been acting in conformity with this prescription. But it was something to have given the unwritten law the sanctity of writing; there is a difference in impression and effect between an unspoken idea and one that has achieved the dignity of the published word; and Machiavelli, by his cynical frankness, appears to have given respectability to much that was known but not held quite respectable before. And so he bequeathed to the future a heritage of disastrous ideas: ideas that, in approving warfare for calculated and self-seeking ends, tended to perpetuate warfare for those same calculated and self-seeking ends. By declaring it legitimate for a sovereign to do whatever he wished for the sake of his sovereignty, regardless of abstract right, Machiavelli lent emphasis to the idea of autocracy, and gave encouragement to those warring rulers who preyed like a pestilence upon the early centuries of the modern era, and who, in their conflicts of political intrigue and personal ambition, showed an arrogant disregard of the welfare of their people. Stalking in the shadows behind many a later leader, we can see the shade of the celebrated Italian, the reflection of his methods, the image of his thought. We can observe it behind Louis XIV, and behind the possibly still more portentous figure of Frederick of Prussia; we can see it reproduced with frightening vividness in the thought and speech and the catastrophic opportunism of the author of *Mein Kampf*. And in the methods of certain other powerful modern rulers, though their professed allegiance is to Karl Marx, we can observe the phantom and the influence of Machiavelli, whether he has come to them first-hand or merely through example.

It is noteworthy that Machiavelli's ideal of the prince was Cesare Borgia, whom he had had a close opportunity to observe—Cesare Borgia, who, as the emissary of a corrupt father, His Holiness Pope Alexander VI, led the armies of the Church in wars that were anything but holy. Apparently not at all taken aback by the suspicion that had attached to him of murdering his brother and various other inconvenient personages, Cesare had embodied in practice the principles that Machiavelli expressed in words. He never, so far as we can observe, let hampering scruples stand in the way of his ambition; he did not hesitate to trump up charges of treachery when he found it to his advantage to invade coveted territory such as that of the unoffending Duchy of Urbino, and drive out its ruler; he was not above enriching himself by fees of thousands of ducats as well as various titles and investitures as a result of warfare allegedly for the benefit of the Pope. Yet this was the man of whom Machiavelli could say:

Upon serious examination, therefore, of the whole conduct of Duke Valentine, I see nothing to be reprehended; it seems rather proper to me to propose him, as I have done, as an example for the imitation of all such as by favour of fortune, or the supplies of other princes, have got into the saddle. . . .

Machiavelli recommends Cesare, obviously, not for moral reasons; moral considerations do not enter into his thought. He recommends him because his methods were calculated to succeed— that is to say, succeed in consummating his own ends. And there is no doubt that not a few later princes did try their best to follow Machiavelli's advice and imitate Cesare's example, though it would be hard to point to many statesmen whose methods were less fitted to preserve peace or further the popular welfare.

IV

Even before the time of Machiavelli, warfare had begun to be transformed by its most momentous innovation since the invention of the bow and arrow. One may doubt if the originators of gunpowder had much conception of its dread potentialities; it is, in fact, not even known for certain who the originators were, though credit has been variously given to the Chinese, the Syrians, and the Egyptians, as well as to Roger Bacon and the fourteenth-century German monk Berthold Schwartz. In any case, gunpowder did come to Europe some time during the fourteenth century, though at first it made but slow headway as a means of hurling projectiles. Despite several earlier uses of cannon, the first important application of the new invention was at the siege of Constantinople in 1453, when the Sultan Mohammed II constructed a monstrous but relatively ineffective instrument capable of hurling eight-hundred-pound rocks, and at the same time made use of fourteen batteries of smaller cannon that were all too effective in pounding breaches in the city walls.

Although men were slow in realizing it, an era had come to an end; the day of impregnable castles, and of knights who rode irresistibly in iron armor through the countryside, was closing forever. By the early sixteenth century the Swiss infantry, who for a while had been the terror of Europe, was undermined by the attacks of cannon, against whose flaming mouths they charged suicidally with their huge pikes. And though the guns were at first crude contraptions, so much so that for a long time it was held necessary for musketeers to be shielded by pikemen, the new weapons had definitely freed warfare from its medieval exclusiveness: thenceforth any commoner might be the equal of the knight or the noble, who previously had trotted forth in costly armor far beyond the means of the average citizen. And this meant that the number of potential combatants was vastly increased.

This meant, also, that war might be much deadlier than of old. It might be deadlier because of the more numerous participants, no less than because of the searing, shattering power of the new invention. But it is notable that the use of gunpowder—a discovery that was to spread flame and terror to later generations, and ruin countrysides and cities and take lives innumerable by means of land batteries and naval shells and air bombs—appeared to make no difference whatever in the basic attitude of mind of those who witnessed its introduction. Not that they did not see in it a tool to be utilized or an enemy to be deplored, but that their point of view toward conflict itself had not perceptibly changed. They did not raise an outcry, "War has now become so horrible, or threatens to become so horrible, that it must cease!" They did not exclaim, "We must not bequeath this grisly implement of death to our sons and our sons' sons!" They did not organize a world movement to outlaw the new weapons—or, more fundamental still, to outlaw war itself. True, as we shall see, various pacifistic-minded writers did exert an influence; in the seventeenth century, Hugo Grotius, Samuel Pufendorf, and other authors did work out a basis for international law, and try to establish a means for the settlement of disputes by peaceful negotiation. But the latter lived long after the day when gunpowder had first demonstrated its ruinous possibilities. And theirs were but the protests of a handful of humane and reasoning men.

The sad truth is that the coming of gunpowder showed, as previous innovations had also shown and future ones were to demonstrate time and again, that the addition of new frightfulness does not tend to end war. The addition of new frightfulness merely makes war more frightful. Human beings, taken as a whole, lack the imaginative capacity to visualize, appraise, or foresee terrors which they have not actually experienced. And those that do experience terrors are, for the most part, either stricken silent by them, or are cowed by the voice of authority or the power of example or by boastfulness and bravado, or else they forget after a time. And that is the chief reason why the introduction of gunpowder did not create a worldwide furor, or any significant change at all in men's attitude toward war.

One must remember, furthermore, that for a thousand years or longer men's minds had been trained in habits of fighting. There had been a peaceful interlude of about two centuries, when the *Pax Romana* had spread its beneficent wings over many lands; but ever since the empire's last tottering era the spectacle of warfare had been almost continuous. First the barbarian invasions, when the world order, once thought to be of imperishable granite, was seen to be crumbling into shreds; then the long succession of centuries, when barons in their castles and knights in their armor lorded it over the land; the private wars, and feuds of dukedoms and dynasties; the Crusades, waged at times not only against the infidel but against dissenting sects of Christians, and notably against the Albigenses and the flourishing culture of Provence; the battles against the Moors in Spain; the piratical raids of the Vikings, and the searing scourge of the Mongols; wars of territorial expropriation; wars of political and commercial rivalry between city-states; the dread Hundred Years' War, and encounters without number waged not only by feudal armies but by mercenaries and professionals of many stripes and species.

In view of the long period of unrest, during which the Church in the case of the Crusades and the temporal rulers in other cases had lent the strife their support and approval, how could the average man look on war otherwise than as the normal order of things, a necessity of nature—a curse from heaven, no doubt, but one that must be accepted along with other curses, such as drought and flood and fever. And the habit of accepting war, of believing war inevitable, would nourish an inhibition against protesting against war under any conceivable circumstances.

Therefore what when this diabolical new weapon, this gunpowder appeared—this force that could propel huge rocks to batter down walls, and batter out the brains of men? This too would be viewed as part of the accursed natural order, perhaps a thing to fear, but as far above the reach of protest as the summer lightning bolt. Even among the more educated and intelligent elements, and those most in a position to make their influence felt, the paralysis of old mental habits would freeze the tongue that might have cried out, and numb the hand that might have acted. And meanwhile the dragon intruder, the power that was so vastly to expand the cost and deadliness of combat, would become established so firmly that nothing could uproot it except a force strong enough to destroy its creator, war.

IV

The Rise of the Modern
Military Tradition

Chapter 18

The Other Side of the Screen

We have just observed a long period of confusion and warfare, and are about to consider another period of confusion and warfare that led toward the world of today. But before we continue the chronological thread of our discussion, let us glance at the other side of the screen.

In considering the psychology of war, we are in danger of overlooking or minimizing something quite as common, and quite as important: the psychology of peace. We see the conflicts of nations and dynasties, the clash of armies, the formation and dissolution of empires; and we tend to conclude that these clashes and conflicts tell the entire story. Actually, this is usually far from the case. A gun battle between gangsters may highlight the day's news stories of a great city; but it does not follow that gun battles are characteristic of the lives of its millions of inhabitants. And, in the same way, warfare even when exceptional may blaze its way into the consciousness of nations by its spectacular flare while undemonstrative anti-war movements are mostly lost to view.

It is impossible to know just how much unorganized opposition to war has smoldered throughout the ages: we can judge mainly from the resistance to military service, the desertions, the self-mutilations, the savage penalties for anti-militaristic acts, the resort to conscription and to mercenaries. All these factors tend to prove that millions in past generations have fought in about the way that a balky mule will pull a load: when driven to it. But few of the unknown and humble war-resisters have had any spokesman.

Nevertheless, now and then throughout the centuries some clear voice has called for peace. It is easily possible to overestimate the importance of such cries in the wilderness; doubtless in many cases, as I remarked of Grotius and Pufendorf in the last chapter, theirs have been but the protests of a handful of humane and reasoning men. Still, the protests of a handful of humane and reasoning men are never negligible; they may be indicative of greater, largely unvocal forces; they may bespeak an undertone of feeling that is general or even universal.

It may therefore repay us to fill out our picture with details of a few of the figures who, in late medieval and modern times, proclaimed their belief that peace was indeed a "pearl beyond price."

Among the earliest was Pierre Dubois, who is supposed to have died about 1312, but whose anti-war views did not see print until 1611. He was not exactly a model pacifist; being a faithful son of his own age, he advocated a crusade against the Turk, though for the good purpose of bringing peace to the Catholic powers. Having established this benign condition, they were not to fight again, but were to submit any disputes to the arbitration of the Pope, who would have the right to call international peace conferences.

A century and a half after Dubois' death, a rather similar scheme was worked out by King George Podiebrad of Bohemia and his envoy, the Frenchman Marini; they planned an international union in which disputes would be settled by arbitration, although again the vision of peace was somewhat sullied by a program for conquering the Holy Land. But again the idea of a peaceful union of Christian states is notable, and suggests an underlying discontent with current Christian feuds.

In the fifteenth and sixteenth centuries, various humanistic writers and philosophers were firm-spoken in the cause of peace. There was Rabelais, who believed that the nations should exhaust every amicable means before resorting to war; there was Montaigne, who placed duty to mankind above duty to a cause or country; there was Erasmus, who in his pamphlet on *The Complaint of Peace*, maintained that even an unjust peace was preferable to a so-called just war; there was Thomas More, who says of the people of his Utopia: "War or battle, as a thing very beastly . . . they do detest and abhor; and, contrary to the custom almost of all other nations, they count nothing so much against glory as glory gotten in war." [1] There was Alberico Gentili (1552–1608), who tried to establish principles of international law, appealing to the highest common sense of mankind to uphold the peace. There was Sully (1559–1641), the famous minister of Henry IV of France, who devised a scheme for peace based on the balance of power and the maintenance of nationality, but thought it necessary to engage in one last contest with Austria—a war to end war! And there was Emeric Crucé (1590–1648), who in some ways had the broadest and most humane peace plan of all, who attacked current ideas of glory, embraced all men without exception in his unifying project, and believed that war should be abolished forever.

In somewhat the same way, Hugo Grotius endeavored to develop a code of international law and find non-warlike methods for settling disputes, based upon principles of justice and morality; while his disciple Pufendorf, holding that the state of nature is a state of peace but that man must exert himself to preserve the state of nature, attempted to supplement and enlarge the theories of Grotius. It is noteworthy that, under Archbishop Philip von Schonburg of Mainz, a league of small Rhineland states was actually established in 1658 in pursuance of Grotius' doctrines, pledged to settle their disputes by peaceful means (an end unfortunately frustrated by the admission of militaristic France into the union).

Another powerful seventeenth-century influence was George Fox (1624–90), the founder of the Society of Friends, or Quakers. He too, like Grotius, was opposed to war, but his basis was religious; he took the simple position that war-making was contrary to the spirit of the Gospels.

Fox's most celebrated follower, William Penn, not only shared the usual Quaker views as to universal peace and brotherhood, but wrote an *Essay Toward the Present and Future Peace of Europe*, and strangely foreshadowed some of the schemes of our own day by advocating the formation of a European Diet, in which all nations should be represented in proportion to their importance, and which would make its decisions by a three-fourths majority, and, if necessary, enforce those decisions by armed might—a departure, to be sure, from strict non-belligerence, but a realistic attempt to put an end to the international chaos.

William Penn, as everyone knows, is conspicuous as a man who not only preached peace but acted in a peaceful way. His relations with the Indians are celebrated: he met them without swords or cannon, bullets or fortifications; and sent them, before coming to the future Pennsylvania, a letter whose sincerity is attested by his subsequent actions:

I have great love and regard toward you [he wrote among other things]; and desire to win your love and friendship, by a kind, just and peaceable life; and the people I send are of the same mind, and shall, in all things, behave themselves accordingly; and if in anything, any shall offend you, or your people, you shall have a speedy satisfaction for the same; that by no means you shall have just occasion of being offended against them.[2]

Voltaire, with his rapier manner, no doubt exaggerated when he remarked that Penn's treaty with the Indians was the only one which was never sworn to and never broken. Yet the agreement was carried out with such justice, and such equal treatment of red man and white that, while all the rest of the border was spouting crimson and few other colonists could consider themselves safe, never an Indian hand was deliberately lifted to take Quaker blood.

II

The late seventeenth and early eighteenth centuries, as we shall have occasion to observe, were periods of bitter European warfare, dominated by the dictatorial figure of Louis XIV. As in the case of most military autocrats from the day of the embattled Pharaohs, the praises of war and the war-maker were spoken by sycophantic court-followers, flattering court poets, and official reporters and story-tellers. Nevertheless, an abundance of anti-war sentiment was manifest even in the fire-hurling days of the most glorious of the French monarchs. Sometimes this is expressed obliquely, as in La Fontaine's fables of the lions and wolves that prey upon defenseless innocents; sometimes the references are less veiled, as in the case of La Bruyère, who sees the source of war and the consequent poverty of the masses in the ideas of glory, honor, riches, and territory entertained in the minds of the sovereigns. Even Boileau, though he can acclaim the King's contemporary triumphs, can go back to Alexander of Macedon and find in his hunger for conquest a sort of madness—an inconsistency that makes it not inconceivable that the poet was also the opportunist when it came to passing judgment on the powerful Louis. More notable in their anti-war sentiments are the views of the celebrated economist and army engineer Vauban, who characterized war as the offspring of self-interest and ambition, and the near-relative of all evil-brewing passions, and who believed in an approaching day when it would be no more than a grim memory.

In the works of the great writer Fénelon, one finds a direct attack upon the war-making methods of Louis XIV. This author calls attention to the waste of lives in needless conflicts in order that the King may embellish his court; with prophetic foresight, he warns of a possible revolt of the masses (even though he himself opposes revolutionary means); and he espouses the view of the brotherhood of man, maintaining that all wars are civil wars, and that he who takes up arms does so in order to strike at the members of his own family. Incidentally, he excoriates the seeker of glory: he who places glory above mankind is a "monster of pride."

Other peace advocates in France of the same general period were Cyrano de Bergerac, whose satirical tale of an expedition to the moon exposes the futility of man's fighting motives; Pierre Bayle, who speaks of the antiquity of wars for conquest, glory, profit, or religion; and the Abbé de Saint-Pierre, who pleaded for a Permanent League of European States, a veritable League of Nations, based upon the compulsory membership of all states, and designed to insure perpetual peace. Many ideas that have since become common—the idea of a World Court, and of an international armed force—were embodied in the Abbé's carefully thought-out project.

Various other anti-war schemes, including an Anonymous Peace Project of 1745, can be traced at least in part to the influence of the Abbé de Saint-Pierre. Doubtless he influenced also Ange Goudar (1720–91), who proposed to abolish war by means of international agreements for twenty-year truces (even though somewhat similar treaties among the city-states of ancient Greece had had no startling success). It is notable, however, that Goudar believed that war-making and peace-making are largely matters of habit, and thereby recognized the psychological forces at work.

A little before Goudar, the great English satirist Jonathan Swift had leveled the blasts of his mockery against the war-makers. He has Gulliver tell us, in all soberness, how an emperor of Lilliput, having had the misfortune to cut one of his fingers on the edge of an egg, published an edict "commanding all his subjects, upon great penalties, to break the smaller ends of their eggs. The people so highly resented this law, that our histories tell us that there have been six rebellions raised on that account; wherein one Emperor lost his life, and another his crown." [3]

After reporting the religious issues involved, and how no less than eleven thousand persons were computed to have suffered death "rather than submit to break their eggs at the smaller end," the author relates:

Now the Big-Endian exiles have found so much credit in the Emperor of Blefuscu's court, and so much private assistance and encouragement from their party here at home, that a bloody war hath been carried on between the two empires for six and thirty moons with various success; during which time we have lost forty capital ships, and a much greater number of smaller vessels, together with thirty thousand of our best seamen and soldiers; and the damage received by the enemy is reckoned somewhat greater than ours. However, they have now equipped a numerous fleet, and are just preparing to make a descent upon us. . . . [4]

Another Englishman, of a slightly later period, likewise attacked war with scourging irony. This was the poet Southey, whose *The Battle of Blenheim* has perhaps been better known to subsequent generations than the struggle it commemorates. The concluding stanza will indicate its flavor:

> And everybody praised the Duke
> Who this great fight did win.
> "But what good came of it at last?"
> Quoth little Peterkin.
> "Why that I cannot tell," said he,
> "But 'twas a famous victory."

In a less known and poetically less meritorious piece, *The March to Moscow*, Southey has displayed a similar irony. Here is the opening:

> The Emperor Nap he would set out
> For a summer excursion to Moscow.
> The fields were green and the sky was blue;
> Morbleu! Parbleu!
> What a pleasant excursion to Moscow!
>
> Four hundred thousand men and more,
> Heigh-ho for Moscow!
> There were marshals by dozens and dukes by the score,
> Princes a few and kings one or two,

While the fields are so green and the sky so blue,
  Morbleu! Parbleu!
What a pleasant excursion to Moscow!

A more direct attack on wars and war-makers occurs in the blank verse of Shelley:

War is the statesman's game, the priest's delight,
The lawyer's jest, the hired assassin's trade,
And to those royal murderers whose mean thrones
Are bought by crimes of treachery and gore,
The bread they eat, the staff on which they lean.
Guards, garbed in blood-red livery, surround
Their palaces, participate the crimes
That force defends, and from a nation's rage
Secure the crown . . . [5]

Pope can write, in one of his *Imitations of Horace:*

                . . . Let Jove encrust
Swords, pikes and guns, with everlasting rust!

And Wordsworth, in the sonnet *1801* on the subject of Bonaparte, can declare:

'Tis not in battle that from youth we train
The Governor who must be wise and good.

But more positive and better known is the vision expressed by Tennyson in *Locksley Hall:*

Till the war-drums throbb'd no longer, and the
  battle-flags were furled
In the Parliament of man, the Federation of the
  world.

Regardless of these examples and others that might be offered, the English poets on the whole do not lift a strong voice against the militarists. Either they say nothing at all on the subject, or they shout with Tennyson himself, "When shall their glory fade? . . . Honor the light brigade," or they exclaim with Scott of patriotism and "One crowded hour of glorious life," or like Campbell they "Sing the glorious day's renown," or speak with Collins of how "Honour comes, a pilgrim grey, To bless the turf that wraps their clay." Thus often the poets have stimulated the war spirit, or at least that love of glory which is one of the props of the war spirit. And the prose writers of England, despite outcries by Hume and Blackstone and others, have as a group been less vocal than those of France in their anti-war protestations—perhaps for the reason that for centuries, and in spite of civil war and the recurrent threat of invasion, the reality of conflict was much more remote from the ordinary Britisher than from the average Continental. Let us therefore return to that more fertile breeding-place of the peace movement, France.

III

In the writings of Montesquieu we find reference to the "sickness" which had infected the European princes, inducing them to keep inordinately large armed forces. The disease being contagious, the malady spread from nation to nation, while the name of peace was given to the "general effort of all against all." In other words, Montesquieu condemns, as Fénelon had done before him, the competition in armaments, whose end results are greater armaments, and greater and earlier wars. Even so, Montesquieu was by no means a thoroughgoing pacifist; he justified wars to repulse aggression, or to aid an ally in repulsing aggression; and he supported the idea of "preventive war," conducted to check the growth of a threatening neighbor—a view fiercely rebutted by Voltaire.

The latter, prominent in the campaign against war as for human liberties in general, expresses himself eloquently. In *Micromegas* he refers to "those sedentary and slothful barbarians, who, from their palaces, give orders for murdering a million of men and then solemnly thank God for their success." [6] In *The Princess of Babylon*, with equally incisive bitterness, he reports that "the men, who were unhappily possessed of power, sent out legions of murderers to ravage unknown countries, and to water with the blood of their children the inheritance of their fathers. Those assassins were called heroes, and their robberies accounted glorious achievements." [7] And in *Candide*, after telling how the protagonist was kidnapped into the army of the Bulgarians, and after describing the "gallant," "spruce," and "brilliant" embattled arrays, he depicts the glorious reality with an unsparing pen:

He passed over heaps of dead and dying, and first reached a neighboring village; it was in cinders, it was an Abara village which the
Bulgarians had burnt according to the laws of war. Here, old men
covered with wounds, beheld their wives, hugging their children
to their bloody breasts, massacred before their faces; there, their
daughters, disembowelled and breathing their last after having satisfied the natural wants of Bulgarian heroes; while others, half
burned in the flames, begged to be dispatched.[8]

Another convinced anti-militarist was Diderot, who maintained
that war was not a part of nature, and indeed was no more natural
in human society than was disease in the human body; he attributed most conflicts to the weakness or glory-lust of kings. Still
another philosopher of the same period who appealed against warfare was the Marquis de Condorcet; he not only believed that war
and civilization could not be reconciled, but advocated the positive
preventive measure of a World Court. And Baron d'Holbach,
otherwise noted for his mechanistic philosophy, condemned wars
for conquest and colonies, contended that just wars were exceedingly rare, and declared that even a defensive war against a treaty-
breaking enemy may not always be just.

A more conspicuous figure was Rousseau, the center of a whole
group of forward-looking writers who had faith in the fellowship
of man, and held that devotion to one's own country did not imply
a desire to rob one's neighbor. Like Pufendorf and Montesquieu,
he believed that man in a state of nature is a peaceful animal; and
like various thinkers before him and since, he was convinced that
the road away from war lay in the formation of a union of states.
And while acknowledging that it was proper to fight in defense
of one's liberties, he preached a creed of humanity, and of consideration to enemy populations. His influence is to be seen in
measures taken by the National Assembly, such as the projected
Code of Twenty-One Articles of the Abbé Grégoire, which takes
cognizance of the duties owed by nations toward their fellow nations, and condemns offensive war as an outrage against the human
race.

It was symptomatic of the spirit of the times that in 1782 a new
anonymous *Peace Plan* appeared—calling for a union of states dominated by the more powerful nations. And yet another peace project, issued anonymously but written by Palier de Saint-Germain,
was published before the outbreak of the Revolution. His scheme

envisaged a union of European states, with a Council or High Tribunal that would be a court of last appeal in disagreements among the nations and would have the support of an international army provided by the member nations.

A little later, even after the storm of the Revolution had descended, an enthusiastic call for peace was heard in the voice of a man christened Jean Baptiste, who had changed his name to Anacharsis Clootz—an aristocrat, a revolutionary, and a destined victim of the Terror. He propounded the idea of a Universal Republic, dominated by an everlasting Constitution. This commonwealth was to embrace men of all races and creeds; its official language was to be French; and the first step toward its establishment might be made by voluntarily extending the boundaries of France to nations desirous of admission. Ultimately, according to this most wide-ranging of eighteenth-century projects, the entire world was to be drawn into the Republic's orbit.

All the above, of course, is meant as no more than a partial résumé. The discussion does not even attempt to take account of many notable figures in the peace movement, such as the English Prime Minister Robert Walpole and Lord Stanhope and the French Cardinal Fleury; nor does it seek to cover many of the writers, such as Jeremy Bentham and the Quaker advocate of a European State, John Bellers, and the German poet-philosopher J. G. Herder, and philosophers such as Fichte and Kant. The fact is that anything approaching a thorough coverage of the peace-making or peace-coveting forces would require not a separate chapter, but a separate book. The above, however, will suffice to show that the will to peace and the desire for peace did exist; in the voices of the figures mentioned above, and of others like them, we hear merely the isolated shouts that happen to have become audible above the mumbling and murmuring of the masses. But we have reason to believe that those shouts have expressed the will of millions. In the peace movement as in all other great movements, it is the few that speak for myriads who must remain forever mute. And those few tell of a great yearning for peace, an aspiration for peace, at times even a passion for peace, which not all the crashing of swords and the clattering of musketry can wholly drown. Although we know that strife has continued despite all the protesting cries, we also know that wars, being matters of the strong arm, can be made and have been made by small organized groups; while beneath all, in a solemn undertone, only occasionally rising to clear expression in the eloquence of some forward-looking spokesman, the pleading and muttering of the peace-craving multitudes ceaselessly continue.

Chapter 19

Modern Wars of Religion

To the student of the history of war, there should be nothing surprising in the religious conflicts that flamed up throughout Europe in the sixteenth and seventeenth centuries. Religious beliefs and practices, as we have seen, are among the earliest sources of war; and in some form or other they tend to inspire strife even with the advance of civilization. We have observed the religious element in the wars of the Aztecs, the Vikings, the Moslems, the Crusaders; and we might go on to note the many phases of religious warfare that mark the Middle Ages. The campaigns against the medieval heretics, including the persecution of the Cathari as far back as 1017 and the subsequent imprisonment, torture, and burning of thousands of Waldenses for the crime of seeking their own road to spiritual fulfillment, were in effect forms of warfare, even though they lacked the benefit of organized sword-battalions. They were, moreover, forms of warfare traceable solely to a psychological persuasion: the persuasion that heresy was the unforgivable offense, the supreme sin against God. That heretics were not necessarily low characters, of which society had to be rid in self-protection, is indicated by the statement of an inquisitor:

Heretics are recognized by their customs and speech, for they are modest and well regulated. They take no pride in their garments, which are neither costly nor vile. They do not engage in trade, to avoid lies and oaths and frauds, but live by their labor as mechanics —their teachers are cobblers. They do not accumulate wealth, but are content with necessaries. They are chaste and temperate in meat and drink. . . . [1]

Judging by this description, one would say that heretics were the very kind of men and women that a sturdy, self-respecting society would want to encourage. Yet these persons were everywhere condemned, were treated ruthlessly, as Lea declares, by "men of the kindliest tempers, the profoundest intelligence, the noblest aspirations, the purest zeal for righteousness, professing a religion founded on love and charity. . . . Dominic and Francis, Bonaventura and Thomas Aquinas, Innocent III and St. Louis, were types, in several ways, of which humanity, in any age, might feel proud, and yet they were as unsparing of the heretic as Ezzelin de Romano was of his enemies. With such men it was not hope of gain or lust of blood or pride of opinion or wanton exercise of power, but sense of duty, and they but represented what was universal public opinion from the thirteenth to the seventeenth century." [2]

I present these facts not merely for the sake of a medieval flash-back. I present them because they are essential for an understanding of the psychological background of the religious wars. When we deal with the late Middle Ages and the early modern period, we treat an era that had worked itself into a psychosis in regard to the heretic. It was an era that had turned the heretic into a bugaboo, a thing of horror, unapproachable by reason, and arousing all the tremors and shudders that witches, vampires, were-wolves, dragons, and other such nightmarish creatures have awakened in the minds of chilled believers. Being scarcely regarded as human, the heretic would be subject to the most inhuman treat-ment—all the more so as the age was one in which military practice had made cruelty a commonplace, and in which human suffer-ing was often shrugged away with a callous nonchalance. But if heretics individually were regarded as monsters on two legs, what when the diabolical beings were banded together to form whole sects? What when a Calvin or a Luther arose, and enlisted his sacrilegious followers to defy the Church and menace the everlast-ing order of things? Would this not kindle the heretic-hater to tumults of fear and paroxysms of rage? Would it not make him rise, and if necessary seize arms and march forth to exterminate the abomination? Particularly when he was goaded by his priests, spurred by his princes and barons, and inflamed by the example of all the countryside, would he not be ready to make an end of heresy?

II

Although the full blaze of the religious wars was not lighted until the sixteenth century, something more than a meager be-ginning had been made in the fifteenth. Immediately after the burning of the religious reformer John Huss in 1413, the followers of the martyred leader burst out with revolutionary violence in a series of riots and wars. In 1419 a large part of Prague was destroyed in a battle between the Hussites and the mercenaries of Queen Sophia of Bohemia; and subsequently the Hussites conquered most of Bohemia, and even invaded Moravia and Germany. But while at first inspired by a fierce religious sentiment, they became divided by internal dissensions; and the fighting force, originally almost one hundred per cent Bohemian, came to include aliens and mercenaries, and took on the qualities of a professional army. Meanwhile the Pope, declaring successive crusades against the rebels, emphasized the religious nature of the struggle; a great number of Crusaders, under the Margrave Frederick of Brandenburg, actually crossed the Bohemian borders in 1431, although they fled ignominiously upon the approach of the Hussites under Prokop the Great.

In many ways, the rise of the Hussites takes its place beside the late medieval peasant revolts of England, France, and other parts of Europe. Religion and property walked hand in hand among the causes; Huss had preached that worldly possessions by the Church and its representatives were contrary to biblical injunction; all Church lands should be returned to their former owners. None but the true believers, Huss thought, had any right to property—a doctrine which, naturally, was popular with the believers, particularly those that were without possessions and were devoutly willing to share with all that had. Peasants and artisans, fired both with religious zeal and zeal for the redistribution of other people's wealth, went forth in armies that regarded themselves as the chosen of God. With curses against believers who would not "bathe and sanctify" their hands in the blood of the enemies of Christ, they gave themselves to their pious work of persecuting, scourging, beheading, drowning, and burning the godless, regardless of rank or sex. And having sacked and fired cloisters, made ashes of libraries and works of art, and murdered priests and monks, they completed the sacred task by annexing such property of the unbelievers as they had not committed to the flames.

In the deeds and precedent of the Hussites, the communistic principles that stimulated them, and their mixture of religious fanaticism and rage at genuine wrongs, we find the background of the greater Social Revolution that erupted in Germany in 1525. This insurrection, like its Bohemian predecessor, was kindled, one might say infuriated, by a religious element; yet it was partly economic in origin, since the poor had been suffering oppression at the hands of the well-to-do, the working classes had been exploited by means of financial trickery and exorbitant profits, combinations in restraint of trade had been formed to create artificial scarcities and keep prices high, and the laboring masses in the towns had been gradually driven toward destitution. At the same time, the peasants had been grumbling against their burdensome tithes, taxes, dues, and rents. And the proletariat in general had been angered and made jealous by the sight of the material indulgences and lavish display of the rich; with the result that they were a receptive audience when agitators urged them to plunge their hands into rich men's coffers—particularly as this sharing was to be a strictly religious observance, a manifestation of Christian brotherhood and charity.

Actually, it was not difficult for many of the peasants to convince themselves—evidently not insincerely, and by a logic not without later analogies—that they did deserve whatever they could take. Since all were equal before God, and the Holy Scriptures ruled out distinctions in class and property, were they not merely carrying out the will of the Most High in looting the wealth of the nobles? What, indeed, was their plundering but a form of piety?

Despite the economic and social features of the outbreak, it has been held that the religious leader Martin Luther was partially if indirectly responsible. For Luther had urged the Germans to strike out at the Church authorities, seize the Church lands, and end the financial tyranny. And the Germans were not reluctant to listen, nor hesitant about combining anti-clericism with economic aspirations. The demands of the peasants, as embodied in their Twelve Articles, would seem reasonable enough today: they include requests for such things as the reform of the clergy and nobility so as to reduce oppression, the readjustment of taxation, the establishment of a uniform coinage, and the elimination of crushing monopolies. But though their objectives on the whole may have been justifiable, they soon yielded to the temptation of most revolutionaries, and leaped to extremes. And after they had attacked not only the Catholic leaders but even Lutheran lords, they aroused the antagonism of Luther, who perceived a peril to the new religion, and, joining the forces of exploitation and repression, counselled the princes to stamp out revolt. "Whoever can should smite, strangle, or stab, secretly or publicly." [3]

But despite Luther's violent about-face, his share in inciting the disturbances remains:

Had Luther and his followers never appeared on the scene, the spirit of discontent and insubordination . . . would still have produced fresh tumult and sedition in the towns and provinces. But it was the special condition of things brought about—or rather developed—by the religious disturbances, which gave this revolution its characteristics of universality and inhuman atrocity.[4]

After the first outbursts, "the work of inflaming the populace by religious preaching was developed into a regular trade. The stormers and ranters who, in Christian phraseology and with lavish use of Biblical texts, proclaimed the gospel of hatred and envy, gathered round them, year after year, a larger concourse of the frenzied masses." [5]

The state of mind of Luther himself may be of interest. In his youth, he had declared that he felt "he might even have become a hideous murderer for the sake of religion. . . . 'I should have been ready to kill any one and every one for daring to refuse obedience to one syllable from the Pope.' . . . 'I implore you,' he wrote to Apalatin in February 1520, 'if you rightly understand the gospel, do not imagine that its cause can be furthered without tumult, distress, and uproar. . . . The word of God is a sword, is warfare, is destruction. . . .'" [6]

Warfare and destruction are to be expected of the followers of such a creed. But the specifically religious ingredients in the strife, the religious preoccupation of the agitators in the Social Revolution, is shown by the frequency with which they aimed their wrath at religious objects and personages. Their offenses were innumerable: for example, "In July 1524 there was a tumultuous rising in the Thurgau; some 5,000 of the common people fell upon the Carthusian monastery of Iltegen, near Fraunfeld, plundered it, burnt it to the ground, and pillaged the houses of the priests who dwelt around." [7] And, again, "On March 19, 6,000 rebels of the Mindel and Kamachthal organized the notoriously ill-famed 'red gangs.' On March 26 the Baltringers and the Allgauers began the plunder of churches, cloisters and castles." [8] And, once more, "This general reign of terror was taken advantage of by the new religionists in Strassbourg for an iconoclastic riot on behalf of the Gospel. The insurgent peasants also considered themselves so deeply versed in the knowledge of the true Gospel that they challenged abbots and priests to a public disputation at their headquarters, with the accompanying threat to visit with chastisement all cloisters that did not send representatives." [9]

At the same time, we learn of cathedrals battered to earth, altars and images destroyed, priests' vestments and books looted and carried away, sacred images broken or decapitated, and baptismal fonts emptied; while grain supplies were plundered, cattle and sheep were slain, villages and cloisters burned, and knights and nobles speared to death.

Amid all this looting and ravaging, a deeply religious spirit continued to move the rebels. How the pious emotions of the fighters were inflamed will be evident from a speech of Thomas Munzer, one of the leaders of the revolt:

. . . Strike, strike, strike! while the iron's hot. Keep your swords warm with the blood of tyrants. It is not possible, while they live, that you should be freed from the fear of man. One cannot speak to you of God, while they rule over you. Strike, strike, strike! while it is still day. God goes before you; do you follow? The history is written in the twenty-fourth chapter of St. Matthew. Let not yourself therefore be intimidated, God the Lord is with you. It is the Lord's battle not yours; it is you who are fighting. Quit yourselves verily like men, and you will have the Lord for your helper. When Jehosaphat heard these words, he fell upon the ground. Therefore, strike with God's help, who will strengthen you, without fear of man, for the true faith. Amen. [10]

Evidently the words took effect; evidently there were many who wished to have the Lord for their helper. Even while Munzer was speaking, his associate Pfeiffer and his host were in a neighboring district, "striking" as the leader had commanded. But perhaps, if you had asked them, they would have said that it was not they but "God the Lord" who was wielding the faggot and sword. It was "God the Lord" that was spreading himself over the country, robbing, burning, and murdering; storming castles, sacking cloisters, setting fire to villages, and forcibly enlisting all the inhabitants who preferred not to feel a spear-point through their vitals.

As the result of the Social Revolution, no permanent good was accomplished—none whatever. The condition of the poor, after the brutal suppression of the revolt by torturings, beheadings, maimings, and blindings, was not ameliorated; the pre-existing evils still existed, although in even more pronounced form. But hundreds of villages lay in ashes, more than a thousand cloisters and castles were cinders and rubble, fields lay unplowed and stripped of farming implements and farm animals, and the wives and children of an estimated hundred thousand slain peasants had been pauperized. And all this, if it was not the outcome of the "Lord's battle," was the fruit of what was called and undoubtedly believed to be the "Lord's battle."

III

Even before the day of the German Social Revolution, religious warfare had been crackling in Spain. It is not at all strange, in view of the long record of human fanaticism, that this strife had been aimed at one of the most advanced and cultured peoples of the age; the Moors had stood at the forefront of European civilization at a time when most of the nations were barely awakening. Nevertheless, they had to be eliminated—and this not because of any pressing material necessity, but because they were infidels; because the cause of the Almighty would be served by the destruction of infidels. Ferdinand and Isabella—and particularly Isabella—were motivated not so much by the need or desire for conquest as by a religious frenzy. The facts have been summarized by Prescott:

Isabella may be regarded as the soul of this war. She engaged in it with the most exalted views, less to acquire territory than to re-establish the empire of the Cross over the ancient domain of Christendom. On this point, she concentrated all the energies of her powerful mind, never suffering herself to be diverted by any subordinate interest from this one great and glorious object.[11]

In other words, the war against the Moors was a form of Crusade, differing little if at all in essential spirit from the Crusades of the Middle Ages.

As a matter of fact, the crusading mood is visible throughout all this period of Spanish history. It is to be seen in the fervor with which Ferdinand and Isabella clamped the Inquisition down upon the country, so enabling them to bring those worthy tools, the rack and the stake, against any of their subjects who had the unhappiness to deviate from the faith. And it is to be observed in actual movements, during the sixteenth century, to conduct crusades against the Eastern infidel. In a sense, a crusade against the Moriscos (or converted Moors) was launched under the Emperor Charles V and his son Philip II. The former in 1526 issued an edict forbidding the use of Arabic, requiring all Moriscos to learn Castilian within three years (but making no provision to teach them), prohibiting the use of Moorish names, dress, or ornaments, invalidating all contracts in Arabic, and ordering the destruction of all public and private baths. And in 1568—forty-nine years before the eventual brutal expulsion of the Moors—Philip issued a still more drastic edict. He imposed upon the Moriscos the supreme indignity of requiring them to surrender their children to be educated by Christian priests; as a result of which a rebellion flared in Granada, and was suppressed with the utmost cruelty by the King, who proclaimed a war of "fire and blood" and gave his army the right to supplement their battle for Christendom by plundering on their own account. And as if this were not sufficient inducement to the God-loving enthusiasts, he materially increased their pay.

As for Philip himself—his motives were those of the true Crusader, the loyal upholder of the faith. The entire record of his leadership makes it reasonable to accept Roger Bigelow Merriman's summary of his motives:

Philip's conception of himself as the true head of Christendom demanded some striking demonstration of his worthiness to champion the cause of the Cross.[12]

Both Charles and Philip, when matters of religion were at issue, were without any profane regard for the ultimate practical welfare of their dominions. The fact is that, though both at times were moved by powerful political considerations, the State in their minds was second in importance to the Church, the Netherlands and Spain were of less consequence than Christendom. In the persecution and expulsion of the Moors, as in Ferdinand and Isabella's exclusion of the Jews, the Spanish sovereigns uprooted an intelligent, industrious, and capable people without whom the country was incalculably poorer—a people whose loss has been cited by historians as a leading cause of the subsequent decline of Spain. But they showed no sign at all of ruing the damage. Perhaps Charles and Philip, like Ferdinand and Isabella, had no inkling of the body blow they were delivering to the country; yet in view of the fanaticism that made them see infidels and heretics as veritable devils in human form, it is unlikely that they would have acted more sagely even had some wise preceptor acquainted them with all that historians now know.

Consider, first of all, the case of Charles. What were the objects that kept this monarch scurrying from corner to corner of his wide-flung domains, fighting to defend the faith, and exhausting his own energies, so that at the age of fifty-six he retired to a monastery, a worn-out old man? One cannot but agree that the episodes of his career "make clear how little Spain's true interests were concerned with those ambitions for which she shed her blood and wasted her treasure." [13]

What benefit did she get from holding the Netherlands, or subjugating Milan? What salvation did she win by leading the cause of the old ecclesiastical order in its bitter struggle with the Reformation? . . . those who are not sure what or where religious truth may be, who fix their eyes on the pages of economic history, see in these magnificent but vain efforts a mere prodigal waste of men and money that inevitably brought about the national decline of later centuries.[14]

This, of course, is a modern uttering a modern point of view. Charles did not share the twentieth-century uncertainties as to religious truth; probably he would have been horrified at the suggestion that he was not a complete master of religious truth. And as for "the pages of economic history"—those are the preoccupation of a later age; there is no more reason to suppose that Charles gave them a thought than to imagine that the North Korean invasion of South Korea or our own counter-invasion were made for ecclesiastical purposes. The man who could introduce the Inquisition into the Netherlands, at the estimated cost of thirty thousand lives and of immense smoldering opposition; the man who could provoke deliberate war in Germany, aiming an attack against such powerful leaders of the Lutheran cause as John Frederick of Saxony and Philip of Hesse (though he called their crime disobedience, and not heresy), was not the man to be governed by mere mundane economic considerations.

But whatever may be said of Charles, his fanaticism does not strike one as so extreme as that of his son Philip. Some of the wars of Philip appear to have been inherited from his father, as we have seen in the case of the Moriscos, in which he outdid his predecessor in pious savagery. But his remote and implacable figure, as in-human-seeming and remorseless as one of his own Inquisitors, gave to his deeds in war and peace the complexion of his own peculiar ideas. An often repeated story—that, upon hearing of the massacre of St. Bartholomew, Philip laughed for the only time in his life—may have no more basis in fact than the tale of Nero's fiddling while Rome burned. Yet this report is certainly not inconsistent with what we know of Philip's character. It is not inconsistent—to take one minor episode, but one that floodlights him in a glare as of full day—with his nature as revealed in his dealings with the French in America.

Under Jean Ribault, a colony of Huguenots had settled at the mouth of the St. John's River in Florida, where they could hardly have been more of a menace to Philip than if entrenched in the wastes of Baffin Land. True, the French were in technical violation of the celebrated Bull of Pope Alexander VI (the infamous Rodrigo Borgia), who partitioned the world between the Spaniards and Portuguese with a noble disregard of little matters such as the claims of other nations and the rights of the natives. But it is questionable whether the theoretical infraction of Spanish sovereignty was half so important in Philip's mind as that the settlers had forsaken the true faith. There was for him no question of "live and let live"; he dispatched one Pedro Menendez against the colonists; and Menendez took their fort and hanged two hundred and thirty of the dissenters. His reason, given with unabashed clarity in a letter to the King, was that the settlers had built the fort "without your Majesty's permission and . . . were scattering their odious Lutheran doctrines in these provinces." [15]

The spirit of the commander, and inferentially of his sovereign, is further illustrated by his treatment of some escaped Huguenots who had offered to surrender if their lives were spared. Their offer was accepted; then they were bound and stabbed to death, Menendez "deeming that to punish them in this manner would be serving God, our Lord, and your Majesty. Hereafter they will leave us free to plant the Gospel and enlighten the natives." [16]

It may be noted parenthetically that the incident had a sequel, when the French adventurer Dominique de Gorgues bore down upon the Spaniards, and put them all to the sword except for a few who were reserved for hanging, while the Spanish inscription for their victims, "Not as to Frenchmen, but as to Lutherans," was replaced by a new legend, "Not as to Spaniards, but as to Traitors, Robbers, and Murderers." And thus religious zeal gave birth to blood vengeance.

However, it is safe to say that no qualm disturbed the serene conscience of Philip. To slay heretics was not, to his mind, like killing men; it was more like hunting man-eating beasts. His outlook, through training and inclination and by the precept and example of his age, had been so conditioned that it was no easier for him to look upon a dissenter from the faith with reason, mercy, or justice than for some modern legislators to regard an alleged Communist sympathizer with a clear-seeing compassion.

The religious incentive, furthermore, is to be seen in his wars against the Turks and against the Mohammedans of North Africa, no less than in the Invincible Armada with which he thought to conquer Protestant England (even though, in all these cases, there were also the provocations of raids upon Spanish shipping). But perhaps the most notable example of Philip's religious war-making occurred in the Netherlands. There is no reason to suppose that he originally thought he was marching into battle; rather, he was doing his conscientious best for the faith, which was menaced by the recalcitrance of thousands of Rome-defying blasphemers. What he was attempting was not war, it was not even persecution; it was merely an effort to put down heresy, and bring the guilty back into the fold. That the result would be revolution, and the eventual loss of the Netherlands, was probably as far from Philip's mind as was the American Revolution and the loss of the colonies from the mind of George III when he attempted his own far less severe repressions.

It is evident that Philip, a Spaniard born and bred, did not understand the people of the Low Countries; if he had understood them, he would not have supposed that they could be controlled by his brutalities. He would not, for example, have appointed the infamous Duke of Alva, who marched on the Netherlands with a force of ten thousand men; nor would he have authorized the establishment of the "Council of Troubles" of 1567, a tribunal of seven which was dominated by its Spanish members, and dealt out executions by the wholesale (thus on January 4, 1568, eighty-four persons were put to death; on February 20 and 21, another hundred and eight; and on the following March 15, an additional fifty-five).

"If necessary, I will send sixty thousand men to the stake," Philip is reported to have said. Apparently he had not learned that one cannot rule ideas with the rod and the faggot. And that was why his attitude was uncompromising: "Though I should lose the Netherlands, I will not yield one jot or tittle in matters of the Holy Catholic faith." And that also was why, on February 16, 1568, he permitted a prescription which, for sheer monstrous inhumanity, may be compared with Hitler's attempt to exterminate all the Jews of Europe.

It is true that the enactment of 1568 was subsequently modified, after thousands had fled the country and other thousands had been burned, imprisoned, hanged, or impoverished; amnesty was granted to all who could prove they had committed no offense and who asked pardon within a prescribed period (pardon for what, one is tempted profanely to ask, if they had committed no offense?). But such relative mildness cannot disguise the ferocious original intention.

One must admit that, as in most revolutions, there were complicating factors behind the revolt of the Netherlands. A powerful ingredient was the Spanish-imposed sales tax—a tax of five per cent on all real estate, and ten per cent on all movable property; a tax which, tripled and quadrupled and more than quadrupled in some cases before the items reached the consumer, was like a straitjacket around the body of trade. Yet even from the religious point of view, the provocation was not exclusively on the Spanish side. Not all the Calvinists were models of propriety, sanity, and sweet good-fellowship; there were fanatics among them; their preaching in some cases was wild and inflammatory, and calculated to stir up riots. And in those riots, as in the German Social Revolution several decades before, the special targets were the churches, whose images and altars were pulled down and whose painted windows and pictures were smashed. It is unquestionable that this Dutch violence was in one sense a reaction to Spanish violence, but in another and deeper sense it was the fruit of the local religious ideas, which were opposed to the religious ideas of the invaders. And while the underlying cause of the disturbances was undoubtedly the Spanish repression, it would be misleading to seek the explanation in a single set of religious views; the explanation, rather, is to be found in two sets of religious views, which clashed like lance clattering against lance. Two groups of believers, each convinced

that they were on the side of holiness, each certain that they were
serving God, stood forth in fiery opposition; and not being subject to logical persuasion, they had to call on that impartial judge
of doctrines, the sword. Had Philip not been an inflexible Catholic,
who felt a sacred duty to drive Protestantism from the earth, the
warfare in the Netherlands would not have occurred; but had there
been no Protestants willing to assert their beliefs in the face of
peril and oppression, there might have been smoldering discontent,
but open conflict would have been unlikely.

IV

During the same general period when Philip was clashing with
the Netherlanders, a series of wars of religion was being waged in
France. While necessarily different in detail, these were similar in
mood and spirit to the persecutions in the Low Countries. Thus
the Edict of Compiègne of July 24, 1557, though it preceded the
savage repressions of Philip and the Duke of Alva by about a
decade, was true to the principles of those gallant champions of
the faith. Its authors, like the Spanish sovereign, did not favor
halfway measures; the penalty of death, and nothing less, was to
be inflicted on anyone who in public or in private embraced any
creed other than orthodox Catholicism. The document, as is usual
with such offerings, was the work of confident collaborators of
the Most High; the preamble mentions "us alone who have received from the hand of God the administration of the public
affairs of the realm."

This edict, however, was apparently not deemed severe enough.
In November, 1559, a new enactment not only ordered the death
of all who went to Protestant assemblies, but prescribed that their
houses should be pulled down, and never rebuilt. Under pain of
the same dire penalties, all persons who knew of Protestant gather-
ings might be called upon to testify; but tattling was not to go un-
rewarded; for betraying his coreligionists the informer was to
be pardoned and given five hundred livres. In Paris meantime the
commissaires des quartiers were to conduct house searches;
throughout the country, curés and vicars were to excommunicate
all who knew of Protestant activities without reporting them;
while in Lorraine images of the Virgin were set up at street cor-
ners, and those who did not kneel and bow were arrested.

It is an indication of the passion of the times that, in response to these and other measures of repression, the Protestants assassinated Minard, vice-president of the Grand Chamber of the Parlement of France. And an incident of the year 1562 further suggests the spirit of the day. On March 1 the Duke of Guise was passing through the city of Vasey; and in a barn on the outskirts he saw a Huguenot congregation at worship. Whether they committed any overt act of provocation is not known; but it is known that, at the sight of the sacrilegious spectacle, the nobleman and his followers fell upon the Huguenots, and ended their day's worship of God by sending them to meet their God.

As in Spain and indeed everywhere in contemporary Europe, the religious motive was interwoven with the political. For men had not yet conceived the idea of the separateness of Church and State, nor did it apparently occur to them that a blow at the doctrines of the former was not necessarily a stroke against the laws and security of the latter. And because religious and political beliefs formed part of a single body of ideas, religious war was the stepping-stone to political war; "the issue of religion raised by the Huguenots," as one historian puts it, "merged imperceptibly into that of the political Huguenots, who not only wanted to alter the foundations of belief, but to change the institutional order of things, and who used the religious opposition as a means to attack the authority of the crown. . . ." [17]

But for many years the aims of the various types of Huguenots were not fused; it required a supreme act of religious persecution to unite the various forces. Even when, on September 25, 1568, an edict proscribed the reformed faith, exiled the pastors, and debarred Protestants from public office and the universities, the oppressed groups did not form one great unified organization. But the thunderclap of the massacre of St. Bartholomew, in August, 1572, when an unknown number of thousands of Huguenots were killed in Paris and in the provinces, consolidated the divergent groups and made them one in the ensuing Fourth Civil War.

The massacre itself, though its supporting causes cannot be traced to any one individual, has been attributed mainly to the machinations of the French Queen, Catherine de Medici. It is known that she attempted the murder of Admiral Coligny, the Protestant leader; and it is also known that the attempt failed. It may therefore be true, as James Westfall Thompson contends, that the miscarriage of her plot "made Catherine frantic with mingled rage and fear lest the Huguenots concentrated in Paris should rise in reprisal." [18] In any case, it is generally agreed that the massacre was not premeditated; but the fact that it could occur at all is testimony to more than the terror and fury of a single distracted woman's mind; it is proof of even more than the political enmities and personal grudges that are known to have played a part, as in the desire of the Guises to avenge themselves on Coligny; it is evidence of something more than ruffianism and a bloodthirsty frenzy in the mob, though all these elements were manifestly present. Above all, it reveals bigotry of such proportions that human life was deemed of little importance by comparison with religious conformity; except for this, it would hardly have been possible for the Pope to raise a *Te Deum* to heaven, and would likewise have been impossible to find crowds of Catholics who would stab and bludgeon Protestants to death. The spirit of the rabble may be compared to that of a lynching mob in our old-time South: the victim's supposed guilt is subordinate to the fact that he is a Negro: were he a white man, he would be left to the civil authorities; and were no racial hatred and prejudice rampant in the country, no lynching would be conceivable. In the same way, had no religious hatred or prejudice prevailed in sixteenth-century France, no massacre of St. Bartholomew could have occurred despite all the pressures of politics and ruffianism.

It is true that as the wars proceeded, men began to lose sight of the issue of religion—which is not inconsistent with the experience of many war-makers, whose original aims, whether of liberating foreign lands or of safeguarding democracy at home, have often been lost in more general motives as the conflict raged on. In the later days of the civil wars, a political feud between the rival houses of Guise and Montmorency tended to take the foreground. "Each party counted not only upon paying its debts, which were enormous, but in establishing the power of its house more permanently than ever for the future." [19] And the rivals of the crown meanwhile "fattened on war, for peace deprived them of their authority, their power, and their partisans." [20] Thus they were a predatory force, living parasitically by means of the sword, and engaging in combats no more related to the popular will or welfare than the transactions of highwaymen. It is significant that the Duke of Guise, in these struggles, had recourse to Walloon and

German mercenaries—which does not indicate any excess of enthusiasm among native fighters. And the effects of the warfare upon the native peasant soldiers are likewise of interest:

The protracted wars by economically ruining and morally debauching this class had generated a breed of men who sprang from the soil like the dragon's teeth of Greek fable, men who by observation and practice were used to the matchlock and the sword, brutalized by oppression, long made desperate by burdensome taxes and the wrong of war.[21]

Thus, by its warping, thwarting effects upon men's minds, war once more generated a brood of evils for the future. It is safe to say that the zealots who piously set out to protect the faith against the heretic, and thereby brought on the succession of religious wars, did not foresee the desperate and debased peasant fighters that were to fill the country like an affliction.

With the sixteenth century, the great epoch of the French religious wars closes. But as late as 1703, following the revocation of the Edict of Nantes (rescinded by Louis XIV in 1685), a flare-up of religious struggles occurred in the Cévennes, where Huguenots known as Camisards battled the royal armies, with such success that the government had to come to terms with them and even grant them pardons.

But by the eighteenth century, wars for the sake of religion were becoming uncommon; and in the seventeenth the religious battlefields were mainly outside France.

v

The most conspicuous flare-up on the Continent during the seventeeth century was the Thirty Years' War (1618–48), one of the most devastating of all the pre-Napoleonic conflicts. Reminding us of the Hundred Years' War of several centuries before, it was something close to a general European contest, in which armies of Germans, Frenchmen, Spaniards, Swedes, and mercenaries from various lands marched and counter-marched. Like most religious struggles, it was not fought over the issue of religion exclusively; and as in the wars of the Catholics and Huguenots in France, the combatants tended gradually to lose sight of religion amid political clashes and ambitions; while terrorism and brutality became so general as to cause a decline in German culture, a marked drop in the German population, and an economic prostration whose marks were not erased in a century. Nothing could be more certain than that no thought of the boundless misery, destitution, and bloodshed of the Thirty Years' War troubled the minds of those who, intent upon religious rights and differences, precipitated the conflict.

Perhaps more than any other individual, the royal Jesuit Ferdinand of Styria (later known as Emperor Ferdinand II) was responsible for the outbreak. The opinion has been expressed that "Few men so honest, pious and consistent have brought upon the world so great an avalanche of misery or have ensured for the intellect of a people so long a period of theological constraint." [22] But whether or not Ferdinand was honest and pious, it is evident that he was bigoted, according to the most approved standards of his times; he shared the general hatred of the orthodox against Protestants, and let that hatred provide the mainspring of his actions. His idea was to abolish heresy entirely; and he seems to have favored no middle course in his persecuting methods, which extirpated the dissenters first in Styria, later in Bohemia, and then throughout the Austrian Empire. This process of establishing Jesuit supremacy, to be sure, required time; it had begun so far back as 1598, and one may therefore say that the seeds of the Thirty Years' War had been sowed that far in advance, and had been nourished and watered during all the interval by assiduous gardeners. The plants began to bear fruit when, after the Protestant church at Klostergrab had been torn down and Protestant preachers at Braunau arrested, the news came that the crusading Ferdinand had been made King, and was shortly to be crowned Emperor. Then, by a celebrated act of violence, the Protestants of Bohemia registered their protest at a stormy meeting; two Catholic ministers, prominently associated with the repressions, were thrown out of a castle window along with a private secretary (although, miraculously, they escaped death). Thus, by an overt act of defiance, the Protestants initiated the rebellion that brought on the Thirty Years' War, at a time when calmer councils and clear-headed negotiation might still have found a solution.

It is the view of at least one authority that the passions of the rulers rather than the antagonisms of the people are to be blamed for the conflict:

There is every reason to believe that if Germany had possessed anything like a popular representation its voice would have spoken in favor of some kind of compromise. There is no trace of mutual hostility between the populations of the Catholic and Protestant districts apart from their rulers.[23]

As in most wars, however, the people had little opportunity to make their feelings known. And by the time the strife was sputtering fast and hot, it was not easy to determine just what anyone had thought or intended. That the original seed was a religious one is, as we have seen, unquestionable; but once the disturbance had become widespread, the way was open for a multitude of forces unrelated to the initial incentive. It was only to be expected that the lust for material possessions, the greed for power, the envy and rivalry of monarchial and territorial ambitions, should come crowding to claim their share.

All the princes and statesmen who came successively to participate in the Thirty Years' War wished to augment their power by triumph. This is true of Ferdinand II and Maximilian of Bavaria; of Louis XIII, and his minister Cardinal Richelieu; of Gustavus Adolphus and Oxenstiern. Having once drawn the sword, the question was the same with all—increase of territory and people. . . .[24]

Over all the leaders alike, even those whose religious convictions were sincerest, the conquering traditions of centuries wove their persuasion. And the thought of conquest, power, and glory was planted so deeply that it required little more than a few sword-strokes to convert a conflict for the salvation of religion into a life-or-death duel for personal or national influence or aggrandizement.

One of the significant results of the Thirty Years' War, though one perhaps little noted at the time, is to be seen in the award to France of Upper and Lower Alsace. This acquisition may have seemed natural enough to the observers of the day, all the more so as France had already entered Alsace and Lorraine in the time of the Emperor Charles V, less than a century before. And it may have seemed a prize due to France for her participation in the Thirty Years' War, in accordance with the principles by which provinces and countries had long been doled among princes like chips in a card game. Any onlooker, however astute, would have had to be endowed with more than human wisdom to have had an inkling of future disturbances: the Franco-Prussian War of more than two centuries later, the much more dire catastrophe of the First World War, and the cataclysm of the Second World War. Yet the psychological currents stirred up by the Treaty of Westphalia in 1648 were to flow throughout succeeding generations; a blow had been struck at the *amour propre* of the German people; and though the results were not immediately evident, they were to become plain enough when ensuing events had developed a clear national feeling, and when the passion of patriotism arose in a wave that the peace-makers of 1648 could little have envisaged.

VI

Even before the Treaty of Westphalia, another in the great series of wars of religion had erupted in England. Unlike most of the religious disturbances, the Puritan Revolt was not a struggle between Catholic and Protestant. But like most of the upheavals, it was not wholly religious in origin; political and economic motives were conspicuous and in some ways predominate in the long conflict between the King and Parliament, which had not begun with the reign of Charles I. And personal excitations and hostilities, and above all the autocratic beliefs of Charles, were prominent factors behind the uprising. In one sense, we have here the clash of two religious doctrines: the convictions of the rebels had come into conflict with the creed bequeathed to the King by his father James I, that his power had come to him from God, and that he owed responsibility to God alone. This faith was transferred into action during the eleven years (1629–40) in which he ruled without Parliament; and it was subsequently manifest in his defiance of the legislative body, when in the company of hundreds of armed retainers he forced his way into Westminster Hall and demanded (unsuccessfully) the surrender of five leading members on a charge of high treason. The presumption is that, except for his instilled views as to divine prerogatives, along with his own supreme confidence in the righteousness of his rule, he would have given less incitement to Parliament, and might have reached a working arrangement that would have averted the civil war altogether.

The most divergent views have been expressed as to the Great Rebellion. On the one hand, we observe an attempt to minimize the influence of religion, as in the following from a biography of Cromwell:

We shall find overwhelming evidence that the Civil War led by Cromwell in England was very much akin to the religious wars of Germany and France; for all alike they were only in a small degree matters of theology and fervent religious faith, being rather political manipulations, craftily managed by worldly men who found a religious dogma just as convenient a banner of war as the Crusaders had found the Cross.[25]

At the opposite extreme from this estimate, with its rather questionable historical side-appraisals, we find the opinion of another writer that "If ever there was in this world a revolution with ideas as well as interests, with principle and not egotism for its mainspring, it was this." [26] The same commentator elsewhere evaluates the moral force behind the revolutionaries:

Calvinism exalted its votaries to a pitch of heroic moral energy that has never been surpassed; and men who were bound to suppose themselves moving in chains inexorably riveted, along a track ordained by a despotic and unseen Will before time began, have yet exhibited an active courage, a resolute endurance, a cheerful self-restraint, an exulting self-sacrifice, that men count among the highest glories of the human conscience.[27]

An example of this sort of moral force occurred at the time of the King's belligerent intrusion into the House of Commons, when he had advanced as far as the Speaker's chair and demanded surrender of the five allegedly treasonable members. Defying the royal authority, at what might have been the cost of his neck had Charles eventually predominated, Speaker William Lenthall made the often-quoted retort: "I have neither eyes to see, nor tongue to speak, in this place but as the House is pleased to direct me, whose servant I am."

An equal moral force was required a little later. In an incident generally regarded as marking the start of the civil war, the King demanded admittance into the port of Hull, which would provide him a channel for arms and troops from the Continent. The governor's response was to shut the gates and draw up the bridge—for which he was pronounced a traitor and would probably have gone to the block had Charles been able to put hands upon him.

Despite the views of those who see in the conflict nothing more than the machinations of economic-minded men, and despite the color lent to this position by Parliament's resistance to the sovereign's money-raising programs, the era was one in which religious beliefs were frequently put ahead of economics. This was evident so far back as 1604, when James I, in pursuance of his belief in Divine Right, ordered the Puritan ministers to conform or be harried out of the land—with the consequence that three hundred pastors gave up their livings. In any case, the spark that gave rise to the Great Rebellion was a religious one, and could not have taken fire in an age with a less fervent set of religious beliefs. We of today would find it difficult to imagine a war arising over the question of a prayer book; yet when Charles in 1637 tried to impose the Anglican Prayer-Book upon the Scots, revolution began to crackle throughout Scotland, armies began to take the field, and early in 1638 almost the entire country expressed its wrath in the bristling words of the celebrated National Covenant, which denounced the doctrines and practices of Rome with a partisan zeal rivaling the most fiery condemnations of Rome itself. Thereafter, with an army of Scots moving toward the border, war between England and her northern neighbor seemed certain; and it was the demands of this war that compelled the King to call upon the people for help, forced the summoning of the Short Parliament and later of the Long Parliament, and brought on the first stage of the Revolution which was to cost England years of turmoil, and eventually would cost the King his head.

It was not unnatural that the leader who came to power in such an age, and who led the rebellion and in time supplanted the King, should be a man of firm religious convictions. The sincerity of Cromwell has been questioned by some critics; but others have pointed out that the charge of hypocrisy is based upon a misconception, which tends to transplant the views of our own age into the seventeenth century. To Cromwell, as to millions of his contemporaries, religion was of supreme importance; both the Old Testament and the New were the Revealed Word, the Truth as uttered by the mouth of God; he believed devoutly in the right of the individual to fight for his own interpretation of the Scriptures; and consequently he saw the strife in which he was engaged as a sort of Holy War. With the irony by which rival claimants often embrace similar claims, he was no less convinced than was Charles of divine leadership; and his victories and almost unparalleled rise were therefore taken by him as manifestations of heavenly guidance. In his ordinary speech, he showed his religious background by his readiness to utter biblical phrases; and in his daily life—if we can leave out of account the excesses in Ireland—he was on the whole temperate, merciful, and restrained in his conduct.

We cannot, however, leave out of account the excesses in Ireland, which show how the passions of war may warp and transform the most pious adventurer. Even Cromwell's apologists must admit that here is a blot upon his career; and if his tactics differed in any essential from those of Tilly and other marauding captains in the long war which had just closed in Europe, that fact was little evident to his Irish victims. Cromwell himself was at no pains to conceal his actions; indeed, we are told of them in his own quaint language, in a way that emphasizes not only the physical details but the psychology behind them. Before embarking in August, 1649, he "did expound some places of Scripture excellently well"; and having reached Ireland, he advanced northward to Droghega, where some encounters occurred and the enemy general Aston was driven to a palisaded height, and there persuaded to surrender. As a reward, Cromwell ordered Aston's men all slain; after which, as he tells us, "Being in the heat of action, I forbade them to spare any that were in arms in the town; and I think that night they put to the sword about two thousand men." About eighty found refuge in the church steeple; at which Cromwell ordered the structure to be set afire, with the result that thirty died in the heat of the flames and the other fifty were slain with cold steel. Various other sanguinary exploits followed, including the deliberate slaughter of all officers that could be found, and the knocking on the head of all friars but two (those two being subsequently killed). "The enemy was about three thousand strong in the town," reports the commander. "I believe we put to the sword the whole number of the defendants. I do not think thirty of the number escaped with their lives."

Being a conscientious man, Cromwell felt that such tactics required an excuse. "I am persuaded," he explains, "that this is a righteous judgment of God upon these barbarous wretches, who have imbued their hands with so much innocent blood; and that it will tend to prevent the effusion of blood in the future." Besides, it was not really Cromwell who was responsible; he had deferred to one greater and wiser than he. "And now give me leave to say how it comes to pass that this work is wrought. It was set upon some of our hearts, that a great thing should be done, not by power or might, but by the spirit of God. And is it not so, clearly? That which caused your men to storm so courageously, it was the spirit of God. . . . And therefore it is good that God alone have all the glory."

Here we have the speech of the typical self-righteous, passionate, prejudiced, and ignorant man. Cromwell was perhaps not far different in his misunderstanding of the Irish than was the Duke of Alva in his misunderstanding of the Netherlands, or than numerous European viceroys have been in their misunderstanding of various colonies in Asia, Africa, and America. The difficulties between the English and Irish were generations old; the latter had (though Cromwell seemingly did not realize it) well-justified grievances dating back to the time of Elizabeth. An outgrowth of the long-standing strife and the long-smoldering sense of wrong had been an uprising in 1641 against the English colonists, accompanied on both sides by bloody outrages, in which an unknown number of thousands died. And this was apparently what Cromwell had in mind when he spoke of a "righteous judgment of God," although here he reminds us of the savage who thinks it justifiable to avenge a crime by slaying the offender's innocent brother. Was it possible that he supposed that any great number of the culprits of eight years before were among those that died at the sword-point or perished in the flames at Droghega? In any case, the strife between the English and Irish had filled Cromwell with a prejudice as profound as his ignorance; and this was one element behind the massacre at Droghega.

Another element was the antagonism between Catholics and Protestants. We must remember that Cromwell lived in an age which was still raw and sore from the wounds dealt in the name of religion in the Thirty Years' War, an age which still preserved the rankling memory of religious conflict in France and the Netherlands of the preceding century, an age in which religious flare-ups had recently occurred in Ireland itself, when the Ulster upheaval of 1641 had led to a virtual blood feud between the Protestants and their rivals of the Church of Rome. Though Cromwell had previously sallied forth in the name of religion, not until his arrival in Ireland had he touched the sensitive nerve of the Protestant-Catholic rivalry; and not until then, accordingly, had the frenzy of the fanatic replaced his relatively humane earlier attitude.

The strong religious ingredient in Cromwell's Irish policy is shown by his response in January, 1650, to a manifesto issued by the Catholic prelates at Clonmacnoise. "I shall not, where I have power, and the Lord is pleased to bless me, suffer the exercise of the Mass. . . . As for the people, what thoughts in the matter of religion they have in their own breasts, I cannot reach; but shall think it my duty, if they walk honestly and peaceably, not to cause them to suffer in the least for the same." In other words, the Catholics could think as they wished, but must not carry out the rites of their religion! It was this sort of contradictory thinking that was behind the severe suppressions and confiscations in Ireland, no less than behind the attempted justification of the outrage at Droghega.

And yet except for the Irish episode—in other words, except when religious and international excitations have turned reason to fanaticism—Cromwell on the whole, as already pointed out, conducted himself well. He has been commended for establishing the principle that an army should pay for whatever it takes in the country it traverses—a memorable advance in military morality, however far the world may still be from honoring this doctrine. And in the formation of his army, he followed principles that are noteworthy in the highest degree. Realizing the importance of morale, he did his best to obtain men of sober life and strong convictions. "I had rather have a plain russet-coated captain that knows what he fights for and loves what he knows, than what you call a gentleman and is nothing else." And so in recruiting his celebrated and victorious Ironsides, he would take shipwrights, carpenters, and stevedores side by side with country gentlemen; social lines meant nothing to him, though religious lines did count; his followers must be "godly" men, and his officers must take the Covenant. From a miscellaneous group, at first unorganized, untrained, undisciplined, riding on cart-horses and defending themselves with fowling-pieces, he welded together the force that put the Cavaliers to rout and established him as a virtual uncrowned king. And the all-important factor in that force was the spirit behind the men.

Yet if one looks closely one will see that Cromwell's army, which was outstanding in its day and which the eminent French general Turenne pronounced to be the finest on earth, did not find in the fighting mood a sufficient spur to the fighters. Even the volunteers, fervid and fanatic though many of them might be, were presumably not immune to the lure of regular pay, particularly as the social disorders of the times had thrown many out of work. But the volunteers, despite all inducements that could be baited before willing eyes, were not numerous enough for the needs of the Roundheads. The strong arm, as we shall see in a later chapter, had to exert itself to obtain men for the Cromwellian armies—and this although the number of combatants on both sides was never more than about two and a half per cent of the population. And so, even if the war would seem to involve more of a spontaneous popular movement than most conflicts, the will to peace predominated over the incentive to fight. As John Buchan summarizes the case: "The ordinary citizen was apathetic and desired only to be left in peace; his sympathies may have inclined slightly to the side of the king or of parliament, but he was not prepared to bestir himself for either. At first not even half the gentry were in arms, and to the end the laborer only fought when he was constrained by his betters. The struggle from first to last was waged by two small but resolute minorities." [28]

Chapter 20

The France of Louis XIV

The sparkling fountains and gilded courts, the mirrors and ornate carvings and silver furniture of Versailles were once a stage setting for the modern King of Kings. Although not a figure of outstanding intellect, nor gifted with genius in any observable direction, Louis XIV has somehow held the imagination not only of his own times but of later generations as the model monarch. This may be owing in part to the non-political accomplishments of his reign— the literature and art, the nascent science; but probably it was more largely because of the pose and pomp, the glitter and display, the ceremonial trappings, and the dignity and authority of the monarch. To a considerable extent also it sprang from the wars waged by Louis, wars in which he fulfilled the sovereign's traditional battling role and covered himself and France with that impalpable mantle known as glory, even while incidentally he paved the way for the decline of France and the horror of the Revolution.

It is impossible to consider Louis as an isolated phenomenon. He was the product of a long historical development, the representative fruit of a tree that grew an abundant crop. His peculiar position and the particular influence he wielded in peace and war are to be explained by the existence of two interwoven sets of ideas, both of them with a far-reaching background. The first has to do with the king's relation to his territory and people; the second, extending beyond the territory and people but also involving them, is concerned with his personal connection with God. Let us therefore consider these two sets of ideas.

The twentieth-century conception of a ruler, derived largely from the example of democratic states, is of a man to whom authority has been delegated so that he may act as an exalted public servant for the public benefit. The seventeenth-century conception, however, as applied to the Continental monarchies, was something far different. The king was not a representative of the people; he was a representative of himself, and of his own royal house. Being

243

a descendant of the feudal lord, and in fact a sort of feudal lord magnified, he was not merely the sheepdog of his domains, nor even the shepherd; he was the proprietor; he owned all the territory, its inhabitants were his virtual vassals, and so far as his eye could range or his voice be heard, he was absolute master. "*L'état c'est moi*" ("I am the State"), was literally his creed. Knowing nothing of the people's governments of democratic lands, he represented the dynastic government; his right of succession came to him as a member of a dynasty; and it might be legitimate for him to send his son or grandson across seas or mountains to rule countries whose people spoke a different language and whose traditions had little in common with his own. Thus we find such anomalies as a Dutch king reigning in England, and the offspring of the French Bourbons accepting the throne of Spain; in such cases the interests, rights, and desires of the people were not even considered, and the people themselves bowed to the prevalent notion that they had no rights.

But though the populace was acquiescent, the laws of dynastic succession were not always worked out clearly or beyond cavil; on the contrary, we find constant intrigues and armed conflicts resulting from the aim of this prince or that to seat his son or nephew on the throne of that land or the other. The consequence in warfare is shown in the very names of some of the struggles: the War of the Austrian Succession, the War of the Polish Succession, the War of the Bavarian Succession, and the like. It would be an undue simplification to suggest that dynastic causes were the only ones behind any of these conflicts; but the peculiar and sometimes predatory ideas regarding royal succession did play a conspicuous part, and gave a pretext and incentive for many contests that might not otherwise have occurred. And this was particularly true, as we shall see, of some of the wars of Louis XIV.

As if the doctrine of dynastic rights were not a sufficient goad to strife, the French monarch was prey to an even older autocratic idea. We have seen that kings as far back as ancient Egypt liked to look upon themselves as holding a special commission from God, or even as *being* God. This assumption, so far as the king-controlled records permit us to see, was generally accepted by the people (at least, by those who wished to survive); and many an Alexander was actually worshipped as a god. However, owing in part to the influence of Christianity, the idea of the god-ruler had

gone out of vogue in more recent times, though this was not quite
true of the conception of divine authority. In view of the struggling rebirth of rational thought, the doctrine could not be accepted by the seventeenth century in its crude earlier form; it had
to be restated and re-emphasized, and this was done early in the
reign of Louis XIV by the French Bishop Bossuet, who but followed the trend observable for some time in various European
countries including the England of James I.

Bossuet believed that, of all forms of government, monarchy
was the most usual and the most ancient, therefore the most natural;
it was similar to the rule of a father in the family, and should be
hereditary in the same way. The position of the king was sacred,
since the priests of the Church had anointed him at the time of
his coronation; his power was absolute, and he was accountable in
its exercise to God alone. And while he did indeed have duties
toward the people, their only recourse in case of misgovernment
was to pray to God. It is not hard to detect a certain inconsistency
in the argument of Bossuet, who wished the king to be regarded as
a father, and at the same time wanted him to be considered superhuman, the source of greater wisdom than all other men, the mortal
image of immortal God, and so by his very nature beyond criticism.

Though this creed of divine right may have been convincing to
many Frenchmen, the censorship imposed by the God-appointed
monarch made it a little difficult for the views of the irreverent to
become known. Certainly, France during the reign of Louis XIV was
enacting a role of great power no less than of lavish display—which
might have sufficed to persuade thousands of the monarch's heaven-
given place. Louis himself, in his soberer moods, may have wondered why, if Providence had especially designed him for kingship,
it had played the mean trick of making him short of stature, so that
he had to wear high red heels in order to look imposing. But perhaps he never entertained such a crude doubt. No profane questions, certainly, deterred him from making his symbol the sun, and
so identifying himself with the source of light, a little in the fashion
of an Assyrian or an Incan emperor. And whether or not in his
secret heart he believed in a divine absolutism, he acted as if he
did believe in it utterly; he managed the national affairs and
plunged into wars as if in pursuit of a self-apotheosis. And thus he
not only altered the destiny of France; he set a precedent to be
followed by other monarchs, and one in which the people of

Europe were to acquiesce until the rude awakening of the Revolution.

II

But if Louis' inspiration was from God, it was not God of the type envisaged by Christ or St. Francis; rather, his deity was of the Machiavellian variety. Its first principle was expediency; it had no objection to feigning, lying, and grasping. We therefore have the spectacle of a man who claims to be God-appointed, and discards in practice all the ethics commonly associated with God. Not that he would not probably have fought even without the justifying God-idea; the military traditions of centuries would still have swayed him; but the thought of a responsibility limited to heaven alone could not help making him irresponsible when it came to hatching pretexts for conflict.

These pretexts, though mostly of a gauzy transparency, were various and ingenious. One was the doctrine that every state had its "natural boundaries," and that those of France were the Pyrenees, the Alps, the Rhine, and the ocean (even though quite a bit of this vast territory had been occupied for centuries by non-Frenchmen). But this claim was so rickety that it required bolstering. Not the least far-fetched of the supporting arguments was the legalistic plea that underlay the War of Devolution (1667–68). In the inheritance of private property in the Netherlands, the custom of "devolution" had prevailed: if a man had children by successive marriages, the offspring of the first union would be his sole heirs. With none but the flimsiest basis in law or logic, Louis applied this principle to the dynastic state; he held that his wife Maria Theresa, eldest daughter of Philip IV of Spain, should take precedence over Charles II, Philip's son by a subsequent marriage, a weakling Spanish king crowned in 1665. And since Philip had claimed the Belgian Netherlands, this region was the property of Philip's daughter Maria Theresa, and therefore belonged to Maria Theresa's husband Louis. Truly, God works in wondrous ways his marvels to perform!

Had it not been for the idea of the dynastic state, this preposterous tissue of pretense would have been impossible. But to a God-appointed leader all fabrications were permitted.

After a second stroke of aggression—the Dutch War which he declared in 1672 for reasons evidently connected in part with trade

and politics—Louis concocted another legalistic excuse for extending his domains. Claiming that some of the conquered territory had
feudal rights over various towns and districts, he established so-
called "Chambers of Reunion," courts of puppet judges who decided that Louis had rights of sovereignty over twenty important
towns of the Holy Roman Empire, including Luxembourg and
Strasbourg. Providentially, the army was ready at the opportune
moment to put these judicial decisions into effect.

Louis' expansive program, despite all his sleek justifications, naturally alarmed those parts of Europe that did not feel God-
appointed to be digested by the French monarchy. The League of
Augsburg, a formidable combination of states that enjoyed the
secret support of the Pope and included Holland, Spain, England,
Sweden, and Savoy, was formed in 1686 by the Emperor Leopold
as a counter-measure against the threatened French disturbance of
the traditional "balance of power." A ten-year struggle ensued,
wherein parts of Europe and particularly the Palatinate were mercilessly devastated, and wherein Louis finally was checked and
compelled to surrender the gifts of the "Chambers of Reunion,"
in addition to Lorraine and the Palatinate. But what reason was
there for the War of the League of Augsburg? What was the gain
to France, or to Europe? It is evident that we have nothing but
the old motive of national aggrandizement by armed theft, along
with the desire of a prince for personal aggrandizement in power,
prestige, and glory. And all this was possible only because of the
inherited traditions of fighting, the traditions of absolutism that
made the King arrogant in his depredations, and made the people
bow in the assumption that a ruler was divinely entitled to light
conflagrations for the sake of his glory.

One might suppose that Louis, who was in his sixtieth year
before he had concluded the War of the League of Augsburg,
would now have learned his lesson. Actually, however, his most
exhausting struggle lay ahead—the dynastic contest known as the
War of the Spanish Succession, a war Louis entered with eyes
open, a war no more necessary than his assault upon the Netherlands or the Palatinate, a war that was to drag on from 1702 to
1713 and do more than any of his previous adventures toward
draining the energies of France.

Except for the idea of predominant royal rights—the idea that
made the nations in effect the private property of their sovereigns

—the War of the Spanish Succession would have been unthinkable. And except for the rivalry of Louis with the Hapsburgs, and his desire to make the Bourbons equal or eclipse that ancient family, he would not have permitted the conflict to descend upon Europe. For this vast struggle, which reached not only throughout the Continent but overseas to the colonies and so (like the conflict of 1688–97) was virtually a World War, was waged over no clear issue but that of seating Louis' grandson upon the throne of Spain.

It was in November, 1700, that the Spanish King died, bequeathing all his imperial possessions to Philip of France, grandson of Louis XIV. This inheritance, which promised to make Spain and the Spanish Empire virtually minions of France, was not disdained by the ambitious Louis; refusal would not have been in line with kingly traditions, though it must have been clear that the other nations would not brook such an overturn of the balance of power and such supremacy as this promised for France. Louis must have anticipated the results; but he did not flinch. In fact, he made the conflict doubly sure by a series of aggressions against the Dutch, during which he wrested from the Spaniards the privilege of slave-trading in the Spanish Indies. And by these encroachments he aroused the commercial fears of the Dutch and English, who accordingly formed the Grand Alliance, which waged the war against France.

All this could, obviously, have been avoided, had Louis risen above the dynastic ideas that had descended to him through many generations. But that would have been too much to expect. And so the people of Europe were called upon to pour out their blood over an issue of little more actual concern to them than the question whether the chimpanzee or gorilla was the king ape of Africa.

A curious fact is that at times they even poured out their blood willingly. The idea of king and country was implanted so strongly in the popular mind that, when the war was turning against Louis beneath the shattering blows of Marlborough, the King appealed to the patriotism of his people—and appealed not in vain. Yes, the monarch who had never had much visible regard for his subjects and had led them into a war in which they had no visible interest whatever, pleaded that the masses should be loyal to him—and found them loyal. Recruits rushed to offer themselves; contributions came in from rich and poor; Louis himself, laboring untiringly, led the nation in an effort that would appear heroic had it served a worthier end. And thus the King was enabled to save his skin—that is to say, his personal prestige, and the prestige of France. The eleven years of fighting did keep his grandson on the Spanish throne, though with the provision that Spain should never be joined to France; but aside from this accomplishment France gained nothing whatever; she even lost valuable colonies, and was laden with a weight of debt and taxation that was to bear down upon her until her house collapsed in the catastrophe of the Revolution.

All of which suggests that Louis and his followers were unable to face reality. For a bubble of fame, a will-o'-the-wisp of power, he was willing to cast aside blood and treasure, world order and tranquillity; he was ready to grasp at a shadow, while letting the substance pass him by. And this was perhaps because, all his life, he had lived in an unreal world. He perched on a seat puffed and padded with gilded straw; he inhaled the dense steamy air of majesty, into which never a breath of the impetuous fresh winds could enter; he stared at the veined marbles, the lavishly painted ceilings, the high arched windows of his palace; he instructed himself in the niceties of etiquette, and underwent complex formalities in the presence of reverent crowds every morning when he arose and every night when he retired; he attended ministerial conferences, and manipulated adroitly in the demi-world of diplomacy; but of the struggling, groping, throbbing, aspiring, passionately feeling universe of men and women he had little more idea than if reared among the satrapies of Mars. All about him were the thick veils of pretense, all about him the draperies of rule and rote were hung with an unsmiling solemnity; he was not treated as a man, he did not treat or even quite regard himself as a man; and in the isolation that haunted him amid the crowd and the ignorance that lay at the depths of his blaze of light, he could not act wholly like a man among men. And therein we can see the explanation of his colossal selfishness in episodes such as the War of the Spanish Succession, and the unlimited demands he made upon the *canaille* to whom he gave nothing in return but an idol for their admiration.

Even in his wars, he seemed not quite in touch with reality. He did indeed go forth with his earlier armies; but he avoided pitched battles whenever possible, and had a penchant for sieges, which the able Vauban was always able to bring to a gratifying conclusion; whenever he saw fit, he would withdraw from the battlefield, and none could question why; and he showed little command of the principles of military strategy. Nevertheless, he would boast mightily; and though some cynics dared privately to dub him "King of Reviews," the controlled and censored press was able time after time to rouse the public to shouts of acclamation. A typical incident—and one in which Louis but followed the most approved precedent for fanning military enthusiasm—occurred during the Dutch War, when the army crossed the Rhine on a series of pontoons. The chosen point was at the shallowest and most sluggish spot on the entire river; and the crossing could hardly have involved extraordinary valor, since it was opposed merely by a few cavalrymen, who wasted no time about retreating. Nevertheless, according to the lyrics of praise published in the newspapers, the redoubtable Louis had led his troops across the deep, swift current, and put to rout an enormously greater body of foes based on the fortress of Tollhus (a stronghold otherwise unknown to history).

If he thus lent more vivid color to a myth, there are reasons to suppose that he himself was one of the subscribers to the myth. Unless he had truly been a god, he could not well have resisted the pomp and show, the adulation, the fawning and flattery that surrounded him; he could not have seen himself otherwise than through a rainbowed mist. There is a story in Saint-Simon that casts light in this regard. A General Villars "had owed all his success to the smiling, rose-tinted account he had given of everything. It was the frequency and the hardihood of his falsehoods in this respect that made the King and Madame de Maintenon look upon him as their sole resource." [1] But one day, "Having arrived at the very summit of favor, he thought he might venture, for the first time in his life, to bring a few truths before the King." Foolhardy blunder! "From that moment they began to regard Villars with other eyes. Finding that he spoke now the language which everybody spoke, they began to look upon him as the world had always looked upon him—to find him ridiculous, silly, impudent, lying, insupportable. . . ." [2]

Only when Villars reverted to his old duplicity was he restored to favor. Evidently what the King wished to hear was not the truth, but confirmation of his illusions. With a perfectly human penchant for pleasant bubbles, he desired to live only in the shining, painless world of fancy that had been created for him. There is, indeed, a sign of an awakening at the last moment of his life, when on August 26, 1715, he said to his small great-grandson: "Try to keep the peace with your neighbors. I have loved war too well; do not copy me in this, nor in the lavish expenditures I have made." [8] But despite this deathbed repentance, it was in no such practical spirit that Louis entered the great warring adventures of his career, wherein he saw not the reality of human blood and agony, but a glowing make-believe world over which he gloriously presided. The unfortunate fact is that millions of his subjects, and indeed onlookers throughout the earth, were likewise deluded by this make-believe world of heroism and majesty.

Chapter 21

Sweden, Russia, and Prussia

While the War of the Spanish Succession was still brewing, a stranger and more daring character than Louis XIV was flashing rocketlike across the northern skies. Far more than Louis, and probably more than any other leader in modern times not excepting Napoleon, Charles XII of Sweden was a convert to the heroic ideal, the old cult of glory and honor that made of fighting an end in itself. To his mind, conquest was its own object; warfare for its own sake was glorious. As Voltaire declared of him, he was "the first who had the ambition to be a conqueror without having a desire to aggrandize his State; he wished to gain empires in order to give them away." [1] By the same token, according to Voltaire, "The only way to influence him was to awaken his sense of honor; by mentioning the word 'glory' you might have obtained anything from him." [2]

An incident of his Russian campaign will illustrate his principles and character. He had reached the walls of Poltava, and halted to await reinforcements. Meanwhile he decided to attack the town "for a diversion."

It was in vain that the uselessness of the enterprise and the impossibility of success was represented to him. What was the good of wasting powder and the munitions of war, which had now become rare in the camp? "Yes," replied the Iron-head to Gyllen-kruk, "we are obliged to do extraordinary things to gain honor and glory. . . ." When had his favorite heroes of the Eddas ever been seen to retreat? [3]

Charles appears to have received an overdose of the glory-idea almost with his mother's milk. The deeds of his grandfather Charles X, an aggressor who had hurled himself at Poland and Denmark and thereby won great triumphs and wrought great havoc, were in the very air he breathed as a child. But not only this recent trouble-maker was before his eyes: the heroes of the old sagas were constantly in his mind, firing him with ambition to follow in their footsteps; and Alexander the Great, surrounded with an artificial brilliance in the biography of the uncritical Quintus Curtius, was to him a lifelong model. "Full of the idea of Alexander and Caesar, he proposed to imitate those two conquerors in everything but their vices," declares Voltaire, who relates an interesting anecdote in illustration. A teacher asked Charles what he thought of Alexander. " 'I think,' said the prince, 'I could wish to be like him.' 'But,' resumed the preceptor, 'he only lived two-and-thirty years.' 'Ah,' he replied, 'and is that not enough when one has conquered kingdoms?' " [4]

The character of Charles and the nature of his motivation have been aptly summarized by Rambaud:

His dominant virtue and vice was a passion for glory. Glory, and glory alone, was to him the end of war. He appears not to have understood that it was possible to acquire it by practicing the arts of peace. . . . His conduct appeared to be regulated, not by the political principles current in the eighteenth century, but by some strange and archaic point of honor. . . . Charles the Twelfth was a hero of the Edda set down by mistake in a matter-of-fact century. . . . Pitiless to himself as well as to others, we find him undergoing useless dangers and fatigues seeking adventures like a sea-king who had only his head to risk; considering war as a single combat between two champions, which could only end, if not with the death, at least with the dethronement of the vanquished; fighting not to gain crowns, but to distribute them; giving largesses to his soldiers as if he had always the treasures of pillage, the "red gold of Fafnir's heat," at his disposal; despising all the luxuries of life, like the Northmen who boasted of never having slept beneath a roof; flying from women, "whose silken hairs," say the sages, "are nets of perfidy"; regarding a backward movement as dishonor, and considering prudent advice as evidence of weakness; ready to face water, as in the marshes of Lithuania, or fire, as in the conflagration of Bender.[5]

A modern psychologist might say that Charles had a "glory complex." His passion for the battlefield bespoke a psychological overdevelopment that approached the pathological, a military fanaticism different in direction but not altogether different in type from the religious fanaticism of the perfervid monk. And in part this frenzy can be traced to the overstressed teaching of tradition, and in part to an egotism that craved boundless distinction.

These conclusions are substantiated by the memoirs of an officer under Charles, Carl Gustafson Klingspor, who in old age wrote a book that depicts the King with surprising realism. One learns a great deal about Charles from a description of the royal games:

The best games of all were those of war—costing often a life or two, but surely as instructive as amusing to us of the Court. We threw bombs made of cardboard instead of iron, and tore the clothes off each other, breaking knuckles and noses with an occasional arm or leg in storming snow bastions and fortresses.[6]

Of much the same type were some of Charles' other pastimes, after he had fought for the possession of snow fortresses "so lustily that many an arm and leg was broken before the walls were demolished":

... and when there were no further bastions to be taken, I remember how the King would on a frosty night break so many window-panes with snowballs that the commanding officers and civil officers did the following day, in deepest submission, petition that a royal glazier might be appointed for the army, to restore the panes,—a petition His Majesty proved his good heart by granting. When this jest no longer amused the King, he devised another, namely, riding into the camp in the calm of the night, imitating the frightful shrieks and cries of the Russians, so that all would tumble out of their beds and rush into the streets with naked swords, ready for the fight.[7]

All this is hardly on an adult level. All this is part of the world of make-believe—the world of games and shows. There is reason to suppose that Charles XII, in common with Louis XIV and many another crowned head of armies, lived and acted in the universe of grand illusion painted by an overheated imagination. And in that toy universe he ordered his troops forth, attacked foreign nations, endured long marches and cruel hardships, dashed down opportunities for reasonable peace settlements, and doomed thousands of his men to suffering or death. Preceding Napoleon by more than a century in invading Russia, he underwent futile prodigies of valor in the attempt to bring that mighty nation to her knees; and after miseries paralleled only by those of Napoleon's own invading force, most of the survivors fell before the Russians at the Battle of Poltava in June, 1709. In this engagement the Swedish infantry was virtually annihilated, and fourteen thousand cavalrymen were taken prisoners; while the King was fortunate to escape into Turkey with fifteen hundred men. Thus ended the great epoch of his career; and though he lived another nine years before being killed by a bullet in battle, he might well have served as the inspiration for Gray's famous line, "The paths of glory lead but to the grave."

However, in this case the paths of glory did not merely lead to the grave. Charles XII completed the work begun by his valorous grandsire Charles X, and reduced Sweden to third rank among the powers of Europe. Yet perhaps in a sense he accomplished a salutary task; he demonstrated to Sweden once and for all the folly of military grandeur; that nation, while never again of first military importance, has since covered herself with a more substantial glory as a leader in the arts of peace.

II

The adversary of Charles XII in the most ambitious of his wars was Peter the Great, under whose radical reign Russia was just awakening from her medievalism. Even more than most European rulers of the day, Peter represented the principle of autocratic absolutism—an absolutism bred into Russia by long experience and tradition, and intimately related to most of her activities in peace and war. Despite the despotic contributions of Peter, this absolutism and its popular acceptance can be traced back to the heavy rule clamped down by the Mongols, particularly over the northeastern half of the country—an influence that must be borne in mind if we would understand not only the Russia of earlier centuries but the Russia of today.

The situation has been summarized by a recent historian, who finds "the most substantial effect" of the Mongolian rule to have been felt "in the political thought of the Russian people":

The Mongolian state was built upon the principle of the unquestioning submission of the individual to the group, first to the clan and through the clan to the whole state. This principle was in the course of time impressed thoroughly upon the Russian people. It led to the system of universal service to the state which all without differentiation were forced to give. . . .

The Mongolians also introduced a new view regarding the power of the prince. The power of the Khan was one of merciless strength. It was autocratic; submission to it was unqualified. This view of the authority of the prince was transferred to the Grand Duke of Moscow when the rule of the Khans was weakened. When the last threads of the Tartar control were broken by Moscow, the dukes of Moscow openly regarded themselves as absolute monarchs and considered the people completely subject to their will.[9]

Beneath the sway of the old authoritarian traditions, it became possible for the Czar to do almost as he wished with his subjects; to treat them no less than their lands as his personal property; to lead them into war with the sovereign complacency of a cattle dealer sending his cows to the slaughter. It is on such grounds that we can understand the frightfulness of Ivan the Terrible, that psychopathic Czar who may be ranked beside Genghis Khan, Tamerlane, and Hitler as one of the most monstrous characters of all time. Other countries than Russia have had mad rulers; but in few others if any do we see a despot of quite this stamp—perverted since childhood by sadistic lusts and orgies, bedeviled by a persecution complex, haunted by a religious mania that made him pay for masses for the souls of the victims whom he offered up by the thousands—the murderer of his own son, the perpetrator not only of bloody oppressions and gruesome tortures but of warlike raids against his own people, the creator of the *Oprichina* that was virtually an embattled state within a state, the leader of a band of several thousand brigands who went about in dogs'-head masks to terrorize the countryside, the slayer of horses and cattle and looter of grain, the collector of plunder from business houses, churches, and monasteries, and the destroyer of the city of Great Novgorod with the accompanying massacre of men, women, and children in numbers variously estimated at from two to sixty thousand.

But there is no reason to linger over this blood-smeared lunatic, except to note his exemplification of a single fact: when the current creed permits one man to wield absolute authority, and when that man happens to be the victim of psychological twists and frenzies, warfare of the most disordered nature may break out; and it is a matter of chance whether the targets happen to be foreign enemies or the monarch's own followers. Particularly in lands where violence has been common, and where there is consequently toleration of violence, an unbalanced autocrat may swing his sword in any direction without evoking effective resistance.

If we pass over the period of a hundred and five years that separates the death of Ivan from the ascension of Peter in 1689, we will find the authoritarian system still strongly entrenched. It was because of this authoritarianism, and partly because of fresh accretions to the Czar's power, that Peter was able to effect a one-man revolution in the institutions of peace and war. Strongly impressed by Western material and mechanistic advances, he strove to bring the West to Russia. It is the view of Arnold Toynbee that the traits of the Occidental appear in his character "unmistakably, both for good and for evil. He displays an American vitality, an American impatience of pomp, an American delight in manual skill, and also an American ruthlessness." [9] Whether American or not, he undoubtedly was ruthless; and he undoubtedly did exhibit the other qualities Toynbee enumerates, not only in his introduction of Western methods but in the vigor with which he put down the old-time military organization, the *Streltsi*, and the equal vigor with which he labored to provide a Russian navy and establish a standing army.

Before Peter's time the army had been composed largely of foreign mercenaries augmented by a small native militia. Peter, however, believed in patronizing home talent, and accordingly required the nobility to provide military service without time limit, and submitted the peasantry to a conscription which, as Rambaud tells us, "was long to be a source of despotism and tyranny," and was to be productive of "a whole popular literature of 'Lamentations of recruits.' " [10] The plan was to draw recruits from all classes of society; to send both the married and the unmarried men from the ages of fifteen to thirty in bands of five hundred or a thousand to the nearest towns, and there to drill them to fill the gaps in old regiments or to form new regiments. The first universal conscription occurred in 1705, and there was a new levy every year until 1709, with the consequence that the army eventually numbered about two hundred and ten thousand men.

And if one country thus planted the roots of the large-scale wars of later years, the soil was, paradoxically, not the people's desire to fight, but their reluctance. Had the country been enthusiastic for the soldier's career, men would have enlisted in such numbers as to make forcible recruitment unnecessary. But once again it was the docility of the common man that made it possible to shepherd him into the barracks.

III

If the observer of present turmoils has little trouble in identifying one source in the militaristic means and principles of Czar Peter, he finds it even less difficult to trace another of the knotted roots in Prussia of the day of Frederick the Great and before.

Frederick, the most brilliant and spectacular agent of Prussian militarism, was the wielder of an inherited sword. It was forged in the days of Elector Frederick William of Brandenburg-Prussia, the so-called "Great Elector," who ruled from 1640 to 1688 and bequeathed to his descendants that useful accessory to a fighting blade, the rod of absolute authority. Not only his military but his social ideas are important to an understanding of the martial state of which he may justly be called the founder; he was in accord with the philosophy of political absolutism current in the France of Louis XIV: the ruler should be unrestrained in his authority, his will should be the law, and his subjects should grant him obedience in all things. If such beliefs are accepted, it becomes comparatively simple to impose military regimentation and establish a military despotism.

It must not be forgotten that Brandenburg-Prussia was but a small country, far down in the list of European states in population and importance: in 1640, when the Great Elector took control, Berlin was a backwoods town of an estimated six thousand population. Yet the Elector set about to give his minor realm a major position; and his chief weapon in this endeavor was the army which he developed. From a mere four or five thousand men in 1641, this instrument had grown until it numbered twenty-five to thirty thousand in 1688—men well trained and equipped, whose use, however, was not confined to the defense of their country, since they were hired out like the *condottieri* of medieval times in wide-flung battles from Warsaw to the valley of the Rhine. Not only the nature of the army, but its effect on social life and thought, has been tellingly described:

It became a state institution, and its officers, chosen from the nobility, acquired a privileged position. It had no medieval history; it made its own reputation; it was sharply distinguished from local and civil life; its sword was the ruler's, and it was encouraged to regard itself as the salt of citizenship and the bulwark of Prussia's strength. It could claim to have made Prussia—to be Prussia. This

militarization of the state meant that the ruler as well as his dominion were militarized, began to interpret life in military categories and to regard their military authority as the first of all duties.
To maintain in poor and scantily populated lands so large a force
involved special taxation, the sacrifice of civil to military expenditure, the development of powerful administrative organs whose
claims were supreme; it meant also ideals of duty, obedience, system, control, management and law from above which infiltrated
into and reacted on all social, civil and political thought.[11]

Here, in the seventeenth century, we already have the political
and military system and the code of thought that were to create
boundless trouble for the world in the latter half of the nineteenth
and the twentieth centuries.

Prussia might very well, however, have amended her ways in
the two hundred years between the Great Elector and Bismarck,
placing less reliance upon her army, and growing more pacifistic-
minded. That she did not do so is in part the responsibility of the
Great Elector's immediate successors.

His son Frederick, who followed him, made the notable step of
conferring a crown upon himself; on January 18, 1701, he converted Prussia into a monarchy by crowning himself at Konigs-
berg. The change, so far as one can see, was almost exclusively
psychological; with great pomp and ceremony, Frederick I emphasized the majesty which he accredited to himself; and human nature being easily affected by gauds and shows, the onlookers could
hardly have helped being impressed and regarding the Monarchy
of Prussia and its King as somehow more imposing and important
than the Electorate of Brandenburg-Prussia and its Elector. But
the ruler's absolute authority remained unaffected.

The son of Frederick, Frederick William I, the father of Frederick the Great, was one of those disagreeable characters who
occasionally get misplaced on a throne when their natural environment would seem to be a taproom. When he was not hunting the wild pigs which he slew by the thousands, or smashing at
some errant officer with his head-breaking cane, or entertaining
his cronies amid the clouds of smoke and guard-room jests of his
"Tobacco-Parliament," his chief interests were the state which he
managed with a miser's niggardliness and the army on which he
lavished about five millions out of the seven millions of national
income. The trend of the man's mind is to be seen in his hobby,

the Potsdam Guard—composed of giants, none of them less than six feet in height, and many of them enlisted by kidnapping. During the twenty-seven years of a bullying reign, he increased his standing army from thirty or forty thousand men to ninety thousand, thus creating the fourth largest force in Europe, although Prussia ranked only twelfth in population among European states. It must be said for Frederick William that, despite this huge army, he preferred diplomacy to war. But apparently he did not realize that one cannot sharpen a sword without sharpening the state of mind that leads to the use of a sword; and he could not have foreseen how the instrument which he and his forebears had welded into shape was to be utilized by his son.

IV

Few crown princes have been reared in a harsher school than Frederick II. A sensitive youth, with a penchant for music, poetry, and the graces of French literature and culture, he had the misfortune to be beneath the thumb of a father who might almost have belonged to a different race. From the age of seven he was subject to a rude discipline; he was taught the lore of the army and of the account book, but had to learn French and Latin and flute-playing by stealth, and at the risk of punishment and derision. Of home and friendship in the usual sense of the term he knew little or nothing; and when in adolescence he did have one comrade, young Lieutenant Katte, the relationship was terminated with the most ruthless brutality. Apprehended along with Katte in an ill-considered but not unnatural attempt to flee the country and paternal tyranny, Frederick was thrown into a dungeon, condemned to solitary confinement, and subjected to a pitiless interrogation; and later he was forced to witness the execution of Katte, whose death had been ordered by Frederick William even though a military court had recommended a less stringent penalty. In order to save his life, Frederick was forced to pretend compliance with his father's will; and thenceforth, drilled in hypocrisy, he submitted to the royal scheme of education, which forbade him all books except the Bible, a hymn book, and a treatise on *True Christianity;* while he was entrusted to the care of three nobles who were enjoined to speak to him on nothing but "the word of

God, the constitution of the land, manufactures, police, agriculture, accounts, leases, and lawsuits." [12]

Is it surprising that by manhood the iron had burnt itself into his soul, that the Crown Prince, taught the lessons of a militarized and irresponsible autocracy in the atmosphere of the illiterate and inhuman barrack of the Prussian court, should have been convinced by a damnably royal persistence that womanhood, love, loyalty, generosity, charity, chivalry were the playthings of the mocking gods; that human virtues, like human vices, were simply counters in the relentless game of destiny; that God, freedom and immortality were the superstition of obscurantist priest and pastor, or baffling riddles? Of stupidity, ignorance, treachery, cruelty, tyranny, coarse animalism he knew far too much—of sympathy very little, of happiness nothing.[13]

If one would understand Frederick the king, one must know Frederick the prince. It is not only possible, it is probable that with a different upbringing, and one encouraging his gentler and more humane side, he would have made a different ruler—and the subsequent history of Europe and of the world would accordingly have been different. Like all men, he was a compound of innate qualities and superimposed experience; the flint and steel of the former might in any case have made him a hard, even a remorseless ruler; but a belief in the purposefulness of life, a faith in an ultimate righteousness, morality, love, and truth, might have caused his fist to unclench, and have turned him from those paths of cynicism, treachery, and aggression that made him a pivotal figure in the history of modern militarism.

Not many commentators have refrained from noting that in 1750, the year of his accession, Frederick published his *Anti-Machiavel*, in which he attempted to refute the doctrines of the celebrated Florentine. Yet this document, paradoxical as it may seem from the pen of one of the most Machiavellian of monarchs, is less anomalous than one might suppose; the fact that Frederick wrote about Machiavelli, even *against* him, shows a concern with Machiavelli, possibly a preoccupation with him; and nothing is more true psychologically than that it is possible to swing to an opposite pole within any category of belief or action: the lover may become the hater, the rabid radical may swerve to rabid reaction, the victim of persecution may wield the persecutor's knout. And thus it was no rare psychological feat for Frederick to turn from his *Anti-Machiavel* to the actual practice of Machiavellianism.

His utterances and his deeds alike show just who was his master. "If there is anything to be gained by being honest, let us be honest; if it is necessary to deceive, let us deceive," [14] was a typical remark —which, curious to relate, does *not* show any intention to deceive. "The jurisprudence of sovereigns is commonly the right of the stronger," [15] was a later pronouncement that summarized his working philosophy. And he proved his faith in this doctrine almost immediately after his rise to power. When the death of the Emperor Charles VI in October, 1740, put the young and inexperienced Maria Theresa on the throne and left Austria apparently weak, what should Frederick do but seize the opportunity to overrun the rich province of Silesia? There was no excuse, except that he wanted Silesia and thought he could take it, thanks to the capable army drilled and equipped by his father. And thus Frederick did more than to break Prussia's promise to respect Austria's integrity, more even than to win valuable territory through unprovoked pillage; he set into action forces that were to dominate the forty-six years of his reign, earn him enemies throughout Europe, plunge him into a succession of conflicts, strengthen the precedent of aggression represented by Louis XIV, and lay many of the building bricks for the terrorized and imperiled world of two centuries later.

Before Frederick's time, some semblance of morality had existed among nations; the honor of a state was stained when a ruler flouted his obligations. The resplendent Louis XIV, however, had not shown too much regard for this principle in his dealings with the Dutch and the Germans; and Frederick was but following in the footsteps of the illustrious Frenchman when he hewed his way into Silesia. As in the case of Louis, love of glory seemed to have mingled with the desire for territorial gain. Having trespassed upon Silesian soil, he wrote to his minister Podewils:

I have crossed the Rubicon with waving banners and resounding music; my troops are full of good-will, the officers ambitious and our generals consumed with greed for fame; all will go as we wish and I have reason to promise myself all possible good from this undertaking. . . . I will either perish or have honor from it.[16]

Like Louis XIV, again, Frederick could weave wormlike pretexts for barefaced robbery. In a document of which a thousand copies had been secretly printed before the invasion, he attempted to assure the people of Silesia of his benevolent aims:

This is by no means intended to injure Her Majesty of Hungary, with whom and with the worshipful House of Austria we rather most eagerly desire to maintain the strictest friendship and to promote their true interest and maintenance according to the example of our glorious forefathers in our realm and electorate. That such is our sole intention in this affair, time will show clearly enough, for we are actually in the course of explanation and agreement with Her Majesty.[17]

The propagandists of two centuries later may have found Frederick's precedent of value in the high art of making words transform facts.

Maria Theresa, however, was not convinced by these well-oiled protestations; throughout her life she regarded Frederick as the wolf that had swooped down on her fold; and her antagonism provided nutriment for later and much more deadly warfare.

But despite Frederick's unquestioned role in precipitating the First Silesian War, he cannot be held wholly responsible for the greater conflict of which it was a part. In 1739 a struggle over trading rights had broken out between England and Spain—the War of Jenkins' Ear it was called, owing to the pretext arising from the alleged damage to the ear of Jenkins, an English seaman (a pretext deliberately used by the English to stir up a warlike sentiment in the people). This conflict was merged in the War of the Austrian Succession, of which the two Silesian wars were also part, and which was not ended until the signing of the Treaty of Aix-la-Chapelle in 1748. Meanwhile the French, making one of the gravest diplomatic blunders in their history, had aligned themselves with Frederick and with Spain, so committing themselves to a land war and facilitating Great Britain's triumph on the seas and overseas. And behind the French participation in the Prussian cause we can see a psychological aberration: the great Seigneur the Comte de Belle Isle, smoldering with ancient hatred of Austria and determined to retrieve his family from an old disgrace, had adroitly maneuvered the peacefully disposed Cardinal Fleury into a war on Frederick's side.

After Frederick had tightened his grip on his stolen property and twice betrayed his allies, the war might have ended had it not been for the intrusion of Great Britain and the desire of Maria Theresa for compensation for her lost Silesia. The Austrian Queen, in organizing a national war against France and sending Prince Charles of Lorraine to take Alsace and Lorraine back from the French, could not have realized that she was adding faggots to a bonfire that was to flare up repeatedly in the following centuries, with disastrous consequences to all Europe. Nor could Frederick, when he invaded Silesia, have foreseen the effect upon Alsace-Lorraine, nor the fanning of those jealousies, antagonisms, and hatreds that were to be the bane of a later world. The outcome was, certainly, implicit in his deeds, as in those of Maria Theresa—but it is a rare statesman that can look beyond the nearest bend.

v

It was in 1756 that Frederick plunged into the greatest of his struggles, the celebrated Seven Years' War. This contest, one of the bitterest the world had witnessed, is notable for several reasons, and not least for the so-called Diplomatic Revolution, by which the nations changed partners like men and girls at a dance. While Prussia had been aligned with France in the conflict of the previous decade, Prussia was now at war with France; Great Britain had shifted to the Prussian orbit, and Russia had turned from Great Britain to Austria. Certainly, this would be sufficient commentary —if our age needed such commentary—on the depth and endurance of friendships between nations. Frederick was not the only monarch for whom the doctrine of expediency, the code of "catch while you can" and "let the end justify the means," was then predominant.

Among the causes of the war were French resentment at Frederick's secret maneuvering to make the so-called Convention of Westminster with the British, and Russian resentment at the clandestine British maneuvering to form the Prussian alliance. But more important were the machinations of the Austrian Count Kaunitz, who imagined that nations could be manipulated with the mathematical assurance of pawns on a board, and exerted every art and pressure to bring France and Russia into the alliance against Prussia. Beyond all this there was the rankling hatred of Maria Theresa against her despoiler Frederick, and her ambition to recoup her losses; and there was Frederick's fear of the alliance being formed against him, his information that this alliance was to strike at him in the spring of 1757, his inability to obtain any unequivocal assurance that Maria Theresa had no aggressive intention, and his evident belief in the idea of "preventive war"—the doctrine that the best defense is to strike the first blow. Some historians have contended that when Frederick precipitated the Seven Years' War by invading Saxony on August 29, 1756, he did so with the purpose of annexing Saxony; but a more plausible explanation seems to be that the gathering international tensions, the subterfuges and the diplomatic shifts and secret alliances, had been creating an atmosphere of suspicion and fear that made the need of attacking seem evident to Frederick, whether or not such a need did actually exist.

A reference to Frederick's own writings should be instructive. While one can discount any autobiographical work to some extent, particularly when it seeks to justify the author's own conduct, Frederick has been credited with being unusually candid and straightforward in his reports. And whether candid or not in regard to matters of objective fact, he could not write without casting revealing sidelights on his own state of mind. First of all, Frederick's words indicate an apprehension of attack:

The dispatches which the king received from Dresden were full of the plans that were formed by the court of Vienna to invade the states of the king. From these he learned that, if no better could be found, the empress queen would make the difference of the king with the duke of Mecklenburgh a pretext for war.[18]

This pretext, says Frederick, was nothing but a pretext; the occasion was a trifle; "the affair had been accommodated; and slumbered." But at the same time trouble brewed on another horizon:

The king had a channel through which he obtained certain advice, relative to the projects of his enemies. . . . From these writings it appeared that the court of Russia excused herself, because of inability, from undertaking war that year, her fleet not being in a condition to put to sea; but in revenge she promised the greatest efforts should be made the next.[19]

Frederick naturally felt obliged to inquire of Maria Theresa as to the meaning of the great armaments that were piling up; but she was not frank when he appealed for a "categorical answer."

The reply of Count Kaunitz was found to be conceived in equivocal and ambiguous terms; but he explained himself with less reserve to Count Flemming, the ambassador from the king of Poland at Vienna, who sent his court an account of this conversation. A copy of his dispatches was immediately sent from Dresden to Berlin. In these Count Flemming said—"Count Kaunitz proposes to incite disquietude in the king by his replies, and to induce him to commit the first hostilities." It is certain that the style was so haughty, so arrogant, that it was sufficiently clear the empress queen was determined on war.[20]

We are now provided an insight into the calculating mind of Frederick, which was not concerned with how to avert war, but when best to stage the supposedly unavoidable conflict.

Considerations like these caused the question to be examined, whether it was more advantageous to anticipate the enemy, by an immediate attack, or wait till they had finished their grand preparations, and suffer them to use their own discretion. . . . Whatever part should be taken, under such circumstances, war was equally inevitable; it was the business of calculation to find whether it would be most advantageous to delay, some months, or to begin immediately.

. . . By deferring war, the king would give an ill-disposed neighbor time to become more formidable; not to add that Russia could not enter into action the present year; and Saxony not having concluded its arrangements, the moment seemed favorable to gain upon the enemy, by obtaining, in the first campaign, advantages which ill-timed delicacy would lose, should military operations be deferred to the following year.[21]

The author now defines "ill-timed delicacy":

At a moment so serious, so important, would it not have been an unpardonable fault, in politics, to have stopped at vain formalities; from which we ought not to depart, in the common course of things, but to which we ought not to submit, in cases so extraordinary as these, when irresolution and delay would have insured destruction, and when safety could only be found by vigorous and prompt resolution, executed with equal activity? [22]

No one can say whether "irresolution and delay would have insured destruction" in Frederick's case, nor whether negotiations for peace would have been "vain formalities." Perhaps they would have been; but Frederick's position made the recourse to gunpowder certain. It is impossible to believe that, with a firm will to peace on the part of the leaders of Austria, France, England, Russia, and Prussia, peace could not have been obtained. But the will to peace was insufficiently strong; fear and jealousy and revenge and enmity, greed for territorial and commercial advantage, and desire for the humiliation of rivals, were too powerful in the minds of the chiefs of state to save the world from a disastrous struggle. Whether the subjects of the several monarchs wished war, was of course a matter too trivial for consideration.

It is true that in England, France, and Austria, the people were not sharers in the war nor directly affected, except by the taxes with which they had to meet the bill. But the situation was different in Prussia, whose provinces, as Frederick tells us, "were laid waste and desolated, by the rapacity and barbarity of enemies." The fact is that ruin and havoc were everywhere; the currency had been debased; destitution, scarcity, and crushingly high prices stalked side by side; the population of 4,500,000 had diminished by an estimated half million; law and order in many districts were a mere memory; the very army which had been Frederick's pride had been shot to tatters; and the country had the devastated appearance that had marked it at the close of the Thirty Years' War.

It is therefore not surprising that Frederick ends his history with a prayer that future rulers may never "be obliged to have recourse to remedies so violent and fatal." One has here the suggestion that some idea of war's futility has bitten into the mind of one of the most aggressive of war-leaders.

Chapter 22

Pre-Revolutionary Armies and Peoples

Thus far we have looked principally at the war-making states and their leaders. But this by no means completes the picture: to understand the forces at work, and particularly the psychological forces, we should observe the peoples, and the parts they have played or refused to play; and the armies, their nature and composition.

Now that the idea of "all-out-war" is overshadowing the world; now that we conceive of international conflicts as the affairs of all the people, the worker in the mill and the housewife in the kitchen no less than the soldier on the front lines, it is difficult for us to remember that our view of warfare is relatively new. A mere two centuries ago, before the frenzied awakening of modern nationalism, wars were regarded as matters between governments, in which the interest of the ordinary man was at most incidental. Though eighteenth-century France and England were embroiled in a blazing series of wars, that was not deemed reason for a Frenchman to hate an Englishman, or an Englishman a Frenchman; the fruits of French civilization were not proscribed in London, nor were the products of British civilization condemned in Paris; nor was it unusual for citizens of the countries to intermingle in friendly intercourse. And all this was natural, in view of the fact that war was ordinarily remote from the average citizen; despite some exceptions, which we shall pause to remark, the merchant, the manufacturer, the farmer, and the mechanic usually went about their work unaffected by the fact that the armies of their country, in remote parts of Europe or still remoter colonies, were exchanging shots with the troops of hostile sovereigns.

In short, the rank and file of the people did not see war, know war, or manifest any warlike combativeness.

And this, as noted above, was in part because war was considered the business of rulers and governments rather than of the masses; and in part it was because the actual fighting was done by

specialized classes: on top, the otherwise idle and often impecuni-
ous nobility; and, below them, the professional killers, the riffraff
of society, who were entrusted with the fighting so that honest
men and women might go about their proper affairs. The mercenary system, while not the exclusive recourse of the recruiting
agents, survived vigorously until late in the eighteenth century;
every schoolchild will remember the hired Hessians who opposed
the colonists in the American Revolution; while German and Swiss
mercenaries were conspicuous in numerous early modern armies,
and mercenaries of some sort comprised from one fourth to two
thirds of the usual Continental army prior to 1789.

Even in the case of the standing armies and the navies, the recruits were not ordinarily drawn from the industrious middle
ranks of society, but from the same two unproductive classes as
the unattached mercenaries: the nobility, who monopolized or
nearly monopolized the officerships; and the drifting dregs, the
scum, the ruffianly elements, who frequently gave more trouble
than they were worth. Yet these adventurers and derelicts did not
always enlist willingly or with open eyes; the army of France,
when taken over by Louis XIV's famous minister Louvois, was
composed of men some of whom had been enrolled while drunk,
and some of whom had been enticed by false promises as to pay
and conditions of service, and some of whom had submitted in
desperation as the only alternative to starving. Throughout the
Continent great numbers of soldiers had been "impressed"—in other
words, kidnapped, snatched from dens, bars, and taverns, swept
up from the jails, seized as fair game upon the dark streets and
alleys of cities.

The situation in the British navy was notorious. If a man were
unlucky enough to be an apprentice and out of work in England
of the mid-eighteenth century, or if he were a vagabond or an
able-bodied beggar, or most of all if he were an experienced seaman, he would be in danger of capture by one of the press-gangs
that bore down upon the defenseless like wolf packs. The law,
indeed, required no more than that the sailor be caught in order
to make him liable to service—away with him, let him fend for
his country on a warship! The poor seaman, returning from a
voyage to the colonies, or even coming home from a fishing expedition, might be snapped up before reaching port by one of the
tenders that prowled about just outside the harbor. But the British

sailors were not the only victims; in America the efforts of His Majesty's servants to impress seamen sometimes led to riots, which in one case in Boston lasted three days.

Equally unsavory conditions prevailed in the French navy. The seamen of France were liable for life to naval service, according to a system of classes by which a man might be made to serve one year out of every four or more. But as this method proved inadequate for large-scale warfare, and as the French seamen showed just about the same warlike spirit as their brothers across the Channel, France also had recourse to the press-gang plan of enlistment. Not only that, but when the supply of involuntary native talent failed, she obtained foreigners to man the French warships and fight their battles, likewise involuntarily. And when the press-gangs were unable to capture seamen enough in Nice, Genoa, and other ports of the Mediterranean, they conferred an opportunity for sea travel upon unappreciative French subjects who had never seen the sea before—peasants, craftsmen, and the like. In view of such facts, it is hardly surprising that France did not shine as a naval power.

II

Virtually the same story is repeated, though with some flagrant variations, in one of the most celebrated of Continental military organizations, the Prussian army. We are wont to think of that famous force marching forth boldly, eagerly, animated by a powerful *esprit de corps*. And while there was such a spirit among those Prussians who enlisted willingly, under local lords whom they had been wont to obey all their lives, the case was quite different with great masses of the troops. In vain the dukes of the small neighboring state of Mecklenburg would grumble to the King and complain to the Emperor at the methods of Prussian press-gangs; whole companies of Prussians would come galloping to the villages on a Sunday morning, surround the churches, snatch as many as they wished of the men attending divine services, and bear them off to worship the King of Prussia from a pew in the infantry.

These Prussian recruiters, like the press-gangs of other nations, appear not to have been over-particular about the type and quality of the soldiers. When enlisted men were in hot demand, age and criminality and disease were no barriers; deserters from foreign armies were welcome whether they wished to be or not, and so also on some occasions were prisoners of war; while Frederick the Great, reverting to methods more common in earlier centuries, attempted in 1756 to compensate himself for his losses at the Battle of Lobositz by enlisting fourteen thousand non-voluntary enemy troops. And later he regularly sent recruiting agents into hostile territory, including that of Austria, so that the natives might have the advantages of employment by the Prussian army, whether or not they appreciated such benefits.

Perhaps it is not surprising, therefore, that the thankless wretches did their best to take informal leave. The rate of desertion from the Prussian army was the highest in Europe; the impressed troops could never be relied upon not to go over to the enemy in the thick of the battle, and apparently missed few opportunities to squirm out of sight even in peacetime. "Reading Frederick's *Principes générales de la guerre*," as one commentator declares, "one gains the impression that the prime function of an officer was to prevent desertion; that to fight the enemy was a secondary consideration. The French traveler, Toulongeon, perhaps the keenest observer of mid-century Prussia, put it aptly when he said that to the native half of the Prussian army was assigned the duty of preventing the foreign half from deserting." [1]

What, therefore, was it that won the battles of these miscellaneous mobs of vagabonds, villagers, farmhands, and other reluctant warriors? The fact is that the impressed men put the most serious limitations on the maneuvers of their generals, since it was dangerous to march too fast, to pursue the enemy too far or come to close grips with him, or to attack at night or in places offering opportunities for concealment, lest the men "missing in action" should suddenly become inordinately numerous. Under such circumstances, there was only one force that would drive the troops forth at all. It was a maxim of Frederick's that the recruit should fear his commander more than he did the enemy; and it is evident that this principle was put into effect, and that the Prussian rank and file—like the Zulus who preferred the danger of pursuing the enemy to the certainty of execution by their own side if they retreated—went forth to fight only because the perils of not fighting seemed greater still.

As all this implies, the discipline imposed by Frederick was merciless. In his *Political Testament* (1752), he insisted on the need for absolute obedience; he prescribed the death penalty for the soldier who murmured against his officer or lifted a hand against him, and for the officer who rebelled against a superior; he stated that generals and colonels should be given "despotic power," and that discipline among the soldiers should be better observed than among monks in a monastery. This discipline was in fact maintained by constant rigorous drill, supplemented by coercion of an unsparing nature: floggings were frequent; imprisonment, seasoned by torture, was far from rare; while a particularly cruel punishment was the running of the gauntlet, in which the victim, stripped to the waist, was forced to run back and forth among hundreds of his comrades armed with rods, which they would apply—often fatally—out of fear of a like penalty if they softened their blows.

Thus, in the most militarized country in modern Europe, the military spirit had to be whipped up by the most brutal and artificial means.

The above, of course, applies specifically to the common soldiers. But the case in regard to the officers is equally illuminating. Unlike the men in the ranks, they sprang from the nobility; Frederick, in fact, manifested a strong class bias, and would rarely bestow a commission upon anyone not of aristocratic lineage; if he did employ untitled men when he needed them, they could expect little in the way of recognition when their term of service was over.

On the other hand, he withheld his favor from nobles who would not serve, or would not serve long enough. And he was aided by the fact that the Prussian nobility, the belated survivals of the feudal age and inheritors of a feudal warlike tradition, provided ideal foundations for a military despotism; besides, many of their members welcomed the King's money as a source of livelihood. In most of the *junker* families there were some army officers —officers, who, under Frederick, were subjected to a rigid training in the Cadettenhaus, the state military academy established in Berlin by Frederick's father. There they were encouraged not only to study military tactics and methods, but to write books on the subject; and for years they were submitted to a meticulous routine of drills and reviews—which were regarded so seriously that, we are told, officers would take their own lives sooner than let the

King catch them in an act of negligence. When we remember that these officers were rarely on leave, that they might not engage in crafts or trades, and that comparatively few of them found the opportunity to marry, we will understand that they represented a warped and narrow class development, with their minds unnaturally channeled toward the one end of building armies and making war. In view of the grip that this exclusive, arrogant, and intolerant officer corps obtained over the nation, it is little wonder that a popular saying declared that Prussia was not a country that had an army; it was an army that had a country.

In England the press-gang did not serve the navy only. Yet in England, except during the Cromwellian period, standing armies were not much in vogue; secure in their insular position, His Majesty's subjects relied in the main upon their navy for defense. And while many British mercenaries were indeed to be found in Continental forces, the English repugnance to professional armies was notable throughout the centuries, and particularly after the Restoration, when the country had had a first-hand glimpse of armies in action. Even before Cromwell's ascendancy, in 1624, the reluctance of the people to serve as soldiers was such that it was found difficult to raise six thousand volunteers to send across the Channel to aid the Dutch against the Spaniards; in the autumn of that year, when a rabble of rude, raw wretches were herded into ships to serve in Lower Germany, they were led in much the manner of trapped animals driven by whips. Years earlier, Shakespeare had referred to the practice of impressing men; he put these words into Falstaff's mouth:

If I be not ashamed of my soldiers, I am a soused gurnet. I have misused the king's press damnably. . . . I press me none but good householders, yeomen's sons; inquire me out contracted bachelors, such as had been asked twice on the banns. . . . I pressed me none but such toasts-and-butter, with hearts in their bellies no bigger than pins'-heads. . . . and now my whole charge consists of ancients, corporals, lieutenants, gentlemen of companies, slaves as ragged as Lazarus in the painted cloth, where the glutton's dogs licked the sores; and such as indeed were never soldiers. . . . No eye hath seen such scarecrows. I'll not march through Coventry with them, that's flat: nay, and the villains march wide between the legs, as if they had gyves on; for indeed I had the most of them out of prison.[2]

Shakespeare was here reporting no more than the current reality. According to another sixteenth-century writer, "In England when service happeneth we disburthen the prison of thieves, we rob the taverns and alehouses of tosspots and ruffians, we scour both town and country of rogues and vagabonds." [3]

A system of home defense did indeed exist in theory; every man had the duty of defending the country, every able-bodied male of sixteen or over might be called to serve, and every possessor of an estate of a certain value could be made to provide armed horsemen. Yet all this was of small military consequence; "trained bands" of untrained men were in fact produced; but a Colonel Ward, writing in 1639, remarked that they learned little except how to drink; and other writers echo this complaint.

In the same year that Colonel Ward condemned the "trained bands," Charles I gathered an army of fifteen thousand for the Scottish wars; but Sir Edmund Verney, who saw them from the King's camp, commented with no great enthusiasm: "I daresay there was never so raw, so unskilful, and so unwilling an army brought to fight." [4] In the following year the King impressed an army of twenty-five thousand men—some of whom, apparently, were more eager to fight each other than to engage the enemy; the religious issue flared forth, and some Devonshire Protestants murdered a supposedly Catholic lieutenant, while some Essex men broke into churches and set fire to communion rails and surplices. But as for victory in battle—with such an army, that was out of the question.

In the civil war, impressed troops were used by both sides—that is, such of them as did not slip back home at the first opportunity. The fact is that there was great difficulty in inducing any of them to serve outside their own districts, where they would bear arms only so long as the enemy was at hand. In 1643 an ordinance of Parliament authorized the impressing of twenty-two thousand men between the ages of eighteen and fifty, but specifically exempted scholars, students in the Inns of Court and universities, clergymen, government officials, and certain others, including sons of the propertied classes. And, eight years later, an army of ten thousand impressed men was raised by the Commonwealth for service in Ireland—fitter fighters, it was said, than the volunteers, many of whom should have been still in school. Nevertheless, volunteers filled all needs between 1651 and 1660, when the lure of the military life evidently began to fade and impressment was again held necessary.

But whether or not the soldiers were products of the press-gang, their martial spirit had to be encouraged by the ancient preceptors: fear and punishment. The penalties were the savage ones usual at the time: whipping, running the gauntlet, mutilation, branding, public disgrace, and—in the more serious cases—shooting or hanging. Evidently Cromwell was no more convinced than were Caesar or Frederick II that the fighting spirit was its own all-sufficient inducement to the warrior.

A century after Cromwell's time, the Englishman was still showing his indisposition to serve in standing armies. Sponsored by Pitt, the Militia Act of 1757 introduced a much watered form of conscription; the conscripts were chosen by lot, a little as in the case of the American Selective Service; but the penalty of being picked was in many cases merely financial; the selected man was permitted to pay for a substitute—as a result of which nothing resembling the expected citizens' army was ever developed. Even the prescription of twenty-eight days' drill each year was considered excessive; while the immense unpopularity of the Act was matched only by the weakness and incompetence of the army it created.

IV

This brings us to the question of conscription in general. While nothing corresponding to modern universal service was known anywhere in Europe prior to the French Revolution, we have seen how a limited form of conscription was introduced in Russia by Peter the Great; and we can trace the ancestry of universal service in the partial conscription adopted by various Continental powers, no less than in the recruiting methods of the press-gang.

It was in Prussia that pre-Revolutionary conscription perhaps gained its greatest impetus. At the same time as the kidnapping crews of Frederick the Great were draining manpower from neighboring states, his conscription agents were calling upon Prussian youths according to a system whereby each canton was expected to keep a regiment perpetually supplied with men. This was far from universal service, since numerous exemptions were allowed and none except certain groups of artisans and peasants actually had to bear arms. But even those did not as a rule give continuous service; when agricultural needs demanded—and the country's straitened economy forbade too severe a drain upon farm laborers—the men might return to their homes on leave in order to work the soil for as much as ten months a year.

In Sweden as far back as the time of Gustavus Adolphus, a system of partial conscription existed, whereby prescribed quotas were sent from various districts. And in France, where foreign mercenaries at times formed as much as half the army, the supply of these hirelings did not always suffice even when supplemented by volunteers; the king's agents therefore began to draft men from the militia, which was supposed to be kept at home to guard the native soil from attack—and this drafting proceeded blandly in the face of a law requiring all enlistments to be voluntary. After 1745, the idea of forced service was accepted in France; and this, along with conscription in Prussia and elsewhere, formed the precedent that paved the way for universal service, the armies of Napoleon, and that subsequent militarization which has become the bane of the modern world.

v

Another factor in the progressive militarization of Europe was the position of the nobility. We have seen how the Prussian nobles had a place of overriding privilege in the army, and how none but the aristocrat had much chance of a commission. And the attitude of the Prussians, though approaching a Spartan extreme in hard-and-fast service requirements, differed only in degree from that of other Europeans. Certainly, no other fact as clearly showed the class nature of modern militarism, its foundation upon the sands of social inequality, its identification with the interests of a group rather than of society as a whole, and its expansion in deliberate support of the desires, pride, bias, social prestige, and economic advantage of a narrow segment of the community. In France the most capable common soldier, assuming that he was no richer than most of his class, had no chance whatever of becoming a colonel or captain; but the most incompetent son of a noble, though without military education and no more than fourteen or sixteen years of age, might receive a colonel's commission—provided that his father had the money to pay for it. Louvois, the minister of Louis XIV, was accomplishing a reform when he restricted sales of commissions to captaincies and colonelships. One must admit, of course, that in the great democracy of wealth, men without blue blood were often able to buy officerships for their sons; after all, their money was as valuable as anyone's. And thus the nobility of means came to edge shoulders with the nobility of descent. But poverty even when wedded to competence still was given no consideration. It is scarcely remarkable therefore that, during the Seven Years' War, the French officers were conspicuous for nothing but their incapacity.

In France of the eighteenth century, it would not have been a great exaggeration to say that the army was an employment agency for needy nobles. Thus in 1702 seven thousand commissions were created for the nobility, who thereby, on the basis of nothing but birth, were elevated above the heads of the ablest non-commissioned men. Later the situation became so bad that, to quote one authority,

in 1775, when the total strength of the army was 170,000 men, the number of the officers was no less than 60,000, and they represented a charge of 47,000,000 *livres* . . . while the total remaining expenditure on the army did not exceed 44,000,000. Yet of these 60,000 officers not more than 10,000 were doing duty with their regiments.[5]

"It is necessary to place the gentlemen" was a cry that beat in the face of reform. And so an order of the year 1781 required candidates for sub-lieutenancies to show their breeding papers in the shape of proof of four noble ancestors—if the applicant's blood chanced to be contaminated by an untitled grandfather of no matter what personal distinction, he was unworthy to lead the troops of his country.

Obviously, matters of war or peace, of the national interest or national defense, were not here at issue. All that was taken into account was the maintenance of a patrician class in a privileged position. And the militarization developed by the patricians, and the warfare springing from it, had no more relationship to the needs, desires, or pugnacious impulses of the people than had the baronial castles, the moats, and tournaments of the Middle Ages. The army, to put matters bluntly, was the nobleman's graft; it was held to be as fitting to the nobleman as was service in the company of a lord to the *samurai* of feudal Japan. And this was true to some degree not only in France and Prussia but in England and wherever the nobility existed.

But the nobility did more than to monopolize the officerships of European armies. They brought with them ancient ideas of combat, honor, and glory—ideas represented in private life by the quixotic but bloody institution of the duel, and sometimes developed on a national scale to the plane of a duel, a contest of honor between nations. Yet this "honor" had little to do with righteousness. It did not mean scrupulous regard for truth, strict fidelity to obligations, a spirit of generosity, justice, love, and human kindness. It meant, rather, respect for the more or less arbitrary code of the heroic ideal, a punctilious class loyalty, an aristocratic hauteur, and an almost pathological readiness to react to insult (an insult being an implication that a man had disobeyed the unwritten caste law). Among individuals such an offense could be wiped out only by means of the blood-letting or threatened blood-letting of an "affair of honor"; and among nations something similar has been the case down to our own day. For while it is nothing unusual for nations to machinate in secret, to break agreements and betray allies, the country that loses most prestige and honor is the one that refuses to knock a chip off its shoulder. Similarly, every reverse, every retreat, however wisely or courageously made, lowers its prestige, its honor in the eyes of the world—which is quite in accordance with the nobleman's ideal, as inherited from feudalism and the heroic age.

All this has been made possible, however, only by the attitude of the common man throughout the centuries: the fact that he has been dazed and humbled before the spectacle of the nobleman's pageantry and pretense, and therefore a willing worshipper before the nobleman's idols. Even in America, where titles have been forbidden, we have seen the respectful if not reverential attitude of the masses toward any foreign count, duke, or baroness; while we have read of English crowds waiting for hours to learn of the birth of a child to their future queen, as though this occurred by some process not usual among other humans. And if this can be reported in our democratic and enlightened century, what of the ages when dukes and princes rode past in aristocratic aloofness, bristled in their rock-hewn castles, or posed in velvety livery with flunkeys fawning in their train? Impressed as by the sight of godhood, the multitude not only accepted the physical domination of the nobles but bowed to the domination of their ideas. And thus they came to mirror the lords' own grandiose conception of themselves, followed their leadership in war and peace, and permitted their standards of honor and glory to be engrafted upon the social fabric.

Though the nobles formed a distinctively military caste, there are some things to be said for the principles of combat they inherited from feudal and pre-feudal days. Since they carried on the idea of war as a game, they did not tend to fight with quite the deadliness of many earlier and later warriors; their conception of honor sometimes forbade the use of tricks and subterfuges; and they did not as a rule involve whole populations in their crimson pastimes. Like the *condottieri*, they indulged in many conflicts of a deliberately limited nature; these struggles, in the eighteenth century, were waged only during the warmer and pleasanter seasons, were not pushed to the dire extreme of destroying the opposing armies, and were built around the idea of defense rather than of offense, so that comparatively bloodless sieges tended to predominate over gory pitched battles. Therefore, despite the exceptions already noted, warfare in the eighteenth century did not tend to exhaust the nations' resources of men or materials to anything approaching the twentieth-century extent.

Yet already the drain was considerable, and premonitory of the prostrating engagements of two centuries later. We have seen that Frederick William I of Prussia devoted five sevenths of his country's income to the army; and the situation under his son Frederick was not vastly improved; in 1786, the year of Frederick's death, between twelve and thirteen million thalers out of a government income of twenty-two or twenty-three million was directly given to support an army of 195,000 men. And in France as far back as the time of Louis XIV, the maintenance of the standing army of over 100,000 constituted a tremendous problem: not only in the direct payments for the soldiers and their equipment, but in the creation of influential vested interests, purveyors of food, clothing, and armaments who depended upon military demands for their livelihood; a huge officers' corps; and a potentially mischievous national pride. On the opposite side of the screen, this pride was reflected in the jealousy, suspicion, and fear that great armaments always arouse in neighbor nations; it spurred these, in imagined national defense, to pile up their own armaments; and thus a start was made in the modern armaments race, wherein the burden of preparedness becomes so onerous that to arm one's self for peace is sometimes equivalent to girding one's self for war.

All this was the direct product of the competitive modern state system, which was itself an outgrowth of feudalism, wherein an immense number of states large and small threatened one another in continual wars. It was the world's misfortune that, at a time when the individuality of peoples was comparatively little recognized and a political amalgamation of many lands would have been far easier than at a later period, all of Europe was split into antagonistic entities responsive to the will or desires of local leaders. And it is an even greater tragedy that this system (or lack of system) and the ideas dependent upon it should have survived to our own day, so that the separateness of states rather than the oneness of peoples has been stressed, and old walls have consequently been fortified and new ones erected at a time when the peaceful needs of all alike demanded a leveling of walls. The fact that Europe continued to divide itself into warlike units, instead of to amalgamate itself into a cooperative whole, is therefore largely to be traced to the old political conception of the State, and of the State's all-powerful autocratic leader. With the dawn of the revolutionary era, a gradually developing dynamic new idea—the idea of modern nationalism—was to take the stage; but this idea, as we shall see, was to be reponsible for further war-producing cleavages, and was to inaugurate the most devastating fighting of all time.

Chapter 23

Colonization and Empire

While warfare was raging with accelerated fury upon the continent of Europe, white civilization was being introduced at the point of the sword into far-distant lands. The solitudes of North American woods, once undisturbed except for the occasional whirring of arrows and the war-whoop of the Iroquois, now resounded to the rattling of musketry; the quiet of South American mountains was broken by the march of European gold-seekers; the jungles of Florida, the plateaus of Mexico, the sweltering plains of India, and the slave-raided coast of Africa all rang with the din of the warfare introduced by the omnipotent invader.

Considered with regard to the number of men and the amount of equipment involved, the wars of colonization and empire were not among the greatest. Frequently the combatants were but a handful; often they represented mere isolated expeditions affecting a single limited district. And yet, taken as a whole, they are among the most important in history, for they incurred the extermination of whole races and civilizations, the subjugation of other races, and the decadence of surviving cultures; and they enabled a single continent to conquer several continents, and a single system of belief and action to predominate over much of the known world.

The question therefore arises: how did all this come about? How was it possible for the inhabitants of one limited section of the globe, within the brief period of several centuries, to march with fire and sword across millions of square miles of strange and mostly unknown territory? What motives were behind them? What forces goaded them to their aggressions and triumphs?

It is a commonplace of psychology that human motives are mixed and not simple; and that a variety of impulses, some of them hidden from the actual doer, may underlie even the most ordinary act. Hence we need not attempt to explain the colonizing wars by any single cause or group of causes. The restlessness of young blood and the greed of adventure; the pressure of population, and the goad of religious oppression; the hope of fabulous Elysiums, and the call of mythical fountains of youth, have all played their much-reported part in the early migrations and the consequent wars. Yet there is another factor that seems even more largely responsible for the drift of Europeans overseas and their conflicts with the natives of the invaded lands. And this is the element of acquisitiveness.

Acquisitiveness in America, Asia, and Africa possessed its usual irrational and predatory quality. True to its European heritage, it was not concerned with basic economic needs or sober economic advantage; it was concerned with the passion of the gold-seeker, the madness of the great god Get Rich Quick. "Follow me, and a genie will open your way to wealth!" that divinity had exclaimed to the faithful. "Follow me, and the doors of power, luxury, and lavish gain will swing wide!" Yet, strangely, the explorers were less eager for things of intrinsic value than for that glittering metal which human belief and desire throughout the centuries had exalted with an artificial worth.

"Europeans," remarks one commentator, "were attracted to other lands in the first place by the hope of finding gold and other treasures; and secondly by the anticipation of free land to be exploited by slave labor." [1] "They were not anxious," declares another, "to possess lands which offered wealth only as the reward of the patient and persistent labor of the herdsman and agriculturist." [2] Only on this ground can we explain why the fertile plains of the Argentine were long neglected while the seekers wandered afar on chimerical and sometimes ruinous expeditions, fighting and looting and murdering, attacking and enslaving the Indians and questing for Eldorado in remote mines.

To make the rich plains of Buenos Aires give up their wealth required persistent labor, but it was not for this that the bulk of the Spaniards sought the New World. In the discovery and development of mines, as they were found in Mexico and Peru, there was always an opportunity for severe labor, but there was also the possibility of great rewards. In carrying war into the wilderness against the Indians, there were, moreover, always difficulties and dangers, but there was also the possibility of capturing a prince, whose ransom might suddenly enrich an army. [3]

Many incidents from the careers of the explorers and *conquistadores* illustrate the unlimited grasping propensity that underlay their wars. It appears to have been the accepted philosophy that any newcomer to any land could claim everything in sight, and not a few things out of sight, in the name of his sovereign—and never for a moment do any of the gallant explorers seem to consider that the natives may have any prior rights. Thus Balboa, upon first seeing the Pacific, was restrained by no hampering modesty, but unblushingly proclaimed the right of the King of Spain to the world's largest ocean, along with all its islands and bordering lands. Since the simple-minded aborigines could not always understand the claims of the most Christian and Holy intruders to whatever they wanted to take, it is hardly surprising that a few battles resulted.

De Soto, who has been called "the best of the Conquistadores," is one example of the Spanish methods and state of mind. Though he may have been a prince among his kind, he was capable of fierce destructive orgies; was capable of exterminating whole native tribes (as in the case of the stronghold of Mauvila, whose men and women he massacred indiscriminately after storming the place). Yet doubtless his murderous frenzies were justified by the fact that they occurred in the course of a search for gold. Side by side with his butcheries, incidentally, De Soto introduced religion; the words "Gold" and "God" were linked in his vocabulary; and priests and monks accompanied the *conquistador* in order to save the souls of the savages whose bodies he destroyed and whose precious metals he came to plunder.

An even more striking example was that of Pizarro, the key to whose character was "insatiable ambition and lust for gold, and willingness to sacrifice everything thereto." [4] A typical instance of his lavishness with other people's property is provided by the renowned compact he made with his comrades Almagro and De Luque, agreeing to an equal distribution of conquered territory in South America, along with the spoils in gold, silver, gems, etc. Their document, like the pronouncements of De Soto, was pervaded with a marked note of sanctity, which certainly deceived no one unless the makers themselves were taken in by it.

But it may be that they themselves were convinced by their own protestations of piety. Prescott apparently is on solid ground when, after assuring us that "Gold was the incentive and the recompense," he remarks of Pizarro, "His courage was sullied with cruelty, the cruelty that flowed equally—strange as it may seem—

from his avarice and his religion; religion as it was understood in that age,—the religion of the Crusader." [5]

But the strength of the religious as compared with the avaricious motive will be evident from Pizarro's actual dealings. Though masses were said and everlasting salvation promised to the faithful, his bosom comrades were plunder and loot, bloodshed and destruction. He showed his true nature at the city of Caxamalca, where he and his fellow gallants made an unprovoked attack, and mercilessly shot to death the unresisting and weaponless citizenry. Subsequently, after he had seized and imprisoned the Inca Atahualpa, he agreed to the sovereign's release on condition that a room twenty-two feet long and seventeen feet across should be filled with gold. And after these extraordinary terms had been met by the natives, Pizarro not only shrugged aside his share of the agreement, but conducted a travesty of a trial wherein the Inca was condemned to be burned to death. And having permitted him the mercy of being strangled, in return for his acceptance of Christianity, Pizarro and his merry crew melted down the irreplaceable art treasures of the Incas—fountains of gold, and golden birds and animals, wrought with exquisite skill.

But they did far more than that, this band of Spanish rogues and adventurers, numbering in all not more than two hundred men. They put an end to one of the most remarkable empires ever known, with its highly organized socialized administration, its incomparable network of roads, its cultivated mountain terraces, its tame herds of llamas, and its flourishing population which, at the most conservative estimate, was "approximately twice as great as that of the same territory today." [6] But essentially the wars of Pizarro, though aided and abetted by a ferocious religious belief, were no more than a series of those raids for booty by which marauders for thousands of years have been preying upon civilized communities. And the fact that they succeeded more strikingly than most may be traced to several causes, largely psychological: the maddening urge of the drive for gold; the Inca's false sense of security, which counseled him to permit the invaders to penetrate far inland, that he might dazzle them with a display of his power; and the Europeans' possession of firearms, which, however, might not have proved decisive except for the paralyzing fear they incited in the Indians.

Cortes, while a less revolting character than Pizarro, waged war for much the same reasons. His religion may have been deeper-rooted; but that it was of a not unmercenary nature is shown by the code that he promulgated before the siege of Mexico. "The instrument," says Prescott, ". . . reminds the army that the conversion of the heathen is the work most acceptable in the eye of the Almighty, and one that will be sure to receive his support. It calls on every soldier to regard this as the prime object of the expedition, *without which the war would be manifestly unjust, and every acquisition made by it a robbery.*" [7]

So once more we can see the sources of warfare in theft sanctified by religion. There were certainly other motives in Cortes' case, including not only the daring of an adventurous nature, but the fact that he had no choice except to be daring; he had to go forward, since his enemy Velasquez was behind him blocking his retreat. Nevertheless, one can see the gold-lust traveling everywhere with the expedition. One can observe it in the famous massacre at Cholula, when Cortes' men, after hewing down the undefended natives with musket and sword, burst into the temples and houses and robbed them eagerly of all valuables, including jewels and articles of gold and silver. One can also notice the passion for gold during the long siege of Mexico, when the conquerors steeled themselves to the ordeal by enticing stories of the treasures that were to reward their efforts—treasures that, in the actual taking, were to belie their expectations. And one can read anything but disdain for riches in the fact that Cortes, upon returning to Spain, "displayed his magnificence in a rich treasure of jewels, among which were emeralds of extraordinary size and luster, gold to the amount of two hundred thousand *pesos de oro*, and fifteen hundred marks of silver." [8]

But if gold was the incentive to Cortes and his followers, psychological forces of a different nature were to give them the victory when they might easily have been crushed. We have seen how the Aztecs, hungry for living captives to offer upon the altars of their gods, enabled the Spaniards time after time to escape. As if this did not give the invaders advantage enough, the natives' terror of the horse was a powerful deterrent to the defense; in their ignorance, they imagined that the creature and its rider made but one animal, with two heads—no doubt chillingly dreadful as it came clattering and thundering down upon them in galloping companies.

Under such circumstances, effective resistance was all but impossible.

But perhaps the decisive factor was an old legend which recited how the benign god Quetzalcoatl, having been banished by his fellow deities to the retreat of Tlapallan, would return some day to Mexico. Strangely, Quetzalcoatl was pictured as tall of frame and white of skin, dark-haired and bearded—so that he perfectly matched the actual appearance of the Spaniards. Nor was this all! The feeling seems to have been growing, at the time of Cortes' arrival, that the approach of the beloved deity was at hand: various natural occurrences, including the unexplained overflow of the lake of Tezcuco and the appearance of three comets and a strange light in the east, are all said to have confirmed the native belief in some approaching prodigy. The royal seer Nezahualpilli actually read in these portents a forecast of the empire's early overthrow. And while we cannot say just how far this prediction went toward paralyzing the hand of the sovereign, Montezuma, the whole series of beliefs regarding Quetzalcoatl apparently bred a fatalistic resignation, and had much to do with the monarch's weakness and indecision when vigorous action might have saved his kingdom.

II

Among the English in the New World, acquisitiveness is less evident than among the Spaniards; the Puritans, for example, were urged overseas mainly by religious and political motives, though as much cannot be said for the southern colonists. But neither southerner nor northerner, in their dealings with the Indians, were ruled exclusively by greed. Their disputes with the red men, and the wars that followed, arose largely from the inability of the newcomers to understand the ideas and mental processes of their adversaries. Judging by their own standards, the white men often dealt fairly with the aborigines; sometimes they even went so far as to pay for the land they occupied. The trouble was not so much in their individual honor or lack of it as in a more basic fault: the structure of their civilization, the background of their beliefs, was saturated by proprietary conceptions foreign to the savage. When the colonists gave money in exchange for land, they assumed that it was theirs for all time, since this was the only way they had known. But when the Indians sold their land, they imagined that they were granting merely the favor of its temporary use, since permanent land transfers were unknown to their people. Hence, when they sought to re-enter their hunting grounds and were driven out, they felt tricked and robbed; their resentment was that of the man who rents his house for the summer, only to be excluded at the point of a rifle when the summer is over. "In all instances," as John Fiske tells us, "the transaction was not like a free bargain and sale between members of a civilized community; it was more like the exercise of eminent domain, in which compensation is allowed." [9] The almost inevitable result, therefore, was strife.

We have observed the example of William Penn, who tried to deal understandingly with the native, and so encouraged harmony and mutual good will. Nor do we lack other evidences that the Indian, if properly treated, could act in a conciliatory manner:

In no clearer way is the spirit of the superior Indian recognized than when in Taunton church a leading chief, disgusted with Philip's cowardice and treachery in signing a treaty he did not mean to keep, threw down his arms and became for all time an ally of the whites. The town of Taunton escaped massacre during King Philip's War, because a family named Leonard had shown a kindness to Philip. This was sure proof that even a bloodthirsty chief was not entirely bad and could return kindness with kindness.[10]

How the fuse for an Indian conflict could be lighted is shown by the incident that precipitated King Philip's War. A converted Indian named Sassamon, an aide of King Philip, was found dead under circumstances pointing to murder; as a result of which the whites seized and hanged three Indians, though the evidence of their guilt was far from conclusive. The Indians' comrades, infuriated, took revenge by killing the oxen of a Swansea colonist, who carried on the blood feud by shooting one of the savages—after which the whole country blazed up in terror and bloodshed. The Sassamon affair, it is true, was no more than the proximate cause of the eruption, which had been brewing for some time; but it indicates the type of incident and the attitude of mind that underlay many of the Indian wars.

Much more enlightened, on the whole, were the French in their relations with the Indian. "The scheme of English colonization," says Francis Parkman, "made no account of the Indian tribes. In the scheme of French colonization they were all in all." [11] Hence we may expect to find the Indians better disposed toward the French, much more frequently their allies, and much more rarely at war with them. The most striking exception occurs in the case of the Iroquois, who became inveterate foes of the French after one French leader had played upon the wrong psychological strings. Their enmity, strangely, originated from the white man's desire to gain the good will of the savage—or, rather, from his fatal error in courting the good will of certain savages at the expense of others. The explorer Champlain, who made the disastrous stroke, no doubt earned the gratitude of the Hurons and Algonquins by joining a war party against the Iroquois. With his European weapons and armor, he had little difficulty in winning; merely to behold him, the enemy was stricken mute; and after two of the Iroquois had been killed and a third wounded, the warriors of the Five Nations precipitately fled—leaving the French one of the most dearly bought of all their colonial victories.

Here was the beginning, and in some measure doubtless the cause, of a long series of murderous conflicts, bearing havoc and flame to generations yet unborn. Champlain had invaded the tiger's den; and now, in smothered fury, the patient savage would lie biding his day of blood.[12]

As if fuel enough had not been added to the fire, Champlain on several later occasions indulged in the exhilarating game of shooting Iroquois. No doubt he did not foresee how, generations after his death, the Iroquois would still be the foes of the French and allies of the English, even though they were to learn how little they could rely upon the latter.

It would be futile to linger over the whole long succession of Indian wars, which continued into the nineteenth century. In many cases, apparently, the Indians were mere guileless children played upon by crafty self-seekers—by usurpers inflated with ideas of racial superiority, blown up with notions of religious sanctity, spurred on by an acquisitiveness quite beyond the comprehension of the native, and too often inspired with no fair-dealing. To the Indian's way of thinking, "the white man was rude and lacking in good manners. He was selfish, and refused to share goods, clothing, etc., even when he had an abundance. He scoffed at the most sacred ideas of the Indian and blasphemed the Powers above." [13] And when we add that the white man invaded the Indian's land, destroyed his fields and forests, slaughtered his game, tortured and slew his men in cold blood, outraged his women, and made treaties only in order to violate them, we can see that there was more than ample justification in the native mind for the assaults on the intruders (even when the latter were not the aggressors). To note one or two incidents of a later date than we have been considering: the Black Hawk War of 1836 broke out after the American government, by a treaty with the Sacs, had taken the land of the Foxes without the formality of asking permission. And the Seminole War in Florida began as a direct result of the slave trade: the traffickers in human flesh had set hands upon Osceola's wife, a handsome young squaw, and the irate husband had been arrested for objecting. But subsequently his pleas were heard to better effect among his own people, and within a year he had taken up arms and become the champion of their cause.

Perhaps more vividly than the historians, a poet of our own times has described the Indian's state of mind:

> These white men here have begged our hunting land.
> Their words are crookéd and their tongues are split;
> For even while they feign to beg for it,
> Their soldiers come to steal it.
>
> . . . .
>
> They cut the land in pieces, fencing out
> Their neighbors from the mother of all men!
> When she is sick, they make her bear again
> With medicines they give her with the seed!
> All this is sacrilegious! Yet they heed
> No word, and like a river in the spring
> They flood the country, sweeping everything
> Before them! 'Twas not many snows ago
> They said that we might hunt the buffalo
> In this our land forever. Now they come
> To break that promise. Shall we cower, dumb?
> Or shall we say: "First kill us—here we stand!" [14]

Though the words are those of a poet, the text is based upon historical documents, and the passage plausibly describes the emotions aroused in the Indian by the faithlessness, arrogance, and cupidity of the white despoiler. Hence we can understand how avoidable wars were caused by the passion of resentment and the conflict of ideas, and how the terrorism that long haunted our frontier might largely have been averted by a greater respect for the Indian as a man, a higher regard for the sworn word, and a less grasping attitude toward native possessions.

III

Throughout most of the vital eighteenth century, Europe was dominated by the economic creed known as mercantilism. It was this cult rather than economic necessity that underlay much of the thrusting and grasping, the shoving of nation against nation, and the exploitation or attempted exploitation of the colonies. According to mercantilist theory, it was essential for a nation to obtain a large supply of the precious metals, and to secure a "favorable balance of trade" (the same coveted excess of exports over imports that we hear of even today); and since this was not possible within the settled countries of Europe, with their stable industries, population, and commerce, it was necessary to maintain trade abroad. And this in turn involved the establishment of colonies, and the control of trade routes; which required the exclusion of foreign powers from those trade routes and colonies, as the eighteenth-century view was that the potential quantity of trade was limited, and that any amount taken by one nation subtracted from the sum total available to its rivals. The inevitable result of this philosophy was a competition for the choice spots of the earth among the great powers; and it followed that national jealousies were fanned, national resentments inflamed, and warfare precipitated in the course of the selfish grab-and-scramble for empire. At the same time, the theory was a guaranty of unrest within the colonies; for these, according to mercantilist theory, were meant to produce raw goods for the mother country, to provide receiving grounds for its manufactures, and to increase its favorable balance of trade. Mercantilism, as we shall see, was to be among the sources of the American Revolution. And it was to be visible behind another great colonial episode, the British conquest of India.

It is a curious fact, often remarked by historians, that England had no original intention of subjugating India: the conquest was accomplished by the agents of a commercial company, in defiance of the wishes of London. And it is equally curious that the great opponents of the English, the French under their celebrated administrator Dupleix, likewise acted in disregard of the home authorities, although "with one all-important difference, that Clive was to make his policy appear profitable to his employers, which Dupleix could never do." [15] The fact that the conquest was accepted, indeed the fact that it was even possible, is to be explained largely by mercantilist theories, in whose pursuit France and England, during much of the mid-eighteenth century, were attempting to benefit themselves by injuring each other's trade. A typical situation was that which arose in September, 1744, when news of the War of the Austrian Succession reached Madras; the natural question, which immediately leaped into men's minds, was whether the war should extend to India.

Both companies were divided on the question. Those who advocated war did not do so because they had any ideas of Empire in their heads, but because they saw a chance to destroy a rival's commerce. Those who advocated peace saw that commerce-destruction was a game that two could play, and doubted whether in the double process their profits and dividends would benefit. The French company was more inclined to peace than the English because its financial position was weaker.[16]

The British, having superior sea power, proved true to mercantilist theory by sweeping the waters clear of every visible French ship and so crippling the French commercial prospects. And, during all this time, their own commercial prospects were improving, until eventually the thought of India aroused a furor of emotion and speculation in the home country, and the idea of easy wealth came to dominate every other consideration. "Men had begun to look upon India as a mine of inestimable fortunes, and rushed to buy the Company's stock, which rose in 1767 to the price of 263 per cent. The rate of dividend to be declared was a question that concerned the greatest." [17]

When such was the attitude at home, it is not remarkable if grasping propensities manifested themselves among the field representatives of the Company. Take, for example, the case of Clive, who in 1757, not long before the Indian hysteria broke out in England, had distinguished himself by winning the Battle of Plassey. This military leader, one of the few generals in all history who officially represented not a government but a commercial company, can hardly be acquitted of waging war with no mercenary motives.

Before Plassey, an agreement was made whereby the army and navy were to receive 400,000 pounds, and 120,000 were to go to the Select Committee of six. As his own share, Clive gained the total of 234,000 pounds—not enough, however, to satisfy him! Subsequently, though he had also an annual revenue of 20,000 pounds as a quit-rent for lands south of Calcutta, he entered a scheme for enriching members of the Company by a Society of Trade formed to conduct a forbidden business in salt, betel-leaves, and opium. From this illegitimate traffic gigantic profits were reaped; and while the directors of the Company disavowed the project, Clive was able to sell his five shares for 32,000 pounds.

Even though at first there was no general desire for a new colony, the English were following a one-way path. If they were to retain their commercial grip over India and exclude other powers, they must also assume political sovereignty, since it is often necessary to dominate those whom we would exploit. Confronted on the one hand by the predatory native power of the Mahrattas, and on the other by the machinations of the French in the Carnatic, the Company had either to step into politics and war or to retire from the scene—and the latter idea probably never seriously occurred to anyone. The assumption of governmental responsibility, so foreign to the ideas of most Englishmen, was urged by Warren Hastings in the effort to rescue the country from chaos—and Hastings at the same time, less greedy for gold than most of his countrymen, did his best to relieve the peasants of their oppression at the hands of their new conquerors. But the movement for British control, once unloosed, rushed along like an avalanche; it was forcefully accelerated by Governor-General Wellesley, who, not content with protecting the existing dominions, conceived the audacious scheme of making the Company supreme in India by the seizure of fresh domains. And so, after a career of wars and annexations, the process was virtually completed, and the whole tremendous territory from the sea to the Himalayas became subject to the Company, and eventually to the Crown.

IV

By one of history's many contradictions, the same East India Company that bequeathed India to the British Empire, provided one of the reasons for the loss of the American colonies. The role of the Company did not unfold, however, until the tea episodes of 1773 and 1774; and meanwhile there had been a multitude of other incitements to rebellion.

On the surface, most of those incentives had an economic tinge; mercantilism, with its idea that the colony should be the tree whose sap the mother country should drain, was behind many of the exactions clamped down by England and the resentments fuming in America. A combination of factors combined to irritate the colonists: various acts of Parliament were aimed directly at American business whenever it competed with British interests; the retention by England of her gold supplies, in accordance with mercantilist theories, produced a serious money shortage in America; the passage of the Molasses Act of 1733, which levied a duty of sixpence a gallon on foreign molasses imported into the colonies, evoked loud cries from New England, the very cries later to be heard so frequently, "Taxation without representation!"; the Sugar Act of 1764, though its prospective revenues were to be only half those of the Molasses Act, likewise called forth shouts of indignation; and the Stamp Act of the following year, which imposed a direct tax amounting to no more than a third of a day's labor each year, produced a crisis featured by riots and widespread harrying of the stamp masters, many of whom were chased by mobs, or burned in effigy. The climax drew near in 1773, when the British government declared a tax on tea in the effort to recoup the collapsing fortunes of the East India Company, which supplied this highly popular colonial beverage. Actually, the tax was not unbearably high; the price of tea, on the contrary, had fallen so low that smuggling had become unprofitable; and the smugglers of New York, Philadelphia, and other communities, deprived of their lucrative traffic, were among the loudest in their opposition to the Tea Act; while the middlemen, whose business was imperiled by low-priced tea sold directly to the consumers, were likewise vociferous in their objections.

But despite the economic excitations, the evidence indicates that the cause of the Revolution was not principally or even largely economic. Though some individuals were adversely affected by British legislation, the colonies on the whole were prosperous; their population was doubling each generation, and their material development was pushing rapidly ahead. Even the most burdensome of the British impositions were far from crushing; numerous colonies have endured worse without revolting. Hence one feels obliged to look elsewhere than to the material effects of the British measures:

The true significance of these acts lies in their effect not so much upon colonial economy as upon the colonial psychology: they helped to establish the conviction in the minds of many Americans that Great Britain regarded the growth of the colonies with implacable jealousy and hostility.[18]

The fact is that, from the beginning, Americans feared for their liberties, and suspected that the economic demands were but the tools of political oppression. The "restraints upon American economic liberty revealed," as Miller points out, "that a handful of English capitalists carried more weight at Westminster than the welfare of millions of Americans." [19] Propaganda—by no means an invention of the twentieth century—served to exaggerate the sense of injury in American minds, and to spread not only the idea that British industrialists were planning illegitimate gains at American expense, but that an insidious campaign against American freedom was being plotted. Even religion was brought into the controversy: after the passage of the Quebec Act, which greatly extended the boundaries of Quebec and guaranteed tolerance for the Roman Catholic faith in the province, colonial propagandists charged that the British government was conspiring with the Pope, and incidentally with the devil, to create a Catholic empire. In this they saw an interference with "the finger of God" and the "manifest destiny" of Americans. Even if the destiny was not quite so "manifest" in English eyes, the appeal to religious bias could hardly fail of an effect.

Fundamentally, there was no reason why the Americans and English should not have agreed, no reason why a bloody eruption should have occurred—no reason, that is, except that the participants did not agree in their minds. The English looked upon the colonists as subjects, who owed them duties politically and economically; the Americans, reared in the traditions of freedom and accustomed to self-reliance in their rugged frontier environment, were impatient even of the slightest restraint. The English were inclined to be arrogant, with the air of lords who cannot stoop to be civil to underlings; the Americans were fiercely proud, and flamingly resentful of any imputation of inferiority. The English were inclined to defend the *status quo;* the Americans were strong individualists, much less interested in the pattern of things-in-being than in the maintenance of their liberties. The Americans, again, believed that they were fighting to acquire the rights of Englishmen; the English felt that the colonists had already received all their due rights, and that it was not unreasonable for them to be taxed in return for the protection they received. The Americans had developed a philosophy, based upon a romantic view of the struggles of the heroes of antiquity, and fortified by the doctrines of John Locke, who pictured a state of nature in which men were wholly free, and proclaimed that the government should not invade the "natural rights" of its citizens; the English regarded the views of Locke as obsolete, and had no belief at all in his "natural rights." The Americans held it wrongful of any government to seize the property of its subjects; the English believed that Americans had contributed far too little of their property, and that the British should follow the principles of taxation observed by the French and Spanish overseas.

The worst of the matter was not only that there was no meeting of minds; the worst of the matter was that every effort to bring about a meeting of minds was frustrated by the supercilious attitude of the English:

British propagandists found that one of the most effective ways of silencing the advocates of conciliation was to remind Englishmen of the low birth and general inferiority of the colonists; and, in consequence, every effort at compromise broke upon this inflexible conviction that it would be an insufferable humiliation to treat the colonists as equals.[20]

Rather than undergo this "insufferable humiliation," the British were to endure the much greater humiliation of losing America. And this was because, as Miller elsewhere declares, "To conquer America, the minds as well as the bodies of the colonists had to be subjugated—but the British government throughout the Revolutionary period failed to perceive this truth."[21] It supposed that it could prevail by means of force; and the result was that no peaceful measures in the end were effective, and that England received its final answer in the tolling of the Liberty Bell, and the rattling and flashing of guns in the Revolutionary War.

V

The Background of Today

Chapter 24

The French Revolution

One is inclined to write warily of the French Revolution. So much has been said on the subject, so many archives are filled with its documents, so many and such diverse views have been expressed as to its nature and consequences, that even to approach the theme is to challenge giants. Nevertheless, the Revolution cannot be ignored in a consideration of warfare and its causes; for while not specifically an act of war in the ordinary sense of the term, it not only entailed civil strife but led directly to the most devastating series of struggles the planet had known; it introduced military innovations of a contagious radical character; and pointed toward the super-conflicts of the twentieth century.

Amid the enormous mass of fact and theories, several truths are strikingly clear. And one is that the Revolution need not have occurred, and would not have occurred except for the particular turn that had been given to men's ideas. Despite many genuine abuses—which gave impetus to the Revolution, but did not make it inevitable—the situation of the French masses as a whole had not been deteriorating prior to the outbreak. The various dues and taxes and in particular the burdensome *taille*, which constituted real peasant grievances, were of long standing; as far back as the time of Henry IV we hear the plaints of countrymen whose cattle and farm implements are distrained to meet this levy. The *corvée*, a form of forced labor which theoretically covered all men between sixteen and sixty years of age, had been regularly in operation ever since 1738, but in the latter part of the century its effects were mitigated; usurious ground rents and crushingly high rates of interest were among the other just complaints of the farmers, but here too there had been some improvement, partly because the decline in the value of money tended to reduce real taxes, partly because the rates in some places were considerably lowered or because payment was avoided (it is said that the peasants in some districts would go for as much as twenty or thirty years without paying anything at all). Judged by the standards of earlier centuries, therefore, the country people were not badly off. Unlike the peasants in many regions, they were free; they were acquiring their own land in increasing amounts; they were gaining in numbers, and in many cases waxing in prosperity.

On the opposite side of the picture, one may point to the numerous cases of actual destitution. An enormous number (which has been reckoned as high as ten to twenty per cent of the nation's manhood) made their living through beggary; whenever the harvests were poor, the *disette* or famine was certain to attack some part of the country; the old impositions and abuses, including not only the unjust taxes, but the overrunning of good farm land by the nobleman's horses and hounds, were too often real even if relatively less severe than of old; and the rise in prices, despite a slightly higher living standard, was greatest in necessities such as food, clothing, and fuel. And in the industrial cities, conditions were more distressing than in the typical country district; a budget published by the strikers of Lyon in 1785 "showed that the average earnings of a family of five members amounted to seventy-six pounds a year, and its expenses of living to a hundred and two pounds." [1] Beyond this, one must take account of certain grave aggravations of the period immediately preceding the outburst: the effects of a particularly severe hail storm of July 13, 1788, which ruined crops throughout much of France; the influence in 1786 of a *laissez faire* attitude, accompanied by a policy approaching free trade, which encouraged an influx of low-priced English goods, with a resultant economic depression and unemployment; and the rumors of famine, which caused peasants to aggravate economic difficulties by hiding their corn.

In any well-rounded general picture, furthermore, one must not overlook the ill-managed, extravagant nature of the government (leading to the financial crisis that, by necessitating the calling of the States-General, was the proximate cause of the Revolution). The story has been often repeated: how, while the poor man groped in penury, 33,000,000 livres were spent each year on the household of the King and princes, 28,000,000 on pensions, 46,000,-000 on the pay of 12,000 army officers, and millions on sinecures; how enormous bounties were paid each year, including 100,000 livres to the daughter of the Duke of Guines on her marriage, 400,000 to the Comtesse de Polognac to pay her debts, double that amount for her daughter's marriage portion, 23,000,000 for the debts of the Count of Artois, and millions for chateaux for the King and Queen—at a time when the poor were taxed for the very salt they used on their bread. We have had abundant descriptions of the nobles in their cloths of gold and silver, their elaborate carriages and festivals, their hunting expeditions and entertainments, their gambling and their debts. And in all this we can see reason for resentment and incitement to revolution.

But reason for resentment and incitement to revolution do not in themselves necessarily produce revolution. For many centuries the poor folk of France and of Europe in general had been struggling against injustice and oppression; as far back as the late Middle Ages, sporadic peasant revolts or *jacqueries* had flared up in France, England, Bohemia, and elsewhere; and the smoldering social and economic evils would have sufficed to produce revolts on a scale rivaling or surpassing the Revolution, had there been any regulator that made the popular reaction proportionate to the justification.

But men throughout the ages have demonstrated a remarkable and sometimes a well-nigh incredible capacity for endurance. They will submit for years, for generations, even for centuries; they will drudge and bow, yield to class arrogance and racial oppression, and humbly consent to be milked and fleeced. And then suddenly, perhaps when the situation is improving, they will run amok in a rebellion. What is behind such erratic, such seemingly unreasonable conduct? If we look for an external explanation, we will seek in vain; the answer can be found solely in the mysterious realm of man's inner being, the realm of his feelings and thoughts. Like a harnessed beast that has stolidly endured its master's blows and then at a sudden whip-stroke breaks away in a stampede, men with the habit of yielding will continue to yield until some psychological flick of a whip releases the long-balked emotions, which then, in their impetuous rush and flow, will try to atone for lost time.

It was something of this sort that happened in the Revolution. The whip-stroke was imposed by the new ideas of equality and freedom that were flashing through the air. In the writings of Rousseau, Voltaire, Diderot, Condorcet, and many more, the age had awakened to the thought that there were such things as "natural rights" of man; the doctrine that government depended on the consent of the governed, already expressed by Locke, was given further scope and emphasis; sovereignty, hitherto supposed to belong exclusively to monarchs, was acclaimed as an inalienable possession of the people—and from this concept the road was not long to the view that the people had a right to revolt against usurpations of authority. Spread by various publicists, from the comparatively little-known Morelly with his *Code de la Nature* (1755) to the celebrated lawyer Simon Linguet with his violent attacks upon private ownership, the new creed rapidly gained hold over men's minds, and so prepared the way for action impossible to an earlier generation. The American Revolution, which seemed to provide an illustration of the new theories in practice, gave them impetus and encouragement, and lent the breath of life to the view that it actually *was* possible to throw off the old tyranny. And in 1789 certain more or less fortuitous economic factors combined with natural catastrophes and political weakness to give an opportunity for a stroke on behalf of the creed.

In order for the Revolution to start, it was not necessary that a great percentage of the rebels should be imbued with the idea of the rights of man. And in order for the Revolution to continue, it was not needful for it to remain true to the ideals that had brought it to birth. In the beginning, an organized handful of flame-scattering leaders was enough to set fire to the multitude, whose rankling resentments kept the flames blazing. And once the conflagration had been kindled, it was as if a chain reaction had been started, and the Revolution crackled on from its comparatively mild opening phases to the sanguinary half-light of the Terror and the ruddy flare of war, all in ways that its original instigators could little have foreseen.

In observing the course of the Revolution, one can detect the rise of a rapid, almost an explosive crusading, religious, and militaristic sentiment. Despite such dramatic well-known episodes as the taking of the Bastille on July 14, 1789, and the suspiciously well-organized march of the women on Versailles in October of the same year, the Revolution at first was accompanied by less bloodshed than one might expect of a social upheaval of the first magnitude; one evidence of this is to be seen in the fact that the King and Queen, though borne from Versailles to Paris as prisoners of the people, were not executed until several years later. That there was a guiding hand behind the various riots, even though it merely took advantage of pre-existing popular discontents, is indicated by all the signs; the occurrences were too well directed to have been altogether matters of chance; hundreds of agitators deliberately fanned the passions of the mob; and the propaganda that followed the fall of the Bastille, in the public appearances of thousands of alleged heroes of the attack, and in songs, pamphlets, and patriotic harangues, shows all the signs of purposive direction. Yet it remains true that the early phases of the Revolution were mild as judged by later standards. But already the forces were brewing that were to carry the movement into its lurid mid-channel.

Something that looks remarkably like an effort to disturb the public mind and prepare it for change and violence, was manifest in the wave of fear that erupted throughout most of France after the taking of the Bastille. Though it traveled irregularly and has been traced to at least six or eight foci, it was as irrational as it was widespread; the report that the "brigands" were coming was enough to cause tocsins to ring and alarms to be sounded, stones and boiling oil to be prepared against the imagined aggressors, pitchforks, hoes, and scythes to be seized by peasants who were determined to sell their lives dearly, young girls to be hidden in attics, countrysides to be scoured for the intruders, and false rumors of fighting and death to be broadcasted. Remembering how in other lands and generations there have been evident efforts to render whole peoples malleable for warfare by creating a fear psychosis, one cannot but agree that "It is difficult to escape the conclusion that the rumors had an interested origin." [2] And one can see how fear paved the path of the Revolutionaries:

The Great Fear was but the start. It was easy for the knowing to profit from this senseless disorder; easy to direct the now aroused peasantry against the tangible enemy, the owner of the château, the *seigneur*. Sometimes violence was not necessary. The *seigneur* peacefully harangued his peasants, promised relief, gave up his feudal titles. . . . Sometimes the château was burned, the hated records on which the dues were based burned up with it. [3]

But violence was not characteristic of the peasant uprising in 1789; the people sought to abolish feudalism rather than to kill; and in this aim they were neither organized, nor so bloodthirsty as many earlier and later revolutionaries.

II

The Revolution was still not old when it came into the control of other men and forces than those that had suckled it. If the original Revolutionaries thought to guide and mold the upheaval, events were to teach them a bitter truth: that one cannot bound or confine a historical movement; that when great forces are set loose in the world, one can neither predict their course nor regulate their future. There are so many imponderables, both of concrete fact and of psychology, that even the shrewdest guess may be at best a gross approximation; it is a little as when a child, playing with fireworks, accidentally sets fire to his house—if the flames are not controlled, not one house alone may burn, the entire block, the entire district, the entire city may be reduced to ashes, and unknown numbers of men and women may writhe and suffer, may lose their lives or fortunes, may be driven into destitution or exile. Thus the original Revolutionaries of France, thinking to tear down the old aristocracy of privilege and exploitation, also tore down many another institution; developed enemies they had not foreseen; gave power to a second, more radical group of insurrectionists; and aroused a wave of feeling on which the Revolution was borne forward toward a tragic climax.

One must smile ironically when one remembers that the original Revolutionaries professed peaceful aims; that the Constituent Assembly, on May 22, 1790, renounced the idea of wars of conquest, and solemnly proclaimed that French forces would never be used against the liberties of any people. Assuming that they were sincere in this declaration, they little realized that they were in effect trying to regulate Pandora's brood of troubles after they had opened the box. One of the troubles, and by no means a minor one, was occasioned by the *émigrés*, the nobles who had fled France, and based on the Rhine, were intriguing with foreign courts. A second trouble centered in the persons of Louis XVI and Marie Antoinette, who likewise were believed to be conspiring against the Revolution. And still another disturbance arose from the inflammatory nationalistic sentiment let loose by the Revolution—a wave whose center was the Girondists, an offshoot of the Jacobins, and a group that, according to the general conviction of recent historians, deliberately goaded the nation on to war.

There seems to be reason for holding that the series of conflicts, which began when the Legislative Assembly on April 20, 1792, declared war against Austria, and ended twenty-three years later on the field of Waterloo, was originated with definite intention for the reason that this was the only apparent means of keeping the Revolutionary spirit alive. Marat has been quoted as saying that "one feels only too well that the Revolution could be no more than a passing crisis and that it was impossible for the Revolution to maintain itself by the means which had brought it about." [4] And it was for this reason that some new method of continuing the Revolution was found necessary:

In order to fan the flames of revolution into life again, and at once stimulate and subjugate the country which was full of doubts and on the point of eluding them, the Girondists did not hesitate to set Europe ablaze. The war was a colossal maneuver in their home policy. By means of it they counted on reawakening revolutionary enthusiasm, converting the measures taken for the national defense into measures for the defense of the Jacobins and using for the benefit of their own party the forces raised for the protection of the country. The Revolution, threatened with paralysis, could only escape by means of an outburst of bloodthirsty madness.[5]

Jacques Pierre Brissot, the journalist who was largely responsible for maneuvering the declaration of war against Austria and the later declaration against England, is credited with the statement that "War at the present moment will be a positive benefit to the nation, and the only calamity to be feared is that there should be no war." [6] And he has further expounded his views:

I have been meditating for the last six months—indeed, ever since the revolution began—what course I ought to follow. . . . The force of reason and of facts has persuaded me that a people which, after a thousand years of slavery, has achieved liberty, needs war. It needs war to consolidate its freedom. It needs war to purge away the vices of despotism. It needs war to banish from its bosom the men who might corrupt its liberty.[7]

In line with this philosophy were the ideas of Camille Desmoulins, as expressed in his newspaper *Les Révolutions de France et de Brabant*:

What does it matter, after all, if the tyrants of Europe unite to make war on us? I would go further, and say that perhaps something of the sort is necessary in order to mature and carry out more rapidly the other national revolutions that are being prepared.

The facts about war, as an instrument of revolutionary policy, are summarized by the French writer, Jean Jaurès:

The war enlarged the theatre of action, liberty and glory. It forced traitors to throw off their masks and obscure intrigues were obliterated like an anthill swept away by a hurricane. The war made it possible for the progressive parties to carry the moderates with them, for their lukewarm attitude toward the Revolution could be denounced as treason to the country itself. Lastly war would revive the energy of the people by producing a sense of the unknown and of danger, and by exciting the national pride. It was no longer possible to lead them to the attack upon the national power by means of internal politics alone.[8]

The Girondists, of course, were only a minority; but they were an organized and a determined minority. They were helped, moreover, by the powerful propaganda of most of the newspapers, which catered to mass emotions by exalting the war frenzy. And they had with them the vast majority of the Legislative Assembly. A small group at the Jacobin club, led by Robespierre, could not bring sufficient weight to bear in its denunciations of soldiers and war-making.

Even while things were hanging in the balance, with the sword of Damocles literally suspended above the head of Europe, the foreign opposition was unwittingly feeding strength to the war party. Far from a negligible element in the declaration of war was the state of mind provoked in the Girondists by Austria's elderly statesman, Count Kaunitz: the resentment, suspicion, and fear aroused by his aspersions against the Revolutionary party. These emotions have been credited with lighting the fuse for the conflagration:

Expressions which might have been passed off with a smile by the chancelleries of the last generation, to whom the octogenarian statesman was accustomed to address himself, roused hot anger when recited in a representative parliament. It was not the Emperor's attitude toward the obligations of an out-of-date treaty, but the suspicion that he despised the National Assembly, and disdained a national army, which finally drove the deputies into war.[9]

Despite the warning of Becquet, deputy for Haute-Marne, that the war could not be localized, only seven votes opposed the plunge into what was to be one of history's most devastating conflicts. Nevertheless, the decree was clothed in pious words, of the immemorial sort used by mouthers of aggressive statements in order to give an impression of sanctity. France was fighting "only to defend her liberty and independence," and "would take every care to mitigate the scourge of war, to observe the rights of property, and to see that the evils inseparable from hostilities fall only on those who are in league against the liberty of their country." [10]

Just how well this stated intention was put into effect has been recorded by all historians of the period. Many onlookers, however, were soothed by these bland announcements into a tolerance of the war or even stirred to a fervor of applause.

It should be remembered, besides, that the declarations of the Assembly were quite in line with previous announcements of the Girondists. A crusading spirit had been developing among them, the idea that they were missionaries for the deliverance of other peoples, the view that the benefits of the glorious freedom and equality now enjoyed by the French nation should be made universal. More than that, the French would be welcomed as liberators in other lands; if they crossed the Rhine, the oppressed peoples of Germany would greet them with shouts of acclamation. Anacharsis Clootz, mentioned elsewhere in these pages as a peace advocate, foresaw the cheers of the downtrodden peasants of Bohemia, Lombardy, Scandinavia, the Low Countries, and a dozen other regions as they trampled their tyrants into the dust and flocked forth to greet the tricolor. These magnificent visions were of the same genus and species as the call issued by that latter-day priest, Brissot, for a modern crusade, "whose aim is nobler and holier, a crusade on behalf of universal liberty."

From all this it follows that the war, into which France recklessly threw herself, was not basically caused by any external dangers, by the intrigues of the émigrés or of the King or Queen, or by the attitude of Austria; these were all immediate influences; but the root sources were deeper, the root sources were in the inflammatory emotions and perfervid religious ideas which induced men to fight not only in order to maintain the pride and glory of the Revolution in France, but to spread its benefits to those benighted regions which had the misfortune of lying beyond the frontiers.

III

If the war had begun as a modern First Crusade, it continued even more in the spirit of the medieval warriors of the Cross (the freedom and equality of man being the pious goal of the aggressors). On November 19, 1792, the Convention sent a chill to every foreign capital in Europe when it announced a program of *fraternité et secours* (brotherhood and assistance) to any people wishing to be liberated. The chained multitudes of the earth, in other words, were to rise against their tyrants, and the French in their altruism were to rush forth as comrades in arms and break their fetters. Glorious aim! a goal to set the imagination afire! It is not remarkable, however, if there were furrowed brows in more chancelleries than one; and if anxious eyes began to look to armies and armaments.

But brotherly love for the oppressed was not so absolute that it would not claim its price. By a decree of December 15, the Convention said something as to its fee. It did not, of course, use this ignoble word: what it stated was that the war was directed against the rich; with the poor it wished to remain at peace. But in battling against wealth, it would confiscate wealth; it would abolish all existing taxes and feudal dues; it would replace all existing governments, and proclaim the rule of the people (who would collaborate with Convention-appointed commissioners); and it would take under its wing all property belonging to governments or corporations. Incidentally, the riches so benevolently seized would make war self-supporting.

It is not surprising if this announcement aroused a new wave of terror. It is little wonder if Pitt, in the British House of Commons, later characterized the decree as "a universal declaration of war against all thrones, and against all civilized governments." And it need cause no amazement if not all the beneficiaries took kindly to the benefits: if, for example, the people of Belgium, from whom the author of the decree drained over six million pounds in little more than a month, manifested a churlish want of cooperation; if the Catholic Church, from whose coffers most of the funds were extracted, was unconvinced of the benign motives of the Girondists; and if, as a result of the liberators' surly reception, it became necessary to cling to the country by military force: in effect, keep it in chains in order to complete its liberation.

Subsequent decrees, all made in the same humane and self-sacrificing spirit, extended the advantages of the annexation to Basle, thirty-five communes of the Palatinate, and the entire region between the Moselle and the Rhine. Such measures, undertaken by a Louis XIV, might have been suspect, as smacking of militarism and aggression; under the auspices of the people's government, it represented no more than an extension of the principles of liberty, equality, and fraternity. So, at least, a Girondist might have told you. But the leaders of Britain, like those of other nations, were slow to be persuaded; French conduct in the Netherlands, in fact, put an end to negotiations to have England serve as mediator and arrange a Franco-Prussian peace.

The road was now wide open to war between France and England. The various French activities, including the seizure of Brussels and the plans for the exploitation of the country, posed a threat which was not lightened by the French zeal for liberating oppressed peoples; it was necessary for England to act in self-defense; and an increase in the navy and a blockade of the French coast were the logical counter-strokes. And thereupon France, in her turn, began to form plans for the subjugation of England; a vice-admiral, Comte de Kersaint, argued that war was unavoidable, and foreshadowed Napoleon's pet schemes of crippling England by destroying her commerce, and of crossing the Channel with an army that would dictate terms of peace "upon the ruins of the tower of London." Such bellicose utterances, since they expressed a common sentiment, were but the natural precursors to a declaration of war.

In that declaration, which hurled a great land power unprepared and needlessly against the world's strongest naval power, not only Revolutionary doctrine but Revolutionary rivalries played a part. So, at least, we may judge from a statement of Brissot. "It was the Committee's doing: if we had hesitated (*to declare war*), the Jacobins would have seized power." [11]

Evidently no prevision of the horrors of the enusing twenty-two years disturbed the minds of the Parisians. We are told how, in celebration, a ceremonial Tree of Liberty was planted in the Place du Carrousel; how the band played the *Carmagnole;* and how the municipal officers, headed by the mayor, led in a dance that lasted for hours. By such means, ever since the days of the first armies, men have woven a glamour about the ugly brow of reality, and lighted the flames of a contagious mass emotion.

IV

In the armies which it flung across Europe, and likewise in its methods of recruitment, the French Revolution was not only unique: it set a precedent that has since been one of the shaping forces of world civilization.

It was merely consistent, since they conceived of their movement as international in scope, that the Revolutionaries should plan to raise international armies. And in these armies they did not disdain the use of propaganda—not precisely a new weapon of psychological warfare, since it had been known to Cromwell, to the makers of the American Revolution and others. But it was now employed with a liberality that foreshadowed its use in still wider theaters. One manifestation of this propaganda is to be seen in the attempts to induce foreign soldiers to desert: thousands of leaflets, translated into German and Spanish, were circulated on the frontiers; and the enemy was not only treated to disquisitions on liberty and equality and the identity of their interests with the French, but were tempted with the practical inducement of a pension of a hundred francs a year and an additional gift of fifty livres if they joined the Revolutionary armies.

Propaganda was likewise prominent in the effort to plant French strongholds abroad—strongholds served by citizens of the countries in question: Belgians in Belgium, Batavians in Batavia, Germans in Germany, etc. Each group was to be generously equipped for waging the battle for men's minds; each was to be spearheaded by a club of patriots, and featured by newspapers, pamphlets, and proclamations designed to spread the enlightenment even to the remotest community. From Strasbourg the converts went forth to bring the Revolutionary gospel to the Rhineland; in London, manifestos expressing sympathy with the Revolutionaries were issued by a historical society; disturbances in Geneva and elsewhere bespoke the activities of the militant missionaries. Here was warfare of a definite and novel nature, even if not waged primarily with guns; and if the trouble-brewers of Moscow, a century and a half later, had been accused of taking a leaf out of the French Revolution, they could hardly have made a plausible defense of "Not guilty."

It had been the original idea of the Revolutionaries to rely upon volunteer troops. But the conception of a willing citizen army, though honored by the thousands who flocked to the colors beneath the glow of the new ideas and the fervor of the new nationalism, very quickly proved inadequate to the nation's purposes; it was found that enthusiasm alone is not basis enough for an army, and that warlike sentiment is something that foams, effervesces, and vanishes like the bubbles in a glass of supercharged water. And so compulsion reared its snarling head.

A limited conscription, permitting the rich to escape by paying a fee, had been enacted in February, 1793. But it was on August 23 of that year that the National Convention made unequivocal recognition that most men in a modern war fight not because they wish but because they must; that the fighting spirit alone will not produce the armies demanded by modern war-makers. A draft of a partial type, as we have noted, had been adopted long before in Prussia, Sweden, and elsewhere; but in decreeing universal conscription, the Convention set the precedent that has since guided most great nations and has made possible the colossal wars of our times: it virtually inaugurated a totalitarian state, more absolute than early modern autocracies, since it proclaimed in effect that all the country's human resources were subject to the nod of its rulers; that all men were henceforth liable to a military regimentation which had little concern for personal welfare or desires; and that the individual was to be regarded as existing for the benefit of the State, rather than the State for the benefit of the individual. If this philosophy was later to be seen behind the maneuverings of our Hitlers, Mussolinis, and Stalins, not only the philosophers such as Hegel, Nietzsche, and Karl Marx are to be held responsible, but the doctrinaires whose enactments made possible the conscripted armies of the French Revolution.

At first the conscription embraced only unmarried men and widowers between the ages of eighteen and twenty-five—and many of these escaped through various exemptions. But it must not be thought that the innovation, though limited in scope and mild by comparison with subsequent conscriptions, was everywhere docilely accepted. The zealots might shout, "The Revolution is in danger!—The country is in danger!"; companies of marching men might stir up a hypnotic enthusiasm by singing the *Marseillaise;* drums might beat, and bugles sound—but millions remained sullenly unconvinced. In the Vendée, a coastal department, an armed rebellion shook almost every recruiting center. At Saint-Florent, three thousand rebels defeated the government force and raided the district headquarters. In the department of Loire Inférieure, fifteen hundred men arose and slew the commandant of the National Guard and other officials. And even in Paris, on the Champs Elysées and at the Luxembourg, uprisings of conscripts flared up on two successive days—to be ruthlessly suppressed after the men had protested with cries of "To the devil with Marat, Danton, and Robespierre!" And even aside from such demonstrations, there were thousands of desertions, which reduced the fighting forces to numbers far below the official listing.

None of this, however, should blind us to an all-important truth. And that truth concerns not only the momentous precedent of conscription and universal service; it concerns something of which these were only a part, the rise of modern nationalism. Despite all the rebellions and defections, uncounted thousands did take up arms beneath a patriotic ardor; uncounted thousands did rush forth with zeal to carry out that fiery injunction of Danton, "Audacity, more audacity, and yet more audacity!" Recruits began to fight with vigor not because they were cogs in a machine but because they wanted to fight; they were eager to defend a land that was theirs as never before, and zealous for principles they had espoused with a crusader's devotion. More than that, they felt a dignity unknown in the old armies, for now any soldier might rise to an officership, and none were subject to the humiliation of corporal punishment; they were assured that this was *their* army, *their* cause; a recrudescence of the old heroic ideal, transformed and modernized but with all its romantic ancient trappings, made them think of themselves as gallants rescuing their country and the world from the genii of evil. But like the old warriors of the Cross, they were more than heroes; they were, as already indicated, bearers of a religious principle, which happened to be not theological but national—the principle of Jacobin nationalism. De Tocqueville nearly a hundred years ago called attention to its essentially religious nature; and other writers have harped upon the same theme. "Voltaire and Rousseau were its prophets, Marat and Lepeletier its martyrs, the veterans of Valmy, the gunners of the *Vengeur,* and other dauntless defenders of the Republic, its more or less mythical heroes. . . ." [12]

La Patrie in Jacobin hearts [expounds another historian] was a God, and a jealous God who would brook the worship of no other. . . . The symbols and the ceremonies which it evolved—the national flag, the national anthem, the national shrines, the liberty caps, the altars to *La Patrie*, the graven tablets of the national law, the republican baptisms and funerals, the solemn parades and eulogies, the inscriptions of *Mort pour la Patrie*—were touching manifestations of the new religion of nationalism which the Jacobins substituted for the older Catholic faith. [13]

Nationalism as an idea was abundantly evident, not only in the establishment of patriotic ceremonies and the flaunting of patriotic insignia, but in more forceful measures that have bequeathed their thunder-toned effects to our own day. It was Jacobin nationalism that, founded upon the preachments of Rousseau, developed a fervor and an intolerance of loyalty to be compared only with that of the papal inquisitors. It was Jacobin nationalism that precipitated the fiery days of the Terror. It was Jacobin nationalism that, as we have seen, introduced the disastrous precedent of universal conscription; it was Jacobin nationalism that sponsored military academies, flung open the doors to imperialism, splashed the face of Europe with blood, and evoked the crimson-spotted, sinister figure of Napoleon Bonaparte. And it was Jacobin nationalism that paved the way for all that has been grimmest and most characteristic in the international picture of the last century and a half.

The new conscript armies of France [Professor Hayes summarizes] were nationalist. They could not have been formed, the rank and file would not have submitted to them, if nationalistic sentiment had not been widespread in the land. . . . But this sentiment was intensified and moulded by the Jacobins, who perceived in the new militarism not only the indispensable means of removing the foreign menace but also the most effective agency for propagating their own nationalistic principles within France. [14]

The methods of the Jacobins are eloquent of the power of an idea fortified by deep emotion. Not only was the State a god; it was a god that would recognize no loyalty save of flags and guns. On the one hand, its priests proclaimed the glory of valorous deeds, the splendor of military renown; on the other hand, they preached the magnificence of self-renunciation . . . and of death. Nor were they content with sermonizing, nor with the glamour and éclat of patriotic hymns, parades, and orations; they realized the need of drilling the desired ideas into the minds of the young. Hence the schools which they established, such as the *Ecole de Mars*, which opened in 1794 as an academy for officers; these, like the very system of conscription, went far toward providing an education in nationalism—and in that militarism which marches side by side with nationalism. For the reluctant or the rebellious there was always the guillotine—and we have seen that the reluctant and the rebellious did exist. But the Jacobins, waving the thought of *la Patrie* like a banner before the eyes of their bemused countrymen, had no difficulty in playing upon the love of glory, upon the dread of foreign foes, upon the spirit of service and sacrifice, upon the racial prejudices and passions and the blind imitativeness of the masses—so that within a few months after the adoption of universal service, France had mustered one of the largest armies in history; an army with an enrollment of well over a million men; an army which, unlike most of its predecessors, was composed of citizens and not of professionals.

V

If the effect of this huge draft of manpower had been merely physical, it would have been epoch-making in its way. But it was accompanied by psychological surges, uprushes, and undercurrents that were to be historically more important than the mere quantities of human material employed. In its immediate influence upon France, and in its repercussions upon Europe and the world, it was probably the most momentous occurrence since the introduction of gunpowder.

Not least important was the attitude of mind produced in the Jacobin war-chiefs by the very abundance of men. They were a little in the position of persons, once impoverished, who suddenly acquire seemingly inexhaustible wealth; in the abandon of their new-found riches, they dispense their dollars with a drunkard's prodigality. Finding themselves in control of apparently limitless multitudes of soldiers—and what are soldiers made for, except to fight and die?—they hurled their regiments against the enemy like projectiles from a bottomless store. After all, was this not clever strategy? For France was more populous than her adversaries, and could afford the expenditure of men. The goal was what counted; men were unimportant except as means to that great end. So it has always been when fanaticism rides afield; so it was during the Inquisition, and during the Crusades, and the religious wars of the Moslems, and of our own sixteenth and seventeenth centuries; and it would have been remarkable if the Jacobin religion had proved an exception. The ruthless hurling of the French masses into the face of death was truly "an outcome of the same Jacobin egalitarianism which, as Robespierre expressed it, would rather see ten thousand men perish than a principle." [15] In the pre-Revolutionary period the commanders had mostly attempted, as we have observed, to be sparing of men; they preferred to indulge in comparatively bloodless tactical movements, or long and equally bloodless sieges; and despite gory episodes such as the Seven Years' War, the attempt to conserve life was general and genuine. This is not necessarily proof of humanitarianism on the part of the generals; it may be construed to mean that the soldiers, being comparatively few and not easy to obtain, were regarded as valuable and by no means expendable property. But when enforced recruiting provided a guaranty of full ranks, the soldiers' lives represented a much depreciated form of currency, which accordingly was spent with a free hand.

Away, therefore, with unheroic blood-saving methods! With a rush and a dash the warriors of the Revolution would gain their victories—and who so craven as to count the cost? This, indeed, would seem to have suited well enough the spirit of the men, who were reckless, impatient, ill-trained, mesmerized by the Revolutionary ideals and ambitions, eager to release their energies in action. In pursuance of the sanguinary new mood, Carnot in 1794 ordered mass formations, and bayonet charges that would rout and annihilate the enemy. This decree was aimed particularly at the émigrés, twenty thousand of whom were fighting for the coalition; these, if taken prisoners, were to be slain. Part and parcel of the same savagery was the command of Robespierre, shortly before he went to the guillotine, that the British and Hanoverian troops be shown no quarter (though the soldiers, less murderous-minded than their chief, disobeyed the order). At about the same time a General Houchard was slain when it was found that, in pursuance of pre-Revolutionary amenities, he had been civilly communicating with the enemy as to an exchange of prisoners. Houchard, in the eyes of his superiors, had committed a grave offense; French decrees of September, 1792, and May, 1793, had forbidden the ransoming of prisoners; and the cold-blooded expediency of the orders was as evident as their inhumanity, since here also the principle applied that populous France was better able than her enemies to bear the loss of men.

In these edicts, with their scorn for human values and human suffering and their impassivity as of a puppet master manipulating his manikins, we can see the genesis of the attitude of our own century—an attitude in which the end counts for everything and the means for little or nothing, an attitude which recognizes no absolute goals but Total Slaughter and Total Annihilation. We can discern the same tendencies even in the French treatment of their own people, as in the notorious decrees providing for the total destruction of the great city of Lyon and the obliteration of its very name; and we can see the contempt for life in the mass shootings at that city on December 4 and 5, 1793. At the same time, we can observe how the military thought of the Revolution drew sustenance from the current political ideas:

. . . the military had been profoundly influenced in their thinking by the Jacobinical class-war notion of totally destroying the enemy, an idea up to then foreign to them. Even when class conflict and Jacobinism were put down, the idea of total destruction was to prove ineradicable; out of it came a new strategy aimed at incapacitating the enemy for further resistance through . . . psychological means. As Clausewitz phrases it: "The destruction of the enemy forces is among all purposes which might be pursued in war always the most imperative one." One of the heritages of Jacobinism is terror in war, in the use of which Napoleon fancied himself a connoisseur.[16]

Here we have the spiritual ancestry of events which even the most nightmarish-minded eighteenth-century propagandist could not have conceived. Here we have the psychological background, the psychological preparation for the total submarine warfare of well over a century later, the air raids on London and Belgrade and Hamburg and Rotterdam, the "scorched earth" policy as practiced in Europe and the Far East, the machine-gun attacks on defenseless refugees and the gas-chamber extermination of helpless civilians, the fire raids on inhabited centers, the atom-doom of Hiroshima and Nagasaki, and the terror that like an evil aura has lain over all the civilized earth.

VI

Not the least unfortunate feature of the upflaring of nationalism was the precedent that it set. It not only provided the incentive, the moral and emotional background behind most of the conscripted armies and consequently most of the bloodshed of the nineteenth century; it reacted upon foreign nations by producing a blast of counter-nationalism. Although in many respects the sentiment abroad was unlike that of the Jacobins; although it was aristocratic rather than democratic and aimed to suppress rather than further the Revolution, in essence it was but the reverse side of the same disk, since it too propagated the idea of the nation, of loyalty to the nation and to national lines and divisions. True, one did hear pleas concerned with humanity, the suppression of despotism and the duty of great states to protect the weak—but was there not something similar in the preachments of Jacobinism itself? In any case—and this is the significant fact—the counter-nationalism was like that of the Jacobins in that it was militant, in that it urged men forth by the thousands to face the perils and the agonies of battle. But it did more than that: it created a legend, the legend of the devouring French monster, whose appetite was insatiable, and whose encroachments all right-minded men would resist. And most men, being right-minded, were given an incentive and a reason for fighting; and the need for protection of the native soil being added to hatred and terror of the regicidal foe, militant nationalism obtained all the nutriment it required.

The most pronounced nationalistic movements outside France took place, to be sure, in the Napoleonic epoch rather than during the Revolution proper. But the Revolution and Napoleonism were manifestations of the same great historic upheaval; and while they may be treated separately, they cannot be altogether dissociated. Before considering further nationalistic developments, therefore, we may turn to the strange and baleful phenomenon of General Bonaparte.

Chapter 25

Napoleon

Among history's innumerable *ifs* and *might-have-beens*, nothing could be much more certain than that if there had been no French Revolution there would have been no Napoleon. It is possible, of course, that a man named Bonaparte would have distinguished himself to some extent in politics or war; but without the downfall of the Bourbon monarchy, the ensuing social and political confusion, the great armies built up by the Jacobins, and the weak government of the Directory, conditions would not have been ripe for dictatorial rule and military conquest by an officer risen from the multitude.

On the other hand, the French Revolution might have occurred without producing a Napoleon. What was needed was a personage not only of boundless audacity and an extraordinary driving power, but of an exceptional ability to command men's minds— a capacity to galvanize them into action, dazzle them, and create an enchanted legend regardless of the wasted nations and the wasted lives of millions. The Revolution might gradually have subsided into peacefulness and order; no French armies might ever have been hurled into Egypt or Austria, or across the Pyrenees or into the withering cold of Russia; there might never have been a Jena, an Austerlitz, or a Waterloo; no brothers of the conquering hero might ever have perched on the thrones of Europe, no Josephine might have been crowned Empress, and no Emperor might have ruled like an ancient Sultan over his ever-expanding domains. It would be stretching speculation too far to suggest that there would have been no approach to the nineteenth century's actual sharp aggressive nationalism and military expansiveness. But we can be sure that, without Napoleon, Europe would be considerably different from the Europe that we know.

For he performed the prodigious feat of accentuating existing currents of action and thought at the same time as he gave a new direction to men's minds. He scattered ideas of military grandeur and glory; he became the center and focus of a cult of hero-worship; he set a new precedent of aggression, and reached perhaps not a new low but certainly a depth of faithlessness in international relations; he supported himself by means of most of the devices more recently familiar in the totalitarian state—censorship, doctored news reports, suppression of free information, and imprisonment without trial; he became a devouring phenomenon that many could admire and many abhor, but that none could disregard. And so, during fifteen active years, he dominated the European scene; and during all succeeding generations his ghost has been more potent than most living men.

But all this, as remarked before, need not have been. Except for one man's colossal ambitions and vaulting ruthlessness, one man's exceptional organizing and war-making capacity, the blight of Napoleonism would not have appeared. And except for the fact that he had the power to impress others with his views and desires, and to whip others into following and applauding, he could no more have succeeded than a lone horseman could make a cavalry charge. He trampled half of Europe primarily for one reason: because he had magnetized men's minds. When the magnetism began to wane, as it did after the Russian campaign, he was on the road to his downfall. The god Napoleon was on the way to becoming the man Napoleon—which, of course, was fatal, since the world will give much more unstintedly of its blood and its devotion when it scents the divine aura than when it perceives a mere human being.

Even so, his original chances would have been slight had it not been for two strong converging sets of ideas: the nationalistic sentiments of the Revolution; and the heroic ideal which for centuries, by precedent and example and in poems and songs and stories, had been drilled into the European mind. On the current of these two he was borne forward; and while caring little for the nationalism of the countries which his armies invaded, he gave fresh impetus to French Revolutionary nationalism by the glamour with which he surcharged the air. At the same time, he himself was a convert to the heroic ideal. This pre-eminently practical man of affairs, the diplomatist, the lawgiver and the leader of armies and nations, was clearly a worshipper before the great romantic illusion of glory, even like Charles of Sweden and Louis XIV and Alexander the Great.

The Macedonian hero, in fact, seems to have been his particular star. "The career of Alexander had for him a charm that even the conquests of Caesar could not rival," writes one biographer.[1] And another, referring to the Egyptian campaign, declares, "It would be easy to prove that the designs of the great Macedonian now engrossed the attention of Napoleon with especial vigor and tempted him to imitate, to surpass his predecessor."[2] A strong case might be made for the view that Alexander was in the background if not in the foreground of Napoleon's mind in the very conception of the Egyptian campaign, based as it was on the grandiose scheme of invading a continent in which Alexander also had won fame; the preoccupation of his thoughts with the ancient conqueror is indicated by one of the items in his proclamation to the troops before reaching Africa: "The first town that we are to occupy was built by Alexander the Great. Every step brings us in contact with old memories, which Frenchmen will do well to emulate."[3] Nor is the case much altered by Napoleon's statement in his *Memoirs*, as dictated at St. Helena, that the expedition was first of all for such eminently down-to-earth ends as the establishment of a French colony on the Nile, the opening of a market for French manufactures in Africa, Arabia, and Syria, and the importation of the products of those countries. Napoleon himself gives an important clue when he mentions the final objective:

Thirdly, setting out from Egypt, as from a place of arms, to lead an army of 60,000 men to the Indus; to excite the Mahrattas and oppressed peoples of those extensive regions to insurrection.[4]

Here was a project that for years was never entirely absent from Napoleon's thoughts, though affairs in Europe forbade its attempted execution. One can say, if one wishes, that it was all a part of his master plan for subjugating Britain (itself never much more than a romantic dream); but it is probably more than a coincidence that the man-god Alexander also had fought in India. In any case, what on the face of things could be more impractical than for a European leader to embark with a great army for far-away India? What useful purpose, what object commensurate with the expenditure of energy and blood, could it serve "to excite the Mahrattas and oppressed peoples of those extensive regions to insurrection"? Is not the man who speaks in such terms a victim of the heroic ideal, the same ideal that led knights-errant forth on fantastic quests, the ideal that would sacrifice a generation and trample a world in fond pursuit of the will-o'-the-wisp, personal glory?

Napoleon's own further pronouncements offer additional evidence. He himself admitted his overwhelming ambition when, twenty years after the engagement at Lodi, he said to Gourgaud:

It is since the evening of Lodi that I have believed myself a superior man and that there has come to me the ambition to accomplish great things, which from that moment has occupied me like a fantastic dream.[5]

A "fantastic dream" it truly was. There is reason to suppose that this apparently mundane earthly ruler, who governed in a realm of mundane affairs, was a treader of the clouds of gigantic fantasy —fantasy that fed on his very successes and blinded him to the actualities. Only so can we explain some of his later undertakings, and in particular the bizarre and ghastly Russian campaign; an expedition conducted at a time when he had an army of over a million men and yet not soldiers enough for his ambitions, nor commanders capable of coping with the generals Cold and Distance and Famine. This campaign reveals, as did many of his later undertakings, that he lacked the first requisite of the practical man: the ability to adjust action to reality. Like most of the dazzled minions of the heroic ideal, he tried to adjust reality to his desires.

The development of a grandeur complex became more and more evident with the years. Just as Alexander surrounded himself with the pomp of an Oriental potentate and even let himself be converted into a god, so Napoleon after the campaign of 1805 arrayed himself in the formality suitable for a super-being. No longer was he a man who walked the earth, and breathed the earth-air; he was a divinity who avoided too close contact with mortal creatures, who dwelt in the midst of a halo of ceremony, and who rapidly corrected himself if he made the error of a familiar remark or gesture. Even the blood-kin of this deity, even his brothers dared not seat themselves in his presence or speak until he deigned to address them; nor did they presume to use the familiar "tu" customary among friends and kindred, but rather employed the remote "vous." Whole assemblages, sometimes composed of as many as a hundred persons, would await in silence the arrival of the divine one, who in turn might show the disdainful rudeness of an immortal toward the perishable herd.

Was this imperial remoteness necessary in order to maintain respect and authority? It had not been necessary in the beginning; nor does it on the face of things indicate anything but a growing egomania, a self-romanticizing resulting from the heroic ideal run riot. Actually, Napoleon's god was Napoleon. The ceremonial upon which he insisted was a form of self-worship. And with a lack of the humor and the humility which are so refreshing in a head of state such as Lincoln, he nourished his self-worship by means of campaigns wherein he saw himself in a magnificent light. Thus the effort to stamp out the rebellion in Spain was in effect an attempt to subdue a revolt against his own prestige. Likewise, the bid for renown is evident in the Gargantuan endeavor to bring Russia to her knees, in which Napoleon but followed in the footsteps of a not less ardent devotee of the heroic ideal, who had thrown a Swedish army to the wolves on the frozen steppes more than a century before.

It was not patriotism, any more than it was the necessities of personal leadership, that fired Napoleon to make thrust after thrust for glory:

It is plain that he was no true Frenchman at heart, fond as he was of representing himself as such. . . . Had he been what he pretended he would have been content with securing for France the leading position among the Powers. But that was precisely wherein he had failed the nation which had put its trust in him. Possessing no spark of French patriotism or of ambition for France . . . he had recognized no natural limits to his ambition, gigantic in truth, since it embraced the whole world, and yet at the same time infinitesimally small, since it was to serve only to satisfy the inordinate passion for glory on the part of a single individual.[6]

II

No matter how Napoleon himself was obsessed by the heroic ideal, he could not have gone far toward his goal unless his followers had shared his enthusiasm. But in this respect, as already remarked, he was aided by the spirit of nationalism, the fever of glory and conquest bequeathed by the French Revolution. He was not content, however, merely to receive his inheritance; with shrewd calculation, he did everything possible to play upon the minds of his men and inculcate a war-making fervor.

One of his methods—a method not unknown to army commanders ever since Roman days—was in the conferring of awards and badges of distinction. Thus he established the celebrated Legion of Honor, composed of 17 Cohorts, each with 20 Commandments, 30 Officers, and 350 Legionaries, all enrolled for life; its insignia, in the shape of crosses, might puff out the shoulders of the common soldier with the same decoration as his officers wore. When chided with the triviality of these awards, Napoleon retorted:

I dare wager that you can name no republic, ancient or modern, which has had no distinction to give away. You may call them playthings and baubles; but it is with such baubles that mankind is led. . . . The French . . . have only one passion, and this is called "honor." This passion must be fostered and encouraged by the granting of distinctions.[7]

Here, then, was tacit recognition that, no matter what men might do out of a fighting spirit or for love of a cause, they would do still more for the sake of their pride.

The fact is that personal pride, in the Napoleonic armies, took something of the place occupied by the ardor for liberty and the religious devotion to *la Patrie* in the forces of the Revolution. And when pride did not suffice, Napoleon had other inducements to offer. Annuities, ranging from 250 to 5,000 francs a year, awaited the members of the Legion of Honor. And for officers who had distinguished themselves, annuities were to reach as high as 10,000 francs. Before the Italian campaign, if we can believe the *Memoirs*, Napoleon spoke to the army of the prospects not only of glory but of wealth. And at various other times, he flaunted before his officers' eyes dazzling visions of the "Empire of Europe," whose member countries would fall into the hands of his devoted followers and offer them prospects of splendor and of treasure unlimited.

The personal loyalty of Napoleon's men has often been remarked. We read that his veterans, though he had deserted them in Egypt and left them to suffer torments beneath the withering sun of Spain or to die miserably amid the snow-wastes of Russia, would murmur no complaint against their leader; while the peasants would give of their sons as to a pagan god. No doubt this was due in part to the legend that had grown up even during his lifetime, and in part it arose from the honors which he permitted his men to share. But to a large extent it appears to have sprung of the feeling, which he nursed, that the individual soldier was important to him: the care that, according to common report, he gave to the soldier's comfort and well-being, even to the details of his apparel; and the impression, which he managed to spread, of remembering the particular heroes of Ulm or Friedland or Jena. One may remark that it was strange, extraordinarily strange that the man who made a probable world's record in throwing away soldiers' lives, the man who allowed blood to be tapped like water in his vainglorious expeditions, should have been revered by the men he was sacrificing, and honored for his attention to their needs. But, as always, it is not objective reality that governs men's deeds so much as what they believe.

One source of Napoleon's power was undoubtedly his ability to influence his followers by his words; as in the case of other great commanders, the tongue was a mighty accessory to the sword. "Nothing in the life of Caesar," as one writer puts it, "is more wonderful than the way in which, by a brief speech, or even a single word he could fire the hearts of his soldiers, and win their devotion to himself. Bonaparte, from the first, struck the same note. At Toulon he had filled a battery with heroes by calling it that of 'les hommes sans peur' " ("men without fear").[8]

An example of his speech-making is to be found in his address to the troops after Austerlitz:

Soldiers, I am satisfied with you! In the battle of Austerlitz you have justified all my expectations of your intrepidity; you have adorned your eagles with immortal glory. . . . Soldiers, when the imperial crown was placed upon my head by the people of France I relied upon you for preserving to it always that refulgent glory which alone could give it value in my sight. . . . When everything should have been accomplished necessary to the assurance of happiness and prosperity to our country I will lead you back to France; there you will be the object of my most tender care. My people will look upon you with joy, and it will be enough for any of you to say, "I was at the battle of Austerlitz," to draw forth the reply, "Here is a brave man." [9]

In twentieth-century ears, these words may sound just a trifle bombastic. Nevertheless, they had their effect; the rank and file took them seriously; each man lifted up his head, feeling that *he* was being personally designated; each saw himself basking in the

admiring glances of the folks at home, and overhearing their lauda-
tory cries: "Here is a brave man!"

The good effect of all this, however, might be impaired were
false impressions to get abroad. Rascally correspondents and publicists, if left to themselves, might throw doubt upon the Emperor's
benevolent intentions; they might even question the extent or value
of his victories. Nothing of the kind, of course, was to be permitted. As part of the battle to control men's minds, Napoleon
took both positive and negative measures to see that truth was
presented only in approved and licensed form.

The negative methods consisted mainly of what we today should
know as censorship. He took steps to prevent any public discussions of his laws; he leveled heavy blows at the heads of authors
so reckless as to make objectionable statements (Chateaubriand,
for example, had to flee the country, and was stripped of all his
property); he regulated stage productions and prescribed that they
must apply to a period earlier than Henry IV; and he permitted
the presentation even of Mozart's *Don Juan* only when convinced
that it contained no subversive material. At the same time, he censored the newspapers, which were in constant danger of suppression; in 1805 he informed them that they must neither do nor say
anything opposed to the interests of the single French party, and
later expressed to Talleyrand the intention to have the political
articles for the *Moniteur* written by officials of the Foreign Office,
while other papers were to accept the *Moniteur* as their model.
In February, 1810, a more elaborate censorship was imposed upon
Paris, with a director-general and fifteen or twenty censors. These
functionaries were most diligent in trimming and cutting truth to
measure; in one case they were so conscientious that they tore out
of a book a word in praise of the British constitution; they forbade
the performance in the Hanseatic cities of such dangerous works
as Schiller's *Wilhelm Tell* and Goethe's *Faust;* and they suppressed
two of the remaining independent Paris papers, and made puppets
of the other two.

Under such circumstances, the people were sure to get the truth,
the whole truth, and nothing but the truth as Napoleon wanted
them to see it. More than that, the man who risked a public criticism of the Emperor would have to be braver than his bravest
death-defying troops. Men would be thrown into prison without
a trial on no better excuse than that they hated Napoleon or had

written letters expressing unfriendly views; in 1811 there were 2,500 such prisoners of the State. This, indeed, may seem a picayune number compared with the lists of later dictators; but it was large enough in the eyes of the 2,500 and their relatives; and it was great enough, likewise, to insure a favorable tone to all public discussions of the Emperor, his policy, and his campaigns.

Apart from these negative methods of mind control, Napoleon resorted to positive means. After the suppression of all but two of the independent papers of Paris, a special *Bureau de l'Esprit Public* provided accounts of victories along with many non-controversial items. And Napoleon himself, long before, had taken care that the proper information, and only the proper information, should be reported from the battlefields; he had prudently written or edited his own war bulletins. Doubtless it was by no coincidence that the phrase "lying like a bulletin" was current at the time. It was not unnatural, furthermore, that Napoleon should have considerable success at the modern art of magnifying victories and minimizing losses. Thus after the Battle of Preussisch-Eylau, according to Kircheisen, "Napoleon had the audacity when writing to his brother Joseph and Cambacérès, to speak of a mere 1,500 dead and 3,000 wounded, and in Bulletin 58 he represents the losses at 1,900 killed and 5,700 wounded. Actually the French lost anything up to 25,000 men."

Similarly, when credit was due, the supervisor of the media of enlightenment was careful to do himself no injustice. It would be hard to point to any of the world's dictators whose policy was precisely self-obliterating; praise and renown may be mundane things, of no ultimate value, but few autocrats hesitate to dish it out to themselves in overflowing bowls. Thus, whatever Napoleon did was far more glorious, more magnificent, more extraordinary than similar performances by other performers. Speaking of the battles of Marengo and Austerlitz, Geoffrey Bruun has some signficant remarks:

As a *chef d'oeuvre* neither of these conflicts can be held to surpass Hohenlinden, where Moreau won an equally conclusive victory by similar methods against similar odds and followed it up more swiftly. Moreover, Moreau's casualties were only five per cent of his effectives, whereas Napoleon's losses were twenty per cent at Marengo and ten per cent at Austerlitz. If despite these figures, the legend still persists that Napoleon constantly achieved miracles against superior forces, and possessed a secret formula for victory which no contemporary general could apply, the answer must be sought in his genius for self-advertisement. He seldom gave his subordinates public credit for performances which might dim the glory of his own; neither Kellerman at Marengo, Moreau at Hohenlinden, nor Davout at Auerstadt received full credit for the initiative and courage which brought them victory.[10]

III

It is worthy of note that, despite all the tools of propaganda, censorship, intimidation, artificially fanned patriotism, and the military glamorization of drums, marches, festivals, speeches, badges, and awards, not all the people were converts to Napoleonism; indeed, great numbers showed a spirit of resistance even at the height of the Emperor's power. In view of the fact that resistance was apt to prove dangerous, and that most men are inclined to bow to oppression when the only alternative is to be crushed, we can compile no statistics on the extent of the hostility; all that we can say is that it must have been much greater than the surface eruptions show.

These eruptions manifest themselves chiefly in two ways: in desertions from the army, and in resistance to conscription. In a sense, these two were products of one state of mind: an anti-military attitude that made men object to entering the army in the first place, and drove them to any available means of leaving after they had been enrolled. The phenomena of draft evasion and desertion, to be sure, were not limited to the Napoleonic epoch; they had likewise, as we have seen, characterized the earlier Revolutionary period. But throughout all the years of Napoleon's domination, they were ever-recurrent problems.

On October 28, 1808, for example, we find Napoleon writing to Minister of War Clarke: "Out of 747 recruits from the Aube Department, 485 have deserted. Give orders to have them arrested and sent back to the army." [11] On July 12, 1811, he notified Vice-Admiral Decres: "I am informed that the recruits whom I assigned to the fleet at Toulon, especially those of the Lower Pyrenees Department, have almost all deserted." [12] And on August 15, 1813, he wrote to Clarke: "I have your letter . . . from which it appears that we have 76,000 deserters from the colors. I believe, however, that this estimate falls short of the truth." [13]

A year previously, at the time of the Russian campaign, deserters were very numerous. In the entire country, it is estimated, there were as many as forty thousand of these fugitives, who roamed the woods of Brittany and La Vendée in great bands, until Napoleon's *colonnes mobiles* or flying columns rounded them up like cattle and herded them back to the wars.

Simultaneously, resistance to conscription was widespread. The draft of 1811, which was to sweep an additional 120,000 men into the Napoleonic armies, was evaded in some cases by the payment of as high as eight thousand francs for substitutes. But what of the poor, who could not afford to buy their way out? Thousands of them took the obvious alternative—they made use of their legs. But the government, with a savagery that must have made many a conscript hesitate to flee, held the families or the communities responsible for the desertions; and the flying columns took care to see that the law was enforced.

Even among Napoleon's old-and-tried troopers, historians have noted a growing disaffection during the Emperor's later years; an increase of insubordination; a war-weariness, and a spreading realization that it was not the needs or glory of the country so much as the ambitions and egotism of their commander that drove them forth to agony and death. The very leaders, the officers up to the rank of marshal, were among those who grumbled most. A story is told of Napoleon's second in command, Berthier, the Prince of Neuchâtel; the Emperor's private secretary Méneval chanced to enter his tent one day during the Russian campaign, and found him with his head buried in his hands, the incarnation of dejection. What, he demanded upon being questioned, was the use of his title, his huge income, his chateau in Paris and his country estate, if he was to be tortured like Tantalus, more unfortunate than any private?

In the course of Napoleon's years of campaigning, the glow and glory somehow seemed to fade; only the back-breaking torment remained. The army and the people were slowly awakening to reality. And that, probably more than any other domestic factor, will explain Napoleon's downfall.

But the wave of feeling he aroused abroad was to be still more decisive. Before we consider this, however, let us take a passing glance at the sources of his wars.

IV

It cannot justly be held that Napoleon's was the exclusive or anything close to the exclusive responsibility for the Napoleonic wars. Like all men, he was the heir to the past; and in his case the immediate past had been especially turbulent and militant. Into his care the armies and the traditions of the Revolution had descended; the Revolutionary methods of conscription; and the religious enthusiasm of the Jacobins for *la Patrie*—all in addition to the actual warfare which he had waged under the Directory before the *coup d'état* that elevated him to be First Consul. And not only did he find himself the master of an army and of a people in which the Revolutionary fervor was still alive, but he was opposed by bristling foreign forces: a Europe unreconciled to the fact of the Revolution, a Europe that was suspected of hatching many a royalist plot, a Europe that abhorred the Republicans of France somewhat as it was to loathe the Bolsheviks of Russia after another of the world's great revolutions. As always in human affairs, opposition aroused resistance; the knowledge of monarchial enmity banded the people together, fired their patriotism, and sharpened the claws of their leader. And since his training and his whole outlook was of a military nature, it is not surprising if he saw no safety except in military methods.

A significant sidelight on Napoleon's state of mind occurs in the *Mémoires* of Miot de Mélito. Whether or not it literally gives us the First Consul's words, this quotation does plausibly indicate how he felt in the summer of 1802, and does illuminate the position of the French Republic:

If these Powers are continually going to cherish war in their hearts so that it will break some day, then the sooner it comes to that the better, for every day helps to dissipate in them the recollection of their last defeats, while it tends to diminish at home the prestige of our last victories. . . . The French government of today bears no resemblance to anything which surrounds it. Hated by its neighbors, compelled to hold in restraint within its domain sundry classes of evil-disposed persons, in order to preserve an imposing appearance in the face of so many enemies it stands in need of brilliant deeds and consequently of war. . . . Situated as we are, I regard every peace as a brief truce and the ten years of my consulship as destined to be an uninterrupted warfare.[14]

It is easy to see how a chief of state, confronted by a ring of enemies, would feel that his only security lay in armed strength—strength which he would have to use in order to keep the pack at bay. Even if he had not been naturally circumspect, the First Consul would have been put on his guard in 1799, when he intimated to London a desire for peace and was told that France's best guaranty would be a return of the Bourbons—in other words, the abdication not only of Napoleon, but of the Revolution. It is futile to speculate whether Napoleon's attitude would have been less bristling had the Powers genuinely tried to understand France and to cooperate with her; but since such a consummation was forbidden by the feeling that the French government was the foe of all vested rights, and was discouraged likewise by Napoleon's usurpations and his disregard of international obligations, the nations were headed along a road of fire and blood.

They had been headed in that direction even at the moment of his rise to power, when the flaming spirit of Jacobinism still rode high, and when the national pride would not permit the Directory to surrender Bonaparte's Italian gains, nor to forsake the revolutionary governments in Italy and elsewhere. Yet the war spirit was fanned only by a comparatively small group of officials and fanatics; the mass of the people grievously felt the need of peace, the need for a government that could maintain peace; they were weary of the long period of war, and longed for a pacifistic change of policy. And this was one of the factors behind popular acceptance of the First Consulship.

But it was the fate of France, as we know, to long for an olive leaf and receive a sword. It was her fate to crave a conciliator and be granted a war-maker. The desires of the many seemed impotent against the traditions of conflict and the will of the few. Not only in France but in England, Russia, Austria, and elsewhere the eyes of the leaders were turned from channels of peace. England, with her gaze upon commercial objectives, significantly increased her armed forces after the general peace of 1802; called up the militia; and added ten thousand men to her navy (largely by the press-gang method); and Napoleon was not without reasons for turning publicly upon the English Ambassador Whitworth, demanding whom the precautions were directed against, and declaring that the British preparations compelled him to follow suit. In Russia the throne was occupied by a man who was part fanatic and part idealist and part a shrewd designer; Alexander I had ideas of playing a gallant role as a benefactor of mankind, and his grandiose scheme involved the restoration of liberty to the lands trampled by France and the establishment of the so-called principle of "natural boundaries"—ends which by preference would be attained peaceably, but if necessary were to be achieved by force of arms; in 1805 he announced with a flourish that no neutral would be permitted in the pending war. In Prussia in 1806 Baron vom Stein and Prince Louis Ferdinand captained a small war party which succeeded in carrying the King and Queen along with them, and was aided by the false report that France intended a separate peace with England. In Austria the war party appears to have been enchanted by General Mack's victory promises (which preceded one of history's most resounding defeats); and for no reason to be identified with Austrian interests, the Emperor on August 9, 1805, directed his ambassador in St. Petersburg to make the country a partner in the Anglo-Russian alliance—which made it also a partner in the Anglo-Russian war with France. Three and a half years later, when it was becoming evident to the dullest-witted that Napoleon desired nothing less than the domination of Europe, Austria professedly fought for more definite and idealistic motives; in the directions to its representative who sought English aid on January 29, 1809, it announced two objectives: the dismemberment of Napoleon's system of tributary nations; and the restoration of all the usurped lands to their original owners.

As for Napoleon himself—did he not provide excuse enough for a coalition against him? In our own day we are unhappily familiar with the methods by which a dictator, annexing "satellite nations" by subterfuges, evasions, treaty violations, and indirect pressure even when he does not actively take up arms, gradually expands the circumference of his power, restricts liberty, and inflames suspicion, fear, and military preparations in his neighbors. This form of expansion, somewhat more novel in Napoleonic times than in our own, has doubtless served as a model for totalitarian rulers in the twentieth century; and the effects, in the case of the French Empire, were not essentially different than among later aggressive entities: a ring of enemies and potential victims is invariably welded together against the usurper.

We can see how Napoleon, step by step, inspired increasing rage, fear, and desperation in the countries of Europe. As far back as April 12, 1801, he decided to annex Piedmont and so to take over the western Alpine passes, regardless of the fact that he was thereby violating the Treaty of Lunéville, which he had signed only two months before. He waited no more than another week before transferring the benefits of his protection to the Ligurian Republic, likewise without regard to treaty stipulations; and the year was not out before he summoned the heads of the Cisalpine Republic, and, thanks to the diplomatic maneuverings of Talleyrand, induced them to tender him their Presidency. In January of the following year he permitted himself to be recognized as the head of an Italian Republic, supposedly independent; and the Kingdom of Etruria, previously the Grand Duchy of Tuscany, followed on the list of vassal states. A little previously (on October 17, 1801), he had forced a new constitution on Holland; at a plebiscite, fifty thousand persons said "No!," and only a third of that number registered a "Yes!"; but as five sixths of the entire electorate had not voted, their abstention was held by Napoleon to be acquiescence, and the measure consequently carried by a handsome majority. Again, in 1802, he ordered the entry of thirty thousand French soldiers into Switzerland, so that Swiss politics might be properly directed. Strangely, there was a uniformity in the ways in which the nations accepted Napoleonism.

It would occupy endless pages to discuss all the diplomatic thrusts, counter-thrusts, and manipulations of the times; the schemes and burrowings of the various Powers; the arrogance with which Napoleon maintained his position, and denied concessions that might have gone far toward soothing the outraged feelings of other nations: his refusal, for example, to treat with England regarding his Continental designs; his confining of the sphere of his possible Russian cooperation to Germany and the eastern Mediterranean; and his emphatic statement to the Emperor Francis II that it was impossible for him to reconsider his position as to states such as Bavaria, Wurttemberg, and Baden. When diplomacy is intractable, war is in danger of intervening—that fact was as manifest in Napoleon's day as in our own, and the presumption therefore is that, when taking his unyielding attitude, Napoleon was not deterred by the prospect of war, or at least waived it aside as a "calculated risk." There are even intimations that he considered war desirable, as the means of insuring the peace of Europe beneath the autonomy of a single supreme ruler.

V

It was characteristic of Napoleon that, like the Revolutionary government before him and like his successors in twentieth-century Germany and elsewhere, he should have embraced a thousand and one details in his world-encompassing designs, and yet overlooked the item that was to be his nemesis. That item was an imponderable, something he could not see, feel, or measure: something that existed only in the minds of men, and specifically in foreign minds. In other words, he disregarded if he ever observed at all the rising resentment, the bitterness, the fury which his encroachments were creating among peoples who had been indifferent or even friendly to his operations.

We have been reminded that Napoleon, like his immediate predecessors, waged war not against peoples but against governments. And yet, paradoxically, after he had subdued the opposing governments, it was the people who arose and knocked him off his pedestal. Had he been as wise as he has been credited with being, he would have recognized that nations are driven not only by clubs but by the thoughts in men's minds; he would have taken warning as early as 1808, when he sought to depose the Spanish Bourbon monarchs in favor of his brother Joseph, actually forced the weak Ferdinand to abdicate, and found himself faced with a popular revolt and such a series of reverses that the Peninsular War was to be a permanent mark against his record.

In Russia, also, he underestimated nationalistic feeling, which he played so large a part in creating. It was not only the northern winter that defeated him in 1812; it was the pertinacity of the Russian people, the patriotic fervor with which they harried and haunted his armies, the zeal that counseled even the Draconian extreme of burning Moscow. But it was in his whipping up of German and particularly Prussian nationalism that he produced his most decisive effects—effects of which we even today have not drained the full grievous measure.

It is notable that this development was not only rapid, it was almost eruptive in its suddenness. We know, of course, that many leading Germans, such as Goethe, could watch the rise of Napoleon and the fall of Germany in unperturbed aloofness; the professors at Leipzig greeted the conqueror as a hero; the rulers of Wurttemberg, Saxony, Bavaria, and Baden bowed obsequiously before him; seven ministers of the Crown and many lesser officials swore allegiance upon his arrival at Berlin, and one general went so far as to disobey the royal orders to supply the fortresses with ammunition. And what was true of those in high station was also true, though perhaps in a lesser degree, of the common people. So little had Prussian nationalism shown itself even in 1806 that, before the Battle of Jena, in which the Prussians were overwhelmed, not one inhabitant brought a word of warning of French intentions to the Prussian army sleeping at Kapellendorf. But a few years later, and particularly in 1812 and immediately afterward, Prussian nationalism was a white flame.

It had been fanned into a flame not only by the fear and hatred of Napoleon and the resentment that takes fuel from defeat, but by the deliberate incitements of propagandists: the patriotic songs of Arndt, Korner, and Schenkendorf, the patriotic pronouncements of Baron vom Stein and his pleas for a war that would liberate Prussia and all Europe, and the patriotic example of such a man as the University of Breslau professor Steffans, who thought he heard a voice telling him to make war on Napoleon, offered himself as a recruit, and induced 200 students from Breslau and 258 from Berlin to join the ranks. And aside from all this the preachments of the philosophers, and of Fichte in particular, ranged many on the side of what appeared to be an idealistic nationalism.

At the same time, there was an indefinable pressure from the military elements. Clausewitz is said to have confided to his fiancee, before the Battle of Jena, that his country needed the war, and that only by means of war could his ambitions be fulfilled. And it was men such as he, along with Scharnhorst and Hardenberg and a comparatively small group of military leaders and politicians, who took advantage of the favorable winds which Napoleon had caused to blow, and led the way to the crowning feature of Prussian nationalism. Paradoxically, this measure proved, as similar measures have proved before and since, that nationalistic feeling and willingness to fight were by no means universal; that it was insufficient to persuade men to make war, that one must coerce them. A system of conscription, adopted on September. 3, 1814, was designed to make a soldier of every able-bodied man, and to abolish all exemptions. And thus the military precedent of the Revolution and of Napoleonism fastened itself upon another great nation. Thus, through war-making and army-making, through armed revolution and armed conquest, the world was clamping down the jaws of a new enslavement . . . an enslavement that was to spread, and take possession not only of men's bodies but of men's minds, and become an instrument for the unprecedented extension of the range, the deadliness, and the menace of warfare.

VI

It is true that the Congress of Vienna of 1814–15 paved the way for forty years of peace through the enactment of a series of anti-nationalistic reactionary agreements. But Europe, sliced and partitioned in a multitude of ways, rested uneasily; the return of the *émigrés* and the restoration of Bourbon rule to France provided an arsenal of arguments for those who regretted the loss of the Revolution's genuine gains, and who saw Napoleon as a golden deliverer by contrast with the prosy, repressive royalists. And the uninspiring if unwarlike period following Waterloo, the lack of any blazing cause or magnetic leader, provided nurture and sustenance for a phenomenon in some ways as striking as Napoleon himself: the Napoleonic legend.

As in the case of Alexander, Caesar, and Charlemagne, King Solomon and King Arthur and many another story-book figure, the actual man became overshadowed by the image of a man, an imaginary being who took powerful hold upon the popular mind. We have already noted, in one or two instances, the ways in which a historical character gives place to a legend; and we have seen that the legend, when revolving about a great warrior chief such as Alexander, may inspire men with warlike ideas and urge them to shine in the supposed light of their hero. But the metamorphosis of reality into fable, and the power of fable to rule like reality, has never been clearer or more amply documented than in the case of Napoleon. As we have observed, the legend began in the days when the man was still tramping with his armies across the plains of Europe; it fed on his victories, was fanned by the pomp and show and imperial pretensions of his court, and converted him in the popular mind into something a little more than human. Doubtless for many the halo vanished after his series of military reverses; but even amid his detention at St. Helena the legend found new nourishment, which Napoleon himself largely supplied.

Perhaps, as he brooded over the stirring past, he was to some extent self-deceived; perhaps he believed that he actually was, as he proclaimed, a martyr "to an immortal cause." Perhaps this man, whose iron hand had clamped down against freedom of expression and who had stricken away the sovereignty of many a land, was persuaded that he had really been struggling against oppression, and that the voice of the nations was for him. Yes, perhaps Napoleon was a convert to the Napoleonic legend. But whether or not this was true, the buzzard with the dripping carrion beak did represent himself as an eagle whose wings were spread wide for liberalism and liberty—an idealist who aimed to carry out the high principles of 1789, and to bring equality and freedom to all peoples. If he had perched upon a throne, that had been because harsh circumstance had decreed him no choice; he had in reality been a "crowned Washington," a "Messiah of the Revolution," who had waged war with the altruistic thought of establishing a United States of Europe. To the men of all lands he would be known as "the emblem of their hopes."

Nothing could be more unsalutary than for such a picture to become common. If we look upon our wolves frankly as wolves, beasts of prey who steal and murder out of wantonness or greed, then it is unlikely that our children will grow up with the idea of imitating the wolf. But if we state that they are not really wolves at all but lions, and that their seeming depredations are actually noble feats, then the next generation is likely to see a large wolf crop. The best thing Napoleon at St. Helena could have done for the world would have been to proclaim, as Asoka had done two thousand years before, that his path had been a grim and ungodly one, and that he saw the error of his ways. But actually he did the worst thing possible: he tried to vindicate and glorify his ways. And, unfortunately, he found a host of trumpeters to carry his message abroad, and thus came to enjoy his last and perhaps his most sinister triumph. The result was a little like what we might have expected in Hitler's case if, instead of perishing in the debacle of 1945, he had lived on in captivity, spreading extravagant tales of his benign activities, and finding auditors who circulated the stories to the ends of the earth, so that millions came to look upon him as a hero and a martyr and Germany clasped him back to her heart and used his name as the rallying call for a new patriotism, a new program of racial persecution, and a new militarism.

Truly, "the evil that men do lives after them"—not only in their deeds, but in the legends that transform those deeds. And the military spirit that Napoleon fostered on the battlefields may in time's long judgment be found to have had less effect than that which sprang of glittering rumor and report.

It is strange how, in the dimness of distance, Napoleon's crimes and usurpations began to recede; men remembered not the ruthlessness that had kidnapped the Duc d'Enghien from the neutral territory of Baden and felled him before a firing squad, nor the cold-blooded expediency that had condemned to death many hundreds of inconvenient Arab prisoners during the Near Eastern campaign, nor all the needless expeditions and battles, and the snuffing out of the liberties and sovereignties of peoples. What they recalled was a shining knight, chivalrous and gallant, a prodigy of daring on the battlefield, a giant in resourcefulness, a genius in the cleverness of his designs, the savior and protector of peoples. It mattered not at all that this paladin had never existed; he was none the less reverenced and lauded.

It was in 1840, nineteen years after his death, that the French people completed the apotheosis of the one-time dictator, whose dying wish had been that his ashes be laid to rest on the banks of the Seine. The Prince de Joinville, under orders from the government of Louis-Philippe, voyaged to St. Helena to bring back the remains of Napoleon, which have ever since reposed in the Invalides; the return of this handful of dust was regarded as a historic occasion. And thus, by the bluster and ceremony, the publicity and sentimentality of a posthumous honor, the French reinforced the Napoleonic legend, and by implication endorsed the man's life-program and exalted his military activity.

Unfortunately the writers, and in particular the poets and historians, did their best to join in the chorus. Béranger sang of the glory of the fallen leader; Victor Hugo and others played their part in fanning the flames of the old heroic ideal. Men who had never seen army life spoke of the splendor of serving in Napoleon's army; supposed historical authorities distorted the relationship of the facts, so that the conqueror was seen in a light that had never surrounded him in life. We have all read the sort of history that sheds a glow on armies, generals, and battles; it is hardly too much to say that most of us, in our early days, have been nursed upon this sort of popular fiction, in which the legend of a Napoleon takes precedence over the man himself. There is evidence to support the view that the authors of this type of work aim not so much to elucidate the facts as to present a preconceived point of view:

A very large part of military history is written, if not for the express purpose of supporting an army's authority and prestige, at least with the intention of not hurting it, not revealing its secrets, avoiding the betrayal of weakness, vacillation, or distemper; it is usually designed with a future war in mind, in its inspiring treatment of some particular war in the past. To doubt and attack such prestige by historical criticism even Moltke regarded as unpatriotic.[15]

Another element in the Napoleonic legend was contributed by the survivors of the campaigns. We have seen how, in our own day, veterans' groups tend to be formed, and organizations of veterans are prone to assert themselves in favor of every militaristic move (militarism, in some curious way, being mistaken for patriotism). We have also observed how, among the loudest blowers of horns and rattlers of sabers, we sometimes find those men who went forth to battle with the greatest mumbling and grumbling. Yet we know that such persons are not necessarily insincere; they are merely converts to the romanticizing of war; they are in part self-deluded, and in part deceived by the legend that surcharges the air about them; their memories, like mirrors that select only the brightest reflections, exaggerate every favorable impression of the wars, create new favorable impressions, and disguise or conceal the agony and horror. And so, when the remnants of the Napoleonic armies were reduced to the occupations of unadventurous peace and had the leisure to magnify and glamorize the past, men could speak of the glory in which every villager had shared, the wonder that had descended upon every hamlet and every cottage roof. And the hearers, lulled by the sonority of the words, would mistake the name of grandeur for its reality; and would forget the mud, the dust, the slime, the tears, the blood, the cruelty, the terror of battle. And the young would listen; and having no basis for judgment, would accept the legend, and be eager to emulate their fathers on the warpath. And all the while, gigantically before them, not at all resembling the small human being he actually was but with the might and dimensions and illumination of an immortal, they would see their hero, and hear him urge them to tread in his footsteps and be magnificent and brave—magnificent and brave like him, the more-than-man, the resplendent deity, Napoleon Bonaparte.

Chapter 26

A Century of Nationalism

Between the Battle of Waterloo and the murder of Archduke Francis Ferdinand at Sarajevo, a period of just under a century intervened. And this interval, though not marked by the same catastrophic struggles as the era immediately preceding and the one to follow, can in no way be regarded as unwarlike.[1] A few of the better known conflicts instantly come to mind: the Crimean War, the American Civil War, the Franco-Prussian War, the Boer War, the Spanish-American War, the Russo-Japanese War, the Balkan Wars, etc. The surface causes of these eruptions varied widely; but basically a single ingredient was predominant in them all: the sentiment of nationalism. And this was true even of a contest which, like our own Civil War, may appear economic at root in its concern with the slavery issue: actually, it was an affair of flaming passions on both sides, and the paramount question turned out to be not slavery but the preservation of the American Union.

So many were the nineteenth-century wars of nationalism and "national self-determination" that Carlton J. H. Hayes can devote more than a page of one of his books to a mere listing of the names, beginning with the Haitian Rebellion of 1804 and proceeding to such outbreaks as the Jameson Raid in South Africa, which preceded the Boer War, and the Philippine insurrection against the United States (1899–1901).[2] And this does not even take account of the many nationalistic struggles of the twentieth century, from the conflicts in Indonesia and China to the war of the Arabs and Israelis.

What then is this nationalism that has been of the very blood and bone of recent wars?

We have seen how, during the French Revolution, a fiery religious worship of *la Patrie* flared up in France. We have observed how this religious spirit was accompanied by the rise of conscripted armies; and how the fervor proved contagious, so that other countries likewise developed an ardent nationalism, and likewise conscripted large armies. And we can trace the development forward in ever-widening circles: to Japan, which, following its "awakening" by the West, adopted compulsory military service in 1872; and to the various other countries of the East, which, according to one characterization, "have found themselves at the beginning of a new epoch in which, upon the European model, nationalism is destined to succeed to the rôle of religion." [3] The fact is that nationalistic movements have been growing at an ever-accelerated rate, until they have become worldwide in their range and gigantic in their effects, and are (and have been for many decades) the most powerful incentives to war and deterrents to peace.

The tenets of nationalism are few and simple, and might be codified in an easily understood set of rules, somewhat as follows:

(1) My country can do no wrong.

(2) My country is the world's greatest, its people the world's choicest, its accomplishments the world's most brilliant.

(3) My country, by virtue of its superiority, has a right to push and shove the lesser inhabitants of the globe.

(4) My country has a right to self-determination, and must resist to the last drop of blood any abridgment of this natural law.

(5) No other country has any right to self-determination if it gets in the way of my own.

(6) My country has unlimited sovereignty. It must be ready at all times to punish any other nations who falsely imagine they have the same privilege.

(7) My country must be ready to fight for its honor. The word honor is subject to be construed as we decide.

(8) My country must maintain an army, navy, and air force to enable it to protect its honor.

(9) Every citizen shares in the distinction gained by my country when it protects its honor, just as he shares in the glory (though not necessarily in the dividends) of the companies that float the national flag above foreign oil or mining concessions.

When these views are solemnly held (as they have been held) by the peoples of neighboring or competing countries, the slightest economic disagreement or the slightest incident involving a national of either side may suffice to precipitate a war. We have seen how, even before the heyday of nationalism, the alleged injury to a single seaman's ear was excuse enough in the popular mind for the so-called War of Jenkins' Ear. More recently, the War of 1812 (which cost far more in life than it saved in personnel to our merchant marine) was caused primarily by the impressment of American seamen; this was an affront to our honor, and resulted in a United States declaration of war, which England did not want, and for which we were pitifully unprepared. At the end of the century the destruction of the battleship *Maine*, believed but not proved to have been caused by Spain, resulted in the Spanish-American War because of the supposed attack upon our honor, even though peaceful negotiations might have settled the difficulty. In 1914 an incident that might have proved equally serious occurred in Mexico: a party from an American naval vessel had been arrested but immediately released by the Huerta forces, a salute to our flag had been vainly demanded by Admiral Fletcher, an ultimatum had been sent by President Wilson but not answered; and finally the President, in defense of our national pride and honor, sent a landing party ashore at Veracruz, with the result that a number of Americans were killed or wounded. A few years later, as we shall see, we rushed into a world war when the Kaiser knocked a chip off our shoulders by attacks on American ships, though the material and human cost was incomparably greater than the possible loss in trade and ships through our non-participation. And, in 1941, one element behind the Japanese-American War was the humbling of Japanese pride and the affront to the Japanese national honor in discriminatory American land-laws and other restrictive acts.

This super-sensitive pride and hyper-delicate regard for national honor, which has driven so many nations toward the battlefield, has been by no means a natural or inevitable outgrowth. It has been inspired and cultivated, sometimes undeliberately and sometimes sedulously and intentionally, not only by the makers of patriotic myths and songs but by the writers and philosophers. Hegel, for example, had no small share in creating the porcupine-like German nationalism by his doctrine that the State was all in all, that the individual was comparatively of no importance, and that since the State owed its existence to force, force was justified in the maintenance of its own especial rights. Not less influential was the military writer Clausewitz, who taught that war was merely an instrument for carrying out political ends in ways otherwise unattainable: a justified and even indispensable means of national self-fulfillment. Likewise important in forming the German mood was

Friedrich List, who emphasized that economic life was subordinate to the will of the national State. And later in the century, a multitude of spokesmen reinforced a militant nationalism: Nietzsche, with his doctrine of masculinity, of pitilessness, of the strong will and the strong arm; the historian Heinrich von Treitschke, who proclaimed the superiority of the nation that survived by virtue of arms, and its right to dominate lesser peoples; Adolf Stocker, who foreshadowed a more celebrated Adolf in his denunciation of Jews and Marxists and his mouthings as to the "majesty" of war; Paul Déroulède, a French organizer and lecturer, who sponsored a "League of Patriots," rifle clubs, and chauvinistic fetes; Gustave Le Bon, whose racial theories were of the same ilk and breed as those of the Nazis, and who favored the sword as a means of keeping the lower species in place; Maurice Barrès, author and spreader of militant propaganda; and many others throughout Europe.

A curious fact about these self-conscious and inflammatory writers and agitators is that, whereas nationalism originally had been liberal and forward-looking, they were mostly narrow, intolerant, anti-liberal. Mazzini, Guizot, and many other nineteenth-century nationalists had embraced a creed that in some ways can only evoke admiration; but their humanitarianism was counterbalanced by one fatal flaw: in order to achieve their ends, they allowed themselves to accept the military standards of an earlier generation, and hence traveled a road of no returning, which led not to peace and brotherhood but to repression and war. When men, aflame with genuinely liberal principles, set out to fulfill their purposes with bombs and bayonets, one may be certain that the bayonets and bombs will remain; but one cannot be so sure as to the liberal principles. And when men are drilled to think more of the nation than of man, they end by concentrating upon the former to the neglect of the latter—the stronger idea, the more forceful emotion is apt to survive the heat of conflict. And so we find that the spokesmen of an exclusive nationalism, from Hegel to Hitler, rally their enthusiastic cohorts, while milder voices are drowned; and we observe that nationalism, as it gains in exclusiveness, grows also in pride, in ruthlessness, in an egocentric regard for its own honor, in military displays and expenditures, and in war-impelling provocations.

II

But let us consider particular cases. Since we cannot follow all the turns and ramifications of nineteenth- and early twentieth-century wars, it will suffice to note one characteristic series of outbreaks: the conflicts precipitated by Bismarck in his attempt to achieve German unity. These, as we shall observe, are not only significant in themselves, but are doubly important since they stand in the direct line of descent to the upheavals of our own day.

As Napoleon was the pivotal figure in European warfare in the early nineteenth century, so Bismarck was the leading actor in the latter half of the century. This is all the more surprising since, unlike Napoleon, who was both sovereign and general, he was above all a civilian leader. Yet there is irrefutable evidence that this statesman, this chancellor who might have held it his duty to steer his country away from storms and feuds, was a conscious apostle of Mars, who deliberately led Prussia into conflict with Denmark, Austria, and France—not because he desired bloodshed for its own sake, but because he was a convert to Clausewitz' view that war was but an extension of the political arm of the State, and because he saw in conflict the one means of firing the German people with a sentiment that would insure the country's unification.

"I did not doubt that a Franco-German war must take place before the construction of a United Germany could be realized," he himself tells us in his memoirs.[4] And, in another passage, he candidly expounds his views as to the nature of war:

The object of war is to conquer peace under conditions which are conformable to the policy pursued by the state. To fix and limit the objects to be attained by the war, and to advise the monarch in respect to them, is and remains during the war just as before it a political function.[5]

In his own way, Bismarck was a follower of Frederick the Great. Like Frederick, and like Cavour and Mussolini and many another statesman whose opportunism has led from momentary success to eventual disaster, he was a Machiavellian, although his Machiavellianism was of a particular type. Whereas the Prince, as described by the celebrated Florentine, held no method unjustifiable for the sake of personal power, Bismarck held no method unjustifiable for the sake of German unity. From the point of view of the victim, however, the distinction was academic; the unscrupulousness of Bismarck was as evident as that of Cesare Borgia had been. Here was a man who espoused no principle but a lack of all principle, who believed that good statesmanship required him to be on both sides of a fence at once, and had no scruple about blowing hot today where he blew cold yesterday, or about striking down the hand that had caressed him. One of his biographers summarizes the facts which are manifest in every treatment of the subject:

Reason of state—for Bismarck the reason of the Prussian State—was the one abiding reality in a world of uncontrollable facts and fluctuating situations. The true statesman must be prepared to be Conservative at home and Liberal abroad, or vice versa; to be a Jacobin in Paris and an Absolutist at Petersburg, if necessary, and must seek to wring out of every opportunity the maximum of advantage for his country, otherwise he was a doctrinaire or a bungler, a professor or a bureaucratic automaton.[6]

A man dominated by such cool disregard of moral canons may be more of a peril than the most flaming fanatic. For a fanatic has at least a particular direction: if he can be stopped once, he can be stopped entirely. But a Bismarck will go in any direction that suits his purposes; he will dodge, feint, zigzag, double back, and profess with one side of his mouth what he will deny with the other. And thus it was with matters of war and peace. There is no reason to suppose that the German people desired the Danish War of 1864, or the subsequent conflict with Austria; as we shall see, we have much evidence to the contrary. Moreover, we have the word of no less an authority than Moltke:

The war of 1866 did not take place because the existence of Prussia was threatened or in obedience to public opinion or the will of the people. It was a war which was foreseen long before, which was prepared with deliberation and recognized as necessary by the Cabinet, not in order to obtain territorial aggrandizement, but for power in order to secure the establishment of Prussian hegemony in Germany.[7]

In regard to the Danish War we have a no less qualified witness:

Bismarck wanted the war, intended and schemed it, from the beginning. For this statement we have his own testimony. He has left it on record that from early days he coveted for Prussia the territories which divided her from the Danish monarchy proper, and that his chief reason for so doing was the knowledge that without the double seaboard which they offered Prusso-Germany could never hope to become a maritime power.[8]

There is no need to go into the details of the Schleswig-Holstein controversy. The essential facts are that Bismarck desired the provinces for Prussia; that he took advantage of a change in the Danish royal succession to level an ultimatum at Denmark, demanding the repeal of a liberal constitution that gave home rule to Holstein while making Schleswig a part of Denmark; that the demands were neither acceptable, nor intended to be acceptable; and that, marching side by side with Austria, Prussia invaded and quickly subdued and gobbled the disputed duchies, though Bismarck's claim was based on the single and (to him) all-sufficient ground of superior might.

It was no coincidence that Austria, Prussia's henchman in the Danish robbery, became her collaborator's next victim. Even while accepting her aid, Bismarck was preparing to strike her down; so far back as December 24, 1863, he had written to Count Holtz in regard to the Hapsburg kingdom: "I am nowise frightened of war. . . . You will perhaps be convinced very soon that war is part of my program." [9] And part of his program it unquestionably was—part of his campaign of "blood and iron." Having negotiated secretly to secure the neutrality of Russia and of France, he spoke enthusiastically for war at a decisive Council of Ministers at Berlin in February, 1866; he harped on the old idea that war was inevitable, and Prussia in a better position to fight at the present time; and he won approval from all the other ministers except one, and all the generals without exception. The Crown Prince did indeed appeal for peace; but Bismarck had convinced the King—and so Mars won the day.

The war, as already suggested, was far from popular; even the army is said not to have strongly desired it; peace demonstrations were organized in many districts; peace petitions were addressed to the King by municipal bodies and other groups; and Bismarck himself was so unpopular that when an attempt on his life failed, the people's sympathy was with the assailant, and the celebrated professor Dubois-Reymond was heard to comment regretfully on the poor quality of the local revolvers. The Diet meanwhile reflected the general feeling by refusing to vote supplies for the army. But the government issued treasury bills to meet the expenses, and the war went on. The war went on not because it was necessary or widely desired but because a small group of wilful men, captained by Bismarck, had decided that it should go on.

Why, then, did he want war? His object, in the Austrian conflict, was not to abase his rival, nor to exact territory or indemnities; the mildness of the Treaty of Prague, which merely provided for Austria's withdrawal from Germany and her acknowledgment of Prussia's claim to Schleswig-Holstein and acquiescence in the establishment of a North German Federation, prove that the Chancellor was looking for something more than tangible fruits. While making good his hold on the Danish steals, he was thinking first of all of the effect on German national feeling; he was aiming to fan that sentiment of national pride, that sense of might and of glorious achievement which may be a people's most powerful annealing force; he was scheming to bring the shaky South German states into the federation, and realized that nothing would be more effective than the display of military might and the sense of heroic national accomplishment. In these schemings, as developments proved, he was uncannily correct so far as short-range results were concerned; it was the long-range effects that he grievously and tragically miscalculated.

III

One might suppose that shame and not fame would have been Bismarck's reward at the hands of the nation whose blood he needlessly spilled. But men's judgment, as so often, made a shining virtue of success; military triumph, in the popular vocabulary, became synonymous with glory; and the means were overlooked or forgotten amid the jubilation at the ends attained. And so, after the Austrian war, Bismarck began to wear a hero's toga. And a hero-worshipping Germany was already forgetting its love of peace and uniting in the self-conscious pride of accomplishment.

Nevertheless, his work was not completed. The third and bloodiest of his wars lay ahead. And the conflict with France, one of the most demonstrably unnecessary of all modern struggles, and one of the most disastrous in its eventual effects, deserves attention as an illustration of the ways in which a war may be artificially induced.

Not all the responsibility, as we shall see, was Bismarck's; blun-

dering French statesmanship and hysterical French public opinion
were powerful contributory causes. But these merely helped to
deliver into Bismarck's hands the victim for which he waited with
watering mouth. The fact is that he got what he wanted, and did
not scruple about methods. He himself has made his motives plain:

... our national sense of honor compelled us, in my opinion, to go to
war; and if we did not act according to the demands of this feeling
we should lose ... the entire impetus toward our national development won in 1866, while the German national feeling south of
the Main, aroused by our military successes in 1866, and shown by
the readiness of the southern states to enter the alliances, would
have to grow cold again. ... The gulf which had been created in
the course of history between the South and the North of the
fatherland by variety of dynastic and racial sentiments and modes
of life, could not be more effectively bridged over than by a joint
national war against the neighbor who had been aggressive for
many centuries.[10]

This reveals the purpose; it says nothing of the means. But the
means are, in large part, well known; they involved intrigue, deception, a deliberate playing upon the emotions of the home audience
and of the volatile enemy populace, as well as a skillful manipula-
tion of the pieces which chance and the adversary's maladroitness
had put into the master player's hands.

A matter of dynastic succession—the same dynastic succession
that had, in earlier centuries, involved Europe in many a gainless,
sanguinary war—provided the spark to ignite the conflagration.
Following a revolution in September, 1868, and the uncrowning of
Isabella II, the throne at Madrid became vacant; and after being
refused by a number of prospects, it was offered to the Hohenzollern Prince Leopold—a candidate certain to arouse frantic opposition in France, since his kingship would mean the virtual
encirclement of the nation by Prussian rulers. The impending
storm was by no means unforeseen by Bismarck, who objected to
asking the assent of Napoleon III to the proposed appointment, and
ignored the warning of the French ambassador Count Benedetti,
that the Emperor viewed the incident with concern. It may be
that actions "speak louder than words"; but in this case there is no
reason to discount Bismarck's subsequent remark that he saw here
the desired chance to pick a quarrel with France. To withdraw the
appointment; to hit upon some other candidate who would not

have been a fountain of international friction—this would certainly not have been beyond Bismarck's powers had it accorded with his wishes. But the disputed candidature remained; and step by step Bismarck inflamed the emotions that were to set off the eruption.

By means of negotiations that were a secret from the King himself, Bismarck maneuvered to give the Spanish crown to Leopold; he even spread the story that France, in the effort to cause a rift in Germany, was herself responsible for the proposed elevation of the Hohenzollern prince. This claim, like the candidature in general, aroused hot resentment in France; and one of the country's most egregious blunderers, the minister of foreign affairs, the Duc de Gramont, issued an appeal to the Spanish people, in which he tempered suasion with the scarcely veiled menace of armed action. "An official international threat, with the hand on the sword-hilt," Bismarck called it. Gramont could not better have served Bismarck's schemes had he been in the pay of the master plotter himself! For he aroused indignation in Berlin, and so impeded negotiation; and he kindled public opinion in France, which was being further whipped into fury by the newspapers. Meanwhile the British government, at Napoleon's prompting, was using its good offices for peace, with the natural suggestion of the withdrawal of the Hohenzollern candidate—a suggestion to which Bismarck did not take kindly.

There are reasons to suppose that the King himself now wished to abandon the candidature if he could do so gracefully; he had written the Queen that he would be "altogether pleased if Leopold were not elected." And he seemed destined to have his way when, on July 12, 1870, the father of Prince Leopold telegraphed his abandonment of his son's candidature. After all, Europe was not to be plunged into war!

And now Bismarck was tasting the cold winds of frustration and defeat. "This impression of a wound to our national honor by the compulsory withdrawal so dominated me that I had already decided to announce my retirement," he reports in his memoirs. But at this all-important moment the Duc de Gramont had to intrude his meddling thumb. Evidently he did not realize that pride and patriotism may be as strong in one country as in another, and that the Prussian sense of honor might be as sensitive as the French. Apparently, also, he did not understand that he was pouring oil on a nearly extinguished fire when he induced the Prussian ambassador to write the King asking for a letter of apology to Napoleon; and when, that same day, he telegraphed Benedetti, seeking a formal assurance that the King would never again endorse Leopold's candidature. The monarch, who had already renounced the candidature, could not but be angered at this apparent questioning of his word and desire to humiliate him; and he made a definite refusal to Count Benedetti, who accosted him as he was walking on the river promenade.

Even so, the affair might have ended with nothing worse than some ill feeling on both sides, had Bismarck not seen an opportunity in the misconceived attempt to wring a statement out of the King. The sequel—one of the most famous documents in modern history—was the altered Ems telegram, by which fraud accomplished its purpose of precipitating war.

It has been said that this celebrated telegram was forged; and the word is correct if applied to the perversion of the spirit of the document. But actually it contained one of those half truths that are more dangerous than a total lie. Bismarck, to quote his own statement, "reduced the telegram by striking out words," [11] with the result that Moltke remarked, "Now it has a different ring; it sounded before like a parley; now it is like a flourish in answer to a challenge." [12] By editing and boiling down the King's report as to the French ambassador, by making it appear that his representations were more peremptory than they actually were and by producing the impression that the King's response had been much ruder and more abrupt than had been the case, Bismarck succeeded in conveying the idea that Benedetti had been snubbed, and that an insult had been hurled at the French people. And thus he stirred up evil passions both in Paris and in Berlin.

In the streets of the latter city, according to the German historian Sybel, "the excited masses swayed to and fro; men embraced one another amid tears of joy, thunderous cheers for King William rent the air." [13] And in the French capital, as Bismarck foresaw, the telegram had "the effect of a red flag upon the Gallic bull." The excitable populace, their old hatred of Germany puffing back to flame, clamored for war; the minister of war, Leboeuf, demanded mobilization, which was granted on his claim that Prussia was already mobilized; while Gramont and the other members of the Cabinet, instead of standing on their own feet, were swept along by the storm of popular feeling. One element, not to be discounted in its effects, was the belief of the French army commanders that, within a week or two, their forces would be on the Rhine. And an element of equal importance was the fact that Prussia had been laying the military groundwork; had carefully surveyed the Franco-Prussian frontier; had collected warlike material, built strategic railways, and honeycombed France with spies. As a result, the German generals also were confident.

It was not the least adroit feature of Bismarck's machinations that he wrested the declaration of war from France instead of putting the odium upon himself. In the face of the objections of Thiers and a very few others, the government at Paris voted the war credits by a majority of 285 to 6. A manifesto of July 15 made the pious claim, "We have done everything in order to avert war. We now prepare to meet the struggle which has been forced upon us. . . ." And Paris received the call to arms with jubilation—at least, that part of Paris which made itself vocal; and the press flamboyantly proclaimed that this was not the war of the Emperor or his ministers, but of the nation. Not that this was strictly the fact, however; an inquiry of the prefects showed that only 16 of the provinces whole-heartedly favored war, 34 strongly opposed it, and 37 were unable to make up their minds.

"To Berlin!" shouted the rabble and the irresponsible journalists in Paris. "To Paris!" yelled their counterparts in Berlin. And the religious emotion of nationalism, the old hatred of the neighbor beyond the Rhine, and the feeling of national pride and honor all had their share in completing what passion and blundering and a Machiavellian design had begun, and in precipitating a war that was to cost hundreds of thousands of lives, that was to harrow and humble France, and to create resentments and prolong antagonisms which were to crackle behind the battlefields of 1914 and 1940.

IV

The Franco-Prussian War may have achieved Bismarck's purpose by putting the final nail in the platform of German unity (and unity with Prussia predominant). But, aside from this, it not only settled nothing but evoked greater problems than it had attempted to solve. The brand-throwing nationalism of Germans such as Treitschke and Stocker and of Frenchmen like Déroulède and Le Bon, which we have noted in passing, was in the main the product of the post-war era, when tensions were high and chauvinistic emotions smoldered and smoked. And though the period did not evoke any great new wars, old rivalries almost burst into a conflagration in 1874 and 1875; rumors of impending strife were flying through the air; and on April 8, 1875, the Berlin *Post* sent a wave of consternation across Europe, when it published an article entitled "Is War in Sight?" and answered the question with an implied affirmative.

The answer of history might also have been an affirmative, except for the bold move of the Czar, who assured France that he would be at her side in the event of war. The relief in France when the danger was over appears to have been equal to the jubilation of the Parisian rabble on the declaration of war several years before.

A main reason for the crisis, apart from the war-bred cat-versus-dog attitude, was stated by the Cologne *Gazette* when on April 5 it explained that the growth of the French army indicated a plan for a war of revenge on Germany. On April 30, 1874, Bismarck had sounded the same note when he informed the Belgian ambassador that he "did not see how Germany could avoid war next year, unless the Great Powers combined to persuade France to reduce her armaments to a reasonable peace establishment." [14] Yet what, after all, did Bismarck expect of France? Could he believe that, having once been torn by German rapacity, she would be content to remain a tempting prey? When he imposed his bitterly severe terms, which included not only a huge indemnity but the surrender of Alsace-Lorraine and the pivotal fortress of Metz, did he not foresee that he would arouse twin enemies against himself in the shape of an abiding resentment and a self-protective frenzy that would express itself in arms and armaments? But perhaps for once the great statesman, with more than a little of that arrogance which overrides prudence, had blinded himself to the facts of history. One must in all charity believe so, for the resistance he evoked in France was not only to be expected, but brewed a situation that in the long run proved no more healthy for Germany than for her adversary, and led straight toward the disaster that was to overwhelm both nations and much of Europe in the twentieth century.

But doubtless nothing of this was foreseen, west of the Rhine any more than east of it, when for the decade that followed the war France labored and sacrificed in order to strengthen her fortifications and build up her armed forces. Universal service for five years, with but few exemptions and with a succeeding fifteen years in the reserves, was now the rule in France—a fact which may well have caused a fluttering in Prussian breasts. And when it is remembered that the peace strength of the French army in 1875 was 461,000 men—greater than that of Prussia—it will be seen why rumors and alarms began to spread in Berlin, and why there was danger of a "preventive war" before France became stronger yet.

Meanwhile, as a result of Bismarck's series of conflicts and the nationalizing processes that preceded and accompanied them, armies throughout Europe had been growing. In the early sixties, Prussia had increased her annual levy from forty thousand to sixty-three thousand men, and had raised the term of service from two to three years—measures of "national protection" without which Bismarck would have been much less prepared for his aggressions. And other countries, if not following the example immediately, did not wait long after the Franco-Prussian War before taking the hint: Russia in 1874 prescribed first six years and later five years of compulsory service; and Italy in 1875 ordained three to five years for all able-bodied young men (though she was actually too poor to train a large percentage of the possible recruits). Even Britain, while not resorting to conscription, took measures to improve and enlarge her army. And meantime the German states associated with Prussia were forced into adopting the Prussian army system, which even Austria copied in 1868. And thus the example and the fear of war, the power of imitativeness, and the growing pressure of nationalism combined to create a situation in which, if wars did occur, they were certain to be large-scale; while even if they did not take place, they would be constantly in the background of the world's thought, a lurking terror, a menace that would drain peacetime energies as never before in modern history.

In the eighties there occurred another crisis in European affairs. While reminiscent in most ways of the affair of the mid-seventies, it is of interest as showing the trend of events, and the fact that the preparations against war had made the threat of war ever-present. In 1886 the fire-eating General Boulanger became French Minister of War; and heading a powerful party, moved to raise the peacetime strength of the army to more than half a million men. This step, naturally, was not well received in Germany; Bismarck instantly introduced a bill to increase the army by over forty thousand; and though the Diet at first resisted him, he maneuvered adroitly for a bargain with the Pope that would reverse the anti-army attitude of the Clericals. At the same time, he played upon the popular emotions to bring him success in the elections of February, 1887.

Now began a bad time for Germany—one of those periodical panics into which nations which lack the steadying influence of a sound and well-informed public opinion are ever prone to fall. The nation's infinite capacity for taking alarm was illustrated as seldom before, and the Government spared no effort to turn to advantage the scare which it had created. Thanks to such stampeding of volatile emotions, more creditable to the heart than the head, a large section of the nation seriously believed that the fatherland was really in danger, and the belief called forth a wave of patriotic enthusiasm. . . .[15]

And who was to question Bismarck's word when he implied that war, if not just around the corner, at least lurked in the neighborhood? "As regards the question of time," he wrote, "war *may* break out in the coming summer, although the probability is greater that it will be postponed for a year or more."[16]

When introducing the army bill into the Reichstag, Bismarck summoned Field-Marshal von Moltke, who expressed the belief that if the government did not get what it asked war would certainly follow. The Chancellor himself, no less a peace advocate, spoke of the danger to European harmony if he did not have his way; swore that Germany would never attack France; but stated that, "whether in ten days or in ten years," aggression was to be expected from the French. "If Napoleon III undertook against us a great and difficult war which cost him his throne—in no way constrained from without, but simply because he believed it would strengthen his government within—why should not General Boulanger, for example, attempt the same thing if he came into power?"[17]

The newspapers, as in 1875, did their best to terrorize the people. They reported incident after incident—such as the purchase of horses or lumber which might have military value—and used these to suggest French bellicose intentions. The Berlin *Post*, which had helped to aggravate the crisis of 1875, printed an article commenting on the increases in French armaments, and stating that General

Boulanger no longer had the power to lead the French people back to peaceful ways even if he desired. Very soon afterward, the German army created further anxiety by assembling seventy-two thousand reservists in Alsace-Lorraine; while diplomatic attacks were leveled against General Boulanger, who for the time was the idol of the French people. Excitement on both sides now ran high; a single misstroke, and war would have descended upon Europe. Out of nothing more substantial than rivalry in armaments and fear and suspicion and hatred, a strain had arisen that might have led to immediate conflict. The fact that the danger receded is once more to be attributed largely to the position of the Czar, who again posed an indefinite threat to Germany, and intimated that he would side with France. But whether or not Bismarck got war—and no one can be certain whether this was what he sought —he did force the army bill across all the hurdles of opposition.

And thereby what did he accomplish? Did he make Germany or Europe any safer? Perhaps he honestly believed he had brought security to the empire which it had been his life's labor to create; but, if so, he had not sufficiently taken to heart his own wise admonition that "One cannot see the cards of Providence far enough ahead to anticipate historical developments according to one's own calculation." What he actually did was to insure the continuance of the armed hostility between Germany and France; to perpetuate the race in armaments, with all the attendant furies of fear and jealousy and bitterness; to intensify and encourage the growth of a narrow and exclusive nationalism throughout Europe and the world, and to lay the groundwork for those wars that were to undermine the very Germanic structure he had been at such pains to erect.

Furthermore, in his reinforcement of the Prussian army system, which under Moltke and Roon had nurtured a military regime of inhuman efficiency, he served to perpetuate the worst of the evils introduced by Frederick the Great. Acting hand in hand with the army commanders, he played upon the docility of the people to reinforce the principle of authority; he forged new links in that psychological training which has made the Germans submissive beyond most other modern peoples, and malleable to the designs of any strong leader. Bismarck's military successes, like Frederick's, insured the continuance of the psychological attitude he had encouraged, for the minds of men are so made that they will grant anything to a conquering leader, even the chains to clamp them down. And so the German respect for a uniform, the German attitude of subservience before a uniform, was strengthened by the military victories that Bismarck had made possible; and the way became easier for the regimentation of the twentieth century. At the same time, he transmitted that method of might over right and that doctrine of "blood and iron" which, while perhaps never wholly absent from the world, was never more conspicuous than in the half century following Bismarck's death.

Considered, therefore, from the long-range point of view, Bismarck was not the success he has been reputed to be; he was one of history's tragic failures. He was a failure because, in his resort to ruthlessness, he made it difficult for the German Empire to exist without ruthlessness; because he had predicated Germany's strength upon a great military establishment, which was certain to fall when it came into conflict with a more powerful establishment; and because he saw the psychological basis of German unity in an assertive national pride, a jingoistic patriotism, a swagger and an arrogance of clannish superiority, an antagonism reflected in counter-antagonisms among Germany's neighbors. That the crises of 1875 and 1887 did not result in war was apparently largely fortuitous; any clear-sighted observer could see the direction in which the nations were moving. And while the actual descent into the maelstrom did not occur until twenty-seven years after the affair of General Boulanger, the seeds planted by Bismarck had been germinating during all the interval, and the time and the immediate excuse were mere incidents compared with the fact that Bismarckianism and the reactions to Bismarckianism had produced a psychological conditioning in Germany, France, and the world, a state of chronic inflammation over Alsace-Lorraine, an alliance of great Powers opposed to Germany, and a tension whose physical manifestations were the armies, the navies, and the great armaments which the Powers were to hurl at one another's throats.

VI

The Epoch of the World Wars

Chapter 27

The Origins of the World Wars

It is hardly possible to trace the world wars to any single set of circumstances or events. There is a sense in which the ancestry of the great conflicts goes back to the first man-killing foray ever organized by hide-draped savages; and the line of descent could plausibly be followed through the wars of the Egyptians and the Assyrians, of Alexander and Caesar, and of all the captains and marauders who cast a pall of crimson and black over much of the ancient and medieval world. More directly and pertinently, one could point to the modern fighting tradition as developed in the Thirty Years' War, the Seven Years' War, and the series of world struggles dominated by France and England; one could flick a finger toward Gustavus Adolphus, Marlborough, Louis XIV, Charles XII, and many another famous or infamous war-leader. But when one comes to the French Revolution, as we have seen, one is almost on home territory; in this great upheaval, and in the Napoleonic furor that followed, we can see the direct even if un-conscious preparations for twentieth-century eruptions; we can observe the specific causation in the development of nationalistic and military institutions and of a military tradition that led from disturbance to disturbance. And finally, accentuating the tenden-cies of preceding centuries, stimulating a nervous and troublesome nationalism and emphasizing the cleavages that led toward strife, we can take note of the portentous figure of Bismarck, and of the spirit of pride and fear, resentment and hostility that he incited among some of the most important states of Europe.

Here, in briefest outline, one may trace the origins of the world wars. Nevertheless, this does not indicate the whole story, or even an approach to the whole story. All the preliminaries, up to and including the aggressions of Bismarck, might have occurred with-out precipitating a world war. To make such an event possible, various other conditions had to be fulfilled. And it is to these other conditions, rather than to the remoter causes, that we ordinarily refer when we speak of the origins of the world wars.

II

We have seen that the ideas of the philosophers, from Locke's views regarding the "rights of man" to the Hegelian concept of the all-important State, have had a part in molding the actions of the war-makers and war-provokers. But it is debatable whether all the abstract philosophers together have had as much effect as the doctrinaires of science who occupied so conspicuous a place on the nineteenth-century rostrum. Literally, science had revealed a new, enormously enlarged universe, one whose expanded realities might have broadened man's outlook, strengthened his faith, and stimulated his spirit. Actually, however, it did nothing of the sort. Instead of being inspired, he felt dwarfed by the infinities unbared by astronomy, the prodigious vistas of time unrolled by paleontology; and instead of seeing in the evolutionary theories of Darwin the signs of a master force coordinating the universe, he read nothing but the evidences of chance development in a world of blind mechanism.

More than that, he saw in the "survival of the fittest" a proof that nature was constantly at war, and that the law of talon and fang was the law of life. This interpretation of natural fact—an interpretation against which it is possible to level a heavy barrage of arguments—was in accordance with the mechanistic conception of life processes, which was likewise a contribution of science, or rather of men who thought they saw in science a key to the ultimate. One result was, inevitably, a decreasing respect for individuality (that is to say, the individuality of others), which could hardly matter in a universe that was no more than a gigantic soulless mechanism; and the corresponding result was that the old religious brakes to anti-social conduct were snatched away, and men were more willing than they might otherwise have been to follow the supposed way of nature, and to rend, slash, and tear in order to prove that they were the fittest.

This is to say that the new science-fostered creed tended to unshackle the fighting arm, and to discard century-old safeguards against the ruthless use of that arm. Just how large a part this played in the explosive nineteenth- and twentieth-century warfare and in the discarding of humane considerations in favor of "total annihilation," is of course anyone's guess; but that it did have a part, and a considerable one, is hardly open to doubt. The war-makers of the school of Bismarck, no less than those of the cult of Hitler and Mussolini, acted as if in the implicit belief that human life is of no value, that human feelings and human suffering do not matter—a belief upheld by a shallow reading of science. It is true that war-makers of all ages, from Sennacherib to Napoleon, have had more or less of the same attitude; but the tremendous impetus given to this point of view, in the latter half of the nineteenth and the first half of the twentieth century, would be hard to explain except for the materialism of science and the contemporaneous decline of religion. It would be too much to suggest that the world wars would not have occurred had science not taken its particular mechanistic turn of thought. But it is certain that they would not have shown precisely the features that we know; it is probable that some well-known practices, such as the bombing and machine-gunning and flame-murder of civilians, the sinking of defenseless merchantmen, and the massacre of innocent hostages, would have been somewhat less common; and it is conceivable that they would not have occurred at all. For these were concerned with humane feeling or its lack quite as much as with war-time necessity; and humane feeling is largely a matter of how one has been trained, what examples one has observed, and what one has been taught to believe.

To a large extent, also, the very question of whether war is to occur is (at least, on the part of the aggressor) a matter of humane feeling. Had Bismarck, for example, had such a feeling firmly developed, he might very well have refrained from his successive wars with Denmark, Austria, and France; and the subsequent history of the world would therefore have been very different. But had Bismarck refrained, he would have been ruled by a set of beliefs not at all like those of the Bismarck of history.

III

A direct stimulus to twentieth-century warfare was the imperialism of the three decades beginning with the late eighteen-seventies. Imperialism, of course, was nothing new; the far-flung hand of European empire-makers had previously reached over wide areas from the Americas to India. But never before had so great a colonial eruption simultaneously struck so many nations. Every great European power except Austria-Hungary succumbed to the fever; and during the three decades, "greater progress was made toward subjecting the world to European domination than had been made during three centuries previous." [1]

Whence arose this gigantic new imperialism? Its sources have been persuasively analyzed by Carlton Hayes:

The fact remains . . . that the founding of the new colonial empires and the fortifying of the old ones antedated the establishment of neo-mercantilism, and that the economic arguments adduced in support of neo-mercantilism seem to have been a rationalization *ex post facto*. . . .

Basically the new imperialism was a nationalistic phenomenon. It followed hard upon the national wars which created an all-powerful Germany and a united Italy, which carried Russia within sight of Constantinople, and which left England fearful and France eclipsed. It expressed a resulting psychological reaction, an ardent desire to maintain or recover national prestige. [2]

France, shorn and humiliated as a result of her war with Prussia, desired to re-establish herself in her own eyes and the world's. And Bismarck, curiously enough, encouraged her colonial ambitions in Africa and China—not, we may be sure, out of new-won love of France, but because, as his private memoranda attest, he desired to take her eyes off Europe, and particularly off the burning issue of Alsace-Lorraine. Meantime German imperialism, though slow and tepid at its start, was stimulated by propagandists such as the one-time explorer Hubbe-Schleiden, who insisted that the strength of a nation was manifested by its imperialistic efforts; and the historian Treitschke, whose lectures at the University of Berlin similarly bore the moral that colonial power was the test of national virility.

Unfortunately, also, British resistance to German imperialism stimulated the latter like the proverbial shot in the arm. By arousing the well-known perversities of human nature, it made imperialists of Germans previously indifferent or hostile; even Bismarck, who had been no more than lukewarm, was encouraged to throw himself combatively into the scramble for empire. The idea became current that England, herself the possessor of boundless expanses, had not treated Germany fairly in opposing her African claims; Bismarck but expressed a common sentiment when he declared that England would have done well to have given more consideration to the modest German expansionist plans. Actually, matters of pride and prestige were involved rather than economic advantage or national need; to have colonies had become a sort of international "keeping up with the Joneses." But this international social climb, like the sort that occupies well-to-do matrons, was not altogether conducive to good will.

Unquestionably the colonial rivalries of those days dislocated and disharmonized the relations between Germany and Great Britain for a long time. It is possible, and even probable, that they contained the germ of all later mistrust and misunderstanding. Germany never forgot that she obtained hardly any of her early protectorates without having first to overcome resistance from the British Government, and that in nearly every case the opposition was based, not upon any claim of prior occupation but upon the tacit assumption that territories adjacent to British possessions . . . could not properly be claimed by any other country.[3]

It may not be true that the imperial rivalries, and the jealousies and hatred they entailed, were among the direct causes of the outbreak of 1914. But they were certainly among the indirect causes, for they emphasized hostile attitudes, created misunderstandings, set up great jealously guarded vested interests, and encouraged the growth of armies and navies. The proof that they produced a warlike state of mind is to be seen in the fact that they actually did evoke war in China in the nineteenth century, and in China, Manchuria, the Philippines, Malaya, etc., in the twentieth. Also, on a number of occasions before 1914, Europe was on the verge of war over colonial matters.

For example, in the summer of 1898, a French explorer reached the village of Fashoda on the upper Nile, brought the French into conflict with hard-won British interests, and for a while threatened to embroil the two countries. Far-sighted French statesmanship, which ordered a withdrawal in the face of public opinion after the fleets had been mobilized, was all that prevented this border incident from expanding into a conflagration. Seven years later the Germans, in the apparent effort to drive a rift into the Anglo-French *entente*, sent the Kaiser on a mission to the Sultan in Tangier, and seemed to threaten the French in Morocco—but were frustrated in their dangerous maneuvers because the British gave the French firm assurances of support. And Morocco was again prominent in 1911, when the Agadir crisis threatened war; Germany was roused to the extent of sending the warship *Panther*, and Lloyd George in a speech of July 21 warned that the peace of Europe, while precious, could not be preserved "by allowing England to be treated, where her interests are vitally affected, as if she were of no account in the Cabinet of nations."

Thus, in incident after incident, imperialism continued to sharpen the knife that was to be plunged into the heart of the world.

IV

If a country is to maintain overseas colonies, thousands of miles from the homeland, it must be able to keep the lines of communication open and to protect the dependencies against attack. Hence the possession of an empire implies the maintenance of an army and navy strong enough to safeguard that empire. Hence, also, any increase in the armed forces of potential enemies must be reflected in a rise in the domestic establishment. And hence, finally, imperialism becomes a prime source of the competition in armaments, at which we have already had a glimpse in connection with Germany and France.

Though the world has not taken the lesson to heart, it has often been pointed out that an increase in armaments does not necessarily bring security. It does not even create the sense of security, at least for any considerable period. It produces unrest and suspicion abroad, inspires increases in armaments among rival nations, provokes further armament expansion at home to counter the foreign measures, imposes a dead weight of taxation that tends to check production in non-military lines, and eventually becomes so burdensome that relief is sought in the very war the defenses were aimed to prevent. The armaments competition of modern nations has something of the quality of a treadmill race. Two or more contestants, each on his separate treadmill, attempt to move as rapidly as possible in the effort to outdistance their adversaries. The faster the one goes, the faster the others go; and the result is that all move so swiftly as to resemble gray blurs, while getting no further than their starting point. Eventually, in exasperation and fear of being overtaken and in dread of early exhaustion, they leave their treadmills and fall upon one another.

Sir Edward Grey has expressed the situation in a few irrefutable lines:

More than one thing may be said about the causes of war, but the statement that comprises most truth is that militarism and the armaments inseparable from it made war inevitable. Armaments were intended to produce a sense of security in each nation—that was the justification put forward in defense of them. What they really did was to produce fear in everybody. Fear causes suspicion and hatred; it is hardly too much to say that, between nations, it stimulates all that is bad, and depresses all that is good.[4]

Consider, for example, the rivalry in naval armaments, in some respects the most important single element in the armaments race prior to 1914. The navy was, obviously, the mainstay of England's security; it was the protector of her lifeline not only to essential raw materials, but to the food without which she could not exist; it was likewise her strongest guaranty against invasion in the event of war. Under the circumstances, she was bound to look warily upon any attempt of a Continental power to come within measurable distance of her naval strength. This must have been known to Germany; nothing could have been more self-evident. Nevertheless, the Kaiser pursued a course certain to arouse fear, antagonism, and counter-measures in Great Britain. He did this partly in the belief that a strong navy would make Germany heeded and honored in the world, and would be a powerful argument toward the achievement of her diplomatic ends. Also, in common with Admiral von Tirpitz, he is said to have believed that, once the German navy had passed the period of relative weakness when England might seek to destroy it, it would not only be secure in its own strength, but would be recognized and respected by the British. From this it followed that the faster Germany built ships, the sooner she would reach her coveted position of assured power. Her leaders seem to have overlooked, or at least to have minimized the importance of the interpretation that England would place upon such conduct, and of the counter-measures England was certain to take. Apparently they did not realize that England would be determined at all costs to maintain her leadership at sea; that British hostility and rivalry would demand eight new dreadnoughts a year to Germany's four; that the full eight would actually be authorized, four being made dependent on German building activities; and that mounting British antagonism would be visible also in opposition to German projects in other directions: for example, the cherished Berlin to Bagdad railway.

But Germany did not take warning. In pursuance of her reckless policy, she rejected the idea of naval limitations at the Second Hague Conference, although England had proposed to reduce her building program by one vessel and to consider further decreases if other countries would reciprocate. Not that England's own hands were spotless; she stood out against the world in her insistence on the right of naval seizure, which she regarded as her most effective maritime weapon. But just as Germany had disregarded or underestimated the effect on British opinion of her insistence on dreadnoughts and more dreadnoughts, so England seems not to have foreseen the propaganda value to the Germans of their assertion to their own people that they must build up their navy to protect their ships from British seizure.

One cannot help agreeing with an opinion that has been expressed as to England and Germany—an opinion seemingly not shared by the policy-makers:

Instead of these two friendly powers cooperating as was advocated by the most convinced, energetic and influential promoters of British imperialism, Joseph Chamberlain and Mr. Cecil Rhodes, they chose opposite paths. The nations with the greatest army and the greatest navy, had they worked together, could have maintained their own interests and kept Europe in order, for the fleet and the army could not fight each other. A proper understanding between the two Governments would have guaranteed the peace of the world; but, instead of alliance, they chose rivalry.[5]

It is difficult to know how much truth if any there is in the charge of Theodor Wolff, the editor of the *Berliner Tageblatt* from 1906 to 1933, that Kaiser Wilhelm's naval policy was dictated in part by a desire to "earn for himself a fame alongside which even Bismarck's constellation would pale." [6] But in any case, there can be no question of the extent to which the naval policy was a matter of a state of mind, rather than of any external need. This was revealed by the Kaiser himself, when he wrote, in regard to a report made by Count Metternich on July 16, 1908:

Count Metternich must be informed that good relations with England at the price of the building of the German navy are *not* de-

sired by me. If England intends graciously to extend us her hand
only with the intimation that we must limit our fleet, this is a
groundless impertinence, which involves a heavy insult to the German people and their Kaiser. . . . The German fleet is not built
against anyone, and also not *against* England! But according to
our need. That is stated quite clearly in the Navy Law, and for
11 years has remained unchanged! This law will be carried out to
the last iota; whether it suits the British or not, is no matter! If
they want war, they can begin it; we do not fear it! [7]

This pride, arrogance, and irascibility, this chip-on-the-shoulder
attitude, could hardly be expected to oil the way to sweet reasonableness, amiability, and peace. But the Kaiser expressed his position
even more crisply when, after Sir Charles Hardinge had told him
that he must either stop his naval building or build more slowly,
he retorted, "Then we shall fight, for it is a question of national
honor and dignity." [8]

National honor and dignity! Once more an outcropping of the
old heroic ideal! Once more the deeds of the nations are regulated
like an "affair of honor" between individuals, according to artificial rules of pride and propriety. Once more the *amour propre*
of nations is like that of duelists who challenge one another to
fight and die—what matters the outpouring of blood so long as
the code is punctiliously followed, so long as insults are avenged
and pride upheld? There is of course this difference, that duelists
risk their own flesh and bone, whereas highly placed militarists
offer of the flesh and bone of their countrymen. But such little
distinctions mean nothing to the lofty-minded devotees of "national
honor and dignity."

And so the Kaiser, though doubtless not desiring war, went his
unyielding way with the strut most likely to bring war nearer. And
so England, instead of working hand in glove with Germany to
preserve peace, was thrown into the arms of France and Russia;
an Anglo-Russian *entente* on Eastern affairs followed the Anglo-
French understanding. And thus the line-up for 1914 continued
to be formed; while Germany, far from realizing that the align-
ment against her was largely bred by her ruler's belligerence and
by the fear she had herself inspired, was goaded to a counter-fear—
a dread of encirclement owing to the machinations of "perfidious
Albion." And the result was that the whole continent was imperiled. It is not without significance that Colonel House, on May

16, 1914, wrote to President Wilson, after a tour of the European capitals:

The situation is extraordinary. It is militarism run stark mad. Unless some one acting for you can bring about a different understanding, there is some day to be an awful cataclysm.[9]

V

It is known that the First World War began less as a conflict of individual nations than as the life-or-death contest of two great associations of nations: on the one hand, the Triple Entente, composed of France, England, and Russia; on the other hand, the Triple Alliance, whose active members included Germany and Austria-Hungary. This leaguing together of nations had, as we have observed, been encouraged by the intractable naval stand of the Kaiser and Tirpitz; but it represented a process more or less in effect ever since 1870. Due to the feeling of insecurity that obsessed even the greatest nations following the trouncing of France by Prussia, the various countries began to look about them for allies who would aid them in case of need; and thus encouragement was given to the vicious system of secret alliances. This system—but perhaps "system" is not the word to designate a labyrinth of underground agreements—was based on the belief that it was permissible for the representatives of the nations to bind millions of men *on their honor* to act in accordance with agreements carefully kept from their knowledge. For example, before the war of 1914 Sir Edward Grey had secret military and naval understandings with France and Russia—arrangements deliberately concealed from the House of Commons, the elected representatives of the people.

In the first of his celebrated Fourteen Points, President Wilson recognized the iniquity of secret diplomacy. Probably he would have agreed with Professor Fay's diagnosis:

The greatest single underlying cause of the War was the system of secret alliances which developed after the Franco-Prussian War. It gradually divided Europe into two hostile groups of Powers who were increasingly suspicious of one another and who steadily built up greater and greater armies and navies. Though this system of alliances in one sense tended to preserve peace, inasmuch as the members within one group often held their friends or allies in restraint for fear of becoming involved in war themselves, the system also made it inevitable that if war did come, it would involve all the Great Powers of Europe. The members of each group felt bound to support each other, even in matters where they had no direct interest, because failure to give support would have weakened the solidarity of the group.[10]

Not only is the question of national honor here involved; we encounter the old belief in the "balance of power," which holds that if the power of the Continent is divided between two great approximately even factions, neither side will be able to break the peace. It is safe to say that, but for this idea, there would have been no secret alliances dividing Europe into two great hostile parties, and accordingly no First World War. The situation has been pointedly analyzed by G. Lowes Dickinson:

As a distinguished historian has wittily put it, the word "balance" has two meanings. It means, on the one hand, an equality, as of two sides when an account is balanced, and on the other hand an inequality, as when one has a "balance" to one's credit at the bank. The balance of power theory professes the former, but pursues the latter. It is thus, in fact, a perpetual effort to get the better of the balance; and as this effort is prosecuted on both sides, the ultimate issue is war. All history shows this, for every balance has ended in war.[11]

Had the defensive alliances remained purely defensive, they might have served a purpose. But groupings of nations, though intended solely for defense, seem to follow the same laws as so-called defensive weapons. Just as a gun may be used by an invading force though manufactured only for repelling invasion, so an alliance may become aggressive even if planned only as a safety measure. We see this in the case of both the great alliances: for example, Germany had no direct interest in backing the ultimatum which Austria hurled at Serbia following the murder of the Archduke, but she felt obliged to do so if she did not wish the alliance to split apart. And as soon as the alliances went into full-scale action, offensive and defensive movements were mingled in such a shambles that it is sometimes hard to say where the one began and the other ended. But this in a way was inevitable, if only because of the orthodox military theory that the best defense is an offense: thanks to this belief, the planning of the General Staffs is based on the idea of hitting the enemy whenever possible.

Another fact, too frequently overlooked, is that international alliances can be built only upon compromise—which implies not merely material concessions, but sacrifices of principle. It is difficult, as we all know, to obtain agreement on matters of principle among individuals; but it is a thousand times more difficult among nations, which are swayed by a multitude of interests and aims, conflicting aspirations and traditions, and the influence of groups of citizens and politicians pulling this way and that. This means that, in order to get a successful working arrangement among the nations, the shrewd diplomat must make concessions here, there, and everywhere, adapting himself to the will and mood of his allies without too scrupulous a regard for ethical minutiae. Thus, if France did not favor Russia's designs in the Balkans or if Germany did not approve of Austria's machinations against Serbia, France and Germany none the less nodded their acquiescence rather than risk dissolution of the alliance upon which each depended for its safety. It is debatable whether all would not have been safer if standing by themselves. That too would have been hazardous, but in that case a thousand warlike provocations need not have been blinked at while the Powers stood silently by, and the whole eruptive world situation need not have developed like the explosion of a bunch of firecrackers touched off by a spark.

VI

The pre-war secrecy did not end with secret alliances, pernicious as these were. The plans of the General Staff were likewise secret—necessarily so, one may say, though incidentally they gave the military a war-making power quite independent of the civil authorities. When it was possible for British Foreign Secretary Sir Edward Grey to be ignorant, as he was from 1906 to 1911, of the Franco-English military plans for mutual action in northern France; and when it was likewise possible for German Chancellor Bethmann-Hollweg to be only vaguely aware of the significance of the scheme to strike at France through Belgium, then we have a situation in which military authorities may commit the nations to warlike actions before the political leaders have had a chance to decide, and may bear down with a powerful compulsion upon the people to accept their pre-arrangements in the name of national urgency, national honor and patriotism. It may even happen that the army commanders do not desire war; they may merely act in accordance with what their training has taught them to regard as military necessity, regardless of political consequences; and like the German strategists who recommended the violation of Belgian neutrality, they may never recognize that military wisdom may be political unwisdom.

Take the matter of general mobilization. A moment may arrive when war seems likely: if it does occur, the nation that has mobilized first will be in a much superior position—and therefore what good army officer would hesitate to move for mobilization? Yet it is known that mobilization is virtually irreversible; it is regarded as tantamount to a declaration of war, and will incite the enemy's immediate counter-mobilization; furthermore, the mobilizations and counter-mobilizations will substitute passion for deliberation and terror for calm, and will forestall any possible arrangements at the conference table.

Something of this sort actually did happen in 1914. On July 29 the Czar had forced his Chief of Staff to cancel instructions for general mobilization; but acting under military pressure, and in great uncertainty of mind owing to his genuine desire for peace, he reversed himself, so that mobilization was ordered for July 31. Once he had uttered the fateful word, the future was out of his hands; military men everywhere interpreted the mobilization as a command to fight—and events in other nations began moving like the whirlwind. On July 31, Austria likewise mobilized, and on August 1 France and Germany followed. The spark which might have been extinguished by deft firemen had become a conflagration, and was raging out of control.

<h2 style="text-align:center">VII</h2>

We have here but one phase of the problem of militarism—a problem inseparable from the existence of a group of men, the professional officers' corps, who have been drilled since youth to see things not as ordinary citizens, but from the point of view of armed action and armed strength. Such a training may produce leaders with acute vision in the sphere of their experience; but since that sphere is bounded by shells and guns, they will strive to solve international problems by means of shells and guns, which will seem the necessary and desirable implements; they will be impatient of what they will judge to be the weak and circumambient ways of civilians. We in the United States have recently had one notorious case in which an outstanding general brought about his own downfall because, in defiance of his commander-in-chief, he had advocated measures that the latter thought likely to involve us in universal conflict. This is but one example, but it indicates what the military outlook will do even to a man of high aims and unquestioned integrity. And the situation becomes still more serious when, as in Japan at the time of the Manchurian crisis, military elements have seized control, and, acting without regard to civilian authorities, manifest a strong impulse to practice their trade.

But even when there is no conflict of authority; even when the generals genuinely wish to avoid battle, the very philosophy of the officers may serve to bring war nearer, particularly when that philosophy includes the assumption of war's inevitability (a doctrine which, as we have seen, has played its part in bringing on hostilities as far back as the Peloponnesian War). Though this creed has not been confined to the military; though thousands have flattered their ignorance by reasoning, "There always has been war, therefore there always will be," nevertheless this idea has been most conspicuous in military circles, or circles strongly affected by the military. And, strangely, the belief that war is inevitable tends to make it really inevitable, by weakening or forestalling the efforts that might have avoided it—just as the conviction that a fire could not be stopped might so slacken the hands of the fire-fighters as to make it unconquerable.

One or two examples will suggest the effect that the belief in inevitability had in precipitating the First World War. During the crucial last days of July, 1914, when the Czar was debating the question of general mobilization, he was persuaded in part by the arguments of Foreign Minister Sazonov, who pleaded that war was inevitable in any case—therefore the Czar need have no self-reproaches if he ordered mobilization. And not less significant had been the action of Poincaré of France and his circle: for two years, in the belief that war was certain to come, he had been cooperating with the Russian Ambassador Izvolsky in the effort to strengthen the Entente; in 1913, moved by the belief in inevitability, he had pushed through an increase in the term of compulsory service from two years to three; in the same year, he had brought pressure upon

Russia to build strategic railroads to the frontier and to enlarge her army: and now, in the all-important last days of July, 1914, when Russia might still have been deterred from mobilizing, he once more relied upon the doctrine of inevitability, so losing almost the last opportunity to make the war less than inevitable.

Thus, both in the preparations for war and in the mobilization, the doctrine of inevitability was to play its part, intruding in the way of clear council and wise decision just when these were most needed. And so the Powers, none of which wanted war, all took precisely the measures best calculated to precipitate war.

An offshoot of the doctrine of inevitability is the idea of preventive war. When a leader takes it for granted that a conflict is certain to come, his efforts will be concentrated not on avoiding it but on choosing the most favorable time and battlefield—in other words, in preventing the enemy from gaining an advantage, or in striking him down while he is still relatively weak. Thus the phrase "preventive war" is really a contradiction in terms; nothing is prevented except the first stroke by the other side. But whether war had really been inevitable or not, it becomes so as soon as a "preventive" blow is dealt. We have seen the preventive creed as a recent threat to peace; and it was not absent before 1914, though authorities differ as to the precise part it had in precipitating the crisis. At least in one crucial respect, however, it did have an influence. It was among the determining factors in Austria-Hungary's attitude toward Serbia, for it was urged—and insistently urged—that war with Serbia would eventually come, and that the sooner the better, since the easier it would be to crush the foe. Except for this idea, Austria might not have framed her arrogant ultimatum, might not have refused to treat with Serbia after the latter had accepted seven of her ten demands, and might not have declared war with precipitate haste. And in that case diplomacy might have been able to block the way to catastrophe.

VIII

In all this we have military attitudes and doctrines as they act from above. But an important factor behind the war of 1914, as behind other modern struggles, was the militarization that had increasingly eaten into the masses. This was a subtle thing, far more noticeable in some lands than in others; and its roots are to be traced to the wars of the preceding century, to the nationalism of a bristling hundred years, to the acclaim of military conquest and domination in popular and patriotic literature, and not least to the fact that every able-bodied man in the leading Continental countries had for generations been subject to military discipline.

Take the case of Germany, in which militarization had progressed as far as elsewhere if not further (though Germany was by no means a solitary offender). The routine of the barracks and of drill, which enforces conformity of stride and tolerates no individual expression, had been a little like a steam-roller over the minds of the people, compelling habits of compliance, and permitting no syllable of dissent. Meanwhile the usual patriotic bathos, praising the accomplishments of the Fatherland and exalting the heroic deeds of '64, '66, and '70, had been blared into the ears of the people, so that each man threw out his chest and felt personally glorified with the glorification of his country; each man wished to emulate the noble deeds of his sires. And each man, if he were of the usual stripe, felt jealous of the imperialistic plans of England and France, which belittled his own loved country; each man shuddered at the peril of "encirclement," which was dinned from official throats; each man trembled for the safety of the Fatherland, and was ready (while goosestepping with thousands of his kind) to give of his blood for the greatest nation that had ever dignified the earth, and the most distinguished race that ever breathed the air.

As an indication of the militarization of the people (and again Germany is merely the example chosen, for there were parallel developments elsewhere), consider the organizations with martial affiliations. A few out of the many existing before 1914 were the Wehrverein, or Military League; the Flottenverein, or Navy League; the Kolonialgesellschaft, or Colonial League, which favored imperial expansion; the Alldeutscher Verband, or Pan-German League, which circulated the view, more recently associated with Nazi ideology, that the superiority of the Herrenvolk entitled them to rule the world; and the Association for Combating Social Democracy, which was aimed against the international spirit. When one adds these and other groups together; when one remembers that the Flottenverein is said to have included a million members, and that the Wehrverein, only a little more than a year after its founding in January, 1912, claimed 255 well-established local groups; and when one observes that most of these organizations offered foci for propaganda, one will begin to realize by how many channels the military spirit might spread itself abroad.

The type of mental fodder distributed by those societies is indicated by the records of some of the speeches. For example, the *Frankfurter Zeitung* of May 20, 1913, reported a speaker before the Wehrverein as saying, among other things:

The peace movement is dangerous, and the peace declaration of the 140 Protestant priests is a grave matter. Such moods are also to be found in the teaching profession. This must be energetically combated. A people that has ceased to regard virility as its chief aim, is lost. There is no separate popular spirit and military spirit. The spirit of the people is the spirit of the army.[12]

In the same mood was a speech made at the Congress of the Pan-German Association, September 9, 1912:

... We must become land hungry and acquire new territories for settlement, otherwise we shall become a declining people, an atrophied race. We must, with true, sincere love, think of the future of our people and its children, even if we are reproached with a lust for war and fighting. If the Teutonic people were afraid of war, its day would be past.[13]

At the same time, many nationalistic papers such as the *German Youth Weekly*, which in one issue spoke of the eventual striking of "the great, glad hour of combat," were showering the country with propaganda. And authors of books chimed in: for instance, General von Bernhardi, whose *Germany and the Next War* (1912), sold by the hundreds of thousands. A revealing passage is the following:

In one way or another we must settle with France if we are to have elbow room for our world policy. That is the first and absolutely most important prerequisite of a sound German policy, and since French hostility cannot be eliminated once for all by peaceful means, it must be done by force of arms.[14]

A long list of other propagandists might be mentioned, including some with world reputations. Very much in the Nazi vein was Professor Edmund Weber, who in 1913 showed himself to be an apostle of Nordic superiority:

We demand elbow room for the Teutonic race, we demand space to increase our power, space to rule. We feel like a merry passage at arms. After all, we are not so senile as to regard peace and quiet as the most desirable thing in our planet. Oh, no, we look forward to a fight against an opponent who is worthy of us. To wrest world power from the British seems to be an aim worthy of noble men. . . .The time must come when the world will have to decide whether it wants to become English or German, whether it wants to obey a nation of 45 millions or a nation of 70 millions. There is no third way.[15]

Racialism, nationalism, the heroic ideal, competition for empire, the doctrine that virility must express itself in physical action, the doctrine that superiority may consist in numbers—one would have to go far to find a more ill-assorted hash of half-conceived ideas. Yet the fact that such provocative fantasies could be circulated— the fact that these very views, and others akin to them, were later trumpeted by Nazi spokesmen to millions of followers—is an indication that they had sympathetic hearers. It is also an indication that a war-making state of mind was being developed. And it suggests one reason why the commanders had such little difficulty in mustering their armies and keeping them fighting for four excruciating years.

An important part of all the above is the racialism by which the multitude may flatter its ego and cater to its desire for superiority. This creed requires not only the exaltation of one's own race (the word "race" being used in a strictly unscientific sense); it requires aspersions against the blood of all the rest of the world, and arouses greatest satisfaction when it selects some particular sacrificial victim. Thus, while European racialists looked down from their tower height upon such lower breeds as Negroes, Malayans, Polynesians, Arabs, and the like, they found especial joy in striking at a people in their very midst. Anti-Semites like Adolf Stocker and Adolf Wagner in Germany and like Edouard Droumont in France were active in the closing decades of the last century; a German anti-Semitic party counted 47,500 votes in 1890, and 285,000 in 1898; while the movement gained impetus in the twentieth century, and was considerably accentuated in 1913, when an army ex-captain, Mueller von Hausen, published the forged *Protocols of the Elders of Zion*, an infamous anti-Semitic libel that gained wide currency.

But what was the connection of all this with warfare? It was

definite enough, as Hitler was to demonstrate; it furnished a rallying call for the masses, which, always unthinking and always ame-
nable to prejudice, could be united beneath some such rousing cry
as "Stamp on the dirty Jew!" It offered a scapegoat around whose
head the leaders could hang their own sins and errors; it supplied
a relief gap for dangerous, rebellious, and even revolutionary emotions; it united the people with a sort of crusading, a religious spirit,
the Infidel being not the enemy outside the gate but the Jew at the
threshold; it provided a fighting mood, which after target practice
against the Hebrew at home, could the more easily be aimed against
the foreign foe.

IX

The campaigns against particular races and peoples may be taken
to indicate a failing in individual morality. But even more decisive
in matters of war and peace was the lack of political and international morality.

In view of the absence of good faith shown in subsequent international dealings, one may wonder whether the era prior to 1914
can be branded as conspicuously wanting in world morality. In
those halcyon pre-war days, certainly, agreements among nations
had greater prospects of being honored than in the era of totali-
tarianism. Nevertheless, the disease from which we suffer today—a
disease of which international bad faith is a major symptom—
was already well advanced. It could claim a long ancestry,
through the Machiavellianism of Frederick II, the treacherous opportunism of Napoleon, and the calculated aggressions and diplomatic switchbacks of Bismarck. Hence when Germany in 1914
horrified the world by the Belgian invasion that converted a treaty
into a "scrap of paper," the Kaiser was by no means a lone monster in an otherwise impeccable planet; he was but giving expression to the cult of ruthlessness and the unmorality that had been
drilled into the nations.

Why, indeed, should the captains and commanders be expected
to be honest and honorable when their representatives in the capitals of the world had been trained to be the opposite?

The classical definition of an ambassador, as a man who "lies
abroad for his country," unfortunately embodies more than a witti-
cism. Despite all their vaunted ideas of "honor," the nations would
regard a diplomat as gravely wanting in a sense of duty if he fol-

lowed the rules of decency recommended for private individuals. To spy, to burrow, to inveigle, to misrepresent, to conceal—these are but the commonplaces of his trade, though perhaps never described in such undiplomatic language. "The policies and ideas of statesmen and historians . . ." as G. Lowes Dickinson declares, "imply in them, as well as in the public which supports them, a morality curiously opposed to all those principles and maxims which are supposed to be valid between individual men. Fraud, indeed, is the natural ally of force, and men who in private life are scrupulously honest and honorable, may descend, in diplomacy, to conduct which they would be the first to reprobate in their personal relations. . . ." [16]

An example of deliberate fraud is the case, already mentioned, of Bismarck's tampering with the Ems telegram. One might also cite instances of the alteration of boundary lines on official maps, and of the making of promises contradicted by secret stipulations to other parties—an illustration, from more recent history, is to be found in the conflicting assurances given by the British to the Jews and Arabs (assurances in large part responsible for the subsequent warfare in Palestine). It should be obvious, however, that just as there can be no successful commercial relationships without some guaranty that agreements will be kept, so there can be no peace-making in a world where no nation can trust the honor or the written word of its neighbors, and where suspicion, hatred, and fear consequently find unlimited nourishment. If the nations before 1914 had been able to trust one another, much more might have been accomplished toward setting up international peace machinery at the Hague Conferences. If the United States Senate after the First World War had been less suspicious of foreign nations, our country would undoubtedly have entered the League of Nations, and so made peace far more likely. And if the West and Russia more recently had each seen reason to respect the integrity of the other side, we would have known little of the world tension that has shaken our generation.

x

We have already taken note of occasional inflammatory newspaper utterances, such as the German statements that spread fear and aggravated the crises of 1875 and 1887. And the daily press was likewise, in many ways, behind the crisis of 1914. While we must not hold the entire press responsible for the derelictions of some of its members, we must remember the nature of a newspaper: it is a private organization established for the sake of profit, an organization that can add to its profits by stirring up popular excitement. And for stirring up excitement, even murders in Hollywood or scandals in Newport are vastly inferior to war or the threat of war. If in creating war interest and spirit, the newspapers incidentally bring disaster nearer; if they happen, in the cause of circulation, to command that first-rate weapon of war, propaganda—that no doubt is unfortunate, but only a business manager of the clearest vision and the highest morality would recognize that the interests of circulation and the public interest are not always identical. There is reason to fear that too often the attitude of the press has been similar to that of Joseph Pulitzer before the American war with Spain. He "decided, as he afterwards confessed, 'that he had rather liked the idea of war—not a big one—but one that would arouse interest and give him a chance to gauge the reflex in his circulation figures.' " [17] And having done his part to stimulate a military emotion, he had a "chance to gauge the reflex in his circulation" to the tune of five million copies sold in a single week.

Of far greater world importance was the part played by the Austrian and Serbian press in the crucial weeks following the murder of the Austrian Archduke:

It would, perhaps, be too much to say that, had it not been for the Austro-Serbian newspaper feud, the War might have been averted. But it is true that the violence of the Serbian press was one of the determining factors which led Count Tisza to change his opinion and to accept war with Serbia, whereas at first he had been stubbornly opposed to it; and without his consent Count Berchtold and the militarists could not have made war on Serbia.[18]

Perhaps the press of the two countries, like our own Pulitzer, was titillated by the idea of a war, but "not a big one." In any case, not only the editors but the correspondents helped to spread the war fever, sometimes with no more evil intent than the journalist's normal desire to turn in "good copy." Theodor Wolff cites an example: Jules Hedermann, of the Paris *Matin*, was passing through Berlin on his way back from Russia, "whence he had been sending to his paper stirring articles about the irresistible Russian army and the enthusiastic reception given to Poincaré. When he had described in a telegram from St. Petersburg the review of the 'wonderful troops,' those of his readers who were more or less susceptible had been inspired with faith in the 'Russian steamroller,' which was to flatten out all opposition on its road to Berlin." [19] But later he changed his tone:

Now he was pale and ill at ease. I said to him that he had now got what he wanted. He had not written in malice; he was simply one of those stylists who are concerned above all else to give their readers something to please them over their morning meal.[20]

Those of us who have followed later war dispatches will recognize that there have been other journalists of the Hedermann breed. But we may be unable to estimate just how much they have done to brew a false confidence if not a bellicose spirit by their stories, "not written in malice," yet capable of monstrous harm.

XI

Another form of private business that skulked in the shadows behind the First World War was the armament industry (which, in the broadest sense, includes not only the makers of guns and armor plate, but the purveyors of every variety of military equipment from ships to uniforms).

Here is an industry which can live only on war and the preparations for war. It is an industry controlled not by the State, but by private individuals, for the sake of private gain, in accordance with the self-seeking philosophy of modern trade, which makes accumulation all in all and cares nothing for humanity.

Consequently, we have a strange situation: the doctrines of the age make it honorable for some citizens to rake in rich returns from the maiming and destruction of their fellow beings. They are even rewarded in rough proportion to the numbers maimed and destroyed. Hence the "merchants of death," the Basil Zaharoffs, the sowers of dissension and sellers of the seeds of ruin, have left a sulphurous stench. And human nature being what it is, and human reason a reed that bends before every gust, even well-intentioned men may convince themselves that the multiplication and spread of the tools of war are as beneficial to the world as to their own financial rating.

We have not forgotten certain recent happenings, such as the shipment of American oil to Russia at a time of international threat and tension, and the business-as-usual export of rubber to the Chinese Communists by the British when their forces were exchanging shots with those same Communists in Korea. But these incidents, disquieting as they may seem, appear pallid by comparison with certain events of World War I. The facts have often been made public: that the armaments industry proceeded by means of international cartels and sold to the highest bidder, whereas all other industries were national in scope; that during the Dardanelles campaign, Englishmen were mowed down by guns delivered into Turkish hands by British firms; that, on the Galician front, guns repaired by the Austrians were used for killing Austrian soldiers; that at the Battle of Skagerak the British ships used gunsights delivered to the Dutch by German concerns; that German guns destroyed German troops at the Battle of Koniggratz; that German steel was exported in large quantities, and that no effort was made "to ascertain whether or not this steel was being in turn exported to the Allies"; [21] that "Two French importing firms stated that, without the least difficulty or hindrance of any sort, they were able on their own account to import from Switzerland during the war sixty thousand tons of German steel"; [22] and that, "Just as German soldiers were caught, abraided and bled by barbed wire that originally came from Germany, so British Tommies were being strafed . . . by grenades lined with copper that reached Germany from England by way of the neutral countries." [23]

It has been asserted by Nobel, the "dynamite king," that if any branch of industry needed to be independent of foreign export, that branch was the armament industry. But this truth was no more honored during World War I than in the course of more recent disturbances, particularly since the arms industry had come to include such a multitude of diverse items as to be virtually a world industry. So deeply intrenched was the idea of private profit, so powerful the inbred desire for profit, that it did not stop even when patriots were bayoneted at the point of the dividends of their fellow citizens. Unfortunately, the *laissez faire* preachments of the eighteenth century, and the overemphasis of the right to profit, have given us a false perspective; we have failed to perceive that it is no less monstrous to permit individuals to make money from the equipment of armies than it would be to allow them to declare war and impose conscription for the sake of corporate returns. It

was largely because of the excessive tolerance of the private en-
trepeneur that there was no effective check on the international
arms traffic during World War I. And while this traffic may not
have caused the war, it certainly was an influence toward war in
its stimulation of the arms race, and it certainly tended to pour oil
on the flames the moment they were burning.

Chapter 28

The First World War: Flare-Up

We have seen the psychological tinder prepared for the conflagration. We have noted the ingredients: the doctrines of the philosophers and scientists, and in particular the materialistic interpretation of science; the imperialism that flared into new life in the closing decades of the nineteenth century; the competitive increase in armies and navies, which was linked with imperialism; nationalism, with its complement, the modern version of the old heroic ideal; secret treaties and alliances, and the secret plans of the General Staffs; militarism, the military outlook, and the existence of professional officers' corps; the creed of war's inevitability, and the corresponding idea of preventive war; racialism, and the conformity of the mass due to military indoctrination; the failure of individual, political, and international morality; the part of the inflammatory daily press, and the weavings and burrowings of the international armament combines.

Here we have, truly, a powerful mass of combustibles. But combustibles in themselves do not make a fire. It takes a spark to touch them off. And the spark for the First World War was provided by individuals, playing parts they could little have realized in a tragedy that transcended the conception of any of them.

It is unbelievable that any man wished a tragedy of the proportions and consequences of World War I. On the other hand, it has been established that there were men who did want war—a limited war, to be sure, and one they could control. And these men, with about the wisdom of small boys experimenting with fire-crackers in the vicinity of dynamite, permitted the eruption when courage might have curbed and perhaps entirely averted it.

Everyone knows that the war stemmed from the assassination of the Archduke Francis Ferdinand and his wife at Sarajevo on June 28, 1914. Not only was the Archduke the heir to the Austrian throne—which in itself would have made his murder extraordinarily serious—but the crime lent fire to a long-standing hostility between

Serbia and Austria. The former, on a wave of nationalistic enthusiasm, was expanding and rising; she had recently triumphed in the Balkan Wars, and her claim to northern Albania and an Adriatic seaport was supported by Russia and vigorously combated by Austria; and she had aroused intense Austrian antagonism by her covetous glances toward parts of the unstable Hapsburg monarchy. An indication is to be seen in the remark of the Serbian Prime Minister Pashitch to the Greek Politis, after the Second Balkan War—a statement to the effect that the first round was over, now the second must be waged against Austria. Not that there were not provocations on both sides; a furor had swept Serbia, and war had been regarded as inevitable as far back as 1908, when Austria had high-handedly announced her annexation of the provinces of Bosnia and Herzegovina. But though war did not break out immediately, Serbia was to cherish her grievance (which likewise represented a Russian grievance, a personal affront to the Czarist Minister Izvolsky, who believed he had been double-crossed). And the enmity was to grow throughout the years, abetted by nationalistic aspirations and by Russia and Rumania . . . until the Austrians came to believe that something had to be done once and for all to solve the "Serbian problem."

It has been acknowledged that there was some justification for the unprecedentedly severe ultimatum which Austria flung at Serbia on July 23. Recent research has made it clear that the Serbian authorities knew of the crime, did nothing to forestall it, and made no effort to apprehend the conspirators after the assassination. All this gave reason for acute provocation—not, however, reason for war, and least of all for world war. But Austria, when she leveled her ten demands against Serbia and allowed but forty-eight hours for a reply, was not looking for conciliation. The terms, which could not have been met without impairment of Serbian sovereignty, were not meant to be accepted; they were meant to provide an excuse for war. The proof of Austrian intentions—even if we had no other evidence, such as the precipitate declaration of war, two weeks before the army was ready to move—would be manifest in the offhand manner in which diplomatic relations were severed. The Serbian reply was handed to the Austrian legation just two minutes before the expiration of the ultimatum, at 6 P.M. on July 25. But though the answer involved intricate details centering about ten distinct points, the Austrian Minister Giesl had time to catch the 6.30 train for Belgrade, having meanwhile rejected the response and broken diplomatic relations.

Within Austria there appears to have been a tug-of-war. The aged Emperor Francis Joseph appears to have been wearily resigned to the struggle rather than willing; he was tricked by a statement of Count Berchtold, later deleted, to the effect that Serbian troops had attacked Austrians. But his Chief of Staff, General Conrad, definitely favored war, and so did Berchtold, one of those small men who are sometimes permitted to mismanage great affairs; but Count Tisza, the Hungarian Minister-President, at first held back, and was with difficulty persuaded. It is perhaps useless to speculate whether the destiny of the world would not have been changed if this man, whose hand was on the controls of the Austrian government, had held to his original convictions. And likewise it may be useless to ask whether calamity might not have been avoided if Sir Edward Grey had made a firm early assertion of English intentions; or if the Kaiser, whose government on July 5 had unwisely allowed Austria freedom of action, had given Vienna prompt unequivocal assurance that he would not be dragged into war over Serbia.

But the fateful ultimatum was sent; the fateful breach in diplomatic relations was accomplished; the fateful declaration of war was made three days after the rejection of the ultimatum. Even so, a world conflict need not have occurred. But haste, fury, unreason, and fear had a hand far more than any desire for war; and in the epoch-making forty-eight hours that followed the Austrian declaration against Serbia, all of Europe and indeed all of the world was diverted to a road red-marked with disaster, a road it has never since been able completely to leave.

II

Many pages might be devoted to the diplomatic maneuverings and scurryings of those tragic last days before the holocaust. Mostly the story is that of men who, befuddled and blinded, pushed the wrong buttons or failed to press the right ones, so producing results they had not intended. After careful inquiry, one cannot accept the theory, so long popular in Allied countries, of the exclusive guilt of the Central Powers; it is now the consensus of the opinion of historians that all the countries were responsible in varying de-

grees, though their faults were in the main those of stupidity, neglect, and panic rather than of warlike intent.

Austria was indeed culpable, as we have seen, in plotting war
against Serbia, even if with what she considered the justifiable aim
of safeguarding her national position. Serbia was culpable in shield-
ing the criminals of Sarajevo and in encouraging Pan-Slavic and
anti-Austrian movements of which the murder of the Archduke
was but the culmination; Russia was culpable in her machinations
to build a Balkan bloc and gain control of the Straits, in her secret
diplomacy, and in her ordering of the mobilization that caused a
fatal stampede of counter-mobilizations. France was culpable in
having a secret military understanding with Russia in order to
maintain the balance of power, and in not trying to avert Nicholas'
catastrophic step by a word spoken in time. Germany was culpable
in giving Austria a blank check to pursue her chastisement of
Serbia, though she did make belated efforts to hold her ally's hands.
England was culpable in sitting by passively at a time when the
world might have been saved by a resounding announcement that
she would or would not maintain her neutrality; and culpable also
in her secret commitments to maintain the same balance of power
that was unbalancing the other nations.

All this adds up to a sorry account of moral cowardice, inertia,
and obtuseness when courage, energy, and intelligence were pre-
eminently necessary. But it is not a tale of viciousness or war-mad-
ness on the part of the nations as a whole; apart from a few
ministers and generals, including Berchtold, Conrad, and Moltke,
who urged that the "unusually favorable situation" be used to
strike, it does not indicate an inclination even for localized warfare.
And with all the official blindness, shortsightedness, and misbegot-
ten designs, obviously, the people had nothing to do. It was the
comparatively small group of national leaders who made the series of missteps immediately responsible for the conflict; and the
masses, who had not willed and did not want the struggle, were
dragged in after them.

Of all the psychological forces of the few days before the outburst, fear was the most conspicuous. It was fear of Serbia and her
allies that dictated the Austrian ultimatum and the subsequent declaration of war. It was fear of Germany and Austria, fear sprung
partly of the belief in war's inevitability, that prompted the Russian
mobilization. It was likewise fear of the inevitable conflict, and also

fear of Germany, that urged France to respond with her own general mobilization on August 1. It was fear of the French and Russian mobilizations, and consequently fear of encirclement, that inspired the German mobilization on the same day. It was fear that, from the beginning of the crisis, had prevented the nations from acting in that bold and outright manner that might have clamped a brake on the cumbrous world chariot. And it was fear of a two-front war that prompted Germany, immediately after the start of hostilities, to violate Belgian neutrality in the hope of overwhelming France and then turning to meet the enemy on her Eastern frontier. As in the case of so many wars, chattering terror and not knightly valor was behind the whole ghastly imbroglio. And terror was accentuated by ancient animosity, intolerance, and distrust, and by the generation-old race in armaments and the long diplomatic thrust-and-parrying; while the men at the steering-wheels of the nations, in so far as panic and hysteria permitted any time for thought, mostly took council from the lips of idiots.

III

"It is a curious psychological phenomenon," remarks Sidney Fay, in the concluding chapter of his monumental work, "that as soon as a country engages in war, there develops or is created among the masses a frenzy of patriotic excitement which is no index of their pre-war desires." [1] In large part, this excitement is instilled by artificial methods, by propaganda, and by the blare of drums and bugles and the waving of flags; and much of the propaganda has been hatched in advance by the inculcation of misleading ideas or of international fantasies and prejudices. An example is cited by Theodor Wolff, who tells of the reaction after his paper, the *Berliner Tageblatt*, published the news of the English entry into the war:

The extra edition . . . created a great impression but by no means a devastating one, since most people had no idea of the significance of British participation in the war; all had been brought up from childhood with mistaken ideas about that country. People had been taught that the British were just football players, and not to be taken seriously as soldiers. . . .

But if there was no particular dismay . . . there did burst forth, for the first time since the outbreak of war, a feeling of passion,

of hatred. Apart from those who had developed a sort of poison
gland, nobody felt any hatred of the French and Russian peoples.
Now, in regard to the British, it was different: that nation of shop-
keepers had hatched the intrigue, assembled the fighting coalition
against Germany, deliberately collected the hounds and unleashed
them, and brought indescribable woe upon Europe.[2]

Thus among the Germans there was brewed an idea as false as
the Allied conviction that the war was the single-handed design of
the Kaiser. Furthermore, the German declaration of war against
France attempted to justify itself on the basis of several bombings
and frontier violations, which, though wholly fictitious, were instru-
mental in producing a warlike emotion in the home population—
much as the false reports of German atrocities in Belgium helped
to create a fighting fervor in Allied countries.

Apparently there is a mass contagion in the very excitement of
war, which bursts like a spectacle across the humdrum of life and
at the same time gives an outlet for old prejudices and antagonisms.
People who were not ill-disposed toward their neighbors nor no-
ticeably pugnacious will shout and stamp and join in the blood-
dance; people whose lives have been blankly unadventurous will
rejoice in the vicarious adventure of battle. And evil emotions will
flash like swords; and the mob, in the way of all mobs, will behave
in a manner of which its members individually would not be capable. The present-day reader may smile ironically upon reading that
on July 25, 1914, when announcement was made of the Austrian
break with Serbia, *The New York Times* could tell of Paris boule-
vard crowds shouting "To Berlin!"; while of the German capital it
could be said:

The capital is afire tonight with war fever. The crowds which had
been waiting since 6 o'clock greeted the announcements with frenzied cheers. Hats were thrown into the air and shouts of "War!
War!" reverberated up and down the street.[3]

It was during the fury of the war's outbreak that Jean Jaurès,
the celebrated French Socialist and peace advocate, was shot to
death by a militarist in Paris. Meantime at St. Petersburg a sub-
scription of about one hundred thousand dollars was collected for
the first soldier to reach Berlin; and throughout Russia patriotic
demonstrations occurred, while a labor strike in the capital ended
forthwith. Bursts of warlike enthusiasm were likewise to be heard

in Austria and Serbia; but England displayed little if any zeal for the struggle, which she was led to accept only by degrees as indignation mounted over the breach of Belgian neutrality. Yet even so outstanding an individual as H. G. Wells could be misled: in *The New York Times* of August 5, he could not only speak of the "righteous" nature of the war but remark that "Now is the sword drawn for peace." When an intellectual, a liberal, and a pacifist could utter such unwisdom, it is little wonder if the common citizen was confused. And little wonder if the Socialists and theoretical friends of peace were everywhere voting war credits and donning uniforms—with some exceptions, as we shall note, including the conscientious objectors, and certain celebrated war opponents, such as Liebknecht and Rosa Luxemburg in Germany and Debs in America, most of whom were crucified for their recalcitrance.

In the United States, we can trace the gradual development of a state of mind foreshadowing our declaration of war in 1917. It was a state of mind confused by prejudice and misinformation, and inducing us to believe what we were disposed to believe. Far from understanding or attempting to understand the historical processes behind the Great War and the complicated division of the guilt, we were ready to accept the ancient wolf-eat-lamb theory. This theory had the advantages of simplicity; even a four-year-old could grasp it; the popular mind was charmed by the fairy tale that ascribed the war solely to the greed of the German beast to devour the Allied Little Red Riding Hood.

Even so, our beliefs were powerfully bolstered by propaganda, no less than by ignorance. One element in that ignorance was the fact that, on August 5, the English cut the German cables, so that all our direct news came from Allied quarters. And another element was that, from the beginning, no American correspondent was allowed on the Allied front; we had to take what we could get, mostly from British sources. Aside from this, most American papers were far from neutral in their attitude; they tended to accept the easy explanation of German war guilt, without examining the thick meshwork of underlying causes; and in this position they were reinforced by the ardent Allied propaganda.

Those whose memories can reach back far enough will recall that the atrocity stories, though afterwards disproved, were believed in America as in France and England. They may also recollect that even when there was a basis for a report the tale was usually but half told. It was indeed grim and terrible, for example, when Belgian civilians were executed, but it was not mentioned that the victims had fired upon and killed German soldiers. Beyond this, when we comb back among the tangled relations of the times, we will find that the provocations to the United States were not confined to either side; there were moments when we seemed close to a brush with the British, whose navy had closed the North Sea to neutral shipping, and who claimed and exercised the privilege (unsanctioned by international law, though defended on grounds of military necessity) of escorting neutral vessels into Allied harbors for examination of their cargo. All this might have led to war with England, and one reason it did not was that the trend of our minds was pro-Allied.

Another reason—and likewise a reason for our drift toward war with Germany—is to be found in the unneutral conduct of our ambassador to London, Walter Hines Page. According to Sir Edward Grey of the British Foreign Office, "From the first he considered that the United States could be brought into the war early on the side of the Allies if the issue were rightly presented to it and a great appeal made by the President." [4] And he took extraordinary measures for the envoy of a supposed neutral:

One incident in particular remains in my memory. Page came to see me at the Foreign Office one day and produced a long dispatch from Washington contesting our claim to act as we were doing in stopping contraband going to neutral ports. "I am instructed," he said, "to read this dispatch to you." He read, and I listened. He then said, "I have now read the dispatch but I do not agree with it; let us consider how it could be answered!" [5]

Similar instances may have occurred of ambassadors in secret league against the will and the neutrality of their own government; but, if so, few of them have been brought to light. Yet in the case of the *Dacia*, a ship owned by an American and under American registry, Page almost outdid himself. Realizing that if the British interfered with it, they "ran the risk of provoking an outburst of opinion in America that might be formidable. . . . Page suggested that the French navy instead of the British should intercept the *Dacia*. This was done, and there was not a murmur in America." [6]

From other points of view, we had not been neutral even from the beginning. While theoretically we stood ready to ship arms to either side, British control of the seas meant that in practice we favored one faction only. And the huge munitions business which we developed produced two results: first, that we contributed substantially to the Allied cause; second, that we came to have a large vested interest in the war. Munition shares went soaring; financiers such as Morgan and Schwab piled up profits; the heart of the stock market missed a beat at the merest rumor of peace. Under the circumstances, some forces at home were certain to oppose peace abroad; were certain to move us toward foreign war rather than suffer the calamity of peace.

And in some ways these forces proved decisive. It was our foreign commerce, devoted largely to the tools of war, that brought us into conflict with the German submarines; it was our foreign commerce that had originally goaded the Germans into unrestricted submarine warfare. This does not, of course, condone the anti-human methods by which the U-boat commanders sank merchant vessels and sent defenseless civilians to salty graves; nor does it supply excuses for a crime such as the sinking of the passenger liner *Lusitania*, with the loss of 1,195 lives. But it is evident that if American businessmen had not sent warlike cargoes across submarine-threatened seas in the quest of profit, there would have been fewer provocations to attack; and we might have been spared the tragedy of involvement in the conflict. This would, it is true, have incurred forfeiture of our prized right to unimpeded trade; it would also have meant more moderate dividends from certain stocks; but one can leave it to the appraiser of historical values to decide how much all this would have weighed in the scale against our saving of blood and treasure and our preservation of a neutral role to help in the adjudication of world affairs.

But the fact is that we did move toward war. And even before the U-boat attacks had goaded us to a declaration against Germany, our fighting psychology had been gradually developing. We have noted how, largely because of our original sympathies but partly because of doctored and one-sided war reports, we had tended to favor the Allies—which meant that some of our citizens, such as Theodore Roosevelt with his extraordinary scheme for leading his own infantry division to the Western front, were willing to plunge in to help the Entente. But perhaps still more remarkable is the fact that tremors for our own safety began to agitate the country. "Prepare! Prepare! Prepare!" the shouts dinned through the air. It was perhaps irrelevant that no one could mention any enemy against whom we had need of preparing; the cry still rang forth, "Prepare! Prepare! Prepare!" And like all reiterated clamors, it persuaded many hearers. Peace advocates such as Jane Addams and Henry Ford were heard with disdain; and the country, after a brush with Mexico that might have ended disastrously, was gradually being whipped up into a more warlike frame of mind.

It is needless to follow the succession of incidents, involving vessels such as the *Arabic,* the *Falaba,* the *Vigilance,* and many others, which posed problems for our government and developed anti-German feeling. Nor is it necessary to dwell upon the continued propaganda; nor the effect of the revelations, blared from newspaper headlines, to the effect that Germany had sought an alliance with Japan and Mexico in the event of war with us. The fact is that the national mind bit by bit was made ready for the leap into the affray. We were horrified, and with good cause, at the frightfulness of German submarine warfare; but we did not pause to wonder whether in the long run it might not be as frightful to blockade whole countries into starvation. Similarly, we did not seriously ask whether the way to limit the terrors of war was not to limit war itself. But we soothed our ears with slogans—phrases that still come back to mock and gibe—"Make the world safe for democracy!"—"The war to end war!" There is no doubt that many of us seriously believed in these catch-words; we had not yet learned that nothing makes the world more unsafe for democracy than war, and nothing does less to end war. And so we let ourselves be dragged to the verge. Even before the actual declaration, the newspapers were reiterating the words of Elihu Root that we were already in the fight. And though a lone Representative—Congressman Fred A. Britten of Illinois—could plead that ninety per cent of the people did not want the declaration and that Congress too was opposed to it at heart, the pro-war vote was overwhelming, and on April 6, 1917, the United States officially set foot on that path of no returning which has led us into a different world, and whose darkness after the passage of decades is even now upon us.

Chapter 29

The First World War: Total Conflict

While America was watching and debating, the war in Europe was developing a conception new in modern times. The phrase may not yet have been current, but we had had our introduction to "total war." In ancient Sparta and various other militant communities, all the people's energies had been directed so far as possible toward war-making; but these communities had been relatively small, and the warrior caste had depended for support upon the much larger strata of productive workers—Helots, serfs, and slaves of various categories. It remained for the modern era, therefore, to mature the notion of the state-in-arms.

We have seen this idea taking shape and expanding in the Prussia of Frederick II and the Germany of Bismarck, and in Revolutionary and Napoleonic France. But these were merely the preliminaries. Not until the First World War was a whole group of states transformed into military engines, with no aim but the aims of warfare, and with the power to commandeer the lives and labor of their citizens. Modern efficiency, sprung of the Industrial Revolution, had made it possible to send a larger proportion of the population than ever before to the battle-lines, and to supply them with fighting instruments of a complexity and a profusion known in no previous age. But it was not only in its utilization of power-driven tools that the twentieth century was different; it was notable also for the doctrine, which had been developing ever since the French Revolution, that the State in wartime was entitled to dispose not only of the fighting arms but of the working hands of its citizens.

When even civilians began to feel the grip of military coercion; when those who could not fight were told that they must work, and when women by the millions were enlisted to do men's labor, the nations had undergone a radical alteration not only in economic structure but in political philosophy. It appears not to have been thoroughly recognized at the time—perhaps it is not thoroughly recognized even today—that a form of socialism began to be adopted in once-conservative countries. True, it was a military socialism; its object was not the relief of social evils but the defeat of the enemy, and it did not take the logical step of matching mobilization of men by mobilization of wealth. And yet the governments, by proclaiming their right to the services of all citizens, did establish temporarily a regime featured by that despotic rule and that suppression of individuality which are among the worst dangers of a socialistic order. And thus they set a precedent more perilous than anyone seemed to realize, and made the road easy for the totalitarian tyrannies of the coming decades.

All the main ingredients of tyranny were already present. A machine organization dominated the various countries; a machine organization ruled not only the recruiting offices but the manufacturing plants and the food supplies; a machine organization took charge of the fountains of public information, supervised the molding of mass psychology, and saw that the people were permitted to read only such statements and opinions as would inflame their minds with warlike frenzy and kindle their hatred of the foe. Censorship, the dragon of a myriad eyes, set himself up as sentinel over all the avenues of public thought; every view that was expressed, every bit of knowledge that was circulated, had to be submitted to his searching gaze; and the question he asked was not "Is it true?," but "Is it propaganda?" If it were propaganda (of the right sort, naturally) he would mark it "Approved!"; if it were truth, he would as often as not stamp it "Forbidden!"

Even the acknowledged intellectual leaders were halted by the monster Censorship and made to speak by rote the words he put into their mouths; if they presumed to refuse, they might regret their indiscretion behind the bars or to the whine of the executioner's bullet. Among the many cases that might be cited are those of Bertrand Russell, who was fined, whose library was seized, and who was jailed for six months; Karl Liebknecht, who was imprisoned for two years, and subsequently murdered by his guards; and Romain Rolland, who, although less severely treated than the above-mentioned, suffered an immense unpopularity for his frankly spoken views, and, as he himself declares in *Afer the Battle*, was so censored that for many months no one in France could know his writings except through the arbitrary excerpts and mutilations of his enemies. This was the more iniquitous since the criticism of Rolland's position was based on words which no one in France was permitted to read. It may have been fortunate for the author of *Jean Christophe* that he was in neutral Switzerland when the war broke out.

In an atmosphere in which freedom of discussion is impossible, there is obviously no accurate way of gauging the reactions of the masses. And in an atmosphere in which a well-founded personal fear restrains the dissenters from speaking, one can be certain that the voices of dissent will be few and far between. For this reason, one would hesitate to say that the apparent unanimity of most modern peoples in the face of a war is not apparent only. There are, as we have seen, large numbers who will demonstrate hilariously, in a fervor of belligerent emotion—but what of the greater multitudes who remain quietly at home? Censorship has effectively silenced their opinions.

Nevertheless, there is one phenomenon that cannot be ignored in an appraisal of wartime psychology: the phenomenon of those who refuse military service on conscientious grounds. These rebels against the expressed national will, though comparatively few, are none the less significant. Some have been the spokesmen of small religious groups, but others have represented deep-seated personal convictions—convictions so strong that they cannot be disregarded in any survey of the popular mind; convictions so severely penalized that, no matter how many persons actually shared them, only the resolute courageous few would dare to make them public.

The case of England—normally a freedom-loving, liberal-minded country—will serve by way of illustration. Confronted by the challenge of men who would not fight, what did that country do? There have been various accounts of the experiences of conscientious objectors, but a particularly revealing one is contained in the *Autobiography* of the well-known English poet, biographer, and literary critic, Gilbert Thomas.[1] Mr. Thomas, whose strong personal objections to taking up arms had seen print even before the war, does not write in bitterness; indeed, he says that he was comparatively fortunate. Nevertheless, he tells how the Conscience Clause of the Military Service Act was frustrated by the local administrators. "A standard decision to give exemption only from combatant service had obviously been arrived at beforehand, and the senators as a whole were not to be moved. The hearing of cases was, in these circumstances, a solemn farce."

Mr. Thomas was not pilloried as were many objectors, who, he tells us, "during the early months of conscription, suffered the worst measures applicable to defaulting soldiers not on active service. They were put repeatedly into dark and lonely cells; they were placed on bread and water diet; they underwent 'crucifixion' and every other worst variety of field punishment. Then a number were taken in irons to France, where, under the law, it would be possible to shoot them." But while Mr. Thomas did escape these particular perils and indignities, his experience was unenviable.

After delivering himself up, he was locked in a cell "of a very old type" with "practically no ventilation. . . ." "The only light came from two small panes of glass near the ceiling; while the weather now turned, and remained, abnormally sultry, with a relentless glare from the sun." After several days of confinement—he speaks of having sat "in a kind of stupor"—the court-martial proceedings must have been almost a relief. He was now sentenced to the "not too severe" term of six months in Wormwood Scrubbs Prison, where, though he does not complain that conditions were particularly bad, he was treated like a convicted housebreaker; was given so little to eat that food was constantly in everyone's mind; was compelled, for the first two weeks, to sleep on a plank bed; was not allowed to talk with other prisoners; was not permitted to write or receive a letter or to have a visitor for eight weeks, and after that was limited to one incoming and one outgoing letter and one visit a month. This medieval stringency was, to be sure, relieved by the possibility of reading; and the work of sewing mailbags, while monotonous, was not especially hard.

If one can take this case as typical—and Mr. Thomas, as noted above, seems to have regarded himself as relatively fortunate—one will realize what heavy discouragements piled up before the conscientious objector. And when one takes account of the contempt and opprobrium that fell upon the objector, the sneers at a man's virility and the disfavor of the other sex, one must suppose that it demanded less courage to face gunfire than to refuse enlistment on the grounds of conscience. One must conclude, furthermore, that the number of declared objectors is no index to the number that actually opposed service. Under modern wartime conditions, with the twin specters of compulsion and disgrace towering in the background, a population might be secretly peaceful-minded and yet stream forth to the colors without manifest reluctance.

II

However, the authorities took care that pacifist sentiment, if common in the beginning, was speedily dispersed. We have noted how censorship kept guard over dangerous information; yet this was but the negative side of the screen. The positive side was represented by propaganda, which, as we have seen, did not originate with the First World War, though it had perhaps never been so extensively used before. In its more obvious phases, it was represented by the preachers who fulminated patriotically from their pulpits, the "four-minute" speakers and the political writers with their flamboyant harangues, the cartoonists with their provoking pictures, the pedagogues with their pleas for the defense of "home and country," the trained writers with their depiction of the foreign hawk in the act of swooping down on the domestic dove, the army leaders with their reiterations of the duty of enlisting and the shame of shirking, the poster-makers with their prominent displays of the joy of combat, and their appeal to the knight-at-arms rescuing imperiled innocence from a vulture or a gorilla. Also, there were the leaflet-writers, whose products were distributed from the air, and were not without success in spreading doubt among the Germans and Russians, and scattering disaffection in the shaky Austrian armies.

But more subtle than all this—because they played upon the normal emotions of the people, while allowing men no opportunity to use their reason in rebuttal—were the stories of enemy atrocities.

It would be reassuring to state that all such false accounts were sheerly accidental. However, we know that this was not the case; the calculated falsehood, in the First World War as in the Second, was a means of arousing warlike sentiment. Hitler and Goebbels were not, as some commentators have supposed, the originators of the technique of the "Big Lie"; it was already well known to the French propagandists of 1914–18. In testimony to this fact, note the following, from *Behind the Scenes in French Journalism*, by "A French Chief Editor":

If you reduce the lie to a scientific system, put it on thick and heavy, and with great effort and heavy finances scatter it all over the world as the pure truth, you can deceive whole nations for a long time and drive them to slaughter for causes in which they have not the slightest interest. We have seen that sufficiently during the last war. . . .[2]

It has been shown how, faithful to these principles, a photograph of Germans engaged in a riding exhibition was falsified through a changing of the captions, so that their trophies of horsemanship were represented as plunder snatched from Polish churches and homes. Alleged German atrocities in Poland, in much the same way, have been proved to have been based on pictures of Russian anti-Jewish atrocities of years before. And a photograph of a train-load of horses on its way to a fertilizer plant was described as depicting the German war-dead being hauled to the rear—and evoked strong anti-German feeling even in China, where reverence for the dead is a deep-seated emotion; and aroused hot anger and encouraged enlistments in England through being displayed to indicate the treatment of fallen Tommies.

Since it is impossible for the people of any country to investigate or appraise such frauds, and since it is man's normal tendency to react emotionally and to accept almost any reports that are uttered loud enough and repeated often enough, what chance has the truth against a well-oiled engine of propaganda?

Need we be surprised, therefore, if populations of scores of millions, most of whom did not desire to fight and felt no hatred of the enemy, were trained almost at a moment's notice not only to tolerate the conflict but to participate actively? Never before had mankind received such a lesson in the malleability of the masses; World War I demonstrated how the actions of men in a state of artificially fanned excitement violate not only the restraints of reason but the dictates of elemental humanity. That the German scholars should have taken up arms against the scholars of France is a fact for which few of those scholars could have given a logical excuse; that the native of Tokyo should have exchanged shots with the native of Berlin, or the citizen of Vancouver with the citizen of Constantinople, or the Indian hillman with the resident of Vienna, is a circumstance that finds its roots in no personal or economic antagonism. One can only conclude that, had the psychological training been reversed, each of the warriors would have fought with equal zest on the opposite side.

The attitude of the typical civilian at the time of the war's outbreak has been indicated by Philip Gibbs:

War with Germany? . . . No, it was inconceivable and impossible. Why should England make war upon Germany or Germany upon England? We were alike in blood and character, bound to each other by a thousand ties of tradition and knowledge and trade and friendship. All the best intellect of Germany was friendly to us. . . .

In Hamburg years ago I had listened to speeches about all that, obviously sincere, emotional in their protestations of racial comradeship. That young poet who had become my friend . . . was he a liar when he spoke fine and stirring words about the German admiration for English literature and life, and when . . . he passed his arm through mine and said, "If ever there were to be a war between our two countries I and all my friends in Hamburg would weep at the crime and the tragedy"? [3]

Perhaps the young poet and his friends did weep at the crime and the tragedy. Yet it is fairly certain that they marched with the armies of their country.

If a being of perfect vision had looked down upon the combatants plodding through the smoke and blood, the sincerity of the men as they blew one another to bits might have struck him as ironic and more than a little pathetic. They had left their peaceful villages, their comfortable towns, their farms and their shops, their mills and their gardens, the arms of their wives and the embraces of their children—and for what? It was an ideal that led them—in almost every land it was an ideal that bade them dig bayonets into the entrails of their fellows or asphyxiate them with lung-devouring fumes! Here was the great sorrow of the war, the supreme tragedy —that the best in human nature had been tricked into the service of the worst. Yet was the German not sincere when he slew the Frenchman in the name of *Kultur?* Was the Frenchman not sincere when he defended *la belle France* from rape by the invader? Was the American not sincere when he fought to "make the world safe for democracy"? Of the earnestness, the absolute conviction with which the soldiers entered the trenches, there can be little doubt; the paradox of it all was that this earnestness, this conviction was not confined to either side: the Berliner eviscerating a Parisian was as fully persuaded that he fought in defense of his homeland as was the Parisian who disemboweled a Berliner; both alike were battling for some intangible cause which—had they only known it—

was the same in both cases although viewed through different glasses.

III

Yet there were times when the Berliner and the Parisian forgot that they were supposed to hate. Ignoring all the prejudice and propaganda, ignoring the fact that they were engaged in a game of "I kill you, you kill me," the men of both sides met in friendly intercourse: Frenchmen and Englishmen would exchange jovial words with the Germans, and Germans with Frenchmen and Englishmen. It is reported that once, when the earthworks collapsed beneath the excessive rains and each side was exposed to the gaze of the other, both went about their work as if unaware of the enemy's existence; while at other times parties of men actually crossed over to the opposite trenches, and, instead of bombs and bullets, exchanged hand-shakes. The first Christmas—with a spirit of "good will on earth" that later Christmases did not duplicate— was a virtual holiday: protected by an unofficial truce, the Germans bore the bodies of the fallen to the Allied lines, and prayers for the departed were read in two languages while detachments of Germans and British stood by.

The authorities, however, scowled upon such amicability. Fraternization was not warfare! It violated the first principles of hatred! It broke all the rules of orthodox death-dealing! How could a soldier fight his best if he saw that his opponent was human? Why, if this sort of thing went on, the men might end by refusing to fight at all!

In all this, of course, the authorities were quite logical. War certainly is not friendship; comradeship and murder do not mix. Though the official mandates forbade fraternization, the next Christmas saw a revival of man's normal tendency to greet his fellow man with a hand-shake rather than a saber-thrust; regardless of the staff officers who strove to keep the men apart, the Germans and British shouted invitations across at one another.

At dawn therefore parties went over, and whole battalions might have followed them had not the artillery at once set up a barrage. It was found also that sentries on both sides had been ordered to fire. Some obeyed, some did not. One Guards sentry was proud of having fired fifteen rounds. But he did not hit anyone. Meantime the troops around Neuve Chapelle and Auburs got across in large bodies. Even on the Guards' front men risked their lives to shake hands. Did not one thus lose his life that morning? [4]

Normal human good will, obviously, is here much more evident than what some writers like to call the "instinct of pugnacity."

But how does it happen that soldiers so eager for kindly association with the foe would on occasion blow them to bits with hand grenades or dash at them with unbared bayonets? First of all, we must remember that most of the fraternization occurred early in the war, before hatred had had a chance to accumulate; and we must not lose sight of the devices employed to fill men's minds with rancor and venom. It is known, for example, that one reason why great attention was paid to bayonet practice was in order to develop antagonism where no natural antagonism was. Note the comments of an American journalist:

Uninstructed civilians, visiting the American, French and British training camps, wondered at the time given to bayonet practice. Why so much stress upon it? Any sergeant could explain that. It was a means of cultivating hate, of making your soldier a bit of a brute. The dummy at which you were thrusting—the instructor encouraged you to imagine him a German, to curse him, to work up a savage delight in mutilating him. It was a part of the higher psychology of modern war.[5]

But if long and intensive training did not instill a proper love of murdering—if bayonet practice, propaganda, atrocity stories, the force of example, and the frenzy of combat did not quench man's natural friendliness for man—there were other methods of guaranteed efficacy. And not the least important involved the use of a well-known stimulant. "Some commanders . . . thought double rum-rations put the necessary devil into the men to carry them through the ordeal of a fray, and it is common talk in the army that some of the units that went into the storming of the Hohenzollern redoubt knew very little of what they were doing." [6]

The last words will apply even to many not under alcoholic influence. In the fury of a bayonet rush, when men dash with bristling points toward grim companies awaiting them with bristling points and bombs, normal emotions are in abeyance; the mind of each man becomes a ravening thing; hatred, fear, and the frenzy of self-preservation mingle in fierce confusion. And while the eyes bring flashes of steel and blood and the ears are assailed with a shrieking and a moaning and a rending of bones, the crazed warrior may commit deeds that will come back to haunt him in nightmares. For he has been drugged, drugged with a blinding, overwhelming excitement; his senses have been blurred and distorted, and the world for him has become chaos; borne on tides of primitive impulse, with no shred of will or reason left, he has become like a wild beast beset with fire or a delirious person wandering down aisles of horror in a dream.

Even when participating in no bayonet charge, the soldier reacted very much like an automaton. "When troops are forced to sit in a trench under the most terrific shell-fire, the nerve-racking noise, the sight of their comrades and their defenses being blown to atoms, and the constant fear that they themselves will be the next to go, all deprive the ordinary mind of vital initiative. Having lost the active mental powers that a human being possesses, they are reduced to the level of machines." [7]

Yet occasionally one of the machines, fired with a flash of human self-assertiveness, would beat desperately at its chains. We read of men blowing off their own toes or fingers in order to be discharged from the army as "wounded"; we read of others that deliberately flung themselves into the enemy's hands, preferring the lot of prisoners to that of fighters; we are told of many who merely cursed and impotently cursed, muttering against their commanders and against the fate that had doomed them to be the sport of machine-guns and high-power explosives.

IV

Owing to its very magnitude, the Great War produced unprecedented reactions upon the world state of mind. And those reactions are to be seen in two chief directions: in the attitudes of the authorities toward combatants and civilians, and in the new social attitudes awakened in the nations.

We of the wartime generations, who have passed through a struggle of even greater duration and wider devastation, may tend to forget the extent of the carnage of World War I. We may not recall that in a routine day of fighting five thousand men might be killed, in addition to many thousands scarred, blinded, or crippled; and that there were four years of such routine days. Time and stress may have obscured for us the fact that 60,000 Britons were lost in the first day's fighting on the Somme; that the total British losses at this one battle have been reported at 410,000, as against 190,000 for the French and half a million for the Germans; and that at the Battle of Passchendaele, in the latter half of 1917, the British lost 300,000 men. When human life is squandered with such recklessness, a new attitude toward human life is inevitable—an outlook which, at the upper levels, may be a little like that of the slaughterhouse proprietor toward domestic animals. And so the tendency which had come to Europe with the French Revolution and had found support in the Napoleonic wars, the Crimean War, the American Civil War, the Franco-Prussian War, and other conflicts—the inclination to value men as mere tools in pursuit of military objectives—was accentuated to a degree unexampled in modern history.

We see this in the treatment by the commanders of their own men. It is known, for example, that during a barrage fire many a man would be blown to fragments by his own side. And such losses were regarded as necessary—even as paying investments. "Infantry soldiers follow the barrage closely," declares one officer, "even if a few men are hit by the shells. . . . If an enemy machine-gunner or bomber can reach his post six or eight seconds before the first line of storming troops arrives, he almost invariably inflicts scores of casualties on the British infantry, in comparison with which a ten per cent loss from their own barrage is of minor importance." [8]

No doubt, from the point of view of the ten per cent, the loss is of more than minor importance.

Philip Gibbs lists several other ways in which losses, presumably also of minor importance, were forced upon the troops by their commanders. He mentions divisions that "set out to attack terrible lines without sufficient artillery support, and without reserves behind them, and without any chance of holding the ground they might capture. They were the pawns of 'strategy,' serving a high purpose in a way that seemed to them without reason. Not for them the glory of a victorious assault. Their job was to 'demonstrate' by exposing their bodies to devouring fire. . . ." [9]

In another place, Gibbs speaks of a time "when from Hooge to the Hohenzollern redoubt our men sat in wet trenches under ceaseless bombardment of heavy guns, and when any small attack they made by the orders of a High Command which believes in small attacks, was only 'asking for trouble' . . . without definite results on either side beyond piling up of the lists of death.

" 'It keeps up the fighting spirit of the men,' said the generals. 'We must maintain an aggressive policy.' " [10]

Doubtless the leaders, who had got used to the spectacle of men blown into a bloody pulp, had been pounded by the war into a state of mind that made it impossible for them to think of the soldiers as each a breathing, thinking, feeling man, with his own life-impulses, his longings, loves, desires, griefs, pangs, ambitions, and desperate craving to live. Men to them had ceased to be men; they were expendable counters in a gigantic game.

And if such was the attitude of the chieftains toward their own followers, what could foreign populations anticipate? Was Germany to be expected to act with a light hand in raped and trampled Belgium, where the town of Dinant was torn stone from stone after 670 of its citizens had been shot, and where 594 civilians were slain in the occupation of Brabant, while the inhabitants crowded in a tragic procession from Louvain, whose cathedral and priceless library along with 1,120 houses were given to the flames? In the horrors that fell upon Belgium, to be sure, "military necessity" justified everything—this was made only too plain by Chancellor Bethmann-Hollweg, who frankly admitted that Germany had violated international law, but stated that she had to do so for the sake of self-preservation. And "military necessity" was the all-sufficient excuse for later infringements that showed a total disregard for civilian lives and rights.

Even when the exactions fell short of indiscriminate havoc and massacre, the philosophy that the end justifies the means was uppermost. In the invasion of Belgium, for example, there was no allegation that the victim had been at fault; Bethmann-Hollweg went so far as to admit that a wrong had been done, and to say that Germany would try to make it good as soon as she had reached her military goal. It is known, of course, that she never did reach her military goal. And before her control ended, she had "made the wrong good" by measures such as the general confiscation of property (in direct breach of the Hague Convention), the visiting upon an entire family of offenses charged against any member of it, the substitution of German judges for the Belgian tribunals, the deportation of men for refusal to accept forced labor, or for the nondescript offense of "undesirability," the appropriation of raw materials and destruction of all machinery not transportable to Germany, the prohibition of work in all shops and mills except by special permission, the requisition of all able-bodied males between the ages of sixteen and seventy, and the removal to Germany of as many as could not be used locally to dig trenches and build railroads, often within range of gunfire (more than 57,000 were actually carted off to Germany, and 2,531 of these died, allegedly from ill treatment).

In all the above, we witness the crumbling of the growth of centuries; we see a return to the system of Assyria and Rome, since the battles were waged not only against armed men but against entire unarmed peoples. We will recall how, in ancient and even in medieval times, all the men of a captured city might be slain, and the women and children enslaved. Yet despite much looting and violence, and despite the barbarities of the Thirty Years' War and other conflicts, recent times had brought an improvement in the lot of the non-combatant and a respect for his life and property. The First World War, however, changed all this, and not in Belgium alone; once again not only the armies but entire populations were assailed. True, there may have been a remorseless logic in all this, since modern war depends not only upon its armies but upon the civilians who produce foodstuffs and munitions. Yet it is questionable whether the terrorization of civilian populations actually brought any great military advantage: what it did was to break down the inhibitions of centuries, to demolish the unwritten law against attacking unarmed men and women, to serve notice that an unshackled ruthlessness again rode abroad, and to set a precedent that was to lead in a direct line to Hiroshima and Nagasaki and a shuddering world that, cowering in dread of its own bombs, has become less secure than in all the ages since the first ape-man left the trees.

Neither side was blameless. The Germans, when their "Big Berthas" hurled shells across a gulf of seventy miles and demolished buildings and slaughtered the Good Friday worshippers at the church of St. Gervais in Paris, had shown little of the old-time regard for human life. And likewise in their Zeppelin raids and airplane attacks upon England, in which a total of 1,413 persons were killed and 3,407 injured, they bespoke the dawning of a new age dominated by a new attitude of mind—a mentality that made the civilian a legitimate target of war, and put human values on the same plane as steel and oil. But how did the Allies react to this challenge? Did they maintain that, when fighting the Vandals, they need not descend to Vandal methods? Did their moral indignation ring to high heaven, along with their refusal to profit from means involving the mangling and dismemberment of old men, and babes in their cradles, and nursing mothers and playing children and blooming young girls? Did they, in their rejection of the cult of mass murder, set a precedent that put an end to the gory practice and lifted a shadow from the future?

We are only too well aware of the answer. We are only too well aware that not restraint but retaliation is what appeals most to men amid the passions of wartime. And just as the white settlers of New England replied to the Indian scalpers by organizing their own scalping parties, so the Allies met the air raids by dropping their own air bombs. While the Germans were extending their attacks to such widely scattered points as Calais and Salonika, the French and British bombarded Stuttgart and Freiburg, Cologne and Karlsruhe, and various other points in western Germany, Albania, and elsewhere. And thus the door was thrown wide for the more sanguinary attacks of later decades. It may be too much to suggest that, during the craze of conflict, a concerted world protest against these assaults on non-combatants would have been immediately effective. But it is not stretching possibilities to imply that it might have led to a post-war agreement to outlaw such assaults. We know, however, that no such protest was made. No such protest was made because, basically, the same attitude of mind dominated both sides. It was an attitude of "Win the war—and humanity be damned!" And so the war was won—and humanity was damned. It is therefore open to question whether humanity might not have been saved from the worst of the dire subsequent disturbances if it had been taken more into account.

Another phase of "Humanity be damned!" was represented by the submarines. The right of search of merchant vessels in war zones had, of course, long been recognized; and the Germans had been understandably aggravated by an Allied blockade to which they had no answer so long as they followed the rules. Nevertheless, there was something callous beyond words in Germany's method of retaliation: unrestricted U-boat warfare, in which commercial vessels were sent without warning to the bottom, and in which the passengers and crews had virtually no chance of rescue from drowning. The case of the *Lusitania*, while the most notorious, was only one of a long series of maritime tragedies precipitated by the attempt to counter the Allied blockade and to starve England. In all these assaults upon mankind we can see the predominance of the Mephistophelean doctrine that the means does not count. Likewise, we can see the reinforcement of a precedent, and the ancestry of the state of mind that was to tolerate the even more ghastly horrors of World War II.

In much the same category we can place the introduction of chemical warfare, even though this was aimed exclusively against combatants. Chemical warfare, to be sure, was nothing new; burning sulphur and pitch had been used as far back as the Peloponnesian War, and the "Greek fire" of the Middle Ages was a chemical weapon. But it is notable that, during the Crimean War, when Lord Dundonald proposed to use burning sulphur at the siege of Sebastopol, the suggestion was vetoed on grounds of humanity. And it is likewise worth mentioning that the Hague Peace Conference of 1899 forbade the use of harmful or asphyxiating gases, while the Hague Convention of 1907 prohibited poison or poisoned arms. The use of gas by the Germans must therefore be construed as a violation of the Hague agreements, no less than as an extension of the creed, "Humanity be damned!" It is all very well to argue that war is cruel in any case, and that it is no more inhuman to burn a man's lungs with corroding gas than to atomize him with a high-power shell: this may be the case, but the answer should be left to those who have suffered the experience. But it is undeniable that chemical warfare did add one new terror to conflict, that it did so in violation of express agreements, that infringements prompted retaliation in kind, and that warfare consequently moved even further from the old chivalric ideal, in which there were levels to which the fighter would not descend.

Fought with no holds barred, the war could not but evoke man's most evil emotions: rage, hatred, terror, sadism, the desire for revenge, along with a blood-frenzy to which men and men's lives were no more than the flies on a barn wall. And the black deeds of the after-war period, which in turn led toward a new and even more grievous struggle, can in large part be traced to the black emotions of the war.

V

Side by side with the new attitudes toward human life, the changed social attitudes are of utmost importance. We have noted how the war forced a form of socialization upon the nations—a military socialization whose one aim was efficiency in war-making. But this socialization, which more recently we have given the name of "regimentation," was not possible without a surrender of civilian liberties—a considerable surrender, as was discovered even in normally free England. And what was the effect of this loss of liberty? Not, unfortunately, to make liberty more prized. Far from the least of the tragedies of World War I was that it reversed the liberal tendencies of more than a century, the impulses felt even in autocratic Russia for growing popular representation in government and increased individual freedom. Henceforth the repressive, narrow, authoritarian forces would be more assertive; the Continent, having clamped itself in chains for the war's duration, was never again to be unshackled as of old, despite all the attempts to establish independent new nations such as Poland and Czechoslovakia; the way was open to the usurpations of a new order of totalitarian rulers.

 Even during the war, Revolution had lifted her crimson head in Europe. The German Revolution, which unseated the Kaiser and established a republic, was a war-born phenomenon, which began in October, 1918, when the crews of three German vessels rebelled against orders to raid British communications and subsequently were joined by all the ships at Kiel. Within a few days, the revolt had spread across the country; Hamburg, Bremen, Hanover, Brunswick, and Cologne fell in rapid succession; in Munich, as the result of an independent insurrection, the Republic of Bavaria was proclaimed; and shortly afterward the Kaiser announced his abdication in favor of the Crown Prince. The country's war-weariness and disillusionment, after more than four years of unprecedented trials and horrors, would sufficiently explain the outbreak even if military defeat had not complicated the picture.

War-weariness and disillusionment were likewise behind another governmental overturn—one of the most momentous in history. Had there been no war, there might still have been a revolution in Russia, though it is arguable that normal historical processes would have resulted in the gradual and peaceable transformation of the Czarist autocracy into something more tolerable and liberal. But the war brought to a head every disruptive force, gave wings to every rebellious emotion, and made it possible for the Bolsheviks to fasten their grip upon the nation. In part this was because of defeats in battle; but in part it was because of the avenues opened by incredible official bungling. The recruitment of over fifteen million men, called to the colors by early 1917, was a source of weakness rather than strength, since the government neither needed them nor was able to arm them adequately; as a result, millions dragged out their days behind the lines in idleness —focal centers for disaffection and enemy propaganda. Combined with a distrust of the government, a disgust at its methods and its weakness, there was a craving for peace—a desire fed by the German troops that, with the calculated approval of their leaders, began to fraternize with the Russians on the Eastern front. The morale of the Russian soldiers is indicated by the fact that, although a wide breach had been made in the enemy lines and success seemed at hand during the Galician offensive of July, 1917, the attack failed because whole regiments refused to obey commands and many deserted; in the end the Russian army, which had numbered two hundred thousand men, crumbled into a disorganized mob of fugitives.

And if such a debacle could occur on the battle-front, what when the soldiers brushed shoulders with the demonstrators of the Revolution? Opposed by troops willing to fight for the government, the Revolution could have amounted to no more than a series of riots, inconsequential in world history. But the doom of Czardom was sealed when the soldiers joined the rebels. In Petrograd, on March 8, 1917, angry demonstrations and attacks on bakers' shops broke out as a result of the scarcity of bread; and large numbers of police, after several days, began firing on the crowds. But the city's immense garrison, including units of the Imperial Guard, refused to join the shooting—or, rather, joined in reverse, since many of the regiments killed their officers and took sides with the rebels. And thus the Revolution began in deadly earnest. And it continued triumphantly on its way when whole trainloads of troops, sent to Petrograd to put down the insurrection, deserted in favor of the people.

Even so, it was generally believed that Russia could simultaneously indulge in a revolution and continue to battle the Central Powers. It became apparent in time, however, that observers had misgauged the Russian mood; one of the reasons for the Revolution—perhaps its strongest immediate cause—was the people's weariness with war-making. The masses wished the endless recruiting of their young men to end; the soldiers wanted to go back to their fields and villages. And a prime appeal of the Bolshevik government, even before its overthrow of the Kerensky regime, was in the propaganda it infiltrated among the people and troops, to the effect that the war was but an imperialistic class struggle, and that the doctrine of "No annexations or indemnities" would bring peace. Its demand for immediate peace, the first point in its program, won it wide favor; and probably not too many of the dispossessed multitudes were troubled by the contradiction in Lenin's cry, "Peace to the village huts, war against the palaces." And so there was war against the palaces, including not only the expropriation of private dwellings but revolts in the country, wherein in some cases mobs of peasants destroyed the landowners' houses, farm buildings, farm machinery, and orchards, and even tortured and slew the landowners themselves.

But when the Soviets had taken over power, they set about to make good their promise of peace with the foreign enemy. That they acted in accordance with army sentiment was shown by the tragic fate of General Dukhonin, the commander-in-chief, who had refused to carry out an order to ask the enemy for a cessation of hostilities; he was not only immediately relieved of his command, but shortly afterward was torn to bits by a mob of soldiers. At about the same time, great bodies of troops on the Western front and in the Caucasus were unceremoniously leaving for home. And the new rulers of Russia were but the spokesmen of the general will when, in the face of Allied protests, they treated for an early peace.

How profound was the desire for peace, and how willing the people to sacrifice almost anything for this end, is shown by the fact that the Russians (despite their slogan of "no annexations or indemnities") were ready to sign the savagely severe treaty of Brest-Litovsk, by which they ceded nearly a quarter of their European territory and more than a third of their population. It may be argued that Russia, powerless and with its armies dissolved, had no choice but to accede; but on the other hand the country had let itself become powerless, and had allowed its armies to dissolve, largely because it lacked the will to fight even to maintain its own integrity.

Chapter 30

The Twenty-One Years' Armistice

"After the end of the world war of 1914," writes Winston Churchill, "there was a deep conviction and almost universal hope that peace would reign in the world. This heart's desire of all peoples could easily have been gained by steadfastness in righteous convictions, and by reasonable common sense and prudence." [1] And yet, as we all know, mankind plunged again into Inferno, even though, as Churchill further declares, "There can hardly ever have been a war easier to prevent than this second Armageddon." Why then was this conflict, with its matchless misfortunes, permitted to engulf an unwilling race?

The answer to this question might fill volumes. Nevertheless, there are a few well-defined causes, mostly centering about war-bred emotions and post-war attitudes of mind. Among these are the following:

(1) *Nationalism.* We have seen that the nineteenth and early twentieth centuries witnessed an enormous expansion of nationalistic sentiment: movements such as Pan-Germanism, Pan-Slavism, etc., were the order of the day; the cleavages between peoples became more sharply accentuated on the basis of nation and race. Although this had been a leading element behind the First World War, this was not taken into account in the Treaty of Versailles; the right of "national self-determination" was acknowledged by the creation of new national units, such as Czechoslovakia, Poland, Hungary, and Yugoslavia, most of which have since become foci of world peril, and the first two of which were among the immediate root-sources of World War II. It was not recognized that the emotions of nationality, being narrow and exclusive, are by their very nature opposed to that spirit of world cooperation without which there can be no lasting peace. Moreover, each of the nationalities was fractured by animosities and conflicting groups within itself: the case of Czechoslovakia, said to have been in some ways the most gratifying creation of the Peace Confer-

ence, is an excellent example: several million Sudetens, of German extraction, objected to the rule of the Czech majority, and gave Hitler a pretext for the aggressions that led to the outburst of 1939.

(2) *Economic provincialism.* The effects of nationalistic creeds and divisions would not have been so serious had they not disregarded the economic realities. There had been a time when each small self-governed unit had been economically self-sufficient: when it could grow its own food, weave its own clothes, produce its own fuel, and manufacture the few wares it required. A heritage from that time had been a jealous guarding of economic sovereignty by each small self-governed unit. More recently, however, there had been a revolution in world economy: the vastly increased productivity made possible by power-driven tools, the specializations necessitated by the use of such tools, the enormous expansion in transportation and communication, had produced a state of affairs in which local units had ceased to be self-sufficient, and in which economics had in fact become international, to the extent that most nations depended upon their neighbors if not upon overseas colonies for the maintenance of an essential trade. Under such circumstances, what was imperatively needed was freedom from arbitrary restrictions: customs barriers, barriers of currency and of travel visas, were all ropes that hobbled the feet of the commerce upon which the nations depended for their well-being. Only the most narrowly provincial policy, therefore, could have insisted on the retention of such ropes. But when one had a multitude of political entities, each hell-bent upon its own sovereignty, these economic fundamentals were lost to mind. And the nations, consequently, were crippled by their own national lines, with the result of economic crisis and tension, hardship and poverty within the countries, and strain and friction among them—all of which led toward the breakdown of governments, usurpation, dictatorship, and war.

(3) *Malice and revenge.* It was hardly to be expected that the people of any land, after four years of history's most harrowing war, would be quite in a normal state of mind. Still writhing from their wounds, the victors were almost pathologically eager to lighten their sufferings by placing the blame on someone else's shoulders—and what more natural than that, in accordance with their wartime propaganda, they force the fallen foe to sign a con-

fession of guilt? We have seen that, as a matter of historical fact, the responsibility for the war was divided. Nevertheless, the Peace Conference obliged the prostrate enemy to admit his guilt—an accomplishment of about the moral worth of the confessions more recently made under duress before totalitarian tribunals. And what was the result of this extorted confession? A fierce feeling of injustice, resentment, outraged pride, and a consequent savage desire for retaliation. This emotion was epitomized in an article entitled "Lest We Forget!" in a German newspaper—the German people were promised that they would "again strive to attain that place among the nations of the world to which it is entitled. Then, vengeance for 1919!" [2]

Instead of trying to heal the wounds of war, the official peace-makers went out of their way to rub them with salt. This was conspicuously true on the occasion of the signing of the Treaty: the German delegates were forced to put their signatures to the document of defeat in the very Hall of Mirrors at Versailles wherein Bismarck, in 1871, had proclaimed the new German Empire. A small thing this may seem, but small things touch off vast emotions. It is obvious today that the leaders would have been wiser to have foregone this deed of historical irony, by which they spewed their bitter malice upon the vanquished. Yet it must be remembered that they but acted in accordance with popular sentiment, which demanded a heel clamped down on the neck of the fallen—demanded to see the agonized grimace on his face, and to hear his piteous self-abasing squeaks.

Exceedingly heavy and humiliating were the terms imposed upon the losers—doubtless not so severe as the Germans themselves had clamped down on the Russians at Brest-Litovsk, nor even so heavy as had been envisaged in secret treaties made during the war, yet onerous enough to contain the copious seeds of strife. And perhaps not the most serious part of it all was the loss of territory to Germany, though she was humiliated by being stripped of her colonies, and though Alsace-Lorraine, ceded back to France, continued to be a center of stormy emotions. Probably even graver in their consequences were the provisions regarding reparations—reparations that were left indefinite in amount, but that were to be the maximum possible, in accordance with the principle that Germany must be squeezed "till the pips squeaked." Apparently it was not realized that, in this closely knit world, it is possible to wrench no one part out of joint without affecting all parts. Nor was it foreseen how, through economic distress and propaganda, the door would be flung wide for one of the most terrible dictators in all recorded history.

(4) *Fear*. An outstanding cause of World War I, as we have observed, was the fear that passed like a contagion among the nations. Yet "the war to end war" did not abolish fear. For about fifteen years, the Allies had no cause to be afraid of Germany; but terror did still grip them—terror of German rearmament, terror of communism, terror of possible involvement in a new war. And Germany also was obsessed by dread—dread likewise of communism, dread of economic ruin, dread of the power of Allied arms, dread of being unable to resume her proper place among the nations. Fear, always ready to focus itself on any roving object, was utilized with sinister purpose by the Nazis in the form of anti-Semitism—the Jews being represented as the incarnation of all evil forces opposed to the German people, and so being used to bind the trembling, superstitious rabble together beneath the swastika. Fear of war in the Far East was behind the refusal of the British to accept the bidding of the American Secretary of State to prompt action when the Japanese began their long series of aggressions by occupying Mukden in Manchuria in September, 1931. And fear underlay the incredible weakness of the Allies and the League of Nations when Hitler took the successive steps of resigning from the League, of tearing up the Treaty of Versailles and announcing first aerial and then general rearmament, and of sending an armed force into the demilitarized area beyond the Rhine.

Fear again—a shrinking, chattering timidity—was one of the cornerstones of the League's refusal to impose effective sanctions upon Italy in her brutal invasion of Ethiopia (general sanctions were, indeed, recommended, but did not include the all-important supplies of coal, oil, and gasoline; and the consequent failure all but ruined the prestige and ended the effectiveness of the League). And fear saturated the hypocritical "Non-Intervention" agreements of the Spanish Civil War, whereby England, France, and the United States, faithful to the letter of their contracts, refused shipment of munitions to either side; while Hitler and Mussolini, faithful to nothing but their own designs, poured out aid to the rebel Franco. And fear was the root source of the appeasements of the year or two immediately preceding the war and particularly of the betrayal at Munich, whereby Chamberlain bought his short-lived "peace in our time" at the price of the dismemberment of Czechoslovakia, while Daladier turned his back on treaty obligations and the honor of France along with the security of her small ally.

There were, of course, complicating elements: international bargainings, intrigues, and alliances, economic aims and suasions, anxieties in regard to communism, lack of moral strength, and the realization (in the later dealings) of the relative weakness of the home front. But fundamentally most of the Allied compromises and timidities of the post-war years can be ascribed to one cause: the apprehension of another conflict, and desire to avoid causes of tension. It was, in other words, a great if blind love of peace that misled the Powers onto the paths of war. And not the least monstrous indictment of Hitler and Mussolini is that they deliberately preyed upon this great desire for peace; made of it a central strand in their machinations; used it as a lever for extorting concession after concession, which became the stepping stones to the very war they were designed to prevent.

(5) *Lack of cohesion among the Allies.* It is strange that stress and peril will weld peoples together into firm alliances that dissolve as soon as the tension has snapped. We have observed this after the close of the Second World War; it was also true at the conclusion of the First. Joined in a solid front and with a unity of aim, the victors might have made renewal of the conflict impossible. But there was no solid front, there was little unity of aim from the start. And the first and most glaring defection was that of the United States. This country, the sponsor of the wise and practical project for a peace-preserving League of Nations, deserted the creature of its creation and left the League half-orphaned. This reversal—which, in European eyes, looked dangerously like betrayal—was due to the isolationist psychology, the view that the affairs of Europe were the affairs of Europe alone, the fear of "entangling alliances" and of strife to which League membership would make us a party. At this late date, it is unnecessary to show the tragic error of this belief; the fact is that the belief did exist, that it was widely and sincerely held, and that (when linked to party politics) it resulted in the devitalization of the League at its very hour of birth, and removed the strong arm that might have saved it from eventual futility.

But if America was to provide the most striking element of disunity, there was little approach to oneness among the other Powers. During the months of bickering that preceded the signing of the Treaty of Versailles, wide breaches among the Allies appeared; and the results were compromises, which in no case appear to have furthered world peace. President Wilson, in order to bring the League to birth, felt obliged to yield in regard to some of his celebrated Fourteen Points; Clemenceau was forced to surrender his demand for a Rhine frontier, and took in return a guaranty for an Anglo-American defense of France, a demilitarized zone, and German disarmament—none of which were to be of lasting value, and the first of which never became effective, owing to the refusal of the United States Senate to ratify the treaty.

One must admit that it would have been impossible in any case for the representatives of a large group of nations to see eye to eye on all matters; many adjustments were therefore inevitable. The unfortunate fact is that the principles of the old statecraft, wherein each country considered only its own immediate welfare, often prevailed over questions of world welfare and world safety; the diplomats, trained in the smaller national view, found it difficult to accept the world view, even if they did not look upon the larger aims with a designing cynicism. Thus, in the case of the whole series of peace treaties, secret agreements often stood in the way of broad principles such as those of Wilson's Fourteen Points. And the grabbing propensities of some nations were as evident as if world security had not been at stake. Lloyd George by no means did badly for Britain (considered from the old nationalistic point of view); he obtained most of the German commercial fleet, spheres of influence in various colonies including Palestine, Mesopotamia, and Tanganyika, and a share in reparations payments. Meantime Italy, whose ambitions appear to have been solely territorial, received Trentino, Trieste, and other points; while her acquisitive desires were evident in her demands for Fiume, which she later took by force, and which Yugoslavia had also claimed.

Even after the peace-making snatch-and-scramble, inter-Allied disagreements stood in the way of that unity of action which might have averted a new catastrophe. For example, in January, 1923, a serious crisis arose; the British thought it not unlikely that reparations would wreck the German economic system, and accordingly wished to lighten the load. But Poincaré of France, holding Germany fully able to pay, threatened to march (and actually did march) into the Ruhr, while the Berlin government set the following Sunday aside as a day of mourning. As subsequent events proved, this unilateral action of France was most ill-advised; the bitterness aroused in Germany was to leave another infected spot for the operations of Hitler and the war-makers; the economic dislocations were to heighten the peril by increasing economic distress and consequent mass discontent and desperation; while the havoc-wreaking inflation, which left multitudes dispossessed and permanently disgruntled, has been blamed on a deliberate attempt to counter the reparations payments, and was certainly connected with reparations, whether or not the intention was deliberate.

A similar costly disagreement arose over disarmament. The English believed that safety lay in the direction of general disarmament; the French, though Germany lay helpless before them, maintained that disarmament was not possible until they were secure from German attack. And so the argument wore on throughout the years, with no conclusion ever reached. And meanwhile Germany, ringed about with the Allied wall of steel, was covetous of her own armaments, and was secretly rearming; some of the very forces that led toward the last war were reappearing. This does not mean that there were not bright moments when the nations seemed to be acting in concert: the guarantees of the Locarno Treaty of 1925, in which not only the victors but Germany were included, did for a time shed a promise of peace. And several years earlier the Washington Conference of 1921–22 had achieved a partial success in naval disarmament: it had obtained a ten-year limitation on the building of capital ships, a pronouncement against the use of poison gas in warfare, and a prohibition of submarine attacks upon merchant and passenger ships. But it did not vote a limitation in other types of naval craft, nor the complete outlawry of the use of submarines in warfare, which Great Britain sought and France opposed. Thus most of the agreements that did occur were incomplete—too little, too weak, too much the result of compromise, too largely dependent on national desires and fears, national ambitions, rivalries, and machinations. And strong united action in the face of a mounting danger remained conspicuously lacking.

II

It is one of the ironies of history that Germany, widely but erroneously believed to have been the chief instigator of the First World War, was in fact directly responsible for the Second World War, in part because of the very accusations which overlay her from the earlier struggle.

There were, of course, a multitude of complicating factors; but most of these centered about a single individual, the one-time Austrian corporal, Adolf Hitler. It is beyond the province of any observer to say that, had there been no Hitler, there would have been no war in 1939; some other rabble-rouser might have fanned the flames with equal fury. Nevertheless, it is conceivable—it may even be said to be probable—that, without Hitler, the war would have been avoided.

This singular figure, a strange and pathological complex of animosities, resentments, frenzies, and ambitions, leaped upon the world stage like a being almost inhuman in his arrant disregard of man's normal attachments and feelings, his satanic want of pity, his brutal self-assertiveness, his obsessions and phobias and his lust to tear down and kill, his Mephistophelean weavings and burrowings, his unscrupulousness and shameless political unmorality, and his fanatical racial theories that made him more like the exponent of some remorseless savage religion than like a spokesman of the urbane modern world. When we find all these in a personality warped by an ancient sense of frustration and inferiority, and pulled by powerful strands of ambition and by a craze for power, we have the markings either of a lunatic or of a tyrant, if not of the two in one. And when this distorted creature descends upon a land that shares some of his own sense of frustration, his own passionate hatreds, his flaming prejudices, and his corroding conviction of old wrong, we have the ingredients ready-made for a leader of the monomaniacal type.

Not often in history—fortunately for our poor embattled race—have the social constituents and the psychology of great masses of people been ready for the reception of a Hitler. And not often have the menaced neighbors of such a ruler fed his prestige and power by submitting as did France and England to his successive usurpations. But it was his fate to seize the reins of a sick world, a world unwell physically and mentally as a result of a wrenching four years' conflict, a world still in large part unspeakably war-weary and eager for peace. And because conditions were ripe for his advance, he did not halt until he had brought the temple walls of civilization crashing down about his head.

A multitude of forces smoothed the way for his rise. One of these, as indicated at the opening of this section, was the long-smoldering rage of the Germans at being branded with the guilt of 1914, the sense of inferiority following defeat, and the desire to find a redeemer. Other factors were the social and political un-balance created by the fall of the Hohenzollerns; the relative weak-ness of the democratic regime, and the absence of a strong will to lead a nation trained in obedience; the military attitudes of mind drilled into the masses, the clandestine military activities of nation-alistic groups, and the rise of private armies; the economic discon-tent and suffering springing first from the inflation, and, later, from the worldwide depression of 1929, which threw multitudes out of work in Germany as elsewhere; the deliberate collaboration of great industrialists, who saw in the Nazis a means of combating communism, suppressing labor, and reinforcing their own power; and—not least nor least shameful—the pressure imposed upon for-eign governments by their own capitalistic elements, who thought they could do business with Hitler and exerted their influence lest the dictator and his allies be handled too roughly.

Beyond and above and underlying all these forces, there were the perverted racialism and nationalism which engulfed all things as in a dense, ill-smelling fog, and which were consciously deep-ened by Nazi propaganda. Here essentially was nothing new; we have seen how scientifically untenable race-ideas had disturbed the closing decades of the nineteenth and early years of the twentieth century; and how nationalism in all its narrowness, pride, arro-gance, and combativeness had been expanding ever since the French Revolution. The post-war racialism and nationalism of Germany therefore had a long ancestry; but it was racialism and nationalism of a frustrated and hence a peculiarly contracted and acrid nature, which would go even to greater extremes than of old in its efforts at self-vindication and self-glorification. Hence the cult arose of a Germany whose god, acknowledged or unacknowl-edged, was not Jehovah but Wotan, whose prophet and leader was not Christ but Loki. And this Germany was ready to listen open-mouthed to the preachments of Hitler, who gave millions that feeling of superiority which they lacked, and aroused that intolerant and ferocious pride which belongs more to trampling warrior castes than to members of a settled civilized community.

If none but Hitler had been ready to accept the ravings of *Mein Kampf*, that famous volume would have suffered the fate of many another offering of the "lunatic fringe." But he stated only what multitudes believed or wanted to believe. When he proclaimed that man is a fighting animal; that only by battle can an individual or a nation survive; that the superlative qualities of a people are shown only by its abilities in combat, and that those abilities are impaired by "impure" foreign elements such as the Jewish—when he mouthed these and various other fantasies, Hitler was speaking for a vast number who saw in his bombast a saving philosophy. But it was impossible for a vast number to accept such a creed without bringing the world nearer to war. This was implicit in *Mein Kampf*, and in most of Hitler's blusterings. If the rest of the world did not take these fumings seriously, that was because they represented a state of mind alien to most of mankind—so alien that it could not be credited without demonstration in action. And when such demonstration came, the world was already in flames.

We know of course that Hitler's views alone, even aided by an organized campaign of falsification and propaganda, were not enough to bring him to world power. In addition, there were the gangster methods by which he and his henchmen clubbed opponents into silence; there was the ruffianism which, aimed at the Jews, provided a means of uniting the anti-Semites in organized bands; there was the political trickery, the crimes such as the burning of the Reichstag building and the liquidations of intellectuals and anti-Nazis; there was the "blood purge" of 1934, by which an unknown number of Hitler's collaborators were unofficially put out of the way; there were the various other repressions, suppressions, and oppressions common to totalitarian regimes, from the burning of the books to the concentration camps provided for holders of inconvenient views and bearers of un-Nordic blood; and there were, as we have noted, the helping hands of watering-mouthed but myopic capitalists at home and abroad. And, of course, there was the fact that Hitler did temporarily solve the unemployment problem—by putting the people to work making the munitions that were to seal their doom.

Beyond this, Hitlerianism was aided by the allies which the Fuehrer was able to find abroad. The first and most notorious was, of course, Mussolini, the one-time Socialist, the "sawdust Caesar," a leader in some ways remarkably like Hitler, in other ways dissimilar: like him in his unscrupulousness, his brutality, his craze for power, his treacherous statesmanship, his repression of political and personal freedom, his rise on the crest of a wave of social discontent; unlike him in acting through cold Machiavellian design rather than in the heat of fanaticism. Not their least important point of resemblance was in their belief in the strong arm; the Italian leader has been quoted as proclaiming, in words which almost echo the Nazi chieftain, that only in war can a people's energies be brought to their highest pitch, only in war can a people find nobility. Certainly, his actions do indicate faith in this creed: the military regime which he introduced, with its parading and armored Black Shirts, bears evidence that his ideal was Rome if not Sparta. Nevertheless, one cannot see anything very noble about the wars waged by Mussolini: the Ethiopian aggression, by which he dropped air bombs and spewed poison gas among Haile Selassie's defenseless subjects; the Spanish Civil War, into which he injected himself without the pretense of an excuse and fought under the protecting robe of "non-intervention"; the Albanian scuffle, in which he jumped upon a small brother who happened to be on his road to Greece; and the Second World War, which he entered, when victory seemed assured, by dealing France the famous "stab in the back."

In any case, Mussolini was like an extra if subsidiary arm to the Nazis; the Rome-Berlin Axis, marked by occasional Hitler-Mussolini conferences that sent shudders through Allied capitals, was one of the outstanding facts of pre-war diplomacy, and gave the Fuehrer added strength and reassurance.

Another ally was Japan, although she did not join the Rome-Berlin Axis until after the start of World War II. But as early as November, 1936, she did enter into an anti-Comintern pact with Germany; and her associations with the Axis, as we learned to our sorrow, were to be of vital importance. Her government, moreover, had many repressive features in common with Germany and Italy; her young men were subject to conscription, she was in the control of military cliques with points of close kinship to the Nazis and Fascists, and she had for years been feeding the military spirit

by her aggressions in China. Added to this, she had received a long
series of psychological excitations, which wounded her pride, irri-
tated her in her sense of inferiority, and made her feel the need
for self-vindication. The discriminatory American land laws had
been one such factor; the abrogation of the treaty with England
may have been even more decisive:

The United States made it clear to Britain that the continuance of
her alliance with Japan, to which the Japanese had punctiliously
conformed, would constitute a barrier in Anglo-American relations. Accordingly, this alliance was brought to an end. The an-
nulment caused a profound impression in Japan, and was viewed
as the spurning of an Asiatic Power by the Western World. Many
links were sundered which might afterwards have proved of decisive value to peace.[3]

While commentators still speak of "the riddle of Moscow," and
while we cannot pretend to have unraveled every strand of the
complex web, it is evident that a varied psychological meshwork
underlay the Russo-German non-aggression pact of August, 1939,
which removed the last great barrier to the war. During the preceding months, England had been seeking a Russian alliance, which
might have stayed Hitler's hand; and it may have been in large
part England's own responsibility that Ribbentrop stole the deal.
Less than a year before, at the Munich conference, Russia had been
ignored—and yet she had had an alliance obliging her to come to
Czechoslovakia's aid if France did likewise. To the Russian leaders
(whether or not they would have kept their word) the imputation
in Chamberlain's and Daladier's methods must have seemed insult-
ing; and we actually have the statement of Marshal Voroshilov,
given to the head of the French mission to Moscow, that Russia
was but waiting for a signal from France at the time that Czechoslovakia was being sacrificed—a signal that never came. This assertion is confirmed by the testimony of the Nuremberg papers:

Certain points stand out clearly from the story as told by the Nazi
documents. The Munich Conference appears as the true turning
point. Having been excluded from it the Soviet Union . . . concluded that she could not rely on concerted action with the western democracies in case of an armed conflict with Germany.
Driven into political isolation, Stalin apparently decided that, in
self-protection, the Soviet Union must sup with the devil.[4]

By 1939, in view of the loss of the Czechoslovakian forces and fortresses, the increases in Hitler's army and his possession of the Skoda munitions works, the strategic situation had been transformed. One would have thought, therefore, that with the tide turned against them and with a life-or-death necessity of enlisting Stalin on their side, the British would have put all efforts into obtaining the Moscow agreement, and would have sent no less than a first-rank emissary. Instead, rejecting the offer of Anthony Eden to serve, Prime Minister Chamberlain picked a minor official, Strang, almost as if to show that he regarded the negotiations as of secondary importance. Perhaps they were; perhaps the game was already lost; but if there was still a fighting chance, Chamberlain made little effort to utilize it.

This is not to excuse the Stalin-Hitler agreement, which was so conscienceless and coolly designing an about-face on the part of both dictators as almost to set a new low even in diplomacy. But it is important to try to understand the psychological forces behind the deal. And we should recognize that plain miscalculation apparently had much to do with the treaty, not only on Hitler's part but on Stalin's.

"We formed the impression," Churchill quotes the Russian leader as confiding during an interview at the Kremlin in August, 1942, "that the British and French Governments were not resolved to go to war if Poland were attacked, but that they hoped the diplomatic line-up of Britain, France and Russia would deter Hitler. We were sure it would not." [5]

A provoking question presents itself as to Stalin's impression that France and Britain would not go to war if Poland were attacked. Had he foreseen that they would fight and so bring on a general conflict in which there was peril of Russia's involvement, would he have signed the non-aggression pact with Germany? We know that, had he not done so, events in Poland might have taken an altogether different course. Upon such a straw the destiny of nations may rest.

It seems that there was also a false estimate in Hitler's mind. After the shrinking timidity displayed by France and England when Hitler announced his rearmament program, when he reoccupied the Rhineland, when he seized Austria, when he grabbed the Sudetenland, and when he intervened in Spain, it was only natural that the Fuehrer should conclude that the Allies would not fight over Poland, particularly as the region was militarily inaccessible. Why should anyone suppose that France and England, having lost many opportunities to be firm when the power lay in their hands, would grit their teeth at the very time when their resolution would only involve them in insoluble difficulties? What Hitler did not realize was that they had been played with and goaded until, out of sheer self-respect as well as regard for their own safety, they could endure no more.

Would he have fought even if he had correctly appraised their attitude? Judging from the way in which he drew in his horns on the few occasions when he met any foreign opposition—the way, for example, in which, just before Munich, he agreed to a discussion after all attempts at negotiation seemed over and the French had called an additional half million reserves to the colors—it seems at least possible that this swaggering bully would have turned tail as most bullies do before a show of force. On the other hand, we have his own word as to his designs. The following is from a speech he made at a secret meeting of the commanders-in-chief shortly after the end of the Polish campaign:

One might accuse me of wanting to fight and fight again. In struggle I see the fate of all beings. I did not organize the armed forces in order not to strike. The decision to strike was always in me. Time is working for our adversary. I shall strike and not capitulate![6]

Equally revealing is the directive issued by General Blomberg, German minister of war, on June 24, 1937. Among other things, he urged "continuous preparation for war" in order "to enable the military exploitation of politically favorable opportunities should they occur." [7] Evidently it was such a "military exploitation of politically favorable opportunities" that Hitler had in mind when on August 23, 1939, he addressed the commanders-in-chief at Berchtesgaden:

Now Poland is in the position in which I want her. . . . I am only afraid that at the last minute some *Schweinhund* will make a proposal for mediation. . . .[8]

When such thoughts dominate the mind of an all-powerful dictator, nothing short of his overthrow or his change of mind or loss of heart can avert war, though this be abhorred by scores of nations and hundreds of millions of men. Unfortunately, he was not overthrown, though there were conspiracies against him, including, it has been reported, a plot of generals at the time of the Czechoslovakian crisis. Far from being hurled down, he was waxing bolder, more arrogant with each triumph of his bludgeoning diplomacy. If war had not come over the Polish issue, and if he had remained in power, war would still have broken out—he would still have forced it upon the reluctant democracies. With a different leader in Germany, and a different state of mind in his followers and supporters, there would have been, there could have been no war. But to produce a different leader in Germany and a different state of mind, much of the history of a hundred, a hundred and fifty, or even two hundred years would have had to be different; we would have had to see the development of other doctrines, emotions, and psychological attitudes than those that made the Germany of Hitler a pathological phenomenon and a world peril.

Chapter 31

The Second World War:
Moods and Weapons

An observer from another age or civilization, unacquainted with our institutions or history, would be bewildered by the bare surface facts of the Second World War. What was it all about? Why all these wide-flung and apparently unrelated struggles? Why should men from Honshu be battling with men from Birmingham in the jungles of Malaya, and citizens of Chicago be exchanging shots with citizens of Hanover among the deserts of North Africa, and British Tommies be dying in Greece, and Germans perishing before the gates of Stalingrad, and Americans giving their lives at Okinawa and Guadalcanal? What was the pattern, what the plan behind this orgy of death and destructiveness that raged from New Guinea to North Africa, from Norway to the Aleutians, from France and Sicily to Japan and the Philippines? And why these air raids on widely scattered points, from Hamburg to Pearl Harbor, and from London to Rotterdam, Belgrade, Warsaw, Berlin, and Tokyo? And why were so many Powers involved? Why did the nations of every continent but one mobilize for active participation in the most truly global war ever known?

It is safe to say that, to a witness possessed only of the surface facts, the war would be an insoluble mystery. Was it waged for political ends? But it caused political disintegration, political overturns in many of the nations; and political power and predominance were forfeited by the very countries that had most to do with bringing it about. Was it fought for economic objectives? But the cost was economic waste or ruin to most of the earth—the gains could not have been a pittance compared with the losses. Was it a deliberate means of ridding the world of surplus population? In that case no more brutal or inefficient method could have been conceived, for when the massacre was not merely indiscriminate it sacrificed the young and able while sparing the diseased and infirm. No matter which way the onlooker turned for a reasonable explanation, he would be balked; there is no reasonable explanation.

In order to understand the war, he would have to look far into history—far beyond those cliques of scheming politicians who set off the fuse. For they touched a spark to a pile of explosives that they did not wholly create—a pile growing throughout the centuries. To find more basic reasons, the observer would have to peer into the mind of a hundred warring generations, and the code of slaughter and destruction they had formulated and strengthened. He would have to revive the raiding traditions of small bands and tribes and of great nations; to follow blood feuds and vengeance trails; to note the flesh-red war gods that have ruled in the religions of many lands; to scrutinize the sword-thrusting or lance-swinging knight, whose glamorous example led long lines of youths forth on the track of glory. He would have to take account of the praises of battle, the songs and stories, the sagas and epics that surrounded war with a golden nimbus and kept its spirit alive from age to age, until it had become so much a part of life that men assumed that it had to be, that it always had been, and always would be—and so made little effort to strike the rod of power from the bearers of the ancient scourge.

Likewise, the observer would have to remark the docility of the masses—their pliability beneath the thumb of unscrupulous leaders, their credulity that made them believe almost anything poured into their ears. He would have to witness how greed, the love of adventure, and the desire for renown, were all complicating factors; how the encouragement and acclaim of the women were additional incentives; how hatred, often artificially cultivated against neighbors and rivals, seethed side by side with suspicion and envy and misunderstanding and the vengeance-lust; how pride was often a goad to the conflict, and fear of disgrace a hidden spur, and ambition an evil councilor. He would have to be particularly aware of the widening scope and influence of war with the growth of civilization; and its increasing mechanization, so that it was more hopelessly beyond individual control than ever in the past. And he would have to measure the increase of armies and navies, the rise of air fleets, the multiplication of scientific weapons, the accumulation of armaments, the fattening of whole groups of men and whole strata of society upon the war-making, while Mars became a great vested interest, the source of livelihood and profits to non-combatant multitudes.

All this the observer would have to weigh and consider, along with every other spur to that psychological preparedness for war which is more important than physical readiness. Otherwise, he would remain unable to comprehend how in the second third of the twentieth century, in an era of unparalleled scientific and material progress, man had permitted himself to be engulfed in the most wide-ranging, the most insensate, the most remorselessly cruel, the most sanguinary, the most devastating, and probably the most enduringly costly war of all time.

II

The great war was the climax, the culmination of three thousand years. It was also the *reductio ad absurdum* of all the means, methods, and aims of war-making; it left all the combatants so much poorer, it turned so much of the world into a ruin and created such far-reaching and well-nigh insoluble problems that it offered history's most decisive proof that war is a monstrous futility, that war itself is the chief enemy to be overcome.

Throughout the millennia, fighting man had developed some restraints. These are manifest, as we have seen, among many so-called savages, whose encounters are conducted in the manner of games; they are likewise evident in early India and Greece, in the chivalry of medieval times, in the battles of the *condottieri* and other mercenaries, and in the typical relatively unsanguinary struggle of pre-Napoleonic days. But, with the French Revolution, restraints on bloodshed were thrown to the winds: we have noted the bloody bayonet charges; the command of Robespierre to give no quarter to the British and Hanoverians; the execution of General Houchard for trying to negotiate an exchange of prisoners. In the Napoleonic era, we find the continuation and spread of the unchecked gory warfare of the Revolution. And this is the warfare that was bequeathed to the twentieth century. Nor were the facts altered by declarations in favor of restraint: the Second Hague Conference, for example, produced agreements for the limitation of floating mines, live torpedoes, the dropping of aerial bombs, the bombardment of undefended places, and the use of poison gas; but these restrictions were disregarded in practice, though they did represent a widespread sentiment. The truth is that, even in the face of general outcries against outrages such as the German violation of Belgium and the sinking of the *Lusitania*, World War I produced no noticeable deterrent whatever to any inhumanity that the leaders supposed to be of military value.

And the same is true of World War II, except that chemical warfare was not employed as had been predicted; cities were not depopulated by means of phosgene gas or even more dreadful new reagents. But this apparent humanity may be explained by the dread of an unspeakably terrible retaliation. Aside from this one limitation, there was no clear restriction at all on the arm of death and destruction. And this, for two reasons, made the Second World War unique for ruthlessness: first, because scientific progress, culminating in the V-weapons and the still more revolutionary atom bombs, had taken Gargantuan strides beyond 1918; and, secondly, because the idea of "total war" had ripened, because the distinction between combatant and civilian had been obscured, and because the doctrine had arisen that a war was not only a contest of armies and navies but a struggle of peoples, in which the rosy prattler in the nursery and the grandame sewing by the fire were as legitimate targets as the armed man flinging a grenade. An equally savage creed may have been held by some Vikings and Indian avengers, some commanders of the early Near East and the more ferocious of the Romans, no less than by the Huns and Mongols who heaped their slain throughout Europe and Asia; it was something different, however, for this view to be exalted into a world code-of-war by the bearers of the very flower of man's culture. And the situation became a thousand times more serious since the weapons were not knives and spears, war clubs and arrows, but the most efficient and ingenious engines for mass murder that a perverted, fantastically capable science had been able to contrive.

It is unlikely that the untutored horse-warriors of Attila or Genghis Khan, had they had the advantages of blockbusters or atom bombs, would have scrupled to use such devices. But it was the world's salvation that these raiders, fearful as they were, enjoyed only comparatively rude weapons. In the Second World War, however, we had the spirit of the Mongol tribesman, and in addition the miraculously effective new tools of annihilation—in other words, the mood and the social morality of the barbarian governing the products of science.

No more anachronistic or disastrous combination was possible; it was as if a mind from some primeval age controlled the throttle of the twentieth century. What we needed above all else, while science expanded its wizard accomplishments, was a psychology geared to our physical advances; what we achieved was a state of mind and a code of action and principles that descended beneath those of other centuries, that plunged all the way back to the level of the ancient Scythians and the Hiung-nu. We did not realize that it was imperatively necessary that science, having immeasurably widened its boundaries, should be subject to moral control; on the contrary, we subordinated it only to political and military control, in the manner of a barbarian prince whose armorer has forged a cunning new sword. And since the morality of our politicians and militarists is, all in all, the morality of might; since they have been taught to fend for narrow and temporal advantages regardless of the universe as a whole, it was not to be expected that the new discoveries of science would be employed except in the fashion of past gifts such as gunpowder and the breech-loading rifle. In other words, they would be used in any way possible. Their potentialities, however, were inconceivably deadlier than those of earlier weapons; and the unrestrained rule of might had consequences paralleled in no former age.

The state of the world from 1939 to 1945 would, obviously, have been far different if we had had an international tribunal empowered to pass on all scientific inventions before their use in war, and to suppress those adjudged a threat to the race. This is not to suggest that, in the present state of our progress, such a court of last appeal would be practicable; unfortunately, our ideas have not advanced to the point of placing *the* nations above *a* nation, and of recognizing that a phenomenon with the revolutionary world possibilities of science should be controlled by a world authority for the sake of world advancement and safety. Nevertheless, had we had such an authority and tolerated its effective working at the time of the Second World War, some of the worst of the tragedies of that encounter might have been averted, and the most grievous of our post-war perils might not overhang us now.

III

In ruthlessness and the state of mind behind ruthlessness, there had been an evolution. In 1914 an outcry had arisen against the German invasion of Belgium and the reported accompanying atrocities; in 1941, the world was hardened to stories of far more extensive barbarities during the German invasion of Russia. But in the intervening twenty-seven years, the world had received an education in frightfulness. As far as science had made possible, the conflict of 1914–18 had been marked by the use of horror weapons and horror methods: we have noted the unrestricted submarine warfare, the chemical warfare, the "Big Berthas," the air bombardments of populated centers, the maltreatment of conquered populations, the sacrifice of troops to strategic considerations. And the years between 1918 and 1939, instead of counteracting the trend toward remorselessness, had provided a new precedent. The invasion of Manchuria and China by the Japanese, with the bombings of civilian populations; Mussolini's air massacres and gassing of defenseless Ethiopians, wherein a son of Il Duce confessed to have felt an esthetic satisfaction; the German naval bombardment of the unoffending citizens of Almeria during the Spanish Civil War; the machine-gunning by Franco forces of herded masses of workers in the bull-ring at Badajoz; the aerial slaughter of the people of Barcelona, and the carefully planned and systematically executed destruction by the Germans, in June, 1937, of the Basque religious center of Guernica, along with seven thousand of its inhabitants and three thousand refugees—these successive outrages against humanity evoked comparatively little protest, comparatively little indignation, and nothing at all of that universal outcry which might have been expected: "Attacks upon civilians must cease! Attacks upon civilians *must* cease!"

Even though one may doubt the immediate effects of such an appeal, one might have seen in it the token of a spirit that would eventually throttle the menace. In the absence of such a regard for the human fundamentals, one could only have anticipated what actually occurred: the expansion of the assaults, limited only by the power of the assailants and their terror of retaliation. In the ruins of Almeria and Guernica, the observer might have seen the crimsoned rubble of Chungking, Coventry, and London, the thirty thousand dead of Rotterdam, and the devastation of wide once-flourishing districts from Germany and Russia to Korea and Japan.

We need not therefore be amazed if World War II outran the expectations of the pre-war years, when Hitler, Mussolini, Franco, and the Japanese war lords were disporting themselves in their testing fields. We may be shocked, we may turn numb with horror, but we should not be totally surprised to observe the barbed wires of concentration camps enclosing their thousands of emaciated wretches, to behold the forcible transplanting of civilian populations, to see dive-bombers machine-gunning the fleeing peasantry of France, nor to witness the massacre of innocent hostages nor the extermination of the men of Lidice. Nor need we be astonished at the outrages upon innocent Norway, nor at the barbarities perpetrated in Russia, which according to all accounts were atrociously severe, nor at testimony such as that of General Holder in the Nuremberg documents, to the effect that since Russia had not signed the Hague Convention, Hitler decided that Russian prisoners of war need not be treated in accordance with the Articles of the Convention.

Once a nation begins to discard the restraints of humanity, there is no telling where it may stop. Once it has said, "Human feelings and human lives do not matter; there is no right but of the strong, and no law but of the striking arm"—then the last bulwark to sane and humane conduct has been toppled, and there is only the gulf beneath. Into such a gulf Rome tumbled in her bloodthirsty assaults upon Carthage and Jerusalem, in her slave raids and her gladiatorial butcheries; into such a gulf the Mongol raiders fell; into such a gulf the Spanish Inquisitors descended when fanaticism lit the fires of the *auto-da-fé*. But the Germans in World War II, having freed themselves from the minimum considerations of humanity, plunged into the deepest pit of all—the pit of the blackest crime and disgrace that ever made a reproach of the name of "man."

It may not be without significance that, having perpetrated this greatest of historical atrocities, the Germans should have given us a new word (one officially recognized by the United Nations), the word "genocide." In their bestially cold-blooded consignment of millions of men, women, and children to the gas chambers and the furnaces for the offense of having come of Jewish stock, the executioners showed to what hitherto unsuspected extremes men may go beneath the pressure of a war-induced philosophy of callousness and expediency, the fanaticism of nationalistic aspirations and racial theories, the contagion of example, and the oxlike submissiveness and passivity of military control. It is futile to blame this particular crime exclusively upon Hitler and his small personal circle, deep-dyed with guilt though they were. The testimony of manufacturers who supplied poison gas knowing it would be used for purposes of murder, indicate a want of moral capacity almost equal to the Fuehrer's; [1] while the stories of the "Extermination Camps" and their incredible brutalities show that there were many little Hitlers. If the Nazi leader had not found thousands to carry out his orders, those orders would have died still-born; and if the thousands had not to some extent shared his prejudices and passions, or had not been shaped by a discipline that commanded, "Obey always, and question never!," then the slaughtering hands would not have been smeared with innocent blood. But the wartime atmosphere, the wartime reckless squandering of life, the wartime disregard of humanity and the overthrow of the moral safeguards distinguishing men from mad wolves, made it possible for the most fiendish deed of all time to be perpetrated not by one man or one small group but by a host of seemingly willing collaborators.

And this evokes a dread question: if such a heinous act of execution could be accomplished against a whole people, at what step short of the deliberate annihilation of all peoples could we expect the leaders of the nations to halt if driven into a corner and guided only by the expediency, the explosive passions, and the anti-human principles of a Hitler?

IV

This question takes on special point in view of the weapons developed toward the close of the war. An indication of the new attitude was to be seen in the bomb-carrying Japanese balloons, which were blown on the trade winds across the Pacific to the American mainland; these accomplished little, aside from killing a few children, but they did show the direction in which combat was moving. They proved once more, if proof was necessary, that warfare was degenerating from the clash of armed forces into indiscriminate assaults upon non-combatants.

Far more potent were the German V-weapons, rocket missiles that introduced a new principle into warfare. In particular the V-2, which could hurtle across scores of miles at a speed outstripping sound and strike before it was either seen or heard, was indicative of the new era—and the new outlook. It was impossible to claim, as in the case of so-called precision bombing, that this projectile was aimed at military installations and targets. The fact was that it could not be aimed at all with any pretense to accuracy; it could only be discharged in a general direction, allowing chance to decide whether it struck an encampment of soldiers, a group of school-children, worshippers in a church, nurses in a hospital, storekeepers in their shops, housewives in their kitchens, or vacant parks or lots. On the laws of probability, however, it could be expected to strike many more non-military than military targets.

Hence it marked a new step in the battle against civilians. It made recognition, more sharply than even the air raids had done, that modern warfare knew no principle except to murder and destroy, and that it cared little what it destroyed or murdered. It was saying, in effect, "Nothing is sacred, nothing is worthy of respect, nothing deserves to be spared." It represented the intro-duction of chaos, of nihilism into human affairs; it illustrated the negation of everything for which man had been painfully striving through all his centuries. It not only reversed the trend of what we had mistaken for progress; it put us on a plane beneath the abo-rigine sneaking through ambush to clip off enemy heads—the Dyak or Jibaro, at least, could see *whose* head he was taking. But it indicated something even more portentous than a plunge into savagery; it implied the failure of man as a moral being, his defeat before the problems of existence on earth. It suggested the dissolu-tion of all the principles and purposes by which alone man can maintain his civilization—the relapse into spiritual and cultural anarchy.

The V-weapons pointed the way; they were ominous enough to justify the grimmest forebodings even if a still more terrible weapon had not been in store. But such a weapon was being pre-pared, though still presaged only in the secret whisperings of scien-tists and the imaginings of science-fiction writers. Those of us who look back to the morning of August 6, 1945, can still remember the stunned feeling with which we learned that a bomb of unprece-dented power had fallen upon Hiroshima, wiping out the heart of the city. As the dread details impressed themselves upon us, and as we realized that thousands of lives had been snuffed out in the fraction of a second while a radioactive threat to countless other lives had been spewed among the ruins, we had the feeling of living on some strange and fantastic planet, in which bizarre and unhuman things were happening. And that feeling, even after the passage of years, has not wholly left us. For on that August day of 1945, we bade farewell once and for all to the past. It may be that the historian of a later age (if any historians remain to later ages) will be able to say whether the introduction of atomic warfare represented a greater turning point than the discovery of the use of metals or the invention of gunpowder; but it is hardly open to question that all commentators will list it among the epoch-making innovations.

But the recorder will be interested in the atom bomb not only for what it tells him of twentieth-century warfare; he will find it equally important for what it says of the twentieth-century mind. He will hold certain facts to be indubitable, not the least of these being that, while the release of atomic power represented a transcendent scientific achievement, that power might have been developed as a treasure for peaceful industrial use. In the fact that it was not immediately so developed, the historian will see something perverse; he will note a preoccupation with the ends of war, a predisposition to destroy rather than build, a domination of science by politics, and a misconception of the place of science in a free society. He may be inclined to ask why the scientists, with their clever minds, permitted themselves to become docile tools of the State; and why the leaders of the State, in control of the miraculous potentialities of the atom, did not take the long-range view and consider the bomb's beneficent effects. The historian will in all probability question the necessity for making the bomb in the first place, and for using it in the second place; he will admit the power of the fear that the enemy would develop it first, but will deny that fear is excuse enough for creating an instrument of world suicide. And he will claim that, even though the bomb were made, it need not have been hurled at living cities; the war was in any event won; and if the missile had to be thrown, a demonstration in some desert spot, before official observers, would have been sufficiently impressive.

Why, then, were Hiroshima and Nagasaki seared by the atom?

Because the atmosphere of the times favored all available means of destruction; because the current passions and the current morality, the idea of "all-out war" and the precedent of air and naval bombardments and of the V-weapons, made the discharge of atomic explosives a logical outgrowth. But the latter-day historian, by way of commenting on our wisdom, need only remind his readers that within a very few years the United States was chilled with fear, general alarms as to our vulnerability to atom attack were being spread, the wide use of subterranean refuges, the transplanting of industry underground, and the dispersion of government offices were being recommended; while not a man could think of our vast uranium-fission projects without knowing that civilization and the human race itself faced a menace such as it had never in all its generations encountered from wild beast, tornado, disease germ, avalanche, earthquake, fire, flood, or volcanic eruption.

Chapter 32

The Second World War: Russia, Japan, and America

In May, 1940, when the German *blitzkrieg* was rumbling on its way; when Belgium had fallen and France was following and the English were facing the supreme trial of Dunkirk, it would have taken a bold prophet to foretell that within five years the conquering armies would have been swept away, that Hitler would be dead and the Nazi power broken. This transformation, unforeseeable and almost unimaginable in 1940, was to be made possible by the participation of two great Powers not originally embroiled: Soviet Russia and the United States.

But by what process were these nations involved?

In the case of Russia, we find the preliminary of an alliance that flew in the face of years of inflammatory preachments in both countries—preachments aimed to develop fear and hatred in the populace, and featured by screams respectively as to the "Bolshevik menace" and "Fascist peril." After the waging of such a war of propaganda, any union of the two nations for years to come would rest upon an unsound psychological basis. For political reasons they might work together at the top levels; but when such reasons ceased to apply, they might fall upon one another with fang and claw.

All the evidence indicates that it was by Hitler's direct will that the Russo-German alliance ceased to be. Winston Churchill, who as Prime Minister of England had unusual access to sources of information, expresses the general view:

To do him justice, Stalin tried his very best to work loyally and faithfully with Hitler, while at the same time gathering all the strength he could in the enormous mass of Soviet Russia. He and Molotov sent their dutiful congratulations on every German victory. They poured a heavy flow of food and essential raw materials into the Reich. Their Fifth Column Communists did what they could to disturb our factories. Their radio diffused its abuse and slanders against us. They were at any time ready to reach a permanent settlement with Nazi Germany upon the numerous important questions open between them. . . .[1]

Nevertheless, Russia was resolved to look out for her own. How else explain the fact that one third of the Soviet budget, according to an announcement of February, 1941, was being applied for so-called purposes of defense? How account for the rise which this represented of twenty-four per cent above the previous year? While Stalin evidently had no prevision of the impending attack and was deaf to attempted warnings, it was apparent that he distrusted the situation in general. Since he could not anticipate an onslaught from embattled England or fallen France or isolated America and could hardly have needed all his extensive preparations against remote Japan, of whom in particular could he have been thinking?

The fact is that two thugs may join in a housebreaking job; but that does not mean that either will scruple to thrust his blade into the other's back. And the two great totalitarian nations, neither with any recognizable moral principles, were casting eyes on the knife-hilt even while they linked arms in comradeship.

Whatever may have been true of Stalin, Hitler's attitude toward Russia had evidently not changed despite the non-aggression pact of 1939 and the new treaty of friendship and extension of the trade agreement signed on January 10, 1941. The Fuehrer might purr like a cat; but his nostrils were scenting prey, and his sheathed claws were ready to strike. That seething, distorted mind of his, with its limitless capacity for hatred, had not relaxed in its enmity toward Russia; nor had he seemingly forgotten the thesis, stated in *Mein Kampf*, that German destiny lay eastward at the expense of the Russians—the thesis elaborated in 1936 before a party Congress in Nuremberg:

If the Urals, with their immeasurable treasure of raw materials, Siberia with its rich forests, and the Ukraine, with its limitless grain fields, were to lie in Germany, this country under National Socialist leadership would swim in plenty.[2]

We know that even while Hitler was negotiating new treaties of friendship with Russia, this master of duplicity was planning the death-blow. According to Churchill,[3] a directive of December

18 had fixed May 15 as the date of the Russian invasion; the stroke, however, was delayed for more than a month by the revolution in Belgrade. And meanwhile a hundred and twenty crack German divisions were ranging themselves along the Russian front. That Stalin was blind to the obvious is no credit to his intelligence service or his intelligence; but that Hitler could make his gigantic invasion preparations, while blandly reaching out the hand of friendship, is another evidence of the type of mind and morality he brought to the leadership of Germany. It is strange, when one reflects upon it, how large a part sheer stupidity plays in tripping up those super-clever men who are above ethical considerations and moral restraints: in Stalin's case, an exceptional obtuseness forbade him to see that he was taking a boa constrictor into his arms; in Hitler's case, an even greater obtuseness prevented him from realizing that he was attacking a huge formless monster that he could bleed but could not conquer. Grave though the Russian's error in not recognizing the deadliness of his new friend, the German's mistake in underestimating his intended victim was more serious yet, and led to his eventual downfall.

But the double miscalculation proved most costly of all to the people of Germany and Russia. For it led them into one of the most sanguinary wars of all history—a war which, aside from its accomplishment in helping to overthrow the Nazi regime, was among the most needlessly wasteful ever waged. It may be that Stalin, even if he had foreseen what lay in store, could not have averted the blow, though he might have eased its force; but it is certain that Hitler, by his own decision, could have avoided the struggle. As clearly as in any case known to history, this was a war that was fought because a single man or a small group of men willed that it be fought.

II

The situation in regard to the American entry was somewhat less simple. And yet, to the casual observer, nothing would seem easier to explain. "The Japanese war lords," the witness would say, "were filled with envy and hatred of the United States, and with greed for territory; and taking advantage of our unreadiness and of the negotiations being conducted in Washington, hit us with the 'sneak attack' at Pearl Harbor. Hence we had no choice but to declare war; the American people were united by anger at the unjust assault; and Germany and Italy being allies of Japan, we were immediately at war with these also."

The above does, of course, contain elements of truth: the Japanese, by their raid on Pearl Harbor, did arouse an all-but-unanimous war spirit in the United States; and their plan of secret attack without declaration of war, though it had its historical precedents, did place them in an indefensible moral position. But this is not to tell the whole story; it is not even to touch upon the underlying causes of our involvement in the war.

In one sense, the sources go back to the opening up of Japan in the nineteenth century, her adoption of Western ways, her penetration by Western commerce, and her espousal of Western militarism. And for this, with all that it brought of benefit and disaster, the West cannot shrug off the responsibility. Churchill, in reviewing the rise of Japan and the prowess she displayed in her defeat of Czarist Russia, offers a pungent comment:

Japan now took her place among the Great Powers. The Japanese were themselves astonished at the respect with which they were viewed. "When we sent you the beautiful products of our ancient arts and culture you despised and laughed at us; but since we have got a first-class Navy and Army with good weapons we are regarded as a highly civilized nation." [4]

Only a strong army and navy, the Japanese had to conclude, could maintain their respected position. When they spread themselves beyond the reach of their striking arm, as in their emigration to America, they were spat upon, treated as an inferior breed, and denied equality before the law. But when they marched in armed panoply, they were greeted with deference. In view of the world's attitude, was it to be expected that they would neglect their armed forces? And when one remembers that modern Japan was but a stone's throw from feudal Japan, with its *samurai* and its deeply engraven conventions of the sword, one will see that we were but blowing sparks upon heaped-up fuel.

This is not to defend Japanese policies, many of which were highly militaristic and aggressive. But it is well not to lose sight of the background. It is well also not to forget that the provocative acts were often willed by martial factions that happened to have control at the time. Ambassador Grew, in a report of October 8,

1932, makes some pregnant remarks as to the Manchurian situation, which set the example for so much later aggression:

Whatever developments may occur in the future, there will therefore enter into the problem the important element of "saving face," so essential in Oriental countries. Here, I think, is the most dangerous factor in the whole situation. If the fanatical military clique finds that its program is being impeded and is likely to fail . . . it is quite capable of plunging the country into any kind of disaster rather than give in to the saner and more moderate elements. . . . [5]

The danger of dominance by such a "fanatical military clique" did not disappear in the years just preceding Japan's entry into the war. One might therefore suppose that foreign governments would have taken every step to bolster the saner, more moderate groups. Yet it appears that they sometimes took the very moves best calculated to trip the moderates in their tracks.

This was conspicuously true in the case of the Konoye cabinet, which, holding office until October 16, 1941, made an extraordinary effort for peace. The Prime Minister spoke for a large and influential element who sincerely desired to avoid war; even when relations with the United States had seriously degenerated, he persisted in the face of the admitted danger of an assassin's thrust. What he desired most of all was a conference with President Roosevelt, so that the differences between the two countries might be amicably ironed out. He was willing, moreover, to come to Hawaii, Alaska, or any other point designated by the President— and this was to make no small concession:

For a Prime Minister of Japan thus to shatter all precedent and tradition in this land of subservience to precedent and tradition, and to wish to come hat in hand, so to speak, to meet the President of the United States on American soil, is a gauge of the determination of the Government to undo the vast harm already accomplished in alienating our powerful and progressively angry country.[6]

No one will ever be able to say whether a meeting between Konoye and Roosevelt would have spared us the terrors of the Japanese war. But no one can deny that the Western attitude of mind militated against the possibility of such a meeting. Not the least powerful deterrents were the distrust, fear, and antagonism toward Japan that had been growing through the years in American minds—emotions fanned to vigorous fire by the Japanese aggressions in Manchuria, China, and Indo-China. Yet these emotions had preceded the aggressions; decades before Pearl Harbor, there had been talk of an impending, even an "inevitable" struggle with the Mikado's empire. And this idea of inevitability may claim no small part of the discredit in our failure to act in time. This point of view was shared by our Ambassador to Japan, who in December 14, 1940, wrote to Roosevelt:

It seems to me to be increasingly clear that we are bound to have a showdown someday, and the principal question is whether it is to our advantage to have that showdown sooner or to have it later.[7]

I find myself in decided agreement with your conclusions [the President replied, under date of January 21]. I believe that the fundamental proposition is that we must recognize that the hostilities in Europe, in Africa and in Asia are all parts of a single world conflict. We must, consequently, recognize that our interests are menaced both in Europe and in the Far East. . . . Our strategy of self-defense must be a global strategy. . . .[8]

Roosevelt's line of reasoning is not difficult to follow: two Powers, unscrupulous as bandits and with the grasping arms of octopi, had arisen in Europe, and would end by devouring all that was left of the free world unless they were checked. Accordingly, he felt bound to anti-Axis measures that stopped short of war, but not very far short: the granting of lend-lease, the permission to British airmen to train in America, the sending of American marines to Iceland in relief of a British garrison, the arming of merchant vessels, the orders to the fleet to protect merchant ships and attack surface raiders between America and Iceland, the freezing of German and Italian funds, the dismissal of consular staffs, and similar measures. However necessary these steps may have appeared, they plainly brought us nearer to war with Germany and Italy. And if the President assumed, as many persons did at the time, that war with the European Axis Powers was inevitable in any case, and that a conflict with these made war with Japan likewise inevitable, this would explain his failure to negotiate with the Konoye government despite its energetic bids for an agreement.

Aside from this, the movers of American policy may have been no more able to understand the workings of the Japanese mind than were the Japanese to comprehend the intricacies of Occidental psychology. And mutual misunderstanding could have led to mutual disaster, as more than once before in history.

Consider, in any case, the succession of measures by which we trod on sensitive Japanese toes and tightened a noose about the Japanese economy. There was the announcement of July 26, 1939, giving six months' notice of the abrogation of the Japanese-American commercial treaty of 1911; there was the licensing, in July, 1940, of the export of various products, including oil, scrap metal, machine tools, chemicals, and aviation gasoline; there was the embargo, effective on October 16 of the same year, upon the export of scrap iron and steel except to Great Britain and the Western hemisphere; there was the loan to China, the American military mission to China, and the permission to American flyers to fight the Japanese in China as a "volunteer group" under General Chennault; there was the closing of the Panama Canal to Japanese shipping; and there was the freezing, on July 25, 1941, of $130,000,000 of Japanese assets in the United States, with the result that Japanese trade was likewise frozen.

From our point of view, unquestionably, the justification was complete. But our error—and this did not represent the shortcomings of one man or one administration or even of one nation but of the entire Western point of view—was in forgetting psychological issues while emphasizing economic; we had permitted a series of stings and jabs such as no proud and sovereign nation would indefinitely endure. Sheer self-esteem, particularly in the case of a people so susceptible to slight and insult as the Japanese, would not brook a continual repetition of the blows; there would come a point when some stroke, perhaps no more severe than many before it, would evoke violent retaliation.

But the psychological pressures, in the case of Japan, were ominously reinforced by the economic excitations. Take the matter of foreign exchange, as a result of the freezing of Japanese credit by the United States, Great Britain, and the Netherlands East Indies. The following is dated October 9, 1941:

According to information received by a member of my staff from what is regarded as a very reliable source, the amount of foreign exchange available to the Japanese Government now is approximately 20,000 reichmarks and under the circumstances the Japanese Government will be unable to avoid defaulting on contracts calling for foreign exchange on maturity.[9]

Further testimony as to the effect of economic sanctions is offered by Churchill:

Conservative elements were shocked and the moderate leaders scared. The domestic prestige of the Japanese army as a constitutional factor in shaping Japanese policy was already involved. Hitherto the navy had exerted its restraining force. But the embargoes which the United States, Britain and Holland had enforced cut off from Japan all supplies of oil, on which the navy, and indeed the whole war-power of Japan, depended. The Japanese navy was at once forced to live on its oil reserves, and at the outbreak of the Pacific war had in fact consumed four out of eighteen months' supply. It was evident that this was a stranglehold, and that the choice before them was either for Japan to reach an agreement with the United States or go to war.[10]

The facts were expressed by Japanese lips no less than by British and American. Consider the radio message of July 31, 1941, from Foreign Minister Toyoda to Ambassador Nomura (intercepted by the Americans owing to our having broken the Japanese code, and presented in Exhibit I to the Joint Congressional Committee investigating Pearl Harbor):

Commercial and economic relations between Japan and third countries, led by England and the United States, are gradually becoming so horribly strained that we cannot endure it much longer. Consequently, our empire, to save its very life, must take measures to secure the raw materials of the South Seas. Our empire must immediately take steps to break asunder this ever strengthening chain of encirclement which is being woven under the guidance and with the participation of England and the United States, acting like a cunning dragon seemingly asleep. That is why we decided to obtain military bases in French Indo-China and to have our troops occupy that territory.[11]

Toyoda proceeds to acknowledge that the Germans were "somewhat dissatisfied" with Japanese negotiations with the United States, but that "we wish at any cost to prevent the United States from getting into war, and we wish to settle the Chinese incident."

It is true that Japan, owing to her treaties with the Axis Powers and her aggressions in China and elsewhere, did not come into court with clean hands. Nevertheless, since we had secret information of the peaceful desires of her Foreign Minister and secret knowledge that our economic measures were driving the nation toward war, the most that can be said for our policies—as for the policies of England and the Dutch East Indies—is that we were ruled by an overconfidence in our position, or by a fatalistic acceptance of the necessity for fighting, along with an ignorance of the psychological drives at work in Japan.

Doubtless in other ways also our officials misgauged and underestimated their potential enemy. "It had seemed impossible," states Churchill, "that Japan would court destruction by war with Britain and the United States, and probably Russia. A declaration of war by Japan could not be reconciled with reason." [12] But other things than reason rule in human affairs; and manifestly those other things were not sufficiently considered.

We should not forget, however, that Churchill fervently desired the United States to be drawn into war with Japan. For this we have his own reiterated word:

If the United States did not come in, we had no means of defending the Dutch East Indies, or indeed our own empire in the East. If, on the other hand, Japanese aggression drew in America I would be content to have it.[13]

My deepest fear was that the Japanese would attack us or the Dutch, and that constitutional difficulties would prevent the United States from declaring war.[14]

No American will think it wrong of me if I proclaim that to have the United States on our side was to me the greatest joy.[15]

One will not deny that Churchill's wish, charged as he was with the duty of preserving the British Empire, was wholly natural. But one would like to know precisely to what extent he influenced the American attitude. It would have been no more than good orthodox diplomacy had he brought the force of his persuasive personality to attack the idea of a rapprochement with Japan. But whether due to his influence or not, the secret American view—according to his own assertion—had remarkable points of concurrence with his own:

We know that all the great Americans round the President and in his confidence felt, as acutely as I did, the awful danger that Japan would attack British and Dutch possessions in the Far East, and would carefully avoid the United States, and that in consequence Congress would not sanction an American declaration of war.[16]

Churchill did have a persuasive case, based on several huge *ifs: if* Japan proceeded to vast conquests; *if* Germany conquered Russia, *if* England were successfully invaded, then the United States would indeed be isolated against a foe of world dimensions.

Even after the fall of Prince Konoye on October 16, the situation was not hopeless. Although headed by an army man and of a generally less moderate complexion, and although bombarded with such militaristic propaganda that the Foreign Minister risked his life by continuing the negotiations, the Tojo ministry did display a desire to come to terms with the United States. Indeed, Tojo on November 20 and 21 made a new offer, looking toward the eventual withdrawal of Japanese troops from Indo-China, the resumption of trade with the United States, and the settlement of the Chinese question. Possibly these proposals fell far short of what we desired or had a right to expect; but in international diplomacy, unacceptable offerings may often be regarded as handles for further negotiations. In this connection, Grew makes a significant statement:

The belief is current among Japanese leaders that the principal difficulty in the way of an understanding with the United States is the question of the removal of Japanese armed forces from China and Indo-China, but these leaders are confident that, provided that Japan is not placed in an impossible position by the insistence on the part of the United States that all troops in these areas be withdrawn at once, such a removal can and will be successfully effected.[17]

An "impossible position"—whose avoidance would have required great tact and understanding and a strong will for peace—was precisely what we did create. The American reply, presented on November 26, made ten demands: Japan was, among other things, to withdraw militarily from China and Indo-China; she was to support no Chinese government but that of Chiang Kai-shek; and she was to subordinate her Axis arrangements to the new agreement. It would be profitless, at this late date, to try to prove or disprove the contentions of certain commentators that all these conditions might have been met in time if presented in a subtler, gradual way; all that we do know is that they hit the Japanese with shattering impact. Even Churchill, for all his sympathy for the American position, could call the removal of all troops from Indo-China "a rightful but a hard demand." And a prominent Japanese, corresponding with Ambassador Grew, could remark that his friends, with no actual knowledge of the American document, seemed to have concluded that the United States had delivered an ultimatum. This correspondent presented what the Ambassador considered "a fair sample of public opinion in Japan":

Such is the regrettable psychology of our people that in my opinion the only way out at the present time is for the United States to accept as a possible basis for a *modus vivendi* the Japanese proposals and later work out a final agreement in line with the American proposal.[18]

Japanese pride and face-saving, American pride and intransigence, Japanese failure to appraise the American mind, American underestimation of the Japanese resolve—all this, when added to a thousand diplomatic, political, economic, and military urges and counter-urges, spelled out a single word: WAR. That the differences between the nations could have been settled, had there been a clear, long-established atmosphere of reasonableness and good will, is as plain as most things in human relations can be. The cards were on the table; but the players were in no state of mind to pick them up. And as always, when mutual understanding and forbearance are found wanting, the strong arm was ready to intervene. And so on December 1 the leaders of Japan reached their momentous decision. Yet that decision was not wholly made by any small group or at any particular time. It was produced more largely by the events, the tensions, fears, incitements, rivalries, ambitions, and antagonisms of nearly a hundred years, which, mounting to a crescendo, and having no effective mind or hand to check them, finally found an outlet in the flights of dive-bombers that cost the lives of 2,326 American officers and men at Pearl Harbor and sank or damaged a major portion of our Pacific fleet.

Chapter 33

The Balance Sheet

If there is any clear lesson in the warfare of three thousand years, it is that the wider the scope of conflict the less likely the fighters are to attain their objectives. The uncivilized people raiding their neighbor's cattle may indeed capture the cattle (though not without danger of costly reprisals). And the tribesmen embarking on a war of vengeance, may actually take their enemies' heads or scalps (though again the reprisals may be inordinately expensive). But Napoleon, scheming to put most of Europe under his thumb, was adventuring in pursuit of a chimera; and Napoleon's foes, though their coalition held together long enough to smite him to his knees, were unable to make any suitable or lasting response to the cry *Vive la paix!* which dinned through the streets of Paris and through the hearts of most Europeans. With more seeming success, the great Bismarck, in a series of three lightning wars, did achieve his object of unifying Germany—but such are the complications of modern nationalism that the long-run result was a failure that ripped Germany apart. And when we move forward to the World Wars, we find that in so far as the contestants had any clear objectives, the storm mostly swept them into the dust-heap.

In the case of the earlier war, how much that was intended was finally brought to pass? The Central Powers were, indeed, defeated; and flags of victory flew above the capitals of battered France and wounded England. But just what else was accomplished? Austria, which had plotted a limited war in order to put Serbia in her place, saw her empire dismembered; Russia, which had cast oblique glances toward the Straits, had been turned upside down by a revolution; France had indeed regained Alsace-Lorraine, but at an extortionate price in blood and treasure; and the United States— we know now that she had neither made the world "safe for democracy" nor fought a "war to end war." After 1918 the world problems were far more acute than before 1914; democracy in many lands tottered, war threatened ever more menacingly; repressions, usurpations, and mass misery were accompanied by such sword-rattling as Europe had rarely seen; and amid the general commotion the pre-war aims of all countries gradually dissolved in a mist; while even the League of Nations, idealistically designed to redeem the woes of four unspeakable years, was gradually weakened to the point of impotence in the atmosphere of vacillation, timidity, and isolation encouraged by the war itself.

And if this was the aftermath of the First World War, what of the Second? To ask this question is to advance toward the unknown future, which will bring new and probably largely unforeseen developments. Nevertheless, the years since the conclusion of the war have shown on what tide we are moving. They have proved that war has remained true to its heritage: that the greater its scope, the more unlikely it makes the fulfillment of any of its original objectives. Once again, one group of participants achieved "victory"; the prime villains, as in the case of the Napoleonic struggles, were dethroned and deprived of the fruits of their thievery— but what happened to all the announced aims of defending the world from aggressors, safeguarding the rights of smaller nations, and insuring peace? True, we founded the United Nations upon the ruins of the old League of Nations; but at the San Francisco Conference of 1945 we took care that it should rise emasculated, its ability to act limited by the veto power; we denied it an effective striking arm to give force to its decisions; and we imposed the old doctrine of national sovereignty in the way of that international sovereignty that alone could have turned it into a world defensive mechanism.

Not only was an effective peace organization not formed—the very idea of peace did not long survive. Welded together by mutual peril, and by the dire necessity of mutual defense, England and the United States could fight side by side with Russia; differences of ideology could be forgotten, animosities could be thrust aside, suspicions, jealousies, and misunderstandings be buried "for the duration." But as soon as the annealing force of danger was removed, the nations returned to their old-time selves; distrust came back, hatred was revived, arrogance reasserted itself, opposing social philosophies glared across fences, old nationalistic traditions invited arms competition, the thrust and drive of conflicting ambitions threatened new clashes, and the tendency to work together was subordinated to the inclination to work apart. And so we had hardly emerged from the furnace of the hot war before we fell into the ice-bath of the "cold war."

The hostility between Russia and the Western Powers, and particularly between Russia and the United States, is clearly the outstanding fact of the post-war years. This, indeed, is not the first historic case of enmity between former comrades-in-arms; diplomatic revolutions, reversing so-called international friendships, have been fairly common in our mobile modern world. Nevertheless, the about-turn in the relations of Russia and the West is exceptional, if not in its suddenness, at least in its implications. Certainly, nothing was less expected during the years between 1941 and 1945 than that the war would barely have ended before the world would again be divided into two armed camps, each aggressively girding itself as if for combat, each hurling taunts and accusations through the throats of its leaders and from the pages of official organs. It would be impossible, even in the fantasy of a master satirist, to picture a greater *reductio ad absurdum* of our war aims, a more glaring self-stultification of the fighting nations, a clearer proof of war's fatuity and futility, and a more trenchant demonstration that the last way to get what one wishes is by means of modern combat.

But how did the cold war come about? As far as we can piece together the picture, it is a revealing study in international psychology.

II

The origins must be traced back at least as far as the Bolshevik Revolution. This introduced a train of events resulting in enduring new cleavages between Russia and the West.

Not the least of those cleavages centered about the Communist ideology. In a way, this was more than an ideology, more even than a philosophy; like the Jacobin creed of the French Revolution, it was a religion. Like the Jacobin creed, furthermore, it was a fighting, an intolerant, a fanatical religion. "Our Lord God is the Proletarian State, and His Prophet is Karl Marx, and there is none other" was in effect the position of the faithful. But the religion, instead of being theological in the old sense of the term, was economic and political. It was economic in seeking material welfare rather than spiritual consummation; it was political both in its connection with the authoritarian state, and in its idea of the World Revolution through which the infidels (namely, the capitalists) would come into the fold of the true believers. In its outlook and its interpretations it was interested mostly in physical facts; it denied orthodox religion; it accepted Marx's belief in the economic motivation of all human affairs; and its disciples never permitted themselves the heresy of asking how, if the ruling forces in life are economic, it was possible for communism and the communistic state to be erected upon the Marxist framework of ideas.

We have here a combination of dangerous doctrines: an emphasis upon concrete and external fact, to the neglect or obliteration of the inner and idealistic elements in life; a preoccupation with a single stratum of society, in pursuance of the cult of the "class war"; the fighting intolerance of a proselytizing religion; and a concern with economic objectives in a way to arouse all those forces of greed, envy, and combativeness that possession has stimulated throughout the ages. This materialism may have been natural enough considering that the Revolution was, in large part, waged by non-possessors against possessors; the danger consisted first in the fact that the creed was embraced with a zeal that was emotional rather than economic; and, secondly, in the tendency of the Communists to ordain to the rest of mankind, "Ours is the one solution of human affairs. All other peoples must end by doing and thinking as we."

Lenin's original program called for the communization of the world after the benefits of the true faith had come to Russia. Yet Lenin did not endorse the project of Trotsky and Zinoviev for widespread foreign propagandizing. And Stalin, as we know, split sharply with Trotsky, who was driven into exile and assassinated. Nevertheless, the existence of the Communist International or Comintern, which penetrated many foreign nations and colonies and was dedicated to the violent overthrow of existing regimes, could not be otherwise than a source of irritation and alarm. And the Western nations had reason to feel that, even when no conquest was being attempted, Russia's attitude was that of a jackal standing by and waiting for the sick capitalistic lion to die; waiting watering-mouthed in the belief that the beast was about to perish of the ravages of depression, the class war, and the Revolution. Had the Soviet government never made any overt act, and had it refrained from sending its missionaries abroad, its attitude would still have been an unhealthy one, not calculated to elicit confidence or win friends. But when communistic propaganda infiltrated the world, the situation became aggravated many times.

Looking at the reverse side of the screen, we find the world long unready to recognize the Communists or treat them even with a grudging respect. Somewhat like the monarchies of Europe, which acted with ill-concealed horror and disdain toward the Republicans of the French Revolution, the nations showed an obstinate tendency to blink in the face of reality. Thus the capitalistic world as a whole was slow in granting the Soviets full recognition. Great Britain did indeed make the move in February, 1924, but this involved a lapse of more than six years since the regime's rise to power (and, even so, England broke diplomatic relations in 1927). Italy, Norway, Austria, and other countries followed the British lead in 1924; but it was not until November, 1933, that the United States acknowledged Soviet Russia as a member of the family of nations; while certain other lands, such as Czechoslovakia and Rumania, did not recognize the Soviet regime until 1934; and it was not until this year that Russia was included in the League of Nations.

Unfortunately, a nation, like an individual, cannot remain for years in isolation without bearing the psychological scars, without feeling a constraint and a subconscious resentment, which are bound to affect its attitude and to crop up in its later relationships.

Nor does non-recognition of Russia and her non-participation in the League tell the whole story. With good reason or not, she had felt herself slighted in other respects; the Powers had refused, in 1919, to recognize her Treaty of Brest-Litovsk with Germany; they had excluded her from the list of original signatories to the Kellogg Non-Aggression Pact of 1928; they had scorned her moves for disarmament, and distrustfully rejected her proposals at Geneva for the reduction of armies, navies, and air fleets; the United States had nettled her by Secretary of State Stimson's offer to mediate the dispute with China; England in 1930 had antagonized her by the protest (justified though it was) against the call of the communistic *Daily Worker* for a violent seizure of the British government; both England and France had given her deep affront at the time of the Munich crisis by ignoring her while dealing directly with Hitler. These and similar sources of friction may not have sufficed in themselves to bring on the cold war; but as contributory psychological factors they cannot be disregarded.

These were all pre-war excitations; but after the war, with its temporary submergence of old grievances, pre-existing antagonisms were revived more sharply than ever. On both sides, there were provocations: the Truman Plan for Greece and Turkey, however necessary it may have seemed to us, could only be construed as an act of warlike preparation against Russia; the formation of the North Atlantic Alliance and the United States aid for European rearmament were still more obvious measures; and even the Marshall Plan, though we originally offered to include the Russian bloc of nations and though its avowed objects were economic, was construed by the Kremlin as an attempted build-up against the Soviets (and have we not indeed crowed that the Plan has helped to contain communism?).

But even aside from such major sources of friction, the Russians have seen cause for complaint in other Western actions: the development of the atom bomb without taking Stalin into consultation, when, according to one account, he believed that by means of this weapon "Millions of Russian soldiers could have been saved from horrible death"; [1] the abrupt ending of lend-lease, upsetting Russian plans for post-war rehabilitation; the subsequent refusal of the Soviet application for a loan, at a time when Britain, France, and other countries were being granted enormous credits; the agreement between the United States and England for the economic merger of their occupied zones in Germany; the discharge of Consul General Lomakin from New York following the scandal arising from the window-jumping of Mme. Kasenkina; the American aid to Yugoslavia; and last, and perhaps not least in their total effect, the unbridled attacks against Russia which blazed in American newspapers and screamed from the lungs of Congressmen, and whose importance the Russians may have vastly overrated.

To list these various sources of dissension is not to suggest that the attitude of the Russians was justified. It is merely to record, as a matter of historical fact, that they did feel resentment for these reasons among others, and that their resentments helped to produce the cold war.

We on our own part felt cause enough for distrust. We knew that Russia was the nation which, by her cynical bargain with Hitler in August, 1939, had done much to bring on the war; we knew that this was the nation which, in November, 1939, had hurled itself against small Finland and bombed the people of Helsinki with little excuse or none except that it wished bases on Finnish territory. We also know that this nation, in June, 1945, had received appeals from the Japanese to transmit peace offers to the United States—and had not transmitted them. Here was no basis for confidence; nor was confidence enforced by anti-democratic measures occurring in Poland and Rumania as early as 1945; nor by Russia's bristling attitude in the councils of the United Nations, nor by her epidemic of vetoes, nor by her refusal to agree on a program permitting United Nations observers for atomic control.

But the most decisive steps were those by which Russia seized power in the "satellite countries," beginning with Poland in the spring of 1947, proceeding through Hungary and Rumania later the same year, and advancing in swift order into Ruthenia and then into all Czechoslovakia. The idea of satellite states was, of course, nothing new; it had not been unfamiliar to Napoleon; and it had been among the blackest features of Hitlerism, to which intimidation, bluster, infiltration, and force were standard technique. But never had satellites been created by a more insidious combination of psychological excitations and physical violence than in the case of the planned accessions of Stalin. Penetrated by propagandists, by saboteurs, by provokers of racial and political riots, and by agents staging pseudo-trials and coups designed to take over the government, a country was gradually undermined; and the methods were all the more iniquitous since Moscow worked behind a screen. Some of the preliminaries have been described by Ferenc Nagy of Hungary:

Those of you living in a free and orderly country cannot conceive the effect of some tens of thousands of workers marching the streets in disorder and threatening some cabinet minister, judge or public official with removal if he denies their demand. The legally constituted government (in which the Communists still represent a minority) is helpless against such mass demonstrators because force cannot be used against them. . . . If there should chance to be a man in the government who resists their demands, they respond with an outbreak of strikes and with production stoppages leading to economic disintegration.[2]

III

The same general philosophy prevails as before the wars of 1914 and 1939: the materialistic philosophy of science, which has discarded the old religious deterrents to merciless action, and has made men regard the human personality as no more than a mechanical entity to be used or discarded like any other mechanical entity in a mechanical universe. In addition, there is a savage new precedent of misbehavior of man to man; a precedent which, gaining impetus from the incidents of the two world wars and of the turbulent interlude, has been maintained since 1945 by means such as the forcible retention of hundreds of thousands of wartime prisoners, and by concentration camps and "slave-labor" camps. Certainly, at few periods of history has there been such widespread and doctrinaire unconcern for the simple human values. And where such unconcern exists, war comes more easily; and so do war's extreme barbarities.

A second type of philosophy—the creed of imperialism—has received some severe setbacks; has been subordinated to permit the peaceable separation of India from Great Britain; has yielded to the principle of nationalism in Indonesia and elsewhere; but has been a source of strife in Indo-China and Tibet, as well as wherever the Soviet Empire has exerted extensive pressure. The present-day potentialities of imperialism are hard to reckon; but it remains true that so long as the nations are dominated by this idea, and so long as they seek to extend their dominions by force or the threat of force, war will continue to be a possibility.

Imperialism, obviously, cannot be maintained without armies and navies—and armies and navies bring us to the crux of the post-war problem. We have seen how a leading factor behind past wars has been the arms race; how each nation, out of rivalry and fear, seeks to protect itself against its neighbors; how the neighbors, also out of rivalry and fear, strive to protect themselves in turn; how the arming of the neighbors provokes new measures in the original nation, and the mad competition seesaws back and forth until a chance spark, which no one may have wanted or intended, touches off the huge accumulated pile of explosives. It was the arms race that made possible the First World War; it was the rearming of Germany, matched by the massive arming and fortification of France, which enabled Hitler to move in the Second World War. Yet all previous arms races are dwarfed by that which marks our own cold war.

Few of us realize how explosively the world's military expenditures have expanded. In 1914, according to Carlton J. H. Hayes,[3] the per capita annual peacetime military outlay in Great Britain was $8.67, in France $6.61, in the United States $5.23, and in other countries appreciably less. These figures, says Hayes, are "staggering and quite unprecedented." But if they are staggering and unprecedented, what of our own era, when the United States alone makes a peacetime military investment of three or four hundred dollars per capita? Our total previous payment would hardly suffice for interest on our present outlay.

It is true that, with the increased intricacy of weapons and the reduced purchasing power of the dollar, the disparity is not actually as great as the bare figures would indicate. Nevertheless, it is fantastically large. Though the statistics regarding Russia are not exposed to the daylight, we know that she also has been making vast military expenditures. And when we remember that the competition is not merely in conventional weapons, terrible as these have come to be; when we recall that we are racing to see who will be first in atomic annihilation, and are spending millions to produce the inconceivably destructive hydrogen bomb, we will have to recognize that here is a situation of a gravity without parallel. Nor is there much protection in the circumstance that our side has (for the time, at least) an apparent lead; it would be rank folly to suppose that the men who happen to be in command at a time of great tension would act with a wise restraint and a humane regard for the future simply because they were on our side. All history shows, in fact, that at a moment of extreme peril or panic men will use whatever weapons seem likely to give them an advantage, regardless of ultimate consequences. All history shows, also, that there is no such thing as an arm for defense only; however originally intended, it may become subject to an offensive will; and there is no government or land that can claim immunity from the possible operation of the worldwide law.

Hence, if ordinary arms races are dangerous, the atomic arms race is portentous beyond words. There is, and there can be no safety for mankind until some way has been found of halting it.

IV

Among the other forces that spread the flames of two world wars, the system of alliances likewise remains. The alignments have been, indeed, somewhat altered; but the essential fact is that two groups of nations, embracing the greater part of the civilized world, are glowering at one another across a fence. And this guarantees that, if the fence breaks down, the conflict will not involve merely the two chief competitors; it will insure universal bloodshed.

By the nature of things, we cannot know how great a part secrecy plays in these alliances. We do know, however, that despite all the disclosures at Congressional investigations, secrecy has much to do with the workings of our own government, as in the projects of the Atomic Commission; and we also know that the plans of the General Staff are and must remain secret. We can only hope that there are no hidden commitments among the nations, such as that which Sir Edward Grey gave to France before the war of 1914, or such as France exchanged with Czarist Russia.

In any case, the problem of militarism has grown more acute. The multiplication of the means and methods of warfare, the building of an increasingly large professional military class in our armies, navies, and air forces, has resulted in an augmented amount of thinking along military lines—thinking which tends to assume that wars, if not right or desirable, are at least inevitable. And the theory of inevitability, as already mentioned, may check the hands of the fire-fighters. Similarly, the idea of preventive war has been suggested in various quarters; we have heard certain intemperate officials urge that we begin by bombing Moscow. It is needless to point out that such a doctrine, even if not carried into effect, can be mischievous in its influence on the mood of our potential enemy as well as on our own state of mind.

At the same time, the militarism of the masses proceeds at an unprecedented rate in some countries, and particularly in the United States, where the peacetime draft has become the law of the land, and where steps have been taken toward the still more radical innovation of universal military training. What the advocates of these measures apparently do not realize is that military training, by its very nature, leaves its stamp upon personality; that of all forms of regimentation, it is the most rigid, since it demands absolute conformity of the body and mind; that, being based upon submission and obedience, it is opposed to nothing so much as the assertiveness of individual will and opinion; and that, because the training it enforces is all in the direction of combat and slaughter, it inculcates precisely those psychological reactions that take us furthest from the likelihood of peace.

This is all, of course, quite aside from the question whether, in the world's present state, conscription or universal service are required for our immediate national safety. It is merely to say that, when they do exist, they make the attainment of peaceful objectives more remote. The rise of veterans' organizations—groups which, in America as in Europe, have usually taken a militaristic turn—are a conspicuous proof of this fact. And the flag-waving and blatant patriotic ceremonies and addresses, the vociferous demonstrations to returning generals, the tendency to offer university presidencies to retired army leaders who, however, notable in their own field, are conspicuously lacking in scholastic qualifications, the sentiment among great numbers of the people for selecting our chief executive from among the four- or five-star generals—all this indicates the rise of a military spirit. And even admitting that a certain amount of this spirit could have been found at any time in our history, one can hardly deny the symptoms to be particularly conspicuous now.

Side by side with a waxing militarism we can see an ever-rising nationalism in many parts of the world—the same nationalism that underlay a majority of the struggles of the past hundred and fifty years. Chinese nationalism, allied with a variety of forces, has been one of the dominant and disturbing facts of recent world history; Korean nationalism, rudely severed by the arbitrary division at the thirty-eighth parallel, has involved us in a cruel and costly war; German nationalism, sullenly resurgent and with a disquieting new Nazi tinge, involves eventual warlike possibilities; Jewish and Arab and Iranian nationalism have left inflammation spots in the Near East; and other forms of nationalism throughout the world are crowding and pushing one another while maintaining an uneasy peace. And all this although the growth of science, and the improvements in methods of production, transportation and communication, have tended to abrogate national lines. But so long as many small nationalities continue to assert themselves in the face of world realities, so long will many points of potential warlike infection remain.

It may be true that extreme racialism, which helped to aggravate the recent war-making mood of Germany, is less of a factor than in Hitlerian days. But in its place we find the communistic and anti-communistic religious crusade, which has risen to new fury on both sides. We for our part realize that the outcries of the Communists against the West are often immoderate and absurd, charged with vitriolic passions, and contemptuous of the facts. But we in our turn almost daily encounter some anti-communistic diatribe, little more rational than the criticism of a Jewish prayer meeting from the lips of a Goebbels; and we conduct our anti-communistic witch-hunts even in the august halls of Congress. Not that we must not be alert to any peril; but perils cannot best be attacked by means of hysteria, which widens the rifts that separate us from our adversaries, increases the hatred and fear of us abroad, deepens the gulfs of misunderstanding, and adds to our own dread and horror of the Communists at the very time when wisdom and healing are most needed. Thus we not only bring war closer, but prepare the popular mind for the acceptance of war. The fact that a similar mind-conditioning is occurring among the Soviet-controlled peoples, makes the situation particularly unhealthy.

All this would not be possible, at least to the same extent, except for the existence of a flame-spouting newspaper press, such as has helped to arouse the passions and prejudices of former wars. In the Communist countries, this press is muzzled or unmuzzled as the dictators decree; among the democracies, it ranges from the sober utterances of responsible journals to the wildly provocative cries of the yellow press (which are joined by the blatancies of many radio commentators and so-called "news analysts"). When, for example, any attempt to settle a war by the normal method of diplomatic negotiations is excoriated as "appeasement," we can understand that the clamor may indeed have an influence against peace. And when we find the spokesmen actually advocating war—or measures likely to lead to war or its extension, such as the bombardment of Manchurian bases or of Chinese industrial centers—we can realize how they may irritate foreign countries, and how, if they do not directly affect national policy, they may prepare our minds for the acceptance of aggressive changes in that policy.

v

The international religious conflict of communism and non-communism is, unfortunately, tempered by few of the moral principles professed by the older religions. World morality has shown little sign of improvement since World War II; we have the same Machiavellianism, the same code of expediency, the same aggressiveness, of which the North Korean attack on South Korea and the Chinese invasion of Tibet are but two examples. The United States itself, with its comradely gestures toward blood-soiled Fascist Franco, and its endorsement of a Chinese leader whose corrupt regime has been discredited and cast out by the Chinese people, and its support of what began as an old-style imperialistic war by the French in Indo-China though it has since developed into an effort to hold back communism and counter Communist supplies of arms, can hardly be said to perform on the world stage with immaculate hands. The sober fact is that we, along with other nations, are showing the very principles—or lack of principles—that have time after time led to disaster.

But the surest clue to the state of world morality is to be found in the attitude toward the horror-weapons, and in the failure to take any effective measures against their spread. What plans may be brewing in governmental secrecy, what lethal new engines may be in the throes of birth, is of course any man's guess. But we do know that there has been much talk of atomic sprays to poison the air above great cities or infect the water supply of vast districts, chemicals to wither the crops of wide countrysides, and disease germs to bring the terrors of pestilence to entire populations. It may be that none of these killers will ever be used; but the fact remains that they are being discussed, that they are mentioned as if they represented no more than new methods of exterminating houseflies, that they are taken almost as a matter of course—no outcry against them is raised, there appears to be little realization that they are as anti-human, as diabolical as the Satan of old demon-lore could ever have conceived.

And when the still more portentous possibility of a hydrogen bomb was first described, and later when newspaper stories indicated the actual completion and testing of such a super-destroyer —said to be capable of extirpating all life within an area as large as Greater New York—where was the storm of protests, "This ungodly thing must not be!"? Instead of objecting, we continued to devote funds to the secret furtherance of the project. And this was not because we were uniquely wicked; it was because we were afraid; because, in the current world chaos, we were doing what almost any nation would have done for the sake of military advantage. Moreover, after the moral unrestraint of the last war, with its blockbusters, incendiary shells, and atom bombs, we had so lost our sense of perspective that we could not see the new tools of massacre in their naked monstrous hideousness.

But this much is evident: when a civilization commands neither the moral restraint nor the intelligence to refrain from building the tools of its own destruction, and when there is no way of insuring that such tools will not fall into the hands of irresponsible and immoral leaders, the survival of the civilization would be more of a miracle than would its annihilation. It is not too much to say that human beings, taken as a group, have nowhere shown themselves to be self-restrained enough or mature enough to be entrusted with weapons of such dire potentiality.

The situation is complicated by the fact that, although the American atomic project is in government hands, the greater part of our arms manufacturing is still controlled by profit-seeking individuals, so that war, however disastrous to the country as a whole, may prove lucrative to many persons. This is in part because of the interlinking nature of modern business, and the fact that there are few articles, from wool, cotton, and rubber to wood, paper, steel, and oil, which are not now of military utility. The attitude of modern business is only too candidly revealed by the fact that, when we are embroiled abroad, the stock market dips sharply at every peace rumor. What does this mean except that, to many stock traders, war is profitable, and peace a depressant? It does not follow that the profit-seekers consciously work against peace; but it does follow that there is a large element with an unwholesome interest in continued hostilities. And so long as such an element exists, there will be at least a passive opposition to peace moves.

It is not to be assumed, however, that the remedy is nationalization of all means of war production; owing to the ramifications of modern industry, this would imply an approach to nationalization of all production—a measure which, in Russia, has been no remedy at all. But so long as the Western world will not act to curb wartime profits, by means of stringent anti-inflationary measures and taxes running as high as one hundred per cent, so long will we continue to have a class of citizens for whom war will seem advantageous. And so long as such a class exists, there will be a psychological atmosphere which will subtly retard all efforts at war-prevention.

VI

Our survey of three thousand years of war-making has shown us that war has been largely if not entirely the product of psychological urges. We have seen that it has sprung from desires stimulated by civilization and the wealth of civilization: from a deliberately inculcated training; from social creeds and doctrines which encourage and reward the warrior; and from traditions that have shed a halo on the battlefield. We have observed the origin of war in raids for booty, covert and quite unwarlike raids for blood revenge, and religious raids in placation of gods or ghosts; and we have noted that, side by side with war in all its forms, a cult of heroism has developed: the heroic ideal has hidden the crimson smear upon the fighter's face beneath a golden veil, and has flashed across the ages in songs and legends of glamour and valor. And so by degrees the idea of war has fastened itself upon the world; our princely Alexanders and our regal Caesars, glorified in wonder tales that bear little relation to sordid fact, have moved the imagination of men, and caused the youth of many lands to reach for the sword. Successive waves of fury have beaten at the world: the pillaging Romans, the pillaging Vandals and Vikings, the pillaging Mongols, and many more; and meanwhile the idea of the virtue of battle has constantly been developed, and the myth of grandeur has continued to stir the imagination.

But for centuries war remained an affair of idle aristocrats and paid mercenaries, and did not affect the common man, unless his village or his fields happened to lie in the path of the marauders. Not until the time of the French Revolution did the military idea, like a baleful new star, expand with a fiery explosiveness. But in the succeeding period of roughly a century and two thirds, the world has seen a new militarism, new military attitudes of mind, and an extension of warfare to the rank and file, who must provide not only the raw material of armies but many of the targets of battle. This, therefore, implies a new military conditioning and outlook, the development of traditions that far outpace those of previous centuries. And it is mostly these new traditions, and the attitude of mind accompanying them, that we must keep in view in our attempt to understand present-day warfare and to meet its menace.

Many proposals have been made for a more effective and truly united world organization than has been created in the United

Nations; and something of this nature is not only desirable, it is indispensable, since the present anarchic conditions with their perennial threat to peace are bound to continue until we have established dependable super-national methods of control. To state this, however—and this has been said so often as to make emphasis of the point superfluous—is not to tell the whole story, nor even the most important part of the story. The world's tragedy, in the sad and futile generation through which we have lived, has not been primarily its inability to devise workable international machinery. Its tragedy has been the inability to adapt the human will, human ideas, and desires to the operations of the machinery. The old League of Nations, as originally conceived, might have served its purpose, but American isolationist sentiments kept the most powerful nation on earth from participating; Soviet Russia for a long time was not a member; Germany and Japan, for reasons of their own, subsequently withdrew; England, France, and the other members declined to bolster the League with sufficient resolution and strength, as in the case of the half-hearted sanctions against Mussolini's Ethiopian aggressions when only full-blooded action could have checked the depredations and lent the League dignity and authority. And something similar may be said of the United Nations: despite the veto power—which itself might have been vetoed by a genuine will to peace—it would have been possible to move toward general arms limitation and international control of atomic weapons; it would have been possible to provide an armed force to preclude an episode such as the Korean War, and a world tribunal in which the dispute could have been adjudicated. But this would have meant that every great nation really had a will for peace, and was ready to cooperate for peace even at the cost of some of its own aspirations. Aided by such a will, defective political machinery might prove adequate; lacking such a will, the most shrewdly designed mechanism would break down.

The situation is like that commonly observed in a narrower setting. A legislature may pass idealistic laws, which experts will recognize as for the community's good; but if most members of the community desire to circumvent the laws for private gain, or out of prejudice or misunderstanding, and if enforcement agents cannot be found to arrest violators, or judges or juries to convict or sentence them, then it will not matter that the law is beneficent in its intention—it will be a dead letter. It will be a dead letter simply because the people are not psychologically ready to receive it.

In the same way, we have not been made psychologically ready for an effective world organization. It may be that we are moving in the right direction; the use of the troops of many nations in Korea may indicate a developing will of the nations to work together. Even so, we have taken but a tentative step or two on a long road. And meanwhile the leaden weight of the past, and the clinging traditions of the past, slow us down and tend to halt us.

Most of us, in the current state of education and belief, begin life with a heritage of military ideas. We come into a world in which war has long existed, and in which we are inclined to think of it as more or less normal; we go to school, and read shining tales of Alexanders and Napoleons, Wellingtons and Jacksons and Grants; we are taught the narrow tenets of a chauvinistic patriotism, and feel ready to leap to our country's defense against base and designing foes; perhaps we see the veterans of former wars, who, with their badges and medals, seem glorious romantic figures; perhaps we ourselves develop a little of the fighting spirit in the rifle-shouldering corps of summer camps or in college military training units. Knowing nothing directly of war, we are apt to be swayed by martial songs and stories; or we may be moved by the glamorizing accounts of the old-style historians, and may see war as something heroic. More than that, if we were born in any of the great nations, we may be filled with a strutting pride of country; we may be jealous of our own sovereignty, and our own right to do as we will in a world where we alone are wise and incorruptible—and we will be unlikely to have much information enabling us to correct our distorted ideas and emotions.

Here, then, is the substructure of our failure. While nothing is more essential than an international political edifice based upon the needs of the twentieth century, nothing is more difficult than to erect such an edifice beneath the buffetings of the mind currents passed down from the nineteenth, the eighteenth, and previous centuries. We try to create peace, yet have inherited the long-cultivated psychology of war; we seek to establish internationalism, yet have lived through the most narrowly assertive period of nationalism in history. We wish to cease fighting, yet the precept of ages has taught us to sharpen swords; we hope to be our brother's friend, but cannot cast off the dagger at our sides. And we elevate and applaud leaders who represent the old traditions—leaders who, even if inclined to follow new trails, would hesitate to incur the risk of denunciation as traitors.

The methods are known; the plans for an international organization have been formulated. Why, then, do they remain in the stage of theory? Because the wars and the warlike moods of three millennia, added to the nationalism and the aggressive national moods of nearly two centuries, stand bristling in our path. This, accordingly, is the barrier that must be cleared away. Just as the world has had a psychological training for war, so it must now have a psychological training for peace. There is no other way; there can be no other ultimate guaranty. No other message of equal importance can be read in all man's past conflicts; no other warning shines forth in letters of such vivid fire. As men have often prepared for war lest they perish, so now they must prepare for peace. And the preparation must be immediate and thorough, and must enlist every mental and emotional resource at our disposal.

VII

One would indeed be an optimist if, in considering the overwhelming importance of war-prevention, he lost sight of either of two grim considerations. The first is that we have already set into action such gigantic forces of destruction that, no matter how we strive, we may no longer have time to reverse the current. And the second is that, regardless of the efforts undertaken in any one nation or group of nations, peace-making is by its very nature not a unilateral matter; we must enlist the cooperation of all the great nations, any one of which, like a mad carouser in an overladen canoe, could upset the balance and tip all the rest overboard.

But we must not let these dangers chill us into defeatism. It is probable that, had men in the past been daunted by perils that looked equally imposing, the human race would not have survived this long. In fact, a realization of the current urgency and the current hazards should make us act with the greater speed and determination.

But how achieve our psychological training for peace? How reverse or counteract the century-old psychological training for war?

Two related courses suggest themselves, one general, the other specific. The general program would be concerned with the re-education of the mass mind, in a way to deglamorize war and teach the truth about conflict. It would of necessity concentrate its attention on youth; it would abolish all flag-waving and saluting and the preaching of that exclusive nationalism which leads to the war-path; it would teach history as a world affair, and would be careful never to glorify one land at the expense of others. It would depict all warfare realistically; would show the base and egotistic motives that have so commonly governed it, the villainy and brutality that have been so much more frequent than the knighthood of the poets and story-tellers. It would exalt the real heroes of the race, who never challenged with a sword: Confucius, Gautama, and Christ, Plato, Spinoza, and Kant, Virgil, Dante, and Shakespeare, Bruno, Galileo, and Newton, Mozart, Mendelssohn, and Beethoven, and a few score more who have led the way in the shining precincts of thought and knowledge and literature and art. These would be represented as figures to admire and emulate, rather than the bully-ing Achilles who happens to have a swifter thrust or a stonier heart than the majority.

Equally necessary would be a new perspective in regard to the nations. It would be taught that the gulfs dividing race from race and land from land are slight compared with the links uniting them; France and England and Germany and Japan and Russia would be given credit for all their accomplishments, and every effort would be made to avoid bias or distortion in treatment; their great men would be applauded as the universal figures that they are; their problems would be considered with an attempt at under-standing; their people would be shown to be as human as we. And the kinship and unity of mankind being proved to be much more fundamental than its cleavages and differences, we would proceed naturally to the idea that it is not only desirable but logical to link all men in one great warless organization. Exchanges of infor-mation with foreign lands, and exchanges of students, would speed the process; and the often-advocated idea of an international lan-guage, not to supersede but to supplement the national tongues, might be a decided help along the way.

Some training in a more humanistic philosophy would also be essential—some creed to counteract the current negative doctrines, which tend to represent life as meaningless, and ethical conduct as the aberration of a superstitious past. Manifestly, a people which regards life as without ultimate value or purpose, and looks on human beings and their thoughts and feelings as the mechanical products of an aimless nature, is not a people that will strain every muscle and put forth every exertion of the spirit in order to survive. It is, of course, not the function of the present work to present a cosmic philosophy; but it is evident that we must do something to combat the materialistic interpretations of science—interpretations not accepted by some of our greatest scientists, though they have powerfully affected the general mind. As an example of the variety of possible ways of reading the evidence: it has been customary in many quarters to regard man as dwarfed by the tremendous vistas of astronomy, with its millions of galaxies and thousands of thousands of millions of suns spread out through the light-years of inconceivable space; here, it is argued, is proof of our insignificance, our ultimate worthlessness. Yet it is equally possible to interpret those same prodigious vistas as proof of some gigantic Purpose, some magnificent Will, some everlasting Reality of which we are a part. The one interpretation is bleak and paltry, and may make us bleak and paltry in our conduct; the other is bright and expansive, and may give our lives a sense of meaning. Under the first, men feel a bid to follow their own desires and grapple for their own interests; and tend to believe that their personalities do not matter. Hence there is no respect for mankind; and no great bar to treachery, plunder, and slaughter. Hence, also, we lack a strong potential brake to ruthlessness and savagery; and are less zealous than we might have been to avert the destruction of civilization or of the very race of man.

VIII

Now let us turn to the more specific course of action mentioned several pages back as necessary to produce a psychological training for peace. This would be concerned not with the masses but with the men who lead the masses.

Time after time, in discussing past wars, we have observed the root of conflict in the desires and machinations of a single individual. And even in our own day, though we sometimes oversimplify by placing the blame at one man's door, we have noticed how powerfully an individual may influence the issue. The case of the dictatorships is self-evident: there was no one to countermand the orders of Hitler or Mussolini. But in the democracies also one man or one man's policies may on occasion be decisive: Stanley Baldwin and later Chamberlain, by taking a firm stand against Hitler, might have averted or blunted the force of World War II; President Truman, no matter what his advisers counseled, had it within his power to make or not make the step leading to our participation in the Korean War. And with the increasing international complications, decisions leading to war or peace are becoming more common rather than less so. It is therefore imperative that only qualified men be enabled to make the decisions.

In any sphere except politics this would be axiomatic. A great manufacturing concern would not leave the question of plant expansion to a shop apprentice; a hospital would not permit a chance bystander to decide whether an operation should be made. Yet the leaders of modern nations, the men who make the moves that preserve the peace or drive us into war, are for the most part men with no more than an amateur's training; their chief requirement for their appalling responsibility is a sufficiency of votes. They pass judgment on delicate and intricate matters of international relationships, yet need have no specific knowledge of foreign nations, their problems, or their people; they make moves of earth-shaking consequence, yet are not required to be informed of the history of similar moves; they deal with the psychological reactions of people on a world stage, yet their psychological training may be that of the beer-hall or the poker-room. To the universal drama in which they play major roles for all mankind and before all futurity, they may bring but the experience of the village crossroads. Under such circumstances, they could no more fulfill the possibilities of their parts than an untrained barroom singer could star at the Metropolitan.

The need is cryingly obvious. Our political leaders, even as the leaders of the pulpit, the bar, and the army, must be trained for their responsibilities. They must have a thorough grounding in the social sciences, including history and anthropology; they must have been drilled in economic theory and practice; they must have studied psychology, ethics, and philosophy; they must be aware of the latest in science and in scientific interpretation; they must if possible have had experience abroad, in foreign capitals and among the people of foreign lands. As men seek diplomas today in medicine or engineering, so they must work for degrees in statecraft

—and only the graduates of acknowledged institutions should be qualified to compete for high government positions.

Would this be a radical change? Certainly. Would it, in the case of the United States, require a constitutional amendment? Undoubtedly. But would it be undemocratic? No more so than the laws which forbid an unqualified person to establish himself in business as a surgeon, a dentist, or a veterinarian. Far from being opposed to democracy in its long-run effects, the innovation would tend to safeguard democracy—and to curtail the power of the war-inducing special interests. There is, of course, no guaranty that even the most competent officials could avoid political decisions leading to war; but it cannot be denied that trained leaders, aware of all man's recorded experience and bringing a lifelong dedication to their task, would be more likely to steer a safe course than would men who reached their high perches along the shabby and sometimes crooked paths of modern politics. The difference can be that between an unskilled layman and a seasoned navigator in combating a storm at sea.

The situation is really as simple in its essence as it is difficult in its details. We face a crisis in which, admittedly, civilization is in danger, and in which mankind itself may not survive. In these precarious circumstances, it is no more than elementary caution and common sense to fight with our best weapons, to put forth our best resources, our most capable and trained minds. If we fail to utilize these, we will have cut down our chances possibly to a fatal extent.

When all is said, war is not a convulsion of nature. It is not caused, like the earthquake, by vast uncontrollable forces shuddering underground; nor is it like the hurricane, which blows out of the waste places of the sea on an irresistible track. It is produced, as we have seen, primarily by one thing: the mind of man—the ideas, the will, and the emotions of man. This means that it can be checked or controlled only by one thing: the mind of man—the ideas, the will, or the emotions of man. There is nothing recondite or supernatural about it, nor anything beyond our grasp; we cannot look for deliverance to any vague mystical entity. We can turn only to our own intelligence and determination, our own energy and resourcefulness—and the fervor of our own desire. The problem stares us in the face, as no previous problem has ever confronted the race of man; and the nets woven throughout the centuries have made it tremendously complex. But it was man who spread the nets; it is man who must tear them apart. If he cannot or will not succeed, he will almost certainly vanish—and the ants, the lice, or the rats that inherit the earth may some day see his bones projecting from the ancient rubble along with those of other species that failed in their life-adaptations.

But one need not suppose that we cannot or will not succeed. It was not by lying down, and blinking in the face of his problems, that man spread out across all the continents of the earth, and mastered all other organic forms of life and many of the giants of nature. If he arouses himself, and bestirs himself swiftly and courageously, the will and the skill that have conquered most of the planet may yet prevail over the most redoubtable enemies of all: the furies fuming in the heart of man. The issue, it may be repeated, will be for man to decide. And the question to be determined will be not only man's survival but his worthiness to survive.

Appendix

Notes

Chapter 1

1. See H. J. Massingham, *Downland Man*, New York, undated, p. 354; also, G. Elliot Smith, *Human History*, New York, 1929.
2. Fridtjof Nansen, *Eskimo Life*, London, 1893.
3. A. L. Kroeber, *Handbook of the Indians of California*, Washington, 1925.
4. Frances Densmore, *Papago Music*, Washington, 1929.
5. Christopher Dawson, *The Age of the Gods: A Study in the Origins of Culture in Prehistoric Europe and the Ancient East*, Boston, 1928.
6. Lieutenant-Colonel T. R. St. Johnston, *The Islanders of the Pacific*, New York, 1921.
7. A. R. Brown, *The Andaman Islanders*, Cambridge, 1922.
8. Baldwin Spencer and F. J. Gillen, *The Native Tribes of Central Australia*, Second Edition, London, 1938.
9. N. W. Thomas, *Natives of Australia*, London, 1906.
10. W. L. Warner, "Murngin Warfare," *Oceania*, 1940, Vol. I.
11. Bronislaw Malinowski, *Argonauts of the Western Pacific*, London, 1922.
12. J. H. Holmes, *In Primitive New Guinea*, London, 1924.
13. Gunnar Landtman, *The Kiwai Papuans of British New Guinea*, London, 1927.
14. Johannes C. Andersen, *Myths and Legends of the Polynesians*, New York, 1928.
15. Dugald Campbell, *In the Heart of Bantuland*, Philadelphia, 1928.
16. Charles K. Meek, *Law and Authority in a Nigerian Tribe: A Study in Indirect Rule*, Oxford, 1937.
17. *David Thompson's Narrative of His Explorations in Western America, 1784–1812*, edited by J. B. Tyrrell, Toronto, 1916.
18. Camilla Wedgewood, "Some Aspects of Warfare in Melanesia," *Oceania*, 1940, Vol. I.
19. Harry Holbert Turney-High, *Primitive War, Its Practice and Concepts*, Columbia, South Carolina, 1949.
20. W. H. R. Rivers, *Social Organization*, New York, 1924.
21. Joseph Dillaway Sawyer, *History of the Pilgrims and Puritans*, edited by William Elliot Griffis, New York, 1922, Vol. II.

Chapter 2

1. Rafael Karsten, *Blood Revenge, War and Victory Feasts Among the Jibaro Indians of Eastern Ecuador*, Bureau of American Ethnology, Washington, 1923.
2. Baldwin Spencer and F. J. Gillen, *The Native Tribes of Central Australia*, Second Edition, London, 1938.
3. Clark Wissler, *Indians of the United States: Four Centuries of Their History and Culture*, The American Museum of Natural History Series, New York, 1940.
4. A. Hyatt Verrill, *The American Indian: North, South and Central America*, Second Edition, New York, 1943.
5. Paul Radin, *Indians of South America*, The American Museum of Natural History Series, New York, 1946.
6. *Ibid.*

Chapter 3

1. William P. Krohn, *In Borneo Jungles*, Indianapolis, 1927.
2. *Ibid.*
3. *Ibid.*
4. Brigadier-General J. B. Glubb, *The Salubba and Other Ignoble Tribes of Southwestern Asia*, General Series in Anthropology No. 10, Menaska, Wisconsin, 1943.
5. Thomas Whiffen, *The North-West Amazons*, London, 1915.
6. *Ibid.*
7. W. H. Prescott, *The Conquest of Mexico*, New York, 1922, Vol. I.
8. *Ibid.*
9. Lewis Spence, *Myths of Mexico and Peru*, New York, undated.

Chapter 4

1. See Alfred V. Kidder, *An Introduction to the Study of Southwestern Archeology, with a Preliminary Account of the Excavation at Pecos*, New Haven, 1924.
2. D. R. Mackenzie, *The Spirit-Ridden Konde*, Philadelphia, 1925.
3. Major G. St.J. Orde Browne, *The Vanishing Tribes of Kenya*, Philadelphia, 1925.
4. Robert H. Lowie, *The Crow Indians*, New York, 1935.
5. *Ibid.*
6. Clark Wissler, *Indians of the United States*, New York, 1940.
7. Lowie, *op. cit.*
8. *Ibid.*
9. George Bird Grinnell, *The Fighting Cheyennes*, New York, 1915.

10. Brigadier-General J. B. Glubb, *The Salubba and Other Ignoble Tribes of Southwestern Asia,* Menaska, Wisconsin, 1943.
11. Henry A. Junod, *The Life of a South African Tribe,* Second Edition, Neuchâtel, 1927. (Cited by Harry Holbert Turney-High, *Primitive War, Its Practice and Concepts.*)
12. Clark Wissler, *The American Indian: An Introduction to the Anthropology of the New World,* New York, 1922.
13. Bronislaw Malinowski, *Crime and Custom in Savage Society,* New York, 1926.

Chapter 5

1. V. Gordon Childe, *What Happened in History,* New York, 1946.
2. V. Gordon Childe, *New Light on the Ancient Near East: The Oriental Prelude to European History,* New York, 1934.
3. F. G. Scott Elliot, *Prehistoric Man and His Story,* London, 1913.
4. Childe, *What Happened in History.*
5. H. J. Massingham, *Downland Man,* New York, undated.
6. *Ibid.*
7. A. T. Olmstead, *History of the Persian Empire,* Chicago, 1948.
8. G. Elliot Smith, *Human History,* New York, 1929.
9. Major John Campbell, *A Personal Narrative of Thirteen Years Service Among the Wild Tribes of Khondistan for the Suppression of Human Sacrifice,* London, 1864.
10. G. Elliot Smith, *Essays on the Evolution of Man,* Oxford, 1924.
11. Philip Ainsworth Means, *Ancient Civilizations of the Andes,* New York, 1931.
12. Smith, *Human History.*
13. W. J. Perry, *The Growth of Civilization,* New York, 1923.

Chapter 6

1. James Henry Breasted, *A History of Egypt: From the Earliest Times to the Persian Conquest,* New York, 1905.
2. *Ibid.*
3. A. Moret and G. Davy, *From Tribe to Empire,* New York, 1926.
4. Breasted, *op. cit.*
5. *Ibid.*
6. See James Henry Breasted, *The Battle of Kadesh,* Chicago, 1903.
7. Carl Holliday, *The Dawn of Literature,* New York, 1931. (Adapted from the translation of Dr. H. K. Brugsch, *History of Egypt,* London, 1881, Vol. II.)
8. *Ibid.*

Chapter 7

1. Morris Jastrow, Jr., *The Civilization of Babylonia and Assyria*, Philadelphia, 1915.
2. Thorkild Jacobsen, in *The Intellectual Adventure of Ancient Man*, by H. and H. A. Frankford *et al.*, Chicago, 1946.
3. A. T. Olmstead, *History of Assyria*, New York, 1923.
4. *Ibid.*

Chapter 8

1. Robert William Rogers, *A History of Ancient Persia*, New York, 1929.
2. *Ibid.*
3. *The Bhagavad-Gita*, translated by Arthur W. Ryder, Chicago, 1929.
4. *Ibid.*
5. William Loftus Hare, *Mysticism of East and West: Studies in Mystical and Moral Philosophy*, New York, 1923.
6. N. K. Sidhanta, *The Heroic Age of India: A Comparative Study*, New York, 1930.
7. Abbé J. A. Dubois, *Hindu Manners, Customs and Ceremonies*, translated by Henry K. Beauchamp, Oxford, 1928.
8. *Ibid.*
9. Hare, *op. cit.*
10. *Ibid.*
11. James Bissett Pratt, *The Pilgrimage of Buddhism*, New York, 1928.
12. Vincent A. Smith, *History of India*, edited by A. V. Williams Jackson, London, 1906, Vol. II.
13. *Ibid.*

Chapter 9

1. All quotations from the *Iliad* are from the translation by William Benjamin Smith and Walter Miller, New York, 1944.
2. J. B. Bury, *A History of Greece to the Death of Alexander*, New York, 1937.

Chapter 10

1. Translation by Benjamin Jowett.
2. Translation by Alfred E. Zimmern.
3. *Ibid.*
4. This and all the succeeding translations from Thucydides are by Benjamin Jowett.
5. Joseph Ward Swain, *The Ancient World*, New York, 1950, Vol. II.

Chapter 11

1. Guglielmo Ferrero, *The Greatness and Decline of Rome*, translated by Alfred E. Zimmern, New York, 1909, Vol. I.
2. Arnold Toynbee, "A Study of History," reprinted in the author's *War and Civilization*, New York, 1950.

Chapter 12

1. Polybius, Book X.
2. Quoted by W. Warde Fowler, *Social Life at Rome in the Age of Cicero*, New York, 1913.
3. Ernest Barker, "The Conception of Empire," in *The Legacy of Rome*, Oxford, undated.
4. Joseph Ward Swain, *The Ancient World*, New York, 1950, Vol. II.

Chapter 13

1. *The Saga of the Volsungs*, translated by Margaret Schlauch, New York, 1930.
2. Margaret Schlauch, in the Introduction to *The Saga of the Volsungs*.
3. Schlauch (trans.), *op. cit.*
4. *Ibid.*
5. The quotations in this section are from *The Dialogues of Publius Cornelius Tacitus*, translated by Sir William Peterson, London and New York, 1920.
6. Leo, *Tactica*, quoted by Charles Oman, *A History of the Art of War, From the Fourth to the Fourteenth Century*, London, 1898.
7. *Ibid.*
8. Ferdinand Lot, *The End of the Ancient World and the Beginnings of the Middle Ages*, New York, 1931.
9. Oman, *op. cit.*
10. Quoted by Douglas Woodruff, *Charlemagne*, New York, 1935.

Chapter 14

1. Marcel Granet, *Chinese Civilization*, New York, 1930.
2. *Ibid.*
3. *Ibid.*
4. *Ibid.*
5. William Elliot Griffis, *The Mikado's Empire*, New York, 1906, Vol. I.
6. *Ibid.*

Chapter 15

1. James Westfall Thompson, *An Economic and Social History of the Middle Ages*, New York, 1928.
2. Dana Carlton Munro, "Christian and Infidel in the Holy Land," *International Quarterly*, 1901.
3. *Ibid.*
4. Henry Osborn Taylor, *The Medieval Mind: A History of the Development of Thought and Emotion in the Middle Ages*, London, 1927, Vol. I.
5. Raymond of Agiles, quoted by Taylor, *op. cit.*

Chapter 16

1. J. Flach, *Les origines de l'ancienne France*, translated in Dana Carlton Munro and George Clarke Sellery, *Medieval Civilization*, New York, 1904.
2. J. Huizinga, *The Waning of the Middle Ages: A Story of the Forms of Life, Thought and Art in France and the Netherlands in the XIVth and XVth Centuries*, London, 1924.
3. William Stearns Davis, *Life on a Medieval Barony: A Picture of a Typical Feudal Community in the Thirteenth Century*, New York, 1923.
4. Alfred Tennyson, "The Passing of Arthur."
5. *Song of Roland*, Crosland version, quoted by Douglas Woodruff, *Charlemagne*, New York, 1935.
6. Roger de Hovenden, quoted by Walter Clifford Meller, *A Knight's Life in the Days of Chivalry*, New York, 1924.
7. Huizinga, *op. cit.*
8. *Ibid.*
9. Edward P. Cheyney, *The Dawn of a New Era, 1250–1453*, New York, 1936.

Chapter 17

1. Sir John Froissart, *Chronicles*, translated by Thomas Johnes, New York, 1901, Vol. II.
2. The quotations from Machiavelli are from *The Prince*, translated by Henry Morley, London, 1883.
3. Carlo Beuf, *Cesare Borgia: The Machiavellian Prince*, New York, 1942.
4. Alfred Vagts, *A History of Militarism: Romance and Realities of a Profession*, New York, 1937.

Chapter 18

1. *The Utopia of Thomas More,* edited by William Dallam Armes, New York, 1912.
2. Quoted by William Henry Hudson and Irwin S. Guernsey, *The United States,* New York, undated.
3. Jonathan Swift, *Gulliver's Travels,* Part I.
4. *Ibid.*
5. *Queen Mab,* IV.
6. *Micromegas,* VI.
7. *The Princess of Babylon,* VI.
8. *Candide,* III.

Chapter 19

1. Henry Charles Lea, *A History of the Inquisition of the Middle Ages,* New York, 1922, Vol. I.
2. *Ibid.*
3. Carlton J. H. Hayes, *A Political and Cultural History of Modern Europe,* New York, 1936, Vol. I.
4. Johannes Janssen, *History of the German People at the Close of the Middle Ages,* translated by A. M. Christie, London, 1900, Vol. IV.
5. *Ibid.*
6. *Ibid.,* Vol. III.
7. *Ibid.,* Vol. IV.
8. *Ibid.*
9. *Ibid.*
10. From a letter in Strobel, *Thomas Munzer,* quoted by Janssen, *op. cit.,* Vol. IV.
11. W. H. Prescott, *History of the Reign of Ferdinand and Isabella,* edition of 1887, Vol. I.
12. Roger Bigelow Merriman, *The Rise of the Spanish Empire,* New York, 1925, Vol. IV.
13. Henry Dwight Sedgwick, *Spain,* Boston, 1925.
14. *Ibid.*
15. Ruth Putnam, *William the Silent, Prince of Orange, and the Revolt of the Netherlands,* New York, 1911.
16. *Ibid.*
17. James Westfall Thompson, *The Wars of Religion in France, 1559–1576,* Chicago, 1909.
18. *Ibid.*
19. *Ibid.*
20. *Ibid.*
21. *Ibid.*

22. H. A. L. Fisher, *A History of Europe*, Boston, 1935, Vol. II.

23. Samuel Rawson Gardiner, *The Thirty Years' War*, New York, 1897.

24. Anton Gindely, *History of the Thirty Years' War*, translated by Andrew Ten Brook, New York, 1884, Vol. I.

25. G. R. Stirling Taylor, *Cromwell*, Boston, 1928.

26. John Morley, *Oliver Cromwell*, New York, 1900.

27. *Ibid.*

28. John Buchan, *Oliver Cromwell*, Boston, 1934.

Chapter 20

1. The Duke of Saint-Simon, *Memoirs of Louis XIV and His Court and of the Regency*, New York, 1910, Ch. liii.

2. *Ibid.*

3. Voltaire, *Siècle de Louis XIV*, cited by Penfield Roberts, *The Quest for Security*, New York, 1947.

Chapter 21

1. Voltaire, *History of Charles XII*, translated by Tobias Smollett, New York, 1901.

2. *Ibid.*

3. Alfred Rambaud, *History of Russia*, translated by L. B. Lang, Boston, 1880, Vol. II.

4. Voltaire, *op. cit.*

5. Rambaud, *op. cit.*

6. John A. Gade, *Charles the Twelfth, King of Sweden*, translated from the manuscript of Carl Gustafson Klingspor, Boston, 1916.

7. *Ibid.*

8. George Vernadsky, *A History of Russia*, New York, 1944.

9. Arnold Toynbee, *A Study of History*, London, 1935, Vol. III.

10. Rambaud, *op. cit.*

11. J. A. R. Marriott and Charles Grant Robertson, *The Evolution of Prussia: The Making of an Empire*, Oxford, 1937.

12. W. A. Reddaway, *Frederick the Great and the Rise of Prussia*, New York, 1904.

13. Marriott and Robertson, *op. cit.*

14. Reddaway, *op. cit.*

15. *Ibid.*

16. *Ibid.*

17. *Ibid.*

18. Frederick the Great, *The History of the Seven Years' War*, translated from the French by Thomas Holcroft, London, 1789, Part I.
19. *Ibid.*
20. *Ibid.*
21. *Ibid.*
22. *Ibid.*

Chapter 22

1. Walter L. Dorn, *Competition for Empire, 1740–1763*, New York, 1940.
2. *Henry IV*, Part I, Act IV, Sc. ii.
3. Barnaby Rich, *A Pathway to Military Practice* (1587), quoted by C. A. Firth, *Cromwell's Army*, London, 1905.
4. John Buchan, *Oliver Cromwell*, Boston, 1934.
5. Spencer Wilkinson, *The French Army Before Napoleon*, Oxford, 1915.

Chapter 23

1. Witt Bowden, *The Industrial History of the United States*, New York, 1930.
2. Bernard Moses, *The Establishment of Spanish Rule in America*, New York, 1907.
3. *Ibid.*
4. Roger Bigelow Merriman, *The Rise of the Spanish Empire*, New York, 1925, Vol. III.
5. W. H. Prescott, *The Conquest of Peru*, Boston, 1856, Vol. I.
6. Philip Ainsworth Means, *Ancient Civilizations of the Andes*, New York, 1931.
7. W. H. Prescott, *The Conquest of Mexico*, New York, 1922, Vol. II.
8. *Ibid.*
9. John Fiske, *The Dutch and Quaker Colonies in America*, Boston, 1899, Vol. II.
10. Joseph Dillaway Sawyer, *History of the Pilgrims and Puritans*, New York, 1922, Vol. III.
11. Francis Parkman, *Pioneers of France in the New World*, Boston, 1892.
12. *Ibid.*
13. Clark Wissler, *Indians of the United States*, New York, 1940.
14. John G. Neihardt, *The Song of the Indian Wars*, New York, 1925.
15. A. Mervyn Davies, *Clive of Plassey*, New York, 1939.
16. *Ibid.*

17. M. E. Monckton Jones, *Warren Hastings in Bengal, 1772–1774*, Oxford, 1918.
18. John C. Miller, *Origins of the American Revolution*, Boston, 1943.
19. *Ibid.*
20. *Ibid.*
21. *Ibid.*

Chapter 24

1. J. H. Thompson, *The French Revolution*, Oxford, 1943.
2. Crane Brinton, *A Decade of Revolution, 1789–1799*, New York, 1934.
3. *Ibid.*
4. Pierre Gaxotte, *The French Revolution*, translated by Walter Alison Phillips, New York, 1932.
5. *Ibid.*
6. Thompson, *op. cit.*
7. Gaxotte, *op. cit.*
8. Jean Jaurès, quoted by Gaxotte, *op. cit.*
9. Thompson, *op. cit.*
10. *Ibid.*
11. *Ibid.*
12. Geoffrey Bruun, *Europe and the French Imperium, 1799–1814*, New York, 1938.
13. Carlton J. H. Hayes, *The Historical Evolution of Modern Nationalism*, New York, 1931.
14. *Ibid.*
15. Alfred Vagts, *A History of Militarism*, New York, 1937.
16. *Ibid.*

Chapter 25

1. John Holland Rose, *The Life of Napoleon I*, New York, 1901, Vol. I.
2. August Fournier, *Napoleon*, translated by Margaret Bacon Corwin and David Dart Bissell, New York, 1903.
3. F. M. Kircheisen, *Napoleon*, translated by Henry St. Lawrence, New York, 1932.
4. *Napoleon's Memoirs*, edited by Somerset de Clair, New York, 1948.
5. Quoted in the original French by Spencer Wilkinson, *The Rise of General Bonaparte*, Oxford, 1930.
6. Fournier, *op. cit.*
7. Kircheisen, *op. cit.*
8. Wilkinson, *op. cit.*

9. Fournier, *op. cit.*
10. Geoffrey Bruun, *Europe and the French Imperium, 1799–1814,* New York, 1938.
11. Kircheisen, *op. cit.*
12. *Ibid.*
13. *Ibid.*
14. Miot de Mélito, *Mémoires,* quoted by Fournier, *op. cit.*
15. Alfred Vagts, *A History of Militarism,* New York, 1937.

Chapter 26

1. Quincy Wright, in *A Study of War* (Chicago, 1942), lists fifty-four wars as having broken out between 1824 and 1877.
2. Carlton J. H. Hayes, *Essays in Nationalism,* New York, 1926.
3. Hans Kohn, *A History of Nationalism in the East,* New York, 1929.
4. *Bismarck, the Man and the Statesman. The Reflections and Reminiscences of Otto, Prince von Bismarck. Written and Dictated by Himself After His Retirement from Office.* Translated from the German under the supervision of A. J. Butler, New York, 1899, Vol. II.
5. *Ibid.*
6. Charles Grant Robertson, *Bismarck,* London, 1918.
7. H. A. L. Fisher, *A History of Europe,* Boston, 1936, Vol. III.
8. William Harbutt Dawson, *The German Empire, 1867–1914, and the Unity Movement,* New York, 1919, Vol. I.
9. *Ibid.*
10. *Bismarck, the Man and the Statesman, op. cit.*
11. *Ibid.*
12. *Ibid.*
13. Dawson, *op. cit.*
14. *Ibid.,* Vol. II.
15. *Ibid.*
16. Joseph Vincent Fuller, *Bismarck's Philosophy at Its Zenith,* Cambridge, Massachusetts, 1922.
17. *Ibid.*

Chapter 27

1. Carlton J. H. Hayes, *A Generation of Materialism, 1871–1900,* New York, 1941.
2. *Ibid.*
3. William Harbutt Dawson, *The German Empire, 1867–1914, and the Unity Movement,* New York, 1919, Vol. II.

4. Sir Edward Grey, *Twenty-Five Years*, New York, 1925, Vol. II.
5. Merze Tate, *The Disarmament Illusion*, New York, 1942.
6. Theodor Wolff, *The Eve of 1914*, translated by E. W. Dickes, New York, 1936.
7. Quoted by Sidney Bradford Fay, *The Origins of the World War*, New York, 1941.
8. *Ibid.*
9. Walter Millis, *The Road to War: America 1914–1917*, Boston, 1935.
10. Fay, *op. cit.*
11. G. Lowes Dickinson, *The International Anarchy*, New York, 1926.
12. Quoted by W. M. Knight-Patterson, *Germany from Defeat to Conquest, 1913–1933*, London, 1945.
13. *Ibid.*
14. *Ibid.*
15. *Ibid.*
16. Dickinson, *op. cit.*
17. Walter Millis, *The Martial Spirit: A Study of Our War with Spain*, Boston, 1931.
18. Fay, *op. cit.*
19. Wolff, *op. cit.*
20. *Ibid.*
21. Otto Lehmann-Russbüldt, *War for Profits*, New York, 1930.
22. *Ibid.*
23. *Ibid.*

Chapter 28

1. Sidney Bradford Fay, *The Origins of the World War*, New York, 1941.
2. Theodor Wolff, *The Eve of 1914*, translated by E. W. Dickes, New York, 1936.
3. Quoted by Walter Millis, *The Road to War*, Boston, 1935.
4. Sir Edward Grey, *Twenty-Five Years*, New York, 1925.
5. *Ibid.*
6. *Ibid.*

Chapter 29

1. Gilbert Thomas, *Autobiography, 1891–1941*, London, 1946.
2. Quoted by Harry Elmer Barnes, *The Genesis of the World War*, New York, 1926.
3. Philip Gibbs, *The Soul of the War*, New York, 1915.
4. Stephen Graham, *The Challenge of the Dead*, London, 1930.
5. Will Irwin, *The Next War*, Evanston, Illinois, 1921.
6. Graham, *op. cit.*

7. Richard Haigh, *Life in a Tank*, Boston, 1918.
8. Eric Fisher Wood, *The Note-Book of an Intelligence Officer*, New York, 1917.
9. Philip Gibbs, *Now It Can Be Told*, New York, 1920.
10. *Ibid.*

Chapter 30

1. Winston S. Churchill, *The Gathering Storm*, Boston, 1948.
2. Walter Millis, *Why Europe Fights*, New York, 1940.
3. Churchill, *op. cit.*
4. Peter de Mendelssohn, *Design for Aggression: The Inside Story of Hitler's War Plans*, New York, 1946.
5. Churchill, *op. cit.*
6. The Nuremberg Documents, quoted by Mendelssohn, *op. cit.*
7. *Ibid.*
8. *Ibid.*

Chapter 31

1. See Howard Watson Ambruster, *Treason's Peace*, New York, 1947, p. 407.

Chapter 32

1. Winston S. Churchill, *Their Finest Hour*, Boston, 1949.
2. Francis Trevelyan Miller, *History of World War II*, Philadelphia, 1945.
3. Winston S. Churchill, *The Grand Alliance*, Boston, 1950.
4. *Ibid.*
5. Joseph C. Grew, *Ten Years in Japan*, New York, 1944.
6. *Ibid.*
7. *Ibid.*
8. *Ibid.*
9. *Ibid.*
10. Churchill, *The Grand Alliance.*
11. Quoted by George Morgenstern, *Pearl Harbor: The Story of the Secret War*, New York, 1947.
12. Churchill, *The Grand Alliance.*
13. *Ibid.*
14. *Ibid.*
15. *Ibid.*
16. *Ibid.*
17. Grew, *op. cit.*
18. *Ibid.*

Chapter 33

1. Ellis M. Zacharias, *Behind Closed Doors: The Secret History of the Cold War*, New York, 1950.
2. House Report No. 1920, Eightieth Congress, Second Session, 1948, quoted by Zacharias, *op. cit.*
3. Carlton J. H. Hayes, *A Political and Cultural History of Modern Europe*, New York, 1936, Vol. II.

Bibliography

I

ANDERSON, J. C. *Myths and Legends of the Polynesians.* New York, 1928.

BROWN, A. R. *The Andaman Islanders.* Cambridge, England, 1922.

BROWNE, G. ST.J. ORDE, *The Vanishing Tribes of Kenya.* Philadelphia, 1925.

CAMPBELL, D. *In the Heart of Bantuland.* Philadelphia, 1922.

CAMPBELL, J. C. B. *A Personal Narrative of Thirteen Years Service Among the Wild Tribes of Khondistan for the Suppression of Human Sacrifice.* London, 1864.

CHILDE, V. G. *New Light on the Ancient Near East: The Oriental Prelude to European History.* New York, 1934.

———. *The Dawn of European Civilization.* New York, 1939.

———. *What Happened in History.* New York, 1946.

COLE, F.-C. *The Peoples of Malaysia.* New York, 1945.

DAWSON, C. *The Age of the Gods: A Study in the Origins of Culture in Prehistoric Europe and the Ancient East.* Boston, 1928.

DEL MAR, F. *A Year Among the Maoris: A Study of Their Arts and Customs.* London, 1924.

DENSMORE, F. *Papago Music.* Bureau of American Ethnology, Bulletin 90. Washington, D.C., 1929.

DIXON, R. B. "The Northern Maidu," *Bulletin American Museum of Natural History,* Vol. XVII, 1905.

DORNAN, S. S. *Pygmies and Bushmen of the Kalahari.* London, 1925.

ELLIOTT, G. F. S. *Prehistoric Man and His Story.* London, 1915.

GLUBB, J. B. *The Salubba and Other Ignoble Tribes of Southwestern Asia.* Menaska, Wisconsin, 1943.

GRINNELL, G. B. *The Fighting Cheyennes.* New York, 1915.

HOEBEL, E. A. *Man in the Primitive World.* New York, 1949.

HOLMES, J. H. *In Primitive New Guinea.* London, 1924.

HOWITT, A. W. *The Native Tribes of Southeast Australia.* London, 1904.

JAMES, E. O. *Primitive Ritual and Belief: An Anthropological Essay.* London, 1917.

KARSTEN, R. *Blood Revenge, War and Victory Feasts Among the Ji-baro Indians of Eastern Ecuador.* Bureau of American Ethnology, Bulletin 79. Washington, D.C., 1923.

——. *The Civilization of the South American Indians.* New York, 1926.

KIDDER, A. V. *An Introduction to the Study of Southwestern Archeology, with a Preliminary Account of the Excavations at Pecos.* New Haven, 1924.

KRIEGER, H. W. *Peoples of the Philippines.* Smithsonian Institution War Background Studies, Number 4. Washington, D.C., 1942.

KROEBER, A. L. *Handbook of the Indians of California.* Washington, D.C., 1925.

KROHN, W. P. *In Borneo Jungles.* Indianapolis, 1927.

LANDTMAN, G. *The Kiwai Papuans of British New Guinea.* London, 1927.

LIPPERT, J. *The Evolution of Culture.* New York, 1931.

LOWIE, R. H. *Primitive Society.* New York, 1925.

——. *The Crow Indians.* New York, 1935.

——. *An Introduction to Cultural Anthropology.* New York, 1947.

MACKENZIE, D. R. *The Spirit-Ridden Konde.* Philadelphia, 1925.

MALINOWSKI, B. *Argonauts of the Western Pacific.* London, 1922.

——. *Crime and Custom in Savage Society.* New York, 1926.

MARKHAM, C. *The Incas of Peru.* New York, 1912.

MASSINGHAM, H. J. *Downland Man.* New York, undated.

McCURDY, G. G. *The Coming of Man.* New York, 1932.

MEANS, P. A. *Ancient Civilizations of the Andes.* New York, 1931.

——. *Fall of the Inca Empire.* New York, 1932.

MEEK, C. B. *Law and Authority in a Nigerian Tribe: A Study in Indirect Rule.* Oxford, 1937.

NANSEN, F. *Eskimo Life.* London, 1893.

PALMER, R. A. (compiler). *The North American Indians: An Account of the American Indians North of Mexico, Compiled from the Original Sources.* Smithsonian Institution Series. New York, 1929.

PERRY, W. J. *The Children of the Sun.* London, 1923.

——. *The Growth of Civilization.* New York, 1923.

PRESCOTT, W. H. *The Conquest of Mexico.* Two volumes. New York, 1922.

RADIN, P. *Indians of South America.* Garden City, 1946.

RIVERS, W. H. R. *Social Organization.* New York, 1924.

ST.-JOHNSTON, T. R. *The Islanders of the Pacific; or, The Children of the Sun.* New York, 1921.

SAWYER, J. D. *History of the Pilgrims and Puritans.* W. E. Griffis, editor. Three volumes. New York, 1922.

SMITH, G. E. *Essays on the Evolution of Man.* Oxford, 1924.

——. *Human History*. New York, 1929.

SOLLAS, W. J. *Ancient Hunters and Their Modern Representatives*. New York, 1924.

SPENCE, L. *The Myths of Mexico and Peru*. New York, undated.

SPENCER, B., and GILLEN, F. J. *The Native Tribes of Central Australia*. London, 1938.

SUMNER, W. G. *War and Other Essays*. New Haven, 1911.

THOMAS, N. W. *Natives of Australia*. London, 1906.

TURNEY-HIGH, H. H. *The Practice of Primitive War: A Study in Comparative Sociology*. Missoula, Montana, 1942.

——. *Primitive War, Its Practice and Concepts*. Columbia, South Carolina, 1949.

TYLOR, E. B. *Primitive Culture*. Two volumes. New York, 1920.

TYRRELL, J. B. (editor). *David Thompson's Narrative of His Explorations in Western America, 1784–1812*. Toronto, 1916.

VERRILL, A. H. *The American Indian: North, South and Central America*. New York, 1927.

VON HANSTEIN, O. *The World of the Incas: A Socialistic State of the Past*. London, 1924.

WARNER, W. L. "Murngin Warfare," *Oceania*, Vol. I, 1940.

WEDGEWOOD, C. "Some Aspects of Warfare in Melanesia," *Oceania*, Vol. I, 1940.

WESTERMARCK, E. *The Origin and Development of the Moral Ideas*. Two volumes. London, 1924.

WHIFFEN, T. *The North-West Amazons: Notes of Some Months Spent Among Cannibal Tribes*. London, 1915.

WISSLER, C. *The American Indian: An Introduction to the Anthropology of the New World*. New York, 1922.

——. *Indians of the United States*. The American Museum of Natural History Series. New York, 1940.

WOODS, J. L. (editor). *The Native Tribes of South Australia*. Adelaide, 1879.

II

APPIAN. Translated by H. White. London, 1899.

ARRIAN. "The Anabasis of Alexander," in R. B. Godolphin, *The Greek Historians*. Two volumes. New York, 1942.

BAIKIE, J. *A History of Egypt*. Two volumes. New York, 1929.

BAILEY, C. (editor). *The Legacy of Rome*. Oxford, undated.

Bhagavad-Gita, The. Translated by A. Ryder. Chicago, 1929.

BOAK, A. E. R. *A History of Rome to 565 A.D.* New York, 1943.

BREASTED, J. H. *The Battle of Kadesh*. Chicago, 1903.

——. *A History of Egypt*. New York, 1912.

————. *Development of Religion and Thought in Ancient Egypt.* New York, 1912.

BURY, J. B. *A History of Greece to the Death of Alexander.* New York, 1937.

Cambridge Ancient History. Twelve volumes. Cambridge, England, 1923–39.

DELAPORTE, L. *Mesopotamia: The Babylonian and Assyrian Civilization.* New York, 1925.

DICKINSON, G. L. *The Greek View of Life.* Garden City, 1928.

DILL, S. *Roman Society from Nero to Marcus Aurelius.* London, 1920.

————. *Roman Society in the Last Century of the Western Empire.* London, 1925.

DODGE, T. A. *Hannibal.* Two volumes. Boston, 1891.

————. *Caesar.* Boston, 1893.

DUBOIS, J. A. *Hindu Manners, Customs and Ceremonies.* Translated by H. K. Beauchamp. Oxford, 1928.

DUTT, R. C. *History of India: From the Earliest Times to the Sixth Century B.C.* Volume I in the nine-volume work edited by A. V. W. Jackson. London, 1906–07.

FERGUSON, W. S. *Greek Imperialism.* Boston, 1913.

FERRERO, G. *The Greatness and Decline of Rome.* Translated by A. E. Zimmern. Five volumes. New York, 1907–09.

FOWLER, W. W. *Julius Caesar.* New York, 1904.   . .

————. *Social Life at Rome in the Age of Cicero.* New York, 1913.

FRANK, T. *Roman Imperialism.* New York, 1914.

FRANKFORD, H., and FRANKFORD, H. A. ET AL. *The Intellectual Adventure of Ancient Man.* Chicago, 1946.

GLOTZ, C. *The Greek City and Its Institutions.* New York, 1930.

GODOLPHIN, R. B. *The Greek Historians.* Two volumes. New York, 1942.

GREENE, W. C. *The Achievement of Greece.* Cambridge, England, 1923.

HARE, W. L. *Mysticism of East and West: Studies in Mystical and Moral Philosophy.* New York, 1923.

HENDERSON, B. W. *The Great War Between Athens and Sparta.* New York, 1927.

HERODOTUS. Translated by G. Rawlinson. New York, 1947. (Published under the title of *The History of Herodotus.*)

Holliday, C. *The Dawn of Literature.* New York, 1931.

Iliad of Homer, The. Translated by W. B. Smith and W. Miller. New York, 1944.

JASTROW, M., JR. *The Civilization of Babylonia and Assyria.* Philadelphia, 1915.

KENT, C. F. *A History of the Jewish People During the Babylonian, Persian and Greek Periods*. New York, 1927.

MACFIE, J. A. *Myths and Legends of India*. Edinburgh, 1924.

MAHAFFY, J. P. *Social Life in Greece from Homer to Menander*. London, 1913.

MASPERO, G. *History of Egypt, Chaldea, Syria, Babylonia and Assyria*. Nine volumes. London, undated.

MOORE, F. G. *The Roman World*. New York, 1936.

MORET, A. *The Nile and Egyptian Civilization*. New York, 1927.

MORET, A., and DAVY, G. *From Tribe to Empire: Social Organization Among Primitives and in the Ancient East*. New York, 1926.

NEPOS, CORNILIUS. *Lives*. Translated by E. O. Windstedt. Oxford, 1904.

NILSSON, M. P. *Imperial Rome*. New York, 1926.

OLMSTEAD, A. T. *History of Assyria*. New York, 1923.

——. *History of Syria and Palestine*. New York, 1931.

——. *History of the Persian Empire*. Chicago, 1948.

PARKER, H. M. D. *The Roman Legions*. Oxford, 1928.

PLUTARCH. Translated by J. Dryden, revised by A. H. Clough. Three volumes, Everyman's Edition, New York. (One-volume edition of the same, The Modern Library, New York.)

POLYBIUS. Selections from his works, edited by Strachan-Davidson. Oxford, 1888.

PRATT, J. B. *The Pilgrimage of Buddhism*. New York, 1928.

RAWLINSON, G. *The Five Great Monarchies of the Ancient Eastern World*. Volume III. New York, undated.

——. *History of Ancient Egypt*. Volume I. New York, 1881.

RENAN, E. *History of the People of Israel*. Volume II. Boston, 1912.

ROBINSON, C. A. *Alexander the Great*. New York, 1947.

ROGERS, R. W. *A History of Ancient Persia*. New York, 1929.

ROSE, H. J. *Primitive Culture in Greece*. New York, 1925.

——. *Primitive Culture in Italy*. London, 1926.

SIDHANTA, N. K. *The Heroic Age of India*. New York, 1930.

SMITH, V. A. *History of India: From the Sixth Century B.C. to the Mohammedan Conquest*. Volume II in the nine-volume work edited by A. V. W. Jackson. London, 1906–07.

SPAETH, J. W. *A Study of the Causes of Rome's Wars from 343 to 265 B.C.* Princeton, 1926.

SPAULDING, O. L. *Pen and Sword in Greece and Rome*. Princeton, 1937.

SPAULDING, O. L., NICKERSON, H., and WRIGHT, J. W. *Warfare*. New York, 1925.

STOBART, J. C. *The Glory That Was Greece*. Philadelphia, 1915.

SUETONIUS. *Julius Caesar*. Butler and Cary translation. Oxford, 1927.

SWAIN, J. W. *The Ancient World*. Two volumes. New York, 1950.

TARN, W. W. *Alexander the Great.* Two volumes. New York, 1948.

THUCYDIDES. Translated by B. Jowett. Two volumes. Oxford, 1883.

WELLS, J., and BARROW, R. H. *A Short History of the Roman Empire to the Death of Marcus Aurelius.* New York, 1931.

WILCKEN, U. *Alexander the Great.* Translated by G. C. Richards. New York, 1932.

WOOLLEY, C. L. *The Sumerians.* Oxford, 1928.

XENOPHON. Complete works, translated by H. G. Dakyns. London, 1890.

ZIMMERN, A. E. *The Greek Commonwealth: Politics and Economics in Fifth Century Athens.* Oxford, 1924.

III

ARNOLD, T. W. *The Preaching of Islam: A History of the Propagation of the Moslem Faith.* New York, 1913.

BAYNES, N. H. *The Byzantine Empire.* London, 1925.

BEUF, C. *Cesare Borgia: The Machiavellian Prince.* New York, 1942.

BOISSONNADE, P. *Life and Work in Medieval Europe.* New York, 1950.

BURY, J. B. *History of the Later Roman Empire from the Death of Theodosius to the Death of Justinian.* Two volumes. London, 1923.

———. *The Invasion of Europe by the Barbarians.* London, 1928.

Cambridge Medieval History. Eight volumes. New York, 1911–36.

CHEYNEY, E. P. *The Dawn of a New Era, 1250–1453.* New York, 1936.

Cid, Poem of the. Translated by A. M. Huntington. New York, 1921.

COULTON, G. G. *Medieval Panorama.* Cambridge, England, 1949.

DAVIES, J. D. G., and WORTS, F. W. *England in the Middle Ages: Its Problems and Legacies.* London, 1928.

DAVIS, W. S. *Life on a Medieval Barony: A Picture of a Typical Feudal Community in the Thirteenth Century.* New York, 1923.

DILL, S. *Roman Society in Gaul in the Merovingian Age.* London, 1926.

DURANT, W. *The Age of Faith.* New York, 1950.

FREEMAN, E. A. *The History and Conquests of the Saracens.* London, 1876.

FROISSART, SIR JOHN. Translated by T. Johnes. Two volumes. New York, 1901.

GRANET, M. *Chinese Civilization.* New York, 1930.

GREGORY OF TOURS. *History of the Franks.* Translated by O. M. Dalton. Two volumes. Oxford, 1927.

GRIFFIS, W. E. *The Mikado's Empire.* Volume I. New York, 1906.

HEARN, L. *Glimpses of Unfamiliar Japan.* Two volumes. Boston, 1894.

———. *Japan: An Attempt at Interpretation.* New York, 1904.

HELL, J. *The Arab Civilization.* Translated by S. Khuda Bukhsh. Cambridge, England, undated.

HODGKIN, T. *Italy and Her Invaders*. Eight volumes. Oxford, 1892–99.

HUIZINGA, J. *The Waning of the Middle Ages: A Study of the Forms of Life, Thought and Art in France and the Netherlands in the XIVth and XVth Centuries*. London, 1924.

JOYCE, P. W. *A Smaller Social History of Ancient Ireland*. New York, 1908.

LANE, E. W. *Arabian Society in the Middle Ages*. London, 1883.

LEA, H. C. *A History of the Inquisition of the Middle Ages*. Three volumes. New York, 1922.

LOT, F. *The End of the Ancient World and the Beginnings of the Middle Ages*. New York, 1931.

LOWELL, F. C. *Joan of Arc*. New York, 1896.

MACHIAVELLI, NICCOLÒ. *The Prince*. Translated by H. Morley. London, 1883.

MARGOLIOUTH, D. A. *The Early Development of Mohammedism*. London, 1914.

MELLER, W. C. *A Knight's Life in the Days of Chivalry*. New York, 1924.

MOSS, H. ST.L. B. *The Birth of the Middle Ages, 395–814*. Oxford, 1935.

MUNRO, D. C. "Christian and Infidel in the Holy Land," *International Quarterly*, 1901.

MUNRO, D. C., and SELLERY, G. C. *Medieval Civilization*. New York, 1904.

NEWHALL, R. *The English Conquest of Normandy, 1416–24*. New Haven, 1924.

OLRIK, A. *Viking Civilization*. New York, 1930.

OMAN, C. *A History of the Art of War, from the Fourth to the Fourteenth Century*. London, 1898.

——. *The Great Revolt of 1281*. Oxford, 1906.

PRESTAGE, E. (editor). *Chivalry: A Series of Studies to Illustrate Its Historical Significance and Civilizing Influences*. New York, 1928.

RUSSELL, C. E. *Charlemagne, First of the Moderns*. Boston, 1930.

Saga of the Volsungs, The. Translated by Margaret Schlauch. New York, 1930.

SANSOM, G. B. *Japan: A Short Cultural History*. New York, 1931.

Song of Roland. Translated by C. S. Moncrieff. New York, 1920. (An excellent later version is that by F. B. Luquiens, New York, 1952.)

TACITUS. Dialogues, translated by W. Peterson. New York, 1920.

TAYLOR, H. O. *The Medieval Mind: A History of the Development of Thought and Emotion in the Middle Ages*. Two volumes. London, 1927.

THATCHER, O. J., and McNEAL, E. H. *A Source Book for Medieval History*. New York, 1905.

THOMPSON, J. W. *Economic and Social History of the Middle Ages*. New York, 1928.

———. *The Middle Ages*. Two volumes. New York, 1931.

TREVELYAN, G. M. *England in the Age of Wyclif*. London, 1904.

WILLIAMS, S. W. *The Middle Kingdom*. Volume II. New York, 1883.

WOODRUFF, D. *Charlemagne*. New York, 1935.

YRIARTE, C. *Cesare Borgia*. Translated by W. Stirling. London, 1947.

IV

BLOK, P. J. *History of the People of the Netherlands*. Translated by O. H. Bierstaat and R. Putnam. Five volumes. New York, 1898–1912.

BOWDEN, W. *The Industrial History of the United States*. New York, 1930.

BRUFORD, W. H. *Germany in the Eighteenth Century*. New York, 1935.

BUCHAN, J. *Oliver Cromwell*. Boston, 1934.

CARR, A. *Juggernaut: The Path of Dictatorship*. New York, 1939.

DAVIES, A. M. *Clive of Plassey*. New York, 1939.

DEUTSCH, H. C. *The Genesis of Napoleonic Imperialism*. Cambridge, Massachusetts, 1938.

DODWELL, H. H. *Dupleix and Clive*. London, 1930.

DORN, W. L. *Competition for Empire, 1740–1763*. New York, 1940.

———. "The Prussian Bureaucracy in the Eighteenth Century," *Political Science Quarterly*, Vol. XLVII, 1931.

ERGANG, R. E. *The Potsdam Fuehrer: Frederick William I, Father of Prussian Militarism*. New York, 1941.

FAY, S. B. *The Rise of Brandenburg-Prussia to 1786*. New York, 1937.

FIGGIS, J. N. *The Divine Right of Kings*. New York, 1914.

FIRTH, C. A. *Cromwell's Army*. London, 1905.

FISKE, J. *The Dutch and Quaker Colonies in America*. Two volumes. Boston, 1899.

FREDERICK THE GREAT. *The History of the Seven Years' War*. Translated by T. Holcroft. London, 1789.

GADE, J. A. *Charles the Twelfth, King of Sweden*. Translated from the manuscript of C. G. Klingspor. Boston, 1916.

GARDINER, S. R. *The Thirty Years' War*. New York, 1897.

GAXOTTE, P. *Frederick the Great*. New Haven, 1942.

GINDELY, A. *History of the Thirty Years' War*. Translated by A. Ten Brook. Two volumes. New York, 1884.

GRETTON, R. H. *The King's Majesty: A Study in the Historical Philosophy of Modern Kingship.* London, 1930.

HALLENDORF, C., and SCHUECK, A. *History of Sweden.* London, 1939.

HASSALL, A. *Louis XIV and the Zenith of the French Monarchy.* New York, 1895.

HERKSHER, E. F. *Mercantilism.* London, 1935.

HUDSON, W. H., and GUERNSEY, I. S. *The United States from the Discovery of the American Continent to the End of the World War.* New York, undated.

JANSSEN, J. *History of the German People at the Close of the Middle Ages.* Translated by A. M. Christie. Volumes III and IV. London, 1900.

JOHNSON, A. H. *The Age of the Enlightened Despots, 1660–1789.* London, 1925.

JONES, M. E. M. *Warren Hastings in Bengal.* Oxford, 1918.

LODGE, R. *Great Britain and Prussia in the Eighteenth Century.* Oxford, 1923.

MARRIOTT, J. A. R., and ROBERTSON, C. G. *The Evolution of Prussia: The Making of an Empire.* Oxford, 1937.

MERRIMAN, R. B. *The Rise of the Spanish Empire.* Four volumes. New York, 1925.

MILLER, J. C. *Origins of the American Revolution.* Boston, 1943.

MORE, SIR THOMAS. *Utopia.* Edited by W. D. Armes. New York, 1912.

MORLEY, J. *Oliver Cromwell.* New York, 1900.

MOSES, B. *The Establishment of Spanish Rule in America.* New York, 1907.

NEIHARDT, J. G. *The Song of the Indian Wars.* New York, 1925.

OGG, D. *Louis XIV.* London, 1933.

PARKMAN, F. *Pioneers of France in the New World.* Boston, 1892.

PRESCOTT, W. H. *History of the Reign of Ferdinand and Isabella.* Two volumes. London, 1851.

———. *The Conquest of Peru.* Two volumes. Boston, 1856.

PUTNAM, R. *William the Silent, Prince of Orange, and the Revolt of the Netherlands.* New York, 1911.

RAMBAUD, A. *History of Russia.* Translated by L. B. Lang. Volume II. Boston, 1880.

REDDAWAY, W. A. *Frederick the Great and the Rise of Prussia.* New York, 1904.

ROBERTS, P. *The Quest for Security, 1715–1740.* New York, 1947.

SAINT-SIMON, DUKE OF. *Memoirs of Louis XIV and His Court and of the Regency.* Two volumes. New York, 1910.

SCHEVILL, F. *The Great Elector.* Chicago, 1947.

SHAKESPEARE, W. *Henry IV.* Part I. (Many editions.)

SHELLEY, P. B. *Queen Mab.* (Many editions.)

SOULEYMAN, E. V. *The Vision of World Peace in Seventeenth and Eighteenth Century France.* New York, 1941.

SPEIER, H. "Militarism in the Eighteenth Century," *Social Research,* Vol. III, 1936.

SWIFT, J. *Gulliver's Travels.* Modern Library Edition, New York, 1931.

TAYLOR, G. R. S. *Cromwell.* Boston, 1928.

THOMPSON, J. W. *The Wars of Religion in France, 1559–1576.* Chicago, 1909.

VAN DOREN, CARL. *Secret History of the American Revolution.* New York, 1941.

VEALE, H. *Frederick the Great.* London, 1935.

VERNADSKY, G. *A History of Russia.* New York, 1944.

VLEKKE, N. H. M. *Evolution of the Dutch Nation.* New York, 1945.

VOLTAIRE. *History of Charles XII.* Translated by T. Smollett. New York, 1901.

———. *The Complete Romances of Voltaire.* New York, 1927.

VON ECKHARDT, C. *Ivan the Terrible.* Translated by C. A. Phillips. New York, 1949.

WILKINSON, S. *The French Army Before Napoleon.* Oxford, 1915.

YOUNG, N. *Frederick the Great.* London, 1932.

V

Bismarck, the Man and the Statesman. The Reflections and Reminiscences of Otto, Prince von Bismarck. Written and Dictated by Himself After His Retirement from Office. Translated under the supervision of A. J. Butler. Two volumes. New York, 1899.

BRINTON, C. *The Jacobins.* New York, 1930.

———. *A Decade of Revolution, 1789–1799.* New York, 1934.

BRUUN, G. *Europe and the French Imperium, 1799–1814.* New York, 1938.

BUTTERFIELD, H. *The Peace Tactics of Napoleon, 1806–08.* Cambridge, England, 1929.

CLAPHAM, J. H. *The Causes of the War of 1792.* London, 1899.

DAWSON, W. H. *Evolution of Modern Germany.* London, 1908.

———. *The German Empire 1867–1914 and the Unity Movement.* Two volumes. New York, 1919.

DEUTSCH, H. C. *The Genesis of Napoleonic Imperialism.* Cambridge, Massachusetts, 1938.

DOCORS, L. *French Society in the Eighteenth Century.* New York, 1927.

DODGE, T. A. *Napoleon: A History of the Art of War, from the Beginnings of the French Revolution to the Battle of Waterloo.* Four volumes. Boston, 1904-07.

ERGANG, R. E. *Herder and the Foundations of German Nationalism.* New York, 1931.

EYCK, E. *Bismarck and the German Empire.* London, 1950.

FAY, B. *The Revolutionary Spirit in France and America.* New York, 1927.

FIFE, R. H. *German Empire Between Two Wars.* New York, 1916.

FOURNIER, A. *Napoleon.* Translated by M. B. Corwin and D. D. Bissell. New York, 1903.

FULLER, J. V. *Bismarck's Philosophy at Its Zenith.* Cambridge, Massachusetts, 1922.

GAXOTTE, P. *The French Revolution.* Translated by W. A. Phillips. New York, 1932.

GERSHOY, L. *From Despotism to Revolution, 1763–1789.* New York, 1944.

GOOCH, G. P. *Franco-German Relations, 1871–1914.* New York, 1923.

HART, L. *The Ghost of Napoleon.* New Haven, 1934.

HAYES, C. J. H. *Essays in Nationalism.* New York, 1926.

———. *The Historical Evolution of Modern Nationalism.* New York, 1931.

HAZEN, C. D. *The French Revolution.* Two volumes. New York, 1932.

HIGGENS, E. L. (editor). *The French Revolution as Told by Contemporaries.* Boston, 1938.

KERKSCHER, E. J. *The Continental System.* Oxford, 1922.

KIRCHEISEN, F. M. *Napoleon.* Translated by H. St. Lawrence. New York, 1932.

KOHN, H. *A History of Nationalism in the East.* New York, 1929.

LANGER, W. L. *European Alliances and Alignments, 1871–1890.* New York, 1931.

LEGG, L. G. W. *Select Documents Illustrative of the History of the French Revolution.* Two volumes. Oxford, 1905.

LORD, R. H. *The Origins of the War of 1870.* Cambridge, England, 1924.

MARRIOTT, J. A. R. *England Since Waterloo.* London, 1913.

MATHIEZ, A. *The French Revolution.* New York, 1929.

MIGNET, F. *History of the French Revolution.* London, 1913.

MOON, P. T. *Imperialism and World Politics.* New York, 1926.

MOWAT, R. B. *The Diplomacy of Napoleon.* London, 1924.

Napoleon's Memoirs. Edited by S. de Clair. New York, 1948.

OMAN, C. *Studies in the Napoleonic Wars.* London, 1929.

ONCKEN, C. *Napoleon III and the Rhine: The Origins of the War of 1870–71.* New York, 1928.

PHIPPS, R. W. *The Armies of the First French Republic.* Three volumes. Oxford, 1926–29.

RISENBERG, A. *The Birth of the German Republic, 1871–1918.* Translated by I. F. D. Morrow. New York, 1931.

ROBERTSON, C. G. *Bismarck.* London, 1918.

ROSE, J. H. *The Life of Napoleon I.* Two volumes. New York, 1901.

STEEFEL, L. D. *The Schleswig-Holstein Question.* Cambridge, Massachusetts, 1932.

STEPHENS, H. M. *History of the French Revolution.* Two volumes. New York, 1886–91.

THOMPSON, J. M. *The French Revolution.* Oxford, 1943.

WARNER, G. T. *How Wars Were Won: A Short History of Napoleon's Times.* London, 1915.

WICKWAR, W. H. *Baron d'Holbach: A Prelude to the French Revolution.* London, 1935.

WILKINSON, S. *The Rise of General Bonaparte.* Oxford, 1930.

VI

ABEL, T. *Why Hitler Came to Power.* New York, 1938.

AMBRUSTER, H. W. *Treason's Peace.* New York, 1947.

BANSE, E. *Germany Prepares for War.* New York, 1941.

BARNES, H. E. *The Genesis of the World War.* New York, 1926.

BIRDSALL, P. *Versailles Treaty Twenty Years After.* New York, 1941.

BORTON, H. *Japan Since 1931.* New York, 1940.

BRUCK, W. F. *Social and Economic History of Germany from William II to Hitler, 1888–1938.* London, 1938.

BUNYAN, J., and FISHER, H. H. *The Bolshevik Revolution, 1917–18: Documents and Materials.* Stanford, California, 1934.

BURCHALL, F. T. *The Storm Breaks: A Panorama of Europe and the Forces That Have Wrecked the Peace.* New York, 1940.

CARNEGIE ENDOWMENT FOR INTERNATIONAL PEACE. *The Treaties of Peace, 1919–23.* Two volumes. New York, 1924.

CARR, E. H. *Twenty Years' Crisis, 1919–39: An Introduction to the Study of International Relations.* New York, 1939.

CHAMBERLAIN, W. H. *The Russian Revolution, 1917–1921.* Two volumes. New York, 1935.

CHURCHILL, W. S. *While England Slept: A Survey of World Affairs, 1932–1938.* New York, 1938.

——. *The Gathering Storm.* Boston, 1948.

——. *Their Finest Hour.* Boston, 1949.

——. *The Grand Alliance.* Boston, 1950.

DAVIS, C., and LINDLEY, E. K. *How War Came.* New York, 1942.

DICKINSON, G. L. *The International Anarchy.* New York, 1926.

DODD, W. E., and DODD, M. (editors). *Ambassador Dodd's Diary, 1933–1938.* New York, 1941.

DURHAM, M. W. *The Serajevo Crime*. New York, 1925.

EINZIG, P. *Hitler's New Order in Europe*. New York, 1941.

EWART, J. S. *The Roots and Causes of the Wars, 1914–1918*. Two volumes. Garden City, 1925.

FALLS, C. W. *The Nature of Modern Warfare*. Oxford, 1941.

FAY, S. B. *The Origins of the World War*. New York, 1941.

FENWICK, C. G. *American Neutrality: Trial and Failure*. New York, 1930.

FLORINSKY, M. T. *Fascism and National Socialism*. New York, 1936.

FOLTZ, C., JR. *The Masquerade in Spain*. Boston, 1948.

GEYDE, G. E. R. *Betrayal in Central Europe: Austria and Czechoslovakia, the Fallen Bastions*. New York, 1939.

GIBBONS, H. A. *The New Map of Africa*. New York, 1925.

GIBBS, P. *The Soul of the War*. New York, 1915.

———. *Now It Can Be Told*. New York, 1920.

GRAHAM, S. *The Challenge of the Dead*. London, 1930.

GREW, J. C. *Ten Years in Japan*. New York, 1944.

GREY, E. *Twenty-Five Years*. Two volumes. New York, 1925.

HAIGH, R. *Life in a Tank*. Boston, 1918.

HAYES, C. J. H. *A Generation of Materialism, 1871–1900*. New York, 1941.

HEIDEN, K. *A History of National Socialism*. New York, 1935.

HITLER, A. *My New Order*. Translated and edited. New York, 1941.

HOLTOM, D. C. *Modern Japan*. Chicago, 1943.

HOSKINS, H. L. *European Imperialism in Africa*. New York, 1930.

IRWIN, W. *The Next War*. Evanston, Illinois, 1921.

KNIGHT-PATTERSON, W. M. *Germany from Defeat to Conquest, 1913–1939*. London, 1945.

LASSWELL, H. D. *Propaganda Technique in the World War*. London, 1927.

LEE, D. E. *Ten Years: The World on the Way to War, 1930–1940*. Boston, 1942.

LEHMANN-RUSSBÜLDT, O. *War for Profits*. New York, 1930.

LICHNOWSKY, K. M. *Heading for the Abyss*. New York, 1928.

LICHTENBERGER, H. *The Third Reich*. New York, 1937.

LOWENSTEIN, K. *Hitler's Germany: The Nazi Background to War*. New York, 1940.

LUCAS, C. P. *Partition and Colonization in Africa*. Oxford, 1922.

MANHART, G. B. *Alliance and Entente, 1871–1914*. New York, 1932.

MEGARO, G. *Mussolini in the Making*. Boston, 1938.

MENDELSSOHN, P. DE. *Design for Aggression: The Inside Story of Hitler's War Plans*. New York, 1946.

MILLER, F. T. *History of World War II.* Philadelphia, 1945.

MILLIS, W. *The Martial Spirit: A Study of Our War with Spain.* Boston, 1931.

——. *Road to War: America, 1914–1917.* Boston, 1935.

——. *Why Europe Fights.* New York, 1940.

MORGENSTERN, G. *Pearl Harbor: The Story of the Secret War.* New York, 1947.

NICHOLSON, H. *Peace-Making, 1919.* New York, 1939.

NOEL-BAKER, P. J. *The Private Manufacture of Arms.* Oxford, 1937.

ORTON, W. *Twenty-Years' Armistice, 1918–1938.* New York, 1938.

PARES, B. *The Fall of the Russian Monarchy: A Study of the Evidence.* New York, 1939.

PETERSON, H. C. *Propaganda for War: The Campaign Against American Neutrality, 1914–1917.* Norman, Oklahoma, 1939.

PFEILER, W. K. *War and the German Mind.* New York, 1941.

RAUSGENBUSH, S. *The March of Fascism.* New Haven, 1939.

ROSINSKI, H. *The German Army.* New York, 1940.

SCHMITT, B. E. *The Coming of the War: 1914.* Two volumes. New York, 1930.

——. *Triple Alliance and Triple Entente.* New York, 1934.

——. *From Versailles to Munich.* Chicago, 1939.

SCHUMAN, F. L. *Europe on the Eve: The Crises of Diplomacy, 1933–1939.* New York, 1939.

——. *Night Over Europe: The Diplomacy of Nemesis, 1939–1940.* New York, 1941.

SCOTT, J. F. *Five Weeks: The Surge of Public Opinion on the Eve of the Great War.* New York, 1927.

SFORZA, C. *The Totalitarian War—and After.* Chicago, 1941.

SHIRER, W. L. *Berlin Diary: The Journal of a Foreign Correspondent, 1934–1941.* New York, 1941.

SHOTWELL, J. T. *At the Paris Peace Conference.* New York, 1937.

SINGTON, D., and WEIDENFELD, A. *The Goebbels Experiment: A Study of the Nazi Propaganda Machine.* New Haven, 1943.

SLOUTSKI, N. M. *The World Armaments Race, 1919-1939.* New York, 1941.

STOLPER, G. *German Economy, 1870–1940.* New York, 1940.

TATE, M. *The Disarmament Illusion.* New York, 1942.

TAYLOR, E. *The Strategy of Terror.* Boston, 1940.

TEMPERLEY, H. W. V. (editor). *A History of the Peace Conference of Paris.* Six volumes. Oxford, 1920–24.

THOMAS, G. *Autobiography, 1891–1941.* London, 1946.

TOLICHUS, O. D. *They Wanted War.* New York, 1940.

TOWNSEND, M. W., and PEAKE, C. H. *European Colonial Expansion Since 1871*. Philadelphia, 1941.

VERNADSKY, G. V. *The Russian Revolution, 1917–1931*. New York, 1932.

WOLFERS, A. *Britain and France Between Two Wars*. New York, 1940.

WOLFF, T. *The Eve of 1914*. Translated by E. W. Dickes. New York, 1936.

WOOD, E. F. *The Note-Book of an Intelligence Officer*. New York, 1920.

WOODWARD, E. L. *Great Britain and the German Navy*. Oxford, 1935.

WOOLF, L. *Empire and Commerce in Africa*. London, 1920.

WORK, E. *Ethiopia, a Pawn in European Diplomacy*. New York, 1936.

ZACHARIAS, E. M. *Behind Closed Doors: The Secret History of the Cold War*. New York, 1950.

ZEIMER, G. *Education for Death—the Making of the Nazi*. Oxford, 1941.

GENERAL

ALLEN, D. *The Fight for Peace*. New York, 1930.

Cambridge History of the British Empire. Eight volumes. Cambridge, England, 1929–40.

Cambridge History of British Foreign Policy, 1783–1919. Three volumes. Cambridge, England, 1922–23.

Cambridge Modern History. Fourteen volumes. New York, 1902-12.

DICKINSON, G. L. *Causes of International War*. London, 1920.

EARLE, M. E. (editor). *The Makers of Modern Strategy: Military Thought from Machiavelli to Hitler*. Princeton, 1943.

FISHER, H. A. L. *A History of Europe*. Three volumes. Boston, 1935–36.

FUETER, E. *World History, 1815–1920*. New York, 1922.

FULLER, J. F. C. *War and Western Civilization, 1832–1932*. London, 1934.

HAYES, C. J. H. *A Political and Cultural History of Modern Europe*. Two volumes. New York, 1936.

KLUCHEVSKY, V. O. *A History of Russia*. Translated by C. J. Hogarth. Five volumes. London, 1911–31.

MONTROSE, L. *War Through the Ages*. New York, 1944.

NICKERSON, H. *The Armed Horde: A Study of the Rise, Survival and Decline of the Mass Army, 1793–1939*. New York, 1941.

PEAR, T. H. (editor). *Psychological Factors of Peace and War*. Published on behalf of the United Nations Association of Great Britain and Northern Ireland. London, 1950.

RUSSELL, B. *Why Men Fight.* New York, 1930.

TOYNBEE, A. J. *A Study of History.* Six volumes. London, 1934–40.

——. *War and Civilization.* New York, 1950.

VAGTS, A. *A History of Militarism: Romance and Realities of a Profession.* New York, 1937.

WRIGHT, Q. *A Study of War.* Two volumes. Chicago, 1942.

Index